ASCENDING AND DESCENDING THE ACROPOLIS

Movement in Athenian Religion

ASCENDING AND DESCENDING THE ACROPOLIS

Movement in Athenian Religion

Edited by

Wiebke Friese, Søren Handberg and Troels Myrup Kristensen

Monographs of the Danish Institute at Athens,
Volume 23

Ascending and Descending the Acropolis. Movement in Athenian Religion.

Monographs of the Danish Institute at Athens, Volume 23

Series editor: Kristina Winther-Jacobsen
Type setting: Ryevad Grafisk
This book is typeset in Minion Pro and printed on Novatech Matt 130g.
Cover: Jørgen Sparre
Cover image: Troels Myrup Kristensen
Printed at Narayana Press, Denmark
ISBN 978 87 7184 467 2
ISSN 1397 1433

AARHUS UNIVERSITY PRESS
Finlandsgade 29
8200 Aarhus N
www.unipress.au.dk

Oxbow Books Ltd.
The Old Music Hall 106–108
Cowley Road Oxford, OX4 1JE
United Kingdom
www.oxbowbooks.com

ISD
70 Enterprise Drive
Bristol, CT 06010
USA
www.isdistribution.com

PEER
REVIEWED

/ In accordance with requirements of the Danish Ministry of Higher Education and Science, the certification means that a PhD level peer has made a written assessment justifying this book's scientific quality.

The publication of this book was financed by:
Danish Council for Independent Research (DFF) and Aarhus University Research Foundation (AUFF)

MIX
Paper from
responsible sources
FSC
www.fsc.org
FSC® C010651

Contents

Preface

The majority of the papers published here were first presented in preliminary form in the "Ascending and Descending the Acropolis: Sacred Travel in Attica and Its Borderlands" workshop held at the Danish Institute at Athens on 15 November 2014 and organized by Wiebke Friese and Søren Handberg. The workshop was organized under the auspices of "The Emergence of Sacred Travel: Experience, Economy and Connectivity in Ancient Mediterranean Pilgrimage" collaborative research project (www.sacredtravel.dk), generously funded by the *Sapere Aude* excellence programme under the Danish Council for Independent Research (DFF) and directed by Troels Myrup Kristensen. We would like to thank the staff of the Danish Institute at Athens for their help in organizing the conference, and the Aarhus University Research Foundation (AUFF) for a generous grant to cover the costs of publishing this volume. For editorial assistance, we are grateful to Nicola Daumann, Martine Petlund Breiby and Isak Roalkvam.

Aarhus, Hamburg, and Oslo
April 2018

INTRODUCTION

New Approaches to Movement in Athenian Religion*

Troels Myrup Kristensen

The aim of this volume is to provide new perspectives on religious movement in the city of Athens and the broader region of Attica from the Late Bronze Age to the 2nd century AD.[1] Since the 1990s, work on the ancient Greek world has increasingly focused on different aspects of movement, such as processions and pilgrimages, and how they feed into the cultural, political, and religious imagination of cities and sanctuaries across the Mediterranean.[2] Athens and Attica are particularly fruitful places in the study of these phenomena, as the region provides rich evidence across a range of textual and material sources for a variety of different types of religious movement – both inside the city of Athens itself (such as to, on, and around the Acropolis) and from its centre to sanctuaries in the hinterland (such as those of Demeter and Kore at Eleusis and that of Artemis at Brauron), as well as to more distant sanctuaries, such as Delphi. The evidence for maenadism in both drama and vase-painting provides another fascinating window into the role that specific kinds of ritualised movement could play within Athenian religious and social imaginary.

This brief introduction consists of three parts. The first outlines some key aspects of movement in Athenian (and more broadly, Greek) religion, and why they matter. The second suggests some ways through which archaeology may contribute to the study of Athenian religious movement by taking inspiration from the so-called "new mobilities paradigm". The third presents a brief overview of the individual case studies presented in the following chapters.

Movement Matters

In spite of the obvious perils and dangers that faced ancient travellers, religious movement on a variety of different scales was integral to the development of Greek religion. From the Greek world at large, there is evidence for some 356 processions (*pompai*) in total, clocking in at varying lengths and durations, but each demonstrating how firmly embedded this form of communal and highly performative movement was in the religious life of cities and sanctuaries.[3] The role of movement in enabling both religious and political constellations is central to François de Polignac's influential study of extramural sanctuar-

* I thank Anna Collar and Søren Handberg for reading drafts of this introduction.

1 For scholarship on later periods, see Kaldellis 2009 and forthcoming work by Elizabeth Key Fowden.

2 Processions: Graf 1996; Agelidis 2017. Pilgrimage: Coleman & Elsner 1995; Dillon 1997; Elsner & Rutherford 2000; Rutherford 2013. For a useful historiography, see Elsner 2017. Outside of the present volume, other work by the *Emergence of Sacred Travel* project focuses on the Mediterranean as a whole; see Kristensen & Friese 2017; Collar & Kristensen forthcoming a and b; Kristensen forthcoming a.

3 True *et al.* 2004.

ies and their role in the rise of the Greek *polis* in the 8th and 7th centuries BC, where his focus is on their role as territorial demarcations of individual cities (see also Handberg, this volume).[4] Processions often served to manifest links between a city and outlying sanctuaries, such as in the case of the procession from Athens to Eleusis that demonstrated Athenian control over the sanctuary of Demeter and Kore and its mystery cult (see Agelidis and Clinton, this volume).

However, it is important not to approach Greek processions as a sort of black box, or indeed "as an empty container for social processes",[5] as this obscures much of their potential significance. The manner in which individual processions were staged and conducted is indeed of pivotal importance. In an important paper on Greek processions, Fritz Graf thus noted that a procession "is not just a journey from A from B: undoubtedly, it matters where A and B are, and who is doing the journey".[6] Graf presents two models of Greek processions, one in which they moved towards the city centre (so-called centripetal processions), and the other in which they moved away from the city to an extra-urban sanctuary (so-called centrifugal processions). This fundamental aspect of direction is one key factor in understanding the contexts and meanings of individual cases of religious movement in the broader religious landscape.

Other key features of Greek processions include the social make-up and structure of the procession itself and the ritual activities of the participants.[7] Visual representations of processions show participants wearing garlands, special dress, and a rich assortment of ritual paraphernalia.[8] Processions were headed by a young man or a maiden, and the *pompe* could accordingly be personified as a young woman in Greek iconography.[9] In this sense, religious movement was also a highly gendered practice (see Konstantinou, this volume). Characteristic forms of movement closely linked with processions included dancing and singing (both on the road and in sanctuaries), as well as the performance of other rituals along the way, contributing to a certain carnivalesque quality.[10] Joan Connelly has, for example, described the spectacle of the Panathenaic procession as "the ultimate multi-media kinetic display" (see also Warford, this volume).[11]

From the Archaic period onwards, religious movement on a more "international" scale was institutionalised through the journeys of civic officials as part of the phenomenon of theoria (sometimes glossed as "state pilgrimage") that has received renewed scholarly interest in recent years.[12] Representatives from individual poleis, so-called theoroi (often translated as "state pilgrims" or "sacred observers"), travelled considerable distances to witness and participate in festivals held in extra-territorial sanctuaries. As with all other forms of Greek religious life, participation in theoria was a means of displaying power and performing civic identities, evident for example in the Athenian procession to Delphi that in the 2nd century BC included more than 500 delegates (see also Pirisino, this volume).[13] This procession, known as the *Pythaïs*, has been described as the "travelling image of the Athenian state".[14] But this kind of movement

4 Polignac 1995.

5 Sheller 2014, 791, making this important point in relation to the study of movement more broadly.

6 Graf 1996, 64, thus foreshadowing key points in Cresswell 2006.

7 On gendered aspects of Greek mobility, see Konstantinou 2018.

8 Stavrianopoulou 2015.

9 *LIMC* VII, 435-6.

10 Kowalzig 2007.

11 Connelly 2011, 318. For a full account of the Panathenaic procession, see Shear 2001, 122-206.

12 The key study is now Rutherford 2013.

13 Rutherford 2013, 157 (on the number of *Pythaïdes*), 222-30 (for a broader discussion of the *Pythaïs*).

14 Rutherford 2013, 230.

was not only about external communication, as moving together in a group of theoroi undoubtedly contributed to a sense of community or belonging among the participants themselves.[15]

Influenced by these developments in religious movement, travel was increasingly seen as a method of acquiring knowledge, as the examples of Herodotus and Solon as well as the more extreme Roman example of Apuleius' *Golden Ass* all attest.[16] Beginning with Plato and Aristotle, the model of theoria came to be understood as a metaphor for philosophical inquiry itself.[17] The metaphorical sense of travel further developed during the Hellenistic period. In Stoic philosophy, wandering constituted a metaphor for life itself in which man (*homo viator*) sought moral firmness.[18] These examples demonstrate how the study of movement offers a window into a whole range of different aspects of Greek society and culture. While by necessity highly impressionistic, this brief overview of why movement matters has highlighted the need to look at individual moments in which movement acquires meaning, as well as the shape, direction, and representation of movement in different contexts and media.

The Matter of Movement

Movement is, by its very nature, an elusive and ephemeral topic that has often been exclusively studied through the singular lenses of texts and inscriptions.[19] An alternative approach to religious movement is to take inspiration from methods and theories developed in studies of contemporary mobilities and apply them to the ancient world, especially those that pay close attention to their materiality.[20]

Since the turn of the millennium, a wave of new and important work on mobility has appeared,[21] occasionally under the banner of the so-called "new mobilities paradigm" or "mobile turn", mainly developed within sociology and geography, but often of a highly interdisciplinary character. Scholarship under this broad banner has repeatedly argued that the study of movement must develop new methods and approaches that are able to study an increasingly mobile world.[22] In a programmatic paper published in 2006, Mimi Sheller and John Urry thus point out how the immense growth in contemporary mobility is rapidly transforming scholarly terminologies and methodologies across a broad range of disciplines (note, for example, the rise of network metaphors in historical studies).[23] Sheller and Urry propose that "mobilities need to be examined in their fluid interdependence and not in their separate spheres".[24]

Observers of contemporary mobility have indeed shown how the ways and means by which people move create new social and cultural practices. The automobile is a classic case that has received considerable attention in scholarship,[25] but even seemingly basic forms of movement, such as walking, can offer insights into a broad range of phenomena, shown, for example, in the extensive literature on the

15 Cf. Adey 2009, 172.
16 Montiglio 2005, 147-79; Pretzler 2007, 48.
17 Rutherford 2013, 325-32.
18 Montiglio 2005, 42-61.
19 See also Kristensen & Friese 2017.

20 This is attempted more comprehensively than is possible here in Kristensen forthcoming a. Kristensen forthcoming b applies a "new mobilities paradigm" perspective to the sanctuary of Asklepios at Epidauros.
21 The geographer Tim Cresswell makes a distinction between movement and mobility (Cresswell 2006, 2-3). In his view, movement is in itself abstract and meaningless, whereas mobility is meaningful and socially produced. However, the two are used interchangeably in the present context.
22 Sheller & Urry 2006; see also Büscher *et al.* 2011; Adey *et al.* 2014.
23 For recent applications of network models in history and archaeology, see Brughmans *et al.* 2016.
24 Sheller & Urry 2006, 212.
25 See, for example, Inglis 2004.

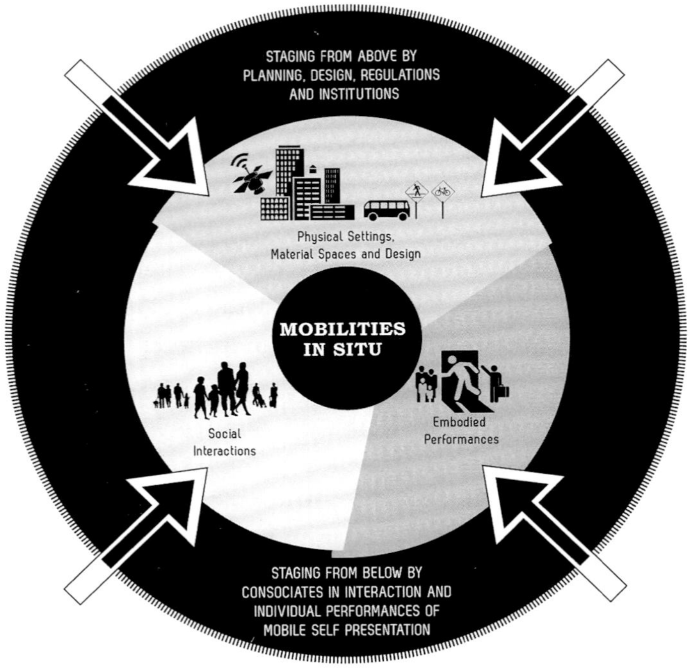

Fig. 1. The "staging mobilities" framework (from Jensen 2013, fig. 1.1, reproduced by permission of Taylor & Francis Books UK).

flâneur.[26] This has profound methodological implications that have been addressed by a number of scholars across a range of disciplines.[27]

In his work on contemporary mobilities, the urban theorist Ole B. Jensen has developed what he calls the "staging mobilities" framework that brings together the study of physical settings (i.e. the material world in which mobility happens), embodied performances (by people), and social interactions (within groups) (Fig. 1).[28] Jensen's framework emphasises how mobilities are always staged, either from above (through careful architectural design or other forms of supervision within a given space) or from below (through the embodied actions and performances of groups and individuals).[29] Jensen furthermore develops the notion of a "mobile situation", defined as "an assemblage of human subjects, physical design and material infrastructures of the built environment" to describe his object of study, thus enabling a study of urban life in motion.[30] Although Jensen's study is limited to contemporary urban spaces, his observations have more general application for two reasons. Firstly, they provide useful terminology for studying movement in both the present and the past, and secondly, they are firmly anchored in material aspects of mobility.

For example, a striking aspect of contemporary mobilities is their dependence on immobile, material infrastructures. Cars need roads, mobile phones need antennae, and so on. Many studies have thus frequently emphasized how different aspects of materiality fundamentally shape movement in the contemporary world.[31] This is particularly helpful for an archaeological approach to past mobility, as many forms of religious movement in the ancient

26 Benjamin 1999.
27 On *flânerie* as a method in ethnography, see Soukop 2013 and Coates 2017.
28 Jensen 2013, 5-10.
29 Jensen 2013.
30 Jensen 2013, 10.
31 Jensen 2013; 2014.

world would have had a material footprint even if the materials and technologies in question were radically different. Most often, archaeology reveals what the geographer Tim Cresswell calls the "places and landscapes of mobility",[32] but this is only the first step in reconstructing the experiences and meanings of mobility itself.

Two recent studies of particular aspects of Athenian archaeology demonstrate these issues in some detail, although their authors do not explicitly draw on methods from the "new mobilities paradigm". The first is Henrik Gerding's discussion of the Athenians' startling decision to rebuild the temple of Athena Polias on the Acropolis after its destruction by the Persians in 480 BC, not in its original position on the so-called Dörpfeld Foundations, but rather slightly to the north at the new location of the Erechtheion.[33] This decision is strikingly at odds with Athenian religious conservatism and stands in stark contrast to the Parthenon, which was finished directly on top of the foundations of its predecessor. As Gerding argues, the decision to relocate the temple of Athena Polias can be explained by the apparently growing need of the participants in the Panathenaic procession to gather in the area around the Great Altar of Athena. The relocation of the temple of Athena Polias created a large open space at the very heart of the Acropolis, allowing large groups of worshippers to convene and participate in the rituals that took place there. Practical needs and the desire to further embellish the Panathenaic festival won over religious tradition in this case, and this new open (and essentially performative) space in turn influenced the ritual practices undertaken (as well as the experiences thereof). Although Gerding does not frame his study from the perspective of movement, his interpretation constitutes a good example of how the movement needs of individual festivals and festivals help us to make sense of architectural developments and topographical changes that are difficult to explain by other factors. Arguably similar spaces were provided in many other sanctuaries that accommodated similar forms of ritual movement, as in the case of the temple of Athena Polias.[34] Yet Classical archaeology often lacks a terminology and methodology to study such spaces and the mobile situations that they would have hosted.

The second case is Nathan Arrington's discussion of the Academy Road that led from the Kerameikos, through its important funerary area and the public cemetery (the *demosion sema*) to the Academy.[35] In some parts, the Academy Road was up to 40 metres wide, which is even more than its extension inside the city walls, the important Panathenaic Way that was between some 10 and 20 metres wide. This extraordinary width suggests that it was constructed not simply to facilitate heavy traffic, but to accommodate grand processions that required considerable space, effectively constituting a kind of moving theatrical stage.[36] The Academy Road was in fact not one of the city's main thoroughfares, as it did not go any further than the Academy and thus constituted a dead end. The materiality and layout of the road instead underlined its use as a public performance space, a role that was especially apt in the public commemoration of Athenians who had died on the battlefield and for the occasion of funerary orations that amassed large crowds. The Academy Road furthermore played a role in several Athenian festivals, notably that of the Dionysia, in which the cult image of Dionysos was taken in procession from his extramural temple that was situated nearby.[37]

Both the case of the Academy Road and that of the temple of Athena Polias on the Acropolis emphasise how individual movement (which Jensen

32 Cresswell 2006, 57.

33 Gerding 2006.

34 Connelly 2011.

35 Arrington 2010.

36 Arrington 2010, 524. On the Panathenaic Way, see Ficuciello 2008, 136-53.

37 Arrington 2010, 527-8.

would classify as "staging from below") can be very difficult to access on the basis of archaeology alone. In fact, it can perhaps only be studied through textual evidence that describes the journeys of single individuals, such as Aelius Aristides or Pausanias (see also Pretzler, this volume). However, what we may term "structural movement" is more readily available for study through material remains. Structural movement relates to a more general level at which movement is shaped and controlled by physical factors, such as buildings and monuments – and how movement through sanctuaries and landscapes is regulated by, for example, sacred ways and sacred regulations that have been inscribed on stone (through what Jensen would call "staging from above"). The study of structural movement also takes in embodied perspectives of experience, such as visibility – what could be seen from where, for example, and, perhaps just as importantly, what could not be seen. The study of sightlines, pioneered as early as 1937 by Doxiadis in his *Raumordnung im griechischen Städtebau*,[38] may be particularly useful for emphasising the experience of arriving at and moving through particular sanctuaries. Doxiadis showed how space in ancient Greece was not a concept that was drawn up on a map, but rather something that was experienced from a particular place in the landscape. But sightlines do not only reveal technical aspects of Greek architecture; they also framed the religious experience of pilgrims and made them participants in liturgical ritual.[39] As such, they constitute an important case of how structural movement was staged in Greek sanctuaries.

The central methodological challenge of the mobility perspective in studying Greek pilgrimage is consequently to see sanctuaries not simply as an assemblage of static buildings, but rather as a series of flows and stages of movement that produced a variety of mobilities that can be partially reconstructed on the basis of material evidence. An important lesson from the study of contemporary mobility is the need to understand Greek religion as a mobile practice that involved not just going to one temple, but visiting several different sanctuaries and doing many different things, complicating our efforts to separate different phenomena and drastically unravelling a field of study that has been rather obsessed with rigid terminology. Indeed, many previous studies of the archaeological evidence for Greek religious movement have focused on static remains, such as individual buildings for the accommodation of pilgrims, or picked up on anecdotal evidence for tents that presumably would have provided a very large proportion of the accommodation for pilgrims. In my view, however, the study of Greek religious movement must be more ambitious and engage in a much broader palette of approaches in order to move forward.[40]

Movement in Athenian Religion: Case Studies

The contributions to this volume provide a range of "mobile" perspectives on Athenian religion. Contributions to the first part of the book, "Movement in the City", focus on religious movement within the *asty* itself. Erin Warford's chapter, "Performing Piety: A Phenomenological Approach to Athenian Processions", thus explores the sensory experiences afforded to participants in processions, particularly focusing on the especially well-documented case of the Panathenaia. In "On the Peripatos: Accessibility and Topography of the Athenian Slope Sanctuaries", Wiebke Friese turns to the sanctuaries situated around the Athenian Acropolis that created a complex and dense network of sacred places. Maria Salta takes us on a

38 Doxiadis 1937.

39 Yasin 2012. Cf. Tonio Hölscher's notion of "sakrale Achsen" (Hölscher 1999, 74-83).

40 Leary 2014 similarly urges us to privilege movement over place.

similar topographical journey to another part of the city in "Under the Care of the Daemons: From the Athenian Acropolis to Kallirhoe on the Ilissos." In contrast, Maria Pretzler focuses squarely on the Acropolis in "Pausanias and the Intellectual Travellers of the Roman Imperial Period: The Acropolis and the Historical Imagination", in which she investigates the significance of visiting Athens in the Roman period through the lens of Roman writers.

The second part of the book, "Movement beyond the City", takes us further afield as it turns to movement that connected the *asty* with sanctuaries placed in the landscapes of Attica, and even beyond in the case of the *Pythaïs*. Søren Handberg looks at the earliest phases of Athenian religious movement in the Late Geometric period when members of the aristocracy not only made dedications on the Athenian Acropolis, but also travelled to sanctuaries in Isthmia and Eretria where they had established guest-friendships, as well as ascending Mounts Parnes and Hymettos to worship Zeus during agricultural festivals. In "'To The Mountain': The Ritual Space of Maenadism in the Athenian Imaginary", Ariadne Konstantinou looks at the ritual movement undertaken by female worshippers of Dionysos, focusing on both textual and visual representations of their so-called "mountain climbing". The following two chapters then investigate movement from Athens to Eleusis during the Eleusinian Mysteries. In "Journeys to the Eleusinian Mysteria", Kevin Clinton offers a close reading of the three inscriptions ("sacred laws") that inform us about the procession itself. In an appendix, he compares this evidence with the procession linked to the Andanian Mysteria. In "Individuals and Polis in Cult: The Procession from Athens to Eleusis in Classical Times", Soi Agelidis studies the Eleusinian procession from the perspective of individual religion, as well as the question of whether it can be considered an example of Greek pilgrimage. Daniele Pirisino's chapter, "The Route of the Athenian Pythaïs across the City and its Territory", offers a detailed investigation of the interaction between the Athenian procession to Delphi with the surrounding landscape. The final chapter by Konstantinos Kalogeropoulos, "Reflections on Pilgrimage at Brauron during the Late Helladic Period", considers the nature and character of religious activity on the acropolis of Brauron by comparing it to other sanctuaries from across the early Greek world. Finally, the volume concludes with an epilogue by Fritz Graf that places its contributions within the larger historiographical context of recent developments in the study of Greek religion more broadly.

Abbreviations

LIMC = Lexicon Iconographicum Mythologiae Classicae (1981-2009)

Bibliography

ADEY, P. 2009
Mobility (Key Ideas in Geography), London and New York.

ADEY, P., D. BISSELL, K. HANNAM, P. MERRIMAN & M. SHELLER (EDS.) 2014
The Routledge Handbook of Mobilities, London.

AGELIDIS, S. 2017
'The "Spatial Turn" in Ancient Greek Festival Research: Venues of the Athenian City Dionysia and the Great Panathenaia *Pompai*', in *Theoretical Approaches to the Archaeology of Ancient Greece,* L.C. Nevett (ed.), Ann Arbor, 230-45.

ARRINGTON, N. 2010
'Topographic Semantics: The Location of the Athenian Public Cemetery and Its Significance for the Nascent Democracy', *Hesperia* 79.4, 499-539.

BENJAMIN, W. 1999
The Arcades Project, Cambridge, MA.

BRUGHMANS, T., A.C.F. COLLAR & F. COWARD (EDS.) 2016
The Connected Past. Challenging Networks in Archaeology and History, Oxford.

BÜSCHER, M., J. URRY & K. WITCHGER (EDS.) 2011
Mobile Methods, London and New York.

COATES, J. 2017
'Key Figures of Mobility: The Flâneur', *Social Anthropology* 25.1, 28-41.

COLEMAN, S. & J. ELSNER 1995
Pilgrimage. Past and Present in the World Religions, London.

COLLAR, A. & T.M. KRISTENSEN (EDS.) FORTHCOMING A
Going, Gathering and Giving. Economies of Sacred Travel in the Ancient Mediterranean (Religions in the Graeco-Roman World), Leiden.

COLLAR, A. & T.M. KRISTENSEN (EDS.) FORTHCOMING B
Comparativism and Ancient Mediterranean Pilgrimage (Aarhus Studies in Mediterranean Antiquity), Aarhus.

CONNELLY, J.B. 2011
'Ritual Movement through Greek Sacred Space: Towards an Archaeology of Performance', in *Ritual Dynamics in the Ancient Mediterranean: Agency, Emotion, Gender, Reception,* A. Chaniotis (ed.), Stuttgart, 313-46.

CRESSWELL, T. 2006
On the Move. Mobility in the Modern Western World, London and New York.

DILLON, M. 1997
Pilgrims and Pilgrimage in Ancient Greece, London and New York.

DOXIADIS, K.A. 1937
Raumordnung im griechischen Städtebau, Heidelberg.

ELSNER, J. 2017
'Excavating Pilgrimage', in *Excavating Pilgrimage. Archaeological Approaches to Sacred Travel and Movement in the Ancient World,* T.M. Kristensen & W. Friese (eds.), London and New York, 265-74.

ELSNER, J. & I. RUTHERFORD (EDS.) 2000
Pilgrimage in Graeco-Roman and Early Christian Antiquity. Seeing the Gods, Oxford.

FICUCIELLO, L. 2008
Le strade di Atene, Athens.

GERDING, H. 2006
'The Erechtheion and the Panathenaic Procession', *AJA* 110.3, 389-401.

GRAF, F. 1996
'*Pompai* in Greece. Some Considerations about Space and Ritual in the Greek *Polis*', in *The Role of Religion in the Early Greek Polis,* R. Hägg (ed.), Stockholm, 55-65.

HÖLSCHER, T. 1999
Öffentliche Räume in frühen griechischen Städten (2nd ed.), Heidelberg.

INGLIS, D. 2004
'Auto Couture. Thinking the Car in Post-War France', *Theory, Culture and Society* 21, 197-219.

JENSEN, O.B. 2013
Staging Mobilities, London and New York.

JENSEN, O.B. 2014
Designing Mobilities, Aalborg.

KALDELLIS, A. 2009
The Christian Parthenon. Classicism and Pilgrimage in Byzantine Athens, Cambridge.

KONSTANTINOU, A. 2018
Female Mobility and Gendered Space in Ancient Greek Myth, London.

KOWALZIG, B. 2007
Singing for the Gods. Performances of Myth and Ritual in Archaic and Classical Greece, Oxford.

KRISTENSEN, T.M. FORTHCOMING A
Materiality and Mobility in Ancient Mediterranean Pilgrimage. Landscapes, Gatherings, Presence, London and New York.

KRISTENSEN, T.M. FORTHCOMING B
'Mobile Situations: *Exedrae* as Stages of Gathering in Greek Sanctuaries', *World Archaeology* 50.2.

KRISTENSEN, T.M. & W. FRIESE (EDS.) 2017
Excavating Pilgrimage. Archaeological Approaches to Sacred Travel and Movement in the Ancient World (Routledge Studies in Pilgrimage, Religious Travel and Tourism), London and New York.

LEARY, J. 2014
'Past Mobility: An Introduction', in *Past Mobilities,* J. Leary (ed.), London and New York, 1-19.

MONTIGLIO, S. 2005
Wandering in Ancient Greek Culture, Chicago.

POLIGNAC, F. DE 1995
Cults, Territory, and the Origins of the Greek City-State, Chicago.

PRETZLER, M. 2007
Pausanias. Travel Writing in Ancient Greece, London.

RUTHERFORD, I. 2013
State Pilgrims and Sacred Observers in Ancient Greece. A Study of Theôriâ and Theôroi, Cambridge.

SHEAR, J. 2001
'Polis and Panathenaia: The History and Development of Athena's Festival', PhD diss., University of Pennsylvania.

SHELLER, M. & J. URRY 2006
'The New Mobilities Paradigm', *Environment and Planning A: Economy and Space* 38.2, 207-26.

SHELLER, M. 2014
'The New Mobilities Paradigm for a Live Sociology', *Current Sociology Review* 62.6, 789-811.

SOUKOP, C. 2013
'The Postmodern Ethnographic Flaneur and the Study of Hyper-Mediated Everyday Life', *Journal of Contemporary Ethnography* 42.3, 226-54.

STAVRIANOPOULOU, E. 2015
'The Archaeology of Processions', in *A Companion to the Archaeology of Religion in the Ancient World,* R. Raja & J. Rüpke (eds.), Malden, MA, 349-61.

TRUE, M., J. DAEHNER, J.B. GROSSMAN, K.D.S. LAPATIN & E.M. NAM, 2004
'Greek Processions', *ThesCRA* 1, 1-20.

YASIN, A.M. 2012
'Sight Lines of Sanctity at Late Antique Martyria', in *Architecture of the Sacred. Space, Ritual, and Experience from Classical Greece to Byzantium,* B.D. Wescoat & R.G. Ousterhout (eds.), Cambridge, 248-80.

PART I

MOVEMENT IN THE CITY

Performing Piety: A Phenomenological Approach to Athenian Processions

Erin Warford

Imagine for a moment that you are a basket-bearer in the Panathenaic procession. In the lead walk the priests and priestesses, setting a steady pace. The basket on your head is beginning to feel heavy, and the handles are slippery in your hands. Your gold jewellery hangs heavy on your neck, jangling with each careful step, and the white paint on your face itches in the summer heat. Ahead of you stretches the wide street, lined with wooden stands which are filled with people, chattering and murmuring as you pass by. You are acutely conscious of all the eyes on you, and the stands channel all the sound down to you. In the distance, you can see the Acropolis, the great rock of Athena. Behind you, you can faintly hear the musicians with their flutes and *kitharai*, matching their solemn tunes to the pace of the procession. Once in a while, the wind carries a whiff of incense to you from the incense-bearers, or the smell of the cattle and sheep who are plodding along behind you to the altar. In your mind's eye, you imagine the procession winding behind you, and you feel giddy and proud. You imagine the altar waiting atop the Acropolis in front of Athena's temple, the goddess watching from her pedestal, the fire lit and waiting for the sacrifice. You can almost taste your share of the roasted meat.

Scholarship on ancient festivals and festival processions tends to be rather clinical, focused on *aitia* and myth, or the mechanics of the ritual. This approach fails to capture the rich sensory experience of these rituals, and especially processions, which combined movement through a landscape with a variety of sights, sounds, and smells, perceived by both the spectators and the participants of the procession.[1] Much of this sensory experience was deeply personal, and it would be impossible to reconstruct any individual's experience. The difficulty does not, however, invalidate the usefulness of attempting to consider this sensory experience, the possible perceptions or meanings of this sensory experience, and the potential ways that these symbols influenced collective memory and identity.

Some scholars studying ancient Greek sacrificial processions have attempted to classify those processions as a way of understanding them. For example, Martin Nilsson organized processions into categories such as processions to the deity, processions with the

1 Angelos Chaniotis has produced welcome and fascinating work (2006, 2011) which injects emotion back into our analysis of festivals and processions and analyzes the ways that these rituals help create "emotional communities", but his work does not focus on the sensory experience of processions. Connelly 2011 focuses mainly on the routes and space of processions, particularly spaces used for dance – an ephemeral but vitally important element of ancient ritual sensory experience. Raja & Rüpke 2015 contains many important articles on experience in ancient religion and the ways we can access that experience through material culture (see especially Huet 2015). However, Stavrianopoulou's chapter on processions focuses on processions as performances and movements through a landscape, and gives little discussion of processional symbols aside from their significance as displays of wealth.

Fig. 1. Wooden plaque from Pitsa with a painted scene of a religious procession. 540-530 BCE. L. 31 cm, max. H. 14.5 cm. A 16464, National Archaeological Museum, Athens (photographer: G. Patrikianos).

deity, and "magical" processions which were originally focused not on a god, but on a specific ritual goal (e.g. processions that carried around a symbol like the phallus or *eiresione*).[2] Fritz Graf, seeking a classification focused on landscape and movement, divided processions into two categories, centripetal (moving toward the city centre) and centrifugal (moving away from the centre).[3] Such classification systems imply that the processions in each category share significant characteristics with each other that they do not share with the processions in other categories, but this is not necessarily true – nor do processions always fit neatly into such categories.[4] What to do, for example, with processions that circumambulate the city, such as the Athenian Thargelia? The processions of each Greek city-state formed a ritual system, in dialogue with and related to each other, sharing symbols, participants, and topography.

Perhaps part of the problem is that processions are complex and difficult to define. What differentiates a procession from a group of people walking down the street? Participants may move in a particular way, as a unified group, perhaps in lines or formations; they may be holding signs or other symbols; they may be escorting a float, a statue, or a distinguished person; they might be shouting slogans or singing hymns; and they might be dressed distinctively, in costumes or priestly vestments.[5] It is by these types of sensory cues that we distinguish a procession from other types of movement. Athina Kavoulaki has proposed a very useful "basic structure" for processions, including human participants, symbols or offerings, musical accompaniment, and

2 Nilsson 1916, 309-23.

3 Graf 1996, 55-65.

4 Kavoulaki 2000, 145 rightly emphasizes the variation in "tone, rhythm and colour" present in processions. Stavrianopoulou 2015, 351-2 criticizes Graf for excluding the element of performance and communication between participants and spectators, as well as the dynamic character of processions.

5 Luginbühl 2015, 47 defines processions as "a number of people moving forward in an orderly fashion as part of a ceremony or other ritual activity, generally of a religious nature".

an established route with a defined start and end point.[6] Additional elements could be added to this basic structure to alter the sensory experience and meaning of the ritual.

The ritual processions of ancient Athens also included these types of sensory cues, so that even a small private sacrificial procession like the one that Dikaiopolis organized with his family in Aristophanes' *Acharnians* would have been immediately recognizable (Fig. 1).[7] Participants in Greek processions were associated with a particular kind of movement that distinguished them from normal walking.[8] Sacrificial animals and other bloodless offerings were escorted or carried, along with other symbols. Auloi were the most common instruments played during processions, although *kitharai*, syrinxes, and drums are also attested.[9] Hymns or songs were also ubiquitous, and certain distinctive types were associated with particular processions.[10] Distinctive dress was also part of ancient Greek ritual processions. Xenophon mentions garments reserved for festivals, something like one's "festival best".[11] Priests and *kanephoroi* dressed in particular clothes, and *kanephoroi* may also have worn makeup to whiten their faces.[12] Demosthenes ordered gold crowns for himself and his chorus and a gold-embroidered robe for himself to wear in the City Dionysia procession.[13]

Literary evocations of processions further emphasise their sensory appeal and draw on their audience's sense-memory. Although a theoria was a different form of sacred travel than a ritual procession, it is still noteworthy that in Aristophanes' *Peace* Trygaios remarks on Theoria's wonderful smell, which evokes for him among other things "sweet fruits, festivals, the Dionysia, the harmony of flutes, the tragic poets".[14] In Aristophanes' *Frogs*, Dionysos and Xanthus first become aware of a procession of initiates in the underworld when they hear the faint sound of pipes and smell torches.[15] Several authors use a phrase vividly translated as "fill the streets with the smell of burnt sacrifice".[16] Incense-burners, or thymiateria, and incense were carried in processions.[17] Both incense, which was imported from afar, and incense-burners, frequently made of precious metals, were symbols of wealth in service of and for the glory of the deity.[18]

Within the procession, participants and spectators alike experienced a rich collection of symbols – items perceived by the senses which possessed meaning for the people who perceived them. These symbols included items worn or objects and offerings carried in procession; the animals led to the sacrifice; hymns, chants, or music that accompanied the procession or marked specific places along the way; dances or movement specific to the processional context; and the monuments, buildings, or art visible along the processional route. Participants and spectators perceived these symbols in different ways, however. Participants walked along the procession's route, seeing all the monuments, buildings, art, and the natural landscape and observing or participating in the minor performances which took place along the route. Spectators were stationary, watching the procession from the side of the road, or perhaps

6 Kavoulaki 2000, 145.
7 Ar. *Ach*. 241-62.
8 Polyaenus, *Strat*. 5.5; Kavoulaki 2000, 154.
9 Haldane 1966, 98-107.
10 The *oschophorikon* at the Oschophoria, see Rutherford & Irvine 1988, 43-51; Kavoulaki 2000, 153. On the "melody of the wild fig. " at the Thargelia, see Bremmer 1983, 313-4.
11 Xen. *Oec*. 9.6.
12 Parker 2005, 93-5, 225 n. 35; Roccos 1995, 641-66.
13 Dem. *Meid*. 16, 22.
14 Ar. *Pax*. 530-2 (trans. O'Neill).
15 Ar. *Ran*. 312-5.
16 Eur. *Alc*. 1156; Ar. *Av*. 1233, *Eq*. 1320; Dem. 43.66.
17 Andoc. 4.29; Parthenon frieze East VIII fig. 56 carries a thymiaterion; Xen. *Ephes*. 1.2.4 describes incense carried in procession (but no thymiateria).
18 Thymiateria made of precious metals as part of the state's processional vessels: Andoc. 4.29; Thuc. 6.46; Diod. Sic. 13.3. Used by private citizens as a mark of luxury: Dem. *Against Androtion*. 22.75; Pl. *Resp*. 373a.

sitting in stands or carts for a better vantage point. They saw the entire procession with all its participants and symbols, but did not experience the landscape in the same manner as the participants. This is not to say that the spectators simply passively absorbed the procession's symbolic spectacle. Eftychia Stavrianopoulou rightly emphasises the central importance of the interplay between participants and spectators, sensory symbols, and landscape elements which can "evoke the creation or collapse of communities".[19] The presence of spectators who were actively watching was an important part of the ritual, since they could bear witness that the procession (and sacrifice) had been properly carried out.[20] The majority of Athenians played the role of spectator most of the time, but this does not diminish the experience of the participant; presumably, if and when an Athenian had the chance to participate in a procession, those memories and impressions influenced his or her later experiences as a spectator.

The meanings of these processional symbols varied from person to person, highly conditioned by personal experience. At least some of these layers of meaning, however, were shared within the community through the links between the symbols and shared myths, history, or knowledge of other rituals. Through their common sensory experience of these rituals and familiarity with the meanings and interpretations of a shared set of symbols, processions brought Athenians together to create, shape, and maintain their communal identity.

Processions were repeated once every year, two years, or four years. Thus, Athenians had the chance to experience the procession and its symbols repeatedly throughout their lives. Such repeated retrieval of memories and cultural knowledge about a procession's symbolism could certainly have reinforced that knowledge in the Athenians' minds.[21] It also allows for the possibility of change in an individual's understanding of religious symbols, as he or she grew older, experienced new rituals, and gained new experiences or insights, and as society itself changed.

These memories of processions and their symbols were also collective, in the sense that they were held by many individual members of a group. While individual emotional experiences during a festival or deeply personal responses to particular symbols were not necessarily shared, the spectators of a procession saw, heard, or smelled roughly the same sensory symbols.[22] As Anthony P. Cohen has observed, just as communities contain a group of individuals with different experiences and views, so symbols accumulate a range of individual meanings.[23] Because the members of a community share the symbols, they overlook the variations in meaning and perceive themselves to be more similar to each other than to the members of other communities, in part based on this shared symbolic language. All who came to see the Panathenaic procession would have seen the peplos with its woven tale of Athena's triumph, or the *kanephoros* walking past in her festival garments bearing her ceremonial basket, or the *thallophoroi* carrying their olive branches. Moreover, since the procession was repeated, two people who had attended the procession in different years would still have shared collective memories about the ritual, since they would have seen much the same set of symbols.

This is not to suggest that processions were static, unchanging rituals. Some things would alter from year to year, for example the identity of the various participants, or perhaps the specific wording of prayers or the tunes played by the musicians. Other

19 Stavrianopoulou 2015, 350.

20 Graf 1996, 57-8.

21 Roediger *et al.* 2009, 138-70.

22 Except performances at particular places along the processional route, which only those nearby would have observed.

23 Cohen 1985, 11-21.

elements of the procession changed to reflect social or political changes in the community, for example the addition of Athenian allies and colonists in the processions of the Panathenaia and City Dionysia during the late 5th century BC. Some symbols, however, were consistently present in these processions, and it is especially with respect to these symbols that we may consider the effects of collective memory.

The concept of collective memory was pioneered by Maurice Halbwachs, who pointed out that the formation and recall of memories was socially structured and conditioned.[24] Geoffrey Cubitt points out that in fact, groups require a collective memory for three reasons: to ensure the satisfactory performance of their own activities, to maintain and communicate their corporate identity, and to maintain and advance their position with respect to other groups or broader institutional structures.[25] The memories collectively held by the group are not necessarily static bodies of information, waiting to be passed on to the newest member as a lump sum of knowledge; rather, the group is itself a place of exchange and interaction, processes which form and maintain the group memory.[26] By participating in the formation and retrieval of these memories, an individual demonstrates and creates a sense of "belonging" to the group. In Athens, these groups existed at many levels, for example the family, the deme, the phratry, the tribe, elite drinking groups, and many more. The group most visible to us, however, is the collective of Athenian citizens. By attending a polis-level festival procession as either a participant or a spectator, an Athenian reaffirmed his or her identity and membership in this group.

Of course, processions could also be attended by non-Athenians, including resident metics and foreign visitors. Non-Athenians lacked access to the shared memories of those who had been raised on Athenian myth and ritual. Some metics who had lived in Athens for longer periods could have become familiar with collective Athenian memory, depending on how enthusiastically they embraced their new home. But they also possessed another set of collective memories tied to their original polis, which differentiated them from Athenians. Also, they would probably not have had the same emotional attachment to Athenian collective memory – for example, they could not say that their ancestors were buried in Athenian cemeteries, or that their ancestors were born from the land itself.

Other scholars have emphasised that memory is also culturally structured and conditioned, embedded in and transmitted through cultural institutions and recurring rituals.[27] As one example, Paul Connerton discusses commemorative rituals – rituals that celebrate their continuity with past observations of the same ritual, and frequently also with a mythical or historical figure or group.[28] Unfortunately, cult myths are not always preserved for the Athenian festivals, and sometimes their associations with mythic figures may be secondary.[29] Connerton suggests that this "rhetoric of re-enactment" is enacted through the recurrence of the ritual at the same time every year, as well as verbal or gestural repetition within the ritual.[30] Athenian festivals did follow a cyclical calendar, but it is harder to find verbal or gestural repetition within the procession itself (the sacrifice is another matter), aside from broader cultural norms of gesture and speech. Hymns and music for the procession could be rewritten, and new ones composed; and we have little evidence for specific gestures during the procession, aside from a sort of

24 Halbwachs 1992 [1925], 37-9. On social memory in 5th-century Athens, see Steinbock 2012, 1-47.

25 Cubitt 2007, 134-5.

26 Cubitt 2007, 166.

27 Connerton 1989, 36-40; Assmann 2011.

28 Connerton 1989, 41-71.

29 For example, Theseus' connections to the Oschophoria, first attested in the 4th century BC. Plut. *Thes.* 23.2; Philoch. F183; Istros *FGrH* 334 F8; Harding 2008, 61-3.

30 Connerton 1989, 65-70.

"processional walk".[31] The important repetition in these rituals was not the content of the hymns or the form of the dances, but the fact of their performance in the right place at the right time, as well as the repetition of meaningful sensory symbols. Each year was another opportunity to delight the deity with a splendid procession, fine offerings, elegant choral dances, and beautiful hymns.[32]

Jan Assmann focused less on the concept of repetition and more on the question of storage. In his view, cultural memory is "disembodied" and "stored away in symbolic forms"; it has to be constantly "circulated and re-embodied".[33] Cultural memory involves the mythical or historical past, communicated through formalized ceremonies and rituals using icons, dances, performances, and archaic language. Participation is hierarchically structured so that only a select few have access to the full range of cultural memory.[34] The symbols in Classical Athenian processions did frequently draw their meaning from the distant mythical or historical past, but they could also commemorate or reference events within living memory (such as prominent military victories, or the relatively recent establishment of democracy). They do not fit comfortably into Jan Assmann's dichotomy between communicative and cultural memory. Nor was the full understanding or appreciation of these symbols (dances, hymns, objects carried, etc.) confined to "specialized carriers of memory".[35]

These concepts of social and cultural memory are not new to the study of Athens. Other scholars have devoted much ink to considering how the Athenians' sense of community and identity was reinforced by myths, monuments, speeches, and political institutions.[36] As yet, no one has thoroughly considered the institution of the *pompe* – how these large, public processions, which reached so many people and were so frequently repeated, contributed to the Athenian memory community and Athenian identity.

The concept of cultural memory is helpful, though not quite as either Paul Connerton or Jan Assmann defines it. Assmann's idea that cultural information is stored in symbols – in the sense that a member of the community perceiving the symbol then remembers the cultural information – fits the emphasis on display and sensory perception present in Greek processions. Connerton's focus on the repetition of commemorative rituals is also an important component of how cultural memory functions, how it is preserved, and how its re-enactment serves to reinforce identity. Sacrifices are somewhat similar in these ways (and in some ways Connerton's description of commemorative rituals better fits Greek sacrifices), but processions remain unique because of their movement, which allows more interaction with the landscape and offers greater opportunity for display and for a larger number of people to see and remember the significance of the symbols involved. In the following sections, I will analyze a few of these symbols, examining who conveyed and observed them, some of the associations that these symbols may have possessed, and other places or rituals where the symbols also appeared – in other words, what shared cultural memories these symbols might have evoked in the minds of Athenians.

31 See n. 8 above.
32 Furley 2007, 119.
33 Assmann 2011, 17.
34 Assmann 2011, 18-22.
35 Assmann 2011, 20-1.

36 This is not a comprehensive list. Shear 2011 focuses on the revolutions at the end of the 5th century; Wolpert 2002 examines the period just after the Thirty, as does Loraux 2002; Loraux 1986 focuses on funeral orations; Loraux 2000, 1993 on myths of autochthony and its implications for gender and citizenship; Bridges *et al.* 2007 looks at the Persian Wars; Castriota 1992 examines the depiction of myths on public monuments following the Persian Wars; Arrington 2014 focuses on the methods and spaces of commemoration for the war dead in 5th-century Athens.

Fig. 2. Block V, the central scene of the east side of the Parthenon Frieze, showing the *peplos* at the head of the Panathenaic procession. 438-432 BCE. H. 1.02 m. British Museum 1816,0610.19 (courtesy of the Trustees of the British Museum).

The Peplos of Athena

Once every four years, a peplos woven with the tale of Athena's victory over the Giants was presented to the goddess at her penteteric festival, the Great Panathenaia (Fig. 2).[37] The peplos was a powerful symbol for the Athenians; in Aristophanes' *Knights*, the chorus describes their fathers as "worthy of the peplos".[38] The Gigantomachy myth connected to the Panathenaia told of Athena's victory, an appropriate myth for a procession where military victory was a prominent theme.[39] Elsewhere in the procession, Athenian hoplites, men in chariots (*apobatai*), and cavalry added to the martial theme.[40] The Gigantomachy myth also expressed the triumph and reaffirmation of Zeus' reign, and thus cosmic order and stability.[41]

The image of Athena conquering a Giant first appeared in Attic vase-painting in the mid-6th century BC, about the same time that the Great Panathenaia was first organised as a penteteric, internationally oriented athletic festival (Fig. 3).[42] Luca Giuliani suggests that the peplos design showing the Gigantomachy was established at this time, perhaps linked to a new poetic version of the Gigantomachy myth, and it was the peplos which inspired the vase-painters.[43] It is most likely that the vase-painters saw the peplos in procession, where it was displayed for maximum

37 Mansfield 1985; Barber 1992, 103-17; Shear 2001, 97-102, 173-85.

38 Ar. *Eq.* 565-8; Shear 2001, 174.

39 Shear 2001, especially chapters 1, 2, and 4.

40 Shear 2001, 155-6; Neils 1996, 181-2 on the 6th-century vase evidence for hoplites and cavalry in the procession; the *apobatai* are attested on the Parthenon frieze and perhaps in Ar. *Nub.* 69-70, see Shear 2001, 161.

41 Sourvinou-Inwood 2011, 270-80.

42 Shapiro 1989, 38; Vian 1952, 246; Giuliani 2000, 266-72; Shear 2001, 35-6.

43 Giuliani 2000, 264-72; Vian 1952, 95-106, 251-3.

Fig. 3. Kantharos fragment depicting the Gigantomachy. 560-550 BCE. L. 14 cm., max. H. 8.3 cm. Acr. 2134a, National Archaeological Museum, Athens (photographer: K. Konstantopoulos).

visual impact on the spectators.[44] However, it is not entirely clear how this display was accomplished in the Classical period. Classical and Hellenistic references suggest the peplos was hoisted on something similar to a ship's mast, but an actual ship-cart is not attested until the Roman period.[45] A piece of clothing like the peplos would be most easily displayed on a pole with a horizontal bar, to spread the fabric out and allow the design to be seen. It seems quite natural that this would be compared to a ship's mast, but it remains unclear how this contraption was conveyed to the Acropolis in the Classical period. Also, the Gigantomachy design is usually thought to have been relatively standardized; the repetition of the procession every four years would have made the image more recognizable and cemented it in the memory of both the artists and the general populace.

While the theme of the peplos' design featured male concerns, the garment itself was most likely produced by Athenian women.[46] Nine months before the Panathenaia, during the Chalkeia festival for Athena and Hephaistos, the priestesses (of Athena, and perhaps Pandrosos) and two of the *arrhephoroi* set up the loom used to weave the peplos.[47] Someone must have prepared the wool for weaving by cleaning, carding, and spinning it. The thread also had to be dyed, because the peplos was saffron and hyacinth coloured.[48] Purple, being a rare dye, was associated with wealth and luxury. Saffron-coloured clothing was closely associated with women, an appropriate choice for Athena's gift and also meaningful to the women who wove and saw the peplos.[49] Unfortunately the age and identities of the girls and women who wove the peplos are not clear. The *arrhephoroi*, who were between seven and 11 years old, may have helped with the weaving in addition to setting up the loom.[50] Well-born citizen women probably also contributed their skills and time.[51]

44 Alternately, the painters could have seen the peplos on display somewhere on the Acropolis. If the peplos was hung on Athena's statue as a garment, it might have been difficult to get a good view of the design. Mansfield's theory that the peplos dedicated at the Great Panathenaia was a tapestry instead of a garment and that it was hung somewhere on the Acropolis for viewing is not universally accepted (Mansfield 1985, accepted by Barber 1992, 103-17; Sourvinou-Inwood 2011, 267; rejected by Aleshire & Lambert 2003, 72; Shear differs on many points, 2001, 173-85).

45 Shear 2001, 143-54.

46 Mansfield 1985, 54 proposed that the penteteric peplos was produced by professional male weavers. A late tradition records that a pair of famous male weavers wove the first peplos (Zen. *Epitome Paroimion* 1.56; Diogenian. 2.7; Ath. 2.48b). Shear rejects Mansfield's theory, but suggests that the male weavers could have been commissioned to produce the first design (Shear 2001, 182-3).

47 *Etym. Magn.* 805.43 s.v. *Chalkeia*; *Suda* s.v. *Chalkeia*; Parker 2005, 464-5.

48 Barber 1992, 116.

49 Håland 2004, 156-8; Barber 1992, 116-7.

50 Mansfield 1985, 277-81; Sourvinou-Inwood 2011, 268-9; Barber 1992, 113, who points out that young girls often participate in detailed traditional weaving because their fingers are small and nimble and their eyesight is still good. Inscriptions from the late 2nd century BC speak of 120 *parthenoi* who either prepared the wool, helped with the weaving, or perhaps did both: Aleshire & Lambert 2003, 65-86.

51 Eur. *Hec.* 466-73 and schol. *Iphigenia in Tauris* 221-4.

Weaving was a prominent part of the lives and identities of Greek women, and was linked to the Panathenaia through myth as well as through the production of the peplos. Pandrosos, a daughter of Kekrops, was supposedly the first to weave woollen clothes, while her sister Aglauros was the first to dress the statue of Athena.[52] Both daughters (as well as a third sister) were entrusted with the infant Erichthonios, mythologized as the founder of the Panathenaia and the fosterling of Athena.[53] Pandrosos received a ewe in sacrifice at the Panathenaia, and also had a kourotrophic role in the development of young girls through the Arrhephoria festival.[54] The *arrhephoroi*, who helped set up the loom for the peplos and perhaps helped with its weaving, occasionally set up commemorative inscriptions to Athena and Pandrosos.[55]

The weaving of the Panathenaic peplos involved many girls and women, and thus would have been a point of interaction for girls still learning their place in society and the married women who could teach them. This point of interaction would also have provided an opportunity for singing and storytelling – passing on a particular type of cultural memory to the next generation.[56] Literary sources frequently mention women singing or telling stories at the loom, whether they were chanting rhythmically as a mnemonic device to remember the patterns or sharing myths, songs, and other wisdom.[57]

The Panathenaic peplos was a potent symbol with many strands of meaning, associations which it might have evoked as it passed by the hundreds of spectators during the Panathenaic procession. Men and women alike could marvel at the skill of the weavers and the beauty of the cloth. The men in particular might have identified with their goddess's inspiring victory over the Giants. All could acknowledge the import of the gods' victory over chaos, the reaffirmation of Olympian rule, and the reassurance of continued stability in the universe.[58] The peplos could have taken on a political meaning, symbolizing the unification of diverse people or viewpoints into a single community.[59] For the women in the crowd, the peplos might have had a very different set of associations. Particularly in times when the Athenians were actively at war, women who had lost fathers, husbands, or sons in war might not have sympathized with the theme of military glory which was so prominent in both the procession and the peplos. On a more positive note, the creation of the peplos was entirely the work of women, and so one can imagine that the peplos itself was viewed as their contribution to honouring Athena, a source of pride. Weaving was an activity with which all the female spectators were very familiar; upon seeing the peplos, these women could easily have imagined the process of production, the painstaking weaving of figures and details, and the atmosphere of female companionship (Fig. 4).[60] The sight of the peplos might have called up other sense-memories, too. There was an auditory element to weaving: the sounds of the shuttle striking the taut threads (frequently described in literature as "singing"), as well as the songs and tales shared among the weavers. As a piece of fabric, the peplos might also have evoked the sense of touch, the feel of the fabric.

52 Phot. s.v. *Pandrosos*. For Aglauros, see Phot. s.v. *Kallynteria*.

53 Sourvinou-Inwood 2011, 36-48. On Erichthonios as founder of the Panathenaia, see Shear 2001, 43-54.

54 Philoch. *FGrH* 328 F10. Aglauros was linked to the Plynteria and Kallynteria instead.

55 Sourvinou-Inwood 2011, 29.

56 I would like to thank Roger Woodard for this suggestion.

57 Posidippos epigram 55, where girls are pictured singing Sappho's songs while weaving; Nagy 2016; Tuck 2006, 539-50; 2009, 151-9; Heath 2011, 69-104; Snyder 1981.

58 Sourvinou-Inwood 2011, 277.

59 Scheid & Svenbro 1996, 9-34, with special reference to Ar. *Lys*. 567-86.

60 Håland 2004, 168-171; weaving was frequently depicted as a communal activity, e.g. the Amasis painter lekythos, MMA 31.11.10, dated 550-530 BC; Bundrick 2008, 283-334.

Fig. 4. Lekythos with a scene of women weaving by the Amasis Painter. 550-530 BCE. H. 17.15 cm. Metropolitan Museum of Art 31.11.10 (Fletcher Fund, 1931).

The peplos was the main type of garment worn by Athenian women in the 5th century, and so was a familiar part of women's daily life and dress.[61] The peplos was thus imbued with many layers of sensory and cultural memory.

Christiane Sourvinou-Inwood, in her analysis of the rituals surrounding the peplos, proposed that the ever-repeating sequence of its production and dedication was designed to provide an experience of "everlasting continuity", emphasizing the cyclical nature of the festival calendar and time in general.[62] This sense of continuity might have been reinforced by the garment itself, which was woven the same size, was made of the same colours, and displayed similar imagery every four years. We cannot be sure who conveyed the peplos to the Acropolis in the procession, but we can suggest the kinds of visual, auditory, and tactile sense-memories it might have evoked in the spectators. The associations of the peplos and its imagery were repeated each time it was offered to Athena, continually interwoven with the cultural memory of the Athenian spectators.

Olive Branches

While the Panathenaic peplos was a symbol used only in the Panathenaic procession, other symbols were used in different ritual contexts, which would have increased the number of times Athenians encountered these symbols during the ritual year and thus embedded them more deeply in the Athenians' cultural memory. By examining the different contexts where these symbols appeared, we can gain a better understanding of their layered meanings.

One such symbol is the olive branch. Olive branches were, in one sense, Panhellenic ritual symbols. Suppliants typically carried branches, sometimes wrapped with wool, to the shrine of the deity where they sought protection or good favour.[63] Olive crowns were also linked to civic and athletic honours. They were given to victors at both Athens and Olympia.[64] Alcibiades on his return from exile was described as decorating his ships with various victory symbols, including olive shoots.[65] Aeschines mentions the awarding of olive-leaf crowns for civic reasons, while Plato discusses awarding olive-leaf crowns to the best soldiers and citizens.[66]

61 Roccos 2000, 245.

62 Sourvinou-Inwood 2011, 208-14.

63 Aesch. *Cho.* 1035; Din. 1.18; Eur. *Supp.* 10; Polyb. 30.9.

64 At Nemea, Delphi, and Isthmia the crowns were made of other foliage.

65 Ath. 12.49. The other symbols were two different kinds of victory crowns.

66 Aeschin. 2.46, 3.187; Pl. *Leg.* 943c proposes awarding olive-leaf crowns to the best of each class of soldier; Pl. *Leg.* 946b awarding olive-leaf crowns to the first, second, and third-best citizens over 50 years old.

The olive also had special resonance for Athenians, however, which coloured its symbolic meaning for those familiar with the myths. The Athenians preserved the myth that Athena had first given them the olive tree during her dispute with Poseidon over who was to become the patron deity of Athens; the tree itself stood on the Acropolis, near the temple of Athena Polias, whose statue was made of olive wood.[67] The olive was considered Athena's sacred tree; in addition to the one on the Acropolis, there was a grove of a dozen sacred olive trees in the Academy, and further trees scattered throughout the Attic countryside on private property.[68] These sacred trees were nominally the providers of the olive oil given as prizes at the Panathenaic games.[69] After the Persian attack on the Acropolis in 480 BC, the sacred olive tree sprouted and became a symbol of Athenian resilience and re-growth.[70] This tree, located beside the charred ruins of Athena's temple, thus acquired a powerful new layer of symbolism. After the completion of the Parthenon in 432 BC, there was a second olive tree on the Acropolis – a sculptured tree in the centre of the west pediment of the Parthenon, which depicted the contest between Athena and Poseidon.[71] The tree's central placement mirrors its importance to the Athenians, who would have seen both the sculpted tree and the live tree when they processed up to the Acropolis for the sacrifice to Athena.

The olive branch also had a symbolic place in the procession itself. Old men called *thallophoroi*, who were perhaps chosen for their beauty, carried olive branches in the procession.[72] The role of the *thallophoroi* supposedly went back to Erichthonios, founder of the Panathenaia, highlighting the significance of this symbol through its perceived antiquity.[73] Why were old men chosen to carry this symbol? Perhaps there is a sense of the same cyclical repetition that Christiane Sourvinou-Inwood saw in the production of the peplos – olive shoots, symbols of new growth, carried by men nearing the end of their life cycle.[74]

Olive branches also carried connotations of supplication. Thus in Mounichion, young girls carried olive branches with wool to Artemis Delphinios in south-eastern Athens.[75] The *thallophoroi* of the Panathenaic procession were also drawing on the imagery of the suppliant, which was entirely appropriate as the procession approached Athena in hopes of securing her blessings for the next year. The association between olive branches and suppliants might explain why this type of foliage was chosen for the begging ritual of the *eiresione*, in which the primary symbol was an olive branch laden with various symbols of agricultural production.[76] An official *eiresione* was carried to the temple of Apollo Delphinios in the Pyanopsia procession by a boy whose parents were both alive, which seems like a symbolic wish for similar blessings on the rest of the city – long life and a lack of disease or misfortune killing people before their time. On the same day, young boys carried their own *eiresione* from house to house in a sort of begging ritual and eventually hung the branch

67 Parker 1987, 198-200.

68 Arist. *Ath. Pol.* 60.1-3; Lys. 7, where the speaker is defending himself against a charge concerning a sacred olive tree on his property. See also Shear 2001, 405; Papazarkadas 2011, 260-84.

69 Shear 2001, 405-6.

70 Hdt. 8.55.1.

71 Hurwit 1999, 174-5; Palagia 1993, 40-52; 2005, 242-53.

72 Xen. *Symp.* 4.17 states that beautiful old men were chosen.

73 Philoch. *FGrH* 328 F9; Schol. on Ar. *Vesp.* 544b; Shear 2001, 53-5, 132-4.

74 Olive branches are also ritually associated with young girls and boys (see following). An olive crown was hung over the door of a house where a newborn boy lived (Hsch. s.v. *stephanon epiferein*; Ath. 9.10).

75 Parke 1977, 137; Simon 1983, 80. Plut. *Thes.* 18.1 explains the practice with reference to Theseus.

76 Parke 1977, 76-7; Parker 2005, 204-6.

over a person's doorway as a symbol of hope for a prosperous year.[77]

Olive leaves and branches thus had a variety of connotations which were at play in several processions in Athens. The olive as a symbol of Athena's commitment as the patron goddess of Athens, as a symbol of the Athenians' rebirth and resilience, and as a symbol of victory and civic honour were all meanings most appropriate at the Panathenaia. As a symbol of rebirth and regrowth (olive trees are difficult to kill), the olive branch might have been an appropriate object for young girls to bear to Artemis or young boys to carry about the city in the *eiresione* ritual. One imagines that whatever the context, in the years after 480/479 BC, the Athenians viewed the olive branch with a new sense of kinship and patriotism as they began to rebuild their city in the aftermath of the Persian destruction.

It is curiously difficult to find any association between the olive branch and peace in this early period, though the association was certainly present among the Romans.[78] Perhaps there are the beginnings of this connotation in the olive branches carried by suppliants, who might be running from harm and seeking asylum at a sanctuary. It has also been suggested that the association with peace derives from the sacred truces of the Olympic games.[79]

Figs

Dried figs also appear as a symbol in several ritual contexts. Figs were considered "the first civilized food" and were linked with the autochthons, the first inhabitants of Attica, who ate them.[80] Just as the Athenians were proud to have originated the cultivation of olives and grain, they also believed that they were the first to grow figs.[81] A rural sanctuary of Demeter and Kore was located near the house of Phytalos, a local Attic king to whom Demeter first revealed the secrets of fig cultivation.[82]

At the Plynteria, a cake of dried figs called the *hegeteria* was carried at the front of the procession – it symbolically "led" it.[83] The procession certainly involved female members of the Praxiergidai clan who were charged with cleaning the statue and its vestments, but it is unknown who carried the *hegeteria*.[84] The procession itself took place at night and probably did not draw a crowd of spectators.[85] The Plynteria procession took the ancient xoanon of Athena Polias down to the sea at Phaleron to receive a purifying bath; the fig-cake may have been intended as a symbolic meal for the statue.[86] The fig's association with Athenian autochthony may have made it an appropriate meal for this ancient cult-statue of Athena housed on the Acropolis, home of the first authochthonous kings.

The association with autochthony, however, has little explanatory use in the Thargelia scapegoat

77 Parker 2005, 205 suggests that the unofficial *eiresione* were probably not identical, but decorated differently according to individual taste, though there were presumably some usual items.

78 Rosenthal 1994, 165-8.

79 Rosenthal 1994, 170-1.

80 Ath. 3.74 says that figs were the first fruit to be cultivated in Attica, and that it was forbidden to export them. Ael. *VH*. 3.38 reports that the olive and fig trees first appeared in Attica. Consumed by the autochthons: Phot., Hsch. s.v. *hegeteria*; *Etym. Magn.* 418, 49 s.v. *hegetoria*.

81 Paus. 1.37.2.

82 Parker 2005, 173-7.

83 Sourvinou-Inwood 2011, 140-1. Phot. and Hsch. s.v. *hegeteria*.

84 Sourvinou-Inwood 2011, 145-51; Robertson 2004, 111-60.

85 It was a time of ill-omen: Xen. *Hell*. 1.4.12; Sourvinou-Inwood 2011, 136-45; Mikalson 1975, 19-27.

86 Sourvinou-Inwood 2011, 183-5 mentions a meal of salt for Artemis at Ephesus and *psaista*, cakes of ground barley, for Hera at the Tonaia. Burkert 1970, 356-69 has an alternate reconstruction, against which see Sourvinou-Inwood 2011, 158-92, 225-62.

ritual, where figs play a major symbolic role. Scapegoat rituals are known from many Greek city-states, and there are some common elements which Jan Bremmer has used to reconstruct what occurred in Athens.[87] The sources referring specifically to Athens mention that there were two scapegoats, one wearing a necklace of dried black figs representing the men of the city, and one wearing dried white figs representing the women of the city (the scapegoats themselves could both be men in actuality).[88] They were paraded around the city, perhaps to the accompaniment of discordant music called the "melody of the wild fig", and then driven away "over the border".[89] Between the necklaces of figs and the melody of the wild fig., figs were clearly an important symbol during the scapegoat ritual.

A necklace of figs is also referenced in a completely different context. According to the chorus of the *Lysistrata*, *kanephoroi* also wore a necklace of dried figs.[90] Robert Parker expresses consternation that the *kanephoroi* and scapegoats at the Thargelia should wear the same symbol, but I believe an explanation can be found.[91] *Kanephoroi* were unmarried virgins, and their purity was a major aspect of their role. Dillon notes that Artemis and Athena were sometimes depicted as *kanephoroi*: "the *kanephoroi* reflect the purity of these two eternally virgin goddesses, and participate in a pure sacrifice to the gods".[92] Barbara Goff points out that the virginity of the *kanephoroi* "emerges as a focus of interest in its own right" during this very public display, as the *kanephoros* stands on the cusp of marriage.[93] The scapegoats at the Thargelia are not themselves pure, but they are the focus of a purification ritual, being cast out along with all the nebulous impurities of the community. The Plynteria festival, where figs played an important symbolic role "leading" the procession, was also concerned with purification. The statue of Athena and perhaps also her garments needed to be cleaned and purified – in the sea, a particularly potent agent of purification. Thus figs might plausibly be associated with purificatory rituals or pure ritual participants. On the surface, these two roles might appear to be a contradiction, but as we will see below, fleece or wool possessed very similar meanings. The association of figs and purification is not unrelated to figs' role as one of the foods of the autochthons. Robert Parker has suggested that certain symbols functioned as purifiers because of their perceived antiquity.[94]

The "Fleece of Zeus" and Wool

The fleece of Zeus is an ambiguous ritual symbol which appears in several poorly known rituals. It was apparently the fleece of a ram sacrificed to Zeus, either Zeus Meilichios or Zeus Ktesios; the *Suda* adds that the fleece was then used by those marching in the procession of the Skirophoria and the *dadouchos* of Eleusis.[95] How the *dadouchos* of Eleusis used the fleece is unclear, though it might have had something to do with the Lesser Mysteries.[96] Additionally, the fleece of Zeus was used in purification rituals for other suppliants, who placed their left (inferior) foot on the fleece, perhaps suggesting it was a receptacle for their impurity.[97] It may also have figured in the preparatory rituals of the Plynteria, where Noel Robertson suggests it might have been spread under

87 Bremmer 1983, 299-320.

88 Harp. s.v. *pharmakos*; Helladius ap. Phot. *Bibl.* 534a 2-12; see Parker 2005, 482-3.

89 Hipponax fr. 153 West; Bremmer 1983, 313-5.

90 Ar. *Lys.* 646-7.

91 Parker 2005, 226.

92 Dillon 2002, 38.

93 Goff 2004, 114.

94 Parker 1983, 228-9.

95 *Suda* s.v. *Dios koidion.*

96 Parker 1983, 285 mentions reliefs showing Herakles undergoing a purification ritual with the fleece of Zeus.

97 Parker 1983, 373; Hsch. s.v. *Dios koidion.*

someone.[98] Perhaps the Praxiergidai had to be purified so that they could perform their ritual bathing of the statue with pure hands. The fleece of Zeus was actively carried in procession during the Pompaia, a festival whose main activity was the *pompe*.[99] The fleece was borne outside the city; Robert Parker characterises it as "an inanimate scapegoat, an object that absorbed evil and was then expelled".[100]

Wool itself could also possess purity. Thus pure wool, perhaps in the form of a cloak, was given to Athena during the Plynteria.[101] Wool was wrapped around the olive branches carried by suppliants, including the young girls who processed to the temple of Artemis Delphinia. Robert Parker suggests that wool fillets sometimes appeared as purifiers because of their antiquity.[102] When Hephaistos pursued Athena and his semen fell on her leg, she used a piece of wool to wipe it clean.[103] She dropped it on the ground, and thus Erichthonios was born from the earth.[104]

Wool, and the fleece of Zeus specifically, is a rare example of a ritual symbol that functioned through the sense of touch – either by sitting on it, stepping on it, or putting on a headband made of wool. Wool was woven into garments that were worn against the skin. It is therefore a decidedly tactile symbol, which limits the group of people who had direct experience of it. However, the fleece was also visible in procession at the Pompaia, and its presence in numerous rituals suggests familiarity with the fleece of Zeus as a symbol of purification.

98 IG I^3, 7.17; Sourvinou-Inwood 2011, 148; Robertson 2004, 121-2 links it with the fleece of Zeus carried in procession at the Skirophorion.

99 Parker 2005, 479; Simon 1983, 14; Parke 1977, 96.

100 Parker 1983, 28-9.

101 Sourvinou-Inwood 2011, 205-14 suggests it might have been raw wool for the peplos. Alternately, the pure wool could be connected with the cloak mentioned in the previous line of the sacrificial calendar, see Lambert 2002, 374.

102 Parker 1983, 229.

103 Apollod. *Bibl.* 3.14.6. See also Shear 2001, 56 n. 99.

104 Parker 1987, 194 n. 31.

Conclusions

These examples of processional symbols clearly demonstrate that processions and their symbolism functioned in a ritual system, repeated cyclically, which resists tidy classification. Processions were recognizable by their sensory cues, especially sight, sound, and smell, all of which constitute symbols endowed with meaning. These symbols could include things carried or worn by the participants, hymns or dances performed during the procession, the sacrificial animals, or the elements of the landscape through which the procession passed.

The sense-memories evoked by these symbols could have encompassed all five senses. Since processions were intended to delight the deity, there was often an emphasis on beauty and wealth, generally perceived through sight: the finest processional vessels, the most beautiful sacrificial animals, the most intricately woven cloth. There were also songs and music, the neighing of horses, the steady beat of footfalls marking the procession's progress, and the hum of the crowd. Whenever food was included in the procession, one can imagine it might have evoked sense-memories of smell and taste; there would also have been the less savoury smells of the sacrificial animals, and perhaps horses if the procession involved the cavalry. Many of the processional objects such as wool and textiles, branches, foods, or hydriai were things that Athenians produced by hand or encountered through touch in the course of their everyday lives. Processional participants also had the experience of walking in procession while carrying these objects, which would have given them a different set of sense-memories tied to processional rituals.

Through the repetition of rituals, these sensory symbols and their meanings became embedded in

Athenian cultural memory. These memories were collective because they were associated with myths, stories, rituals, and experiences that were widely shared by most Athenians, and sometimes even on a Panhellenic level. This is not to deny or devalue more personal perceptions of these symbols – for example, the Panathenaic peplos might have held different meanings and associations for Athenian men and women. Each symbol, as it was paraded past the spectators year after year, prompted them to recall their associations with that symbol – both those collectively shared and those which were deeply personal. The individual element is virtually impossible to uncover, but the commonly held cultural memory may be reconstructed from the available evidence about myths, stories, and meanings which were linked to these symbols, and the rituals in which these symbols played an important part.

Thus the Panathenaic peplos with its representation of the Gigantomachy influenced vase-painters who sought to use their art to tap into the Athenian cultural memory of this myth. The idea of weaving a peplos or garment for a deity was reflected in references or episodes in both tragedy and comedy, which played on Athenians' memories of that symbol and all it meant. The olive branch drew on collective associations with supplication, as well as the common memory of the myth of Athena's contest with Poseidon and the story of the regrowth of the olive tree on the Acropolis. The figs present in the Plynteria, Thargelia, and necklace of the *kanephoros* shared the common thread of purification or purity, perhaps through their association with earliest Athens. Purification was also an important aspect of the fleece of Zeus and wool in ritual contexts; though few people would have had direct experience of using a fleece to purify themselves, this interpretation of the symbol was also prominent at the Pompaia, where a very public procession utilized the fleece's power to absorb impurities from the city and cast them out.

It is these threads of common cultural memory, myths, and associations that an Athenian could depend on his or her fellow Athenians to remember and understand, and which Athenians wove together in their writings, speeches, plays, and rituals to form their common identity. As the meanings of a particular symbol changed, as it acquired new layers of significance, so too could the identity of the Athenians change (and vice versa). It is in this way, through the symbols displayed and the associations they possessed, that a procession like the Panathenaia could express a uniquely Athenian identity.

Bibliography

ALESHIRE, S.B. & S.D. LAMBERT 2003
'Making the "Peplos" for Athena: A New Edition of "IG" II² 1060 + "IG" II² 1036', *ZPE* 142, 65-86.

ARRINGTON, N. 2014
Ashes, Images, and Memories: The Presence of the War Dead in Fifth-Century Athens, Oxford.

ASSMANN, J. 2011
'Communicative and Cultural Memory', in *Cultural Memories: The Geographical Point of View*, P. Meusburger, M. Heffernan & E. Wunder (eds.), Dordrecht, 15-28.

BARBER, E.W. 1992
'The Peplos of Athena', in *Goddess and Polis: The Panathenaic Festival in Ancient Athens*, J. Neils (ed.), Hanover, NH, 103-18.

BREMMER, J. 1983
'Scapegoat Rituals in Ancient Greece', *HSCP* 87, 299-320.

BRIDGES, E., E. HALL & P.J. RHODES (EDS.) 2007
Cultural Responses to the Persian Wars: Antiquity to the Third Millennium, Oxford.

BUNDRICK, S.D. 2008
'Imaging Textiles Production in Classical Athens', *Hesperia* 77, 283-334.

BURKERT, W. 1970
'Buzyge und Palladion', *Zeitschrift für Religions- und Geistesgeschichte* 22, 356-69.

CASTRIOTA, D. 1992
Myth, Ethos, and Actuality: Official Art in Fifth-Century B.C. Athens, Madison, WI.

CHANIOTIS, A. 2006
'Rituals Between Norms and Emotions: Rituals as Shared Experience and Memory', in *Ritual and Communication in the Graeco-Roman World*, E. Stavrianopoulou (ed.), Liège, 211-38.

CHANIOTIS, A. 2011
'Emotional Community through Ritual: Initiates, Citizens, and Pilgrims as Emotional Communities in the Greek World', in *Ritual Dynamics in the Ancient Mediterranean*, A. Chaniotis (ed.), Dresden, 263-90.

COHEN, A.P. 1985
The Symbolic Construction of Community, London.

CONNELLY, J. 2011
'Ritual Movement in Sacred Space: Towards an Archaeology of Performance', in *Ritual Dynamics in the Ancient Mediterranean*, A. Chaniotis (ed.), Dresden, 313-46.

CONNERTON, P. 1989
How Societies Remember, Cambridge.

CUBITT, G. 2007
History and Memory, Manchester.

DILLON, M. 2002
Girls and Women in Classical Greek Religion, London.

FURLEY, W. 2007
'Prayers and Hymns', in *A Companion to Greek Religion*, D. Ogden (ed.), Malden, MA, 117-31.

GIULIANI, L. 2000
'Die Giganten als Gegenbilder der attischen Bürger im 6. und 5. Jahrhundert v. Chr.', in *Gegenwelten: zu den Kulturen Griechenlands und Roms in der Antike*, T. Hölscher (ed.), München, 263-86.

GOFF, B. 2004
Citizen Bacchae: Women's Ritual Practice in Ancient Greece, Berkeley.

GRAF, F. 1996
'*Pompai* in Greece. Some Considerations about Space and Ritual in the Greek *Polis*', in *The Role of Religion in the Early Greek Polis: Proceedings of the Third International Seminar on Ancient Greek Cult, organized by the Swedish Institute at Athens, 16-18 October 1992*, R. Hägg (ed.), Stockholm, 55-65.

HÅLAND, E.J. 2004
'Athena's Peplos: Weaving as a Core Female Activity in Ancient and Modern Greece', *Cosmos* 20, 155-82.

HALBWACHS, M. 1992
On Collective Memory, translated by L. Coser, Chicago (Originally published 1925 as *Les cadres sociaux de le mémoire*, Paris).

HALDANE, J.A. 1966
'Musical Instruments in Greek Worship', *GaR* 13, 98-107.

HARDING, P. 2008
The Story of Athens: The Fragments of the Local Chronicles of Attika, London.

HEATH, J. 2011
'Women's Work: Female Transmission of Mythical Narrative', *TAPA* 141, 69-104.

HUET, V. 2015
'Watching Rituals', in *A Companion to the Archaeology of Religion in the Ancient World*, R. Raja & J. Rüpke (eds.), Chichester, West Sussex, 144-54.

HURWIT, J. 1999
The Athenian Acropolis: History, Mythology, and Archaeology from the Neolithic Era to the Present, Cambridge.

KAVOULAKI, A. 2000
'The Ritual Performance of a Pompe: Aspects and Alternatives', in *Dōrēma: A Tribute to the A.G. Leventis Foundation on the Occasion of its 20th Anniversary*, A.G. Leventis Foundation (ed.), Nicosia, 145-58.

LAMBERT, S.D. 2002
'The Sacrificial Calendar of Athens', *BSA* 97, 353-99.

LORAUX, N. 1986
The Invention of Athens: The Funeral Oration in the Classical City, translated by A. Sheridan, Cambridge, MA. (Originally published 1981 as *L'invention d'Athènes: histoire de l'oraison funèbre dans la "cité classique"*, Paris.)

LORAUX, N. 1993
The Children of Athena: Athenian Ideas about Citizenship and the Division between the Sexes, translated by C. Levine, Princeton. (Originally published 1981 as *Les enfants d'Athéna: idées athéniennes sur la citoyenneté et la division des sexes*, Paris.)

LORAUX, N. 2000
Born of the Earth: Myth and Politics in Athens, translated by S. Stewart, Ithaca. (Originally published 1996 as *Né de la terre: mythe et politique à Athènes*, Paris.)

LORAUX, N. 2002
The Divided City: On Memory and Forgetting in Ancient Athens, translated by C. Pache and J. Fort, New York. (Originally published 1997 as *La cité diverse: l'oubi dans mémoire d'Athènes*, Paris,)

LUGINBÜHL, T. 2015
'Ritual Activities, Processions and Pilgrimages', in *A Companion to the Archaeology of Religion in the Ancient World*, R. Raja & J. Rüpke (eds.), Chichester, West Sussex, 41-59.

MANSFIELD, J.M. 1985
'The Robe of Athena and the Panathenaic "Peplos"', PhD diss., University of California, Berkeley.

MIKALSON, J. 1975
'HMERA APOFRAS', *AJP* 96, 19-27.

NAGY, G. 2016
'Weaving While Singing Sappho's Songs in Epigram 55 of Posidippus', *Classical Inquiries: Studies on the Ancient World from the Center for Hellenic Studies*, C. Filos & K. Stone (eds), https://classical-inquiries.chs.harvard.edu/weaving-while-singing-sapphos-songs-in-epigram-55-of-posidippus/ (accessed 10.06.2016).

NEILS, J. 1996
'Pride, Pomp, and Circumstance: The Iconography of Procession', in *Worshipping Athena: Panathenaia and Parthenon*, J. Neils (ed.), Madison, WI, 177-97.

NILSSON, M. 1916
'Die Prozessionstypen im griechischen Kult', *Jahrbuch des kaiserlich deutschen archäologischen Instituts* 31, 309-39.

PALAGIA, O. 1993
The Pediments of the Parthenon, Leiden.

PALAGIA, O. 2005
'Fire from Heaven: Pediments and Akroteria of the Parthenon', in *The Parthenon from Antiquity to the Present*, J. Neils (ed.), Cambridge, 224-59.

PAPAZARKADAS, N. 2011
Sacred and Public Land in Ancient Athens, Oxford.

PARKE, H.W. 1977
Festivals of the Athenians, Ithaca, NY.

PARKER, R. 1983
Miasma: Pollution and Purification in Early Greek Religion, Oxford.

PARKER, R. 1987
'Myths of Early Athens', in *Interpretations of Greek Mythology*, J. Bremmer (ed.), London, 187-214.

PARKER, R. 2005
Polytheism and Society at Athens, Oxford.

RAJA, R. & J. RÜPKE (EDS.) 2015
A Companion to the Archaeology of Religion in the Ancient World, Chichester, West Sussex.

ROBERTSON, N. 2004
'The Praxiergidae Decree (IG I³ 7) and the Dressing of Athena's Statue with the *Peplos*', *GRBS* 44, 111-60.

ROCCOS, L.J. 1995
'The Kanephoros and Her Festival Mantle in Greek Art', *AJA* 99, 641-66.

ROCCOS, L.J. 2000
'Back-Mantle and Peplos: The Special Costume of Greek Maidens in 4th-Century Funerary and Votive Reliefs', *Hesperia* 69, 235-65.

ROEDIGER, H.L., III, F.M. ZAROMB & A.C. BUTLER 2009
'The Role of Repeated Retrieval in Shaping Collective Memory', in *Memory in Mind and Culture*, P. Boyer & J. Wertsch (eds.), 138-70.

ROSENTHAL, P. 1994
'How on Earth Does an Olive Branch Mean Peace?', *Peace & Change* 19, 165-79.

RUTHERFORD, I. & J. IRVINE 1988
'The Race in the Athenian Oschophoria and an Oschophorikon by Pindar', *ZPE* 72, 43-51.

SCHEID, J. & J. SVENBRO 1996
The Craft of Zeus: Myths of Weaving and Fabric, Cambridge, MA.

SHAPIRO, H.A. 1989
Art and Cult under the Tyrants in Athens, Mainz.

SHEAR, J.L. 2001
'Polis and Panathenaia: The History and Development of Athena's Festival', PhD diss., University of Pennsylvania.

SHEAR, J.L. 2011
Polis and Revolution: Responding to Oligarchy in Classical Athens, Cambridge.

SIMON, E. 1983
Festivals of Attica: An Archaeological Commentary, Madison, WI.

SNYDER, J. MCINTOSH 1981
'The Web of Song: Weaving Imagery in Homer and the Lyric Poets', *CJ* 76.3, 193-6.

SOURVINOU-INWOOD, C. 2011
Athenian Myths and Festivals: Aglauros, Erechtheus, Plynteria, Panathenaia, Dionysia, R. Parker (ed.), Oxford.

STAVRIANOPOULOU, E. 2015
'The Archaeology of Processions', in *A Companion to the Archaeology of Religion in the Ancient World*, R. Raja & J. Rüpke (eds.), Chichester, West Sussex, 349-61.

STEINBOCK, B. 2012
Social Memory in Athenian Public Discourse: Uses and Meanings of the Past, Ann Arbor.

TUCK, A. 2006
'Singing the Rug: Patterned Textiles and the Origins of Indo-European Metrical Poetry', *AJA* 110, 539-50.

TUCK, A. 2009
'Stories at the Loom: Patterned Textiles and the Recitation of Myth in Euripides', *Arethusa* 42, 151-9.

VIAN, F. 1952
La guerre des géants: le mythe avant l'époque hellénistique, Paris.

WOLPERT, A. 2002
Remembering Defeat: Civil War and Civic Memory in Ancient Athens, Baltimore.

On the Peripatos: Accessibility and Topography of the Acropolis Slope Sanctuaries

Wiebke Friese

Introduction

For the inhabitants of ancient Athens, religion was ubiquitous. While fetching water from the fountain house, attending to business, or socialising on the Agora, they passed numerous religious spaces for worship that was both incidental and organised, individual and communal.[1] The Acropolis in the centre of the polis was merely passed by. As a large outcrop of limestone about 150 metres above sea level, measuring some 270 metres by 150 metres, it was an impressive monument. Surrounded with massive fortification walls built in the Bronze Age and covered with various buildings and artworks of outstanding and famous size and quality, it was not only the political and religious focal point of the polis, but, from at least the 6th century BC, it was also the centre of a major road network and the start and end point of several urban and extra-urban processions and individual pilgrimages around Attica and the rest of the Mediterranean religious landscape.[2]

The sanctuaries on its summit are extensively discussed throughout Classical and archaeological scholarship: as individual cult places, but also and especially as places of communal or polis religious practice and as an interlinking political and religious building project.[3] The impact of the many cults on its slopes, however, has long been neglected. Except for the sanctuaries of Dionysos and Asklepios on the south slope, these so-called "smaller sanctuaries" have only been marginally investigated. The architecture devoted to the deities worshipped here is sometimes described as "primitive looking".[4] Robert Parker attested it a rather "problematic" and "ambiguous" character,[5] and Fritz Graf called the cults of this area of the Acropolis "liminal".[6] In summary, these "periakropolitan" cults are traditionally linked to "personal" or "rustic" religion – in contrast to the grander and more communal cults on the top.[7] Their "minor significance" was further reflected in their "minor" topography – on the slopes of the Acropolis instead of the top, as well as their "minor" monumentality and accessibility, as they usually lacked a grander architecture or a monumental access road and propylon.[8] But what signifies a "personal" or "rustic" cult?

1 On roads in Athens, see Ficuciello 2008. Generally, see Goette 2002. On roadside sanctuaries, see Best 2015.

2 On the general topography of the Athenian Acropolis, see Travlos 1971; Camp 2001; Hurwit 2004; Greco 2010. On the spatial organization of cults generally, see Horster 2010, 435-58; Raja & Rüpke 2015, 29-30, 37. For the religious landscape of Athens, see Scott 2017.

3 E.g. Rhodes 1995; Keesling 2003.

4 Rosenzweig 2004, 37.

5 Parker 2005, 52 argues concerning the cult of Pan that this area was near the heart of the city, but also respected the strange wildness of the god, which made him unsuitable for a sanctuary on the summit.

6 Graf 1992, 170.

7 Parker 2005, 52.

8 Except for the Asklepieion and the Dionysos temenos.

For a long time, Classical scholars ignored or even argued against the existence of individual religious experience.[9] Ancient Greek religion was said to be based on communal (polis) ritual practice, or, as Walter Burkert wrote, "Greek religion, bound to the polis, is public religion to an extreme degree."[10] Individual religious experience or personal piety as an aspect of Greek and Roman religious history has only emerged in the last decade. The term originated in Egyptology, but was especially taken over by the interdisciplinary study of religion.[11] "Personal piety" is a rather broad and amorphous category, which is expressed in various religious beliefs and practices: The so-called mystery cults and the re-evaluation of magical rituals, particularly since Hellenistic times, are only two of the various examples.[12] A strict separation between "individual" and "communal" religion is not possible. On the one hand, civic cults could also address the emotional and intellectual needs of an individual, as proven by the thousands of votives and amulets in major intra-urban sanctuaries.[13] Moreover, being still engaged in cults concerning the polis, an individual may have felt drawn to different deities at different stages of his life. Concerning ritual itself, Julia Kindt recently argued that "personal religion should not simply be set in contrast to official Greek religion", and followed that in ancient Greece there was no single belief or practice which qualified as either individual or official *per se*.[14] Individuals rather adopted, modified, and diversified religious traditions and practices concerning their own ideas and needs, but used the same religious "language". Therefore, one and the same ritual addressing a particular deity could be used for the expression of different needs, which could be communal or individual. And as Emily Kearns has shown for the ritual practice of cursing, whether a religious practice qualifies as "individual" or "communal" depends only on its context (setting) and perspective or aim.[15]

The archaeological material could be of significant help in obtaining a more specific idea of a worshipper's motives. Most civic religious architecture was created and financed by the social elite of a polis, which is why it was generally much larger in size and number. Individual religious space was smaller and often bound to natural niches and caves.[16] The same could be said for the accessibility of a sanctuary. This communal sacred space, which was the venue of a festival or the start or end point of a procession, must surely have been connected to a paved road, perhaps a *hiera odos*, and could have been entered through a monumental propylon of some kind/of unknown size.[17] Finally, the production, use, and distribution of small religious artefacts, such as the votive figurines, amulets, or lamps found in a particular sanctuary, could reveal an individual contact with a particular deity which did not involve communal issues.[18]

9 Not mentioned in e.g. Burkert 1985; Ogden 2007. Against: Price 1999, 3.

10 Burkert 1985, 276.

11 It was first described as "Persönliche Frömmigkeit" by A. Erman and J.H. Breasted at the beginning of the 20th century. Erman 1911; Breasted 1912. On the development of the term, see Lang, in Friese *et al.* 2012, 9-36; Kindt, 2015, 35-50. See also Morgan 2006; Instone 2009. On the discussion of the binary system of "private" and "polis" cult, see Sourvinou-Inwood 2000a; 2000b. On the individual in Greco-Roman religion, see Rüpke 2013, 3-40, 115-35; Rüpke & Rebillard 2015; Kindt 2015.

12 For mysteries, see Bremmer 2014. For magic, see Graf 1997; Eckert in Friese *et al.* 2012, 99-124.

13 Rüpke 2013, 5-6. See also the example of the Eleusinian Mysteries in this volume.

14 Kindt 2015, 37.

15 Kearns 2010, 151-90.

16 For Pan in Athens, see Scott 2017; Brommer 1938.

17 On the accessibility of sanctuaries, see Wescoat 2017, 67-86 for a discussion of Samothrace.

18 However, only a written dedication on an artefact allows a concrete conclusion about the donor. Without it, it is unknown whether a worshipper donated an artefact in an individual or a communal ritual. However, the wishes and hopes going along with it could be very individual and private. See e.g. for the sanctuary of Po-

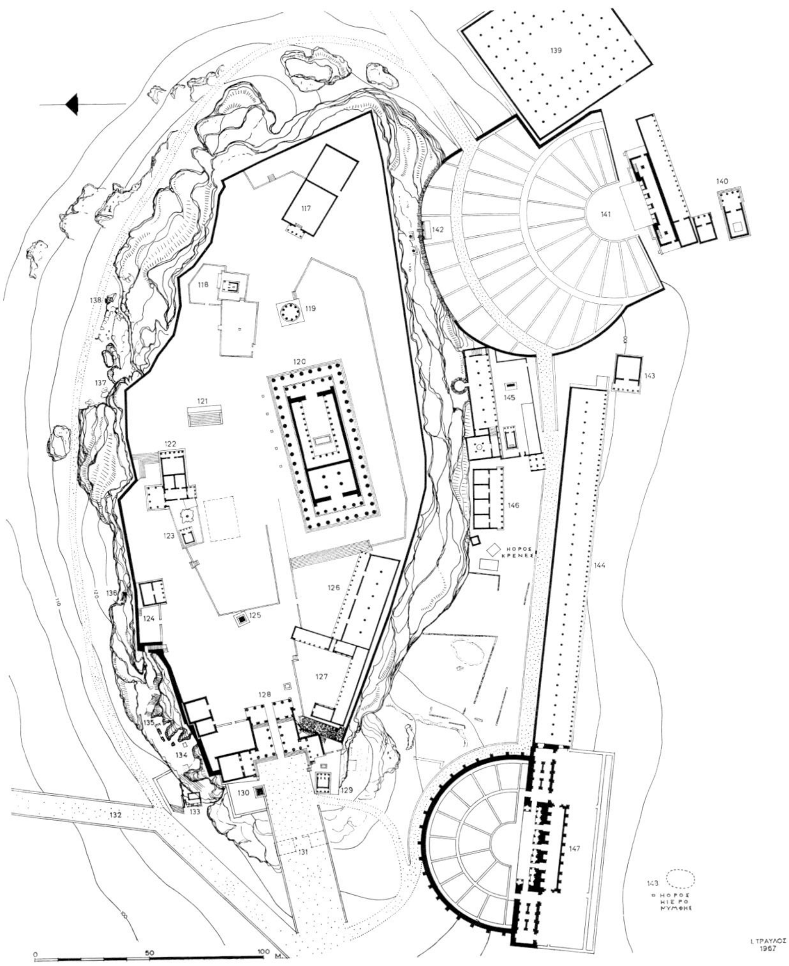

Fig. 1. Plan of the Acropolis (after Travlos 1971, 71, Abb. 91).

By focusing on the archaeological evidence and combining it with the literary and epigraphical material, this paper should offer a rather dynamic approach to the religious topography of ancient Athens. Topographically, the cults on the Acropolis' slope will be integrated into the urban road network and residential districts of ancient Athens. Religiously, they will be classified into the religious system of the ancient Greek cult spectrum. Through an exploration of their accessibility, visibility and architecture, and of the rituals and festivals taking place in the slope sanctuaries, the traditional categorization of public, private, polis, and personal religion will be questioned.

Roads to and around the Acropolis

Thycidides mentioned that the sanctuaries upon the Acropolis slope were built within an area called the Pelasgian ground, on which it was forbidden to build or quarry (Fig. 1).[19] A *horos* found in the

seidon in Isthmia Gebhard 1998; Kron 1998. For dedications in oracle sanctuaries, see Eidinow 2007, 42-55; for those in the Amphiaraion of Oropos, see Petsalis-Diomedis 2017, 106-29. Generally, see Iossif 2005; Scott 2011.

19 According to the Pythian oracle: see Thuc. 2.17.

peribolos wall of the nymph sanctuary on the south slope might have marked the southern boundary of this area.[20] As it is possibly shown on the backside of the so-called Telemachus stele, which was found in the nearby Asklepieion, the *pelasgikon* must have been a rocky but vegetated area interspersed with several sanctuaries of various sizes, which, especially on the north slope, incorporated the natural features of the Acropolis rock.[21] The area was accessible from the north by the most frequented access road to the Acropolis, the *hiera odos*. It crossed the Agora from the northeast to the southwest and climbed the northwest corner of the Acropolis up the steps of the propyleia. It was paved and wide enough to be an appropriate stage for the several processions which ran from the Agora to the sanctuaries on the Acropolis and back. [22] Coming from the Agora, right at the bottom of the rock, in front of the courtyard of the Klepsydra spring, a small paved path, the peripatos, turned to the east.[23] An inscription on a boulder of Acropolis limestone found at the north slope describes the "length of the peripatos: five stades and 18 feet", which is about 1 kilometre.[24] While the inscription is dated to the 4th century BC, the path itself probably already existed in the 5th century BC. Due to building projects on the Acropolis slopes, it was continuously modified until at least the 2nd century AD,[25] when Pausanias partially followed the path coming down from the summit: "On descending, not to the lower city, but to just beneath the Gateway, you see a fountain and near it a sanctuary of Apollo in a cave."[26] The path circles the Acropolis and gives access to several sanctuaries. On the north slope it leads to the terrace with the sanctuaries of Apollon Hypoakraios, Zeus Olympios (?), and Pan and the terrace with the sanctuary of Aphrodite and Eros. On the east side, it passes the peribolos of the Aglaurion. On the south slope, it uses the upper diazoma of the Dionysos theatre *koilon* and then passes the Asklepieion, the area for the Nymphs, Pan, Aphrodite, Hermes, and Isis, and right before the Propyleia, the sanctuary for Aphrodite Ourania, Blaute, and Ge Kourotrophos.[27] Since at least the 2nd century BC, it has been bordered by the Stoa of Eumenes to the south. Since the construction of the Odeion of Herodes Atticus in the 2nd century AD, the path has followed its upper *koilon* line before ending in the courtyard in front of the Propyleia. It was reconstructed by the Ephoria in 1969.[28] Another important road, the *hodos tripodon* (road of the tripods), reached the Acropolis from the south and ended in front of the peribolos of the Dionysos sanctuary.[29]

The Sanctuaries of the North Slope

Terrace of Zeus, Apollo and Pan

Past the Klepsydra spring, the *peripatos* reaches a terrace with four large caves carved into the Acropolis slope (Fig. 2).[30] It was excavated in 1896/1897 by Panagiotis Kavvadias.[31] Cave A right above the fountain contained the remains of steps or benches and was probably used as a tribune from which to

20 *IG* I³, 1064.

21 The stork on the tree trunk depicted on the back face of the plaque. 420/410 BC. Athens, National Archaeological Museum 2490.

22 For more on the sacred way used for the processions from Athens to Eleuisis and for the Panatheneia in this volume, see Clinton, Agelidis, and Warford. On the Athenian road system, see generally Ficuciello 2008.

23 Broneer 1935, 109-25; Beschi 1967/1968, 511-28; Ficuciello 2008, 65-6; Greco 2010, 156-7.

24 *IG* II², 2639.

25 When the Odeion of Herodes Atticus was built in 160-170 AD. See Greco 2010, 156.

26 Paus. 1.28.4. Unfortunately, in what follows, Pausanias did not follow the peripatos completely.

27 Paus. 1.21.4; 1.22.3.

28 Dontas 1983, 49.

29 Ficuciello 2008, 66-71.

30 Travlos 1971, 93, Abb.116; 418, Abb. 536-7.

31 Kavvadias 1897.

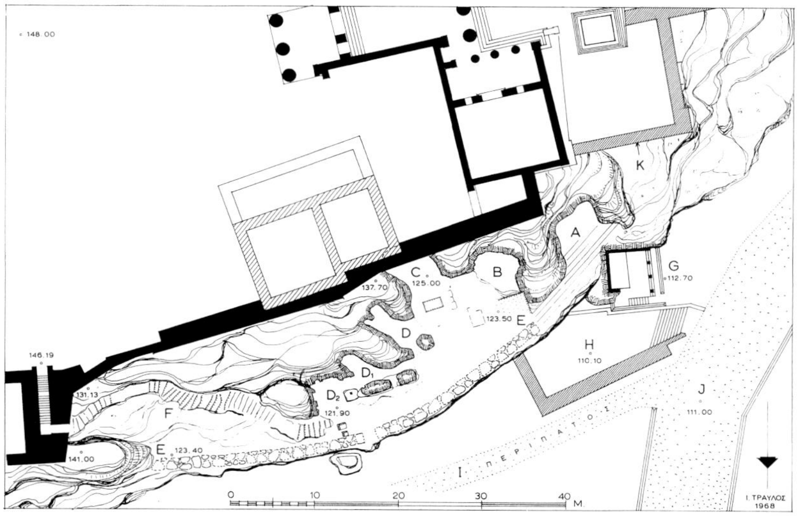

Fig. 2. Terrace of Apollon and Pan. North Slope. Acropolis (after Travlos 1971, 93 Abb.116).

watch festivals such as the Panathenaen procession coming down from the Acropolis and continuing to the Agora. It is also associated with the depositing of the Panathenaen ship during the annual festival.[32] The three caves further east (B, C, and D) were used as cult places.

The first one, cave B, was dedicated to Apollo "Hyp' Akrais" (below the summit).[33] According to Pausanias, this was the place where Apollo slept with Kreousa, the daughter of King Erechtheus, who lived on top of the Acropolis.[34] The cave (4.3/4.8 m x 2.4/3 m x 7.3/8 m) still shows various niches cut into the rock.[35] A low wall closed the cave to the northwest. A small bench on the terrace might have been used as an altar or a place for depositing votives. No figurative dedications or inscriptions were found in front of cave B to give an idea of the deity who was worshipped there.[36] However, Panagiotis Kavvadias excavated 10 marble plaques nearby, which might have resided in its niches. They all feature a crown in relief and an inscription detailing that they are a dedication to Apollo on behalf of the nine archons.[37] Antonios Keramopoullos suggested that, given that they are combined with the *stephanoi* of myrtle, the symbol of their office, the dedications were made by the archons in an official capacity.[38] The cave might therefore have been the place where the oaths of the archons took place. However, all the plaques date to the Roman period, which leaves little idea as to earlier dedications.[39] Several older scholars connected a cult of Apollon Pythios and Apollon Patroos mentioned by Euripides and Demosthenes to cave B.[40] If this is true, then the Pythaistai procession to Delphi also started from here. According to Strabo (9.2.11), before their procession to Delphi the Pythaistai waited here "at the altar of Jupiter As-

32 Philostr. *V S* 2.1.5.

33 Eur. *Ion* 494, 937, 1400.

34 Paus. 1.28.4.

35 Kavvadias 1897, 1-26; Travlos 1971, 91-5; Greco 2010, 151-2, fig. 78.

36 In the 5th century AD, a Christian chapel was built on the terrace (Hag. Athanasios or Hg. Ioannis Chrysostomos). See Greco 2010, 153.

37 IG II^2 2891, 2893, 2894; Travlos 1971, 95, Abb. 120-2. More of the same type were excavated in the Agora. See Travlos 1971, 91.

38 Keramopoullos 1929, 86-92.

39 The Roman date of the archaeological evidence for cult practice, however, offers an opportunity for a later interpretation of the cult's function. See Nulton 2003.

40 For Pythion, see Eur. *Ion* 283-5; Thuc. 2.15; Strabo 9.404. For Patroos, see Dem. *18,* 141; Travlos 1971, 91. Against, see Parker 2005, 52 no. 8; Nulton 2003; Gawlinski 2007; Greco 2010, 152.

trapius, … in the wall between the Pythium and the Olympium" to see the lightning of Zeus appear over Mount Parnas as a sign for them to begin.[41]

It is still controversial whether the second cave, C, might have been dedicated to Zeus Keraunios or Olympios, in his capacity as the god of thunder, as the spot had been struck by lightning.[42] No archaeological or epigraphical remains have been able to prove this assumption. However, according to Antonios Keramopoullos and many other scholars, the remains of an altar in front of the cave belonged to Zeus Astrapaios.[43]

In the third and perhaps most important cave, D (with D1/D2), the Athenians worshipped the god Pan.[44] This cave was dedicated to him as a reward for the help he gave the Athenians against the Persians in the Battle of Marathon in 490 BC.[45] Pausanias mentioned his cult on his way down the Acropolis as being situated next to the Klepsydra spring and the cave of Apollon.[46] The cult place incorporated two caves (D-D1), which are interlinked by a narrow passage. Once more, the several niches inside the cave were archaeologically bare, but probably held both the cult statue of Pan and dedications to him. Except for the literary sources, the only reason we have been able to identify the cave is because two votive reliefs were found on the terrace nearby the cave. The first represents Pan and the Nymphs,[47] and the other shows the god next to many other deities, amongst them Zeus and Hermes.[48] The latter was dedicated by a private person, Neoptolemos, son of Antikles Melite in Ionia (apparently, the sanctuary was famous enough to attract visitors from a great distance) in 330 BC. Herodotus details that an annual ceremony took place at the Pan sanctuary with a torch race and sacrifices' to ensure Pan's continuing protection over the polis.[49] He also mentions that the torch race was in commemoration of Philippides' run to and from Sparta on the eve of the battle of Marathon. Right next to cave D2, a narrow stairway leads up to the Acropolis.

Terrace of Aphrodite and Eros

A little further east on the peripatos, a narrow path leads up to another 30 m x 14 m terrace with an open-air sanctuary (Fig. 3). It was excavated in 1932 by Oscar Broneer, who referred the remains to Aphrodite and Eros.[50] It is separated by a wall in the so-called Middle and Eastern Sanctuary. At its back, a number of small niches were cut into the rock. They probably housed small statuettes (Aphrodite, women, maidens, babies) or other votive gifts such as vases or lamps, mostly datable to the late 3rd and early 2nd century BC, which were found in great numbers on the terrace in front of the caves.[51] The oldest material allows us to date the cult to as early as the mid-5th century BC.[52] Particularly characteristic are the many small marble reliefs of male or

41 Strabo 9.2.11. Trans. George Bell & Sons 1903. See also *horos* from the sacred road to Delphi, 4th century BC. Agora I 5476. See also Pirisino, this volume.

42 See again Strabo 9.404.

43 Keramopoullos 1929, 86-90. Similarly, Dörpfeld 1937, 11-8, 106-7. Again, against this theory, see Parker 2005, 52 no.8; Nulton 2003; Gawlinski 2007; Greco 2010, 152.

44 Kavvadias 1897, 1-32; Travlos 1971, 417-21, Abb.116 D-D1; Greco 2010, 152-4.

45 Hdt. 6.105; Paus. 1.28.4; Luc. *Dial. D.* 22.3; Schol. Clem. Al. *Protr.* 3.45 (39 ed. Potter).

46 Paus. 1.28.4. Also Eur. *Ion* 936-8; Ar. *Lys.* 911-3; Lucian *Bis Accusatus* 9; *Anth. Plan.* 259; Schol. Clem. Al. *Protr.* 3.3.4.

47 Two fragments, 1st century AD. Acr. Mus. 1345 and 6464.

48 Brommer 1938, 376-81.

49 Hdt. 6.105. An annual sacrifice of a he-goat by the Athenians is attested by Schol. Clem. Al. *Protr.* 3.45 (39 ed. Potter).

50 Broneer 1932; 1935; Travlos 1971, 228-31; Pirenne-Delforge 1994, 48-74; Rosenzweig 2004, 45-8; Greco 2010, 154-5; Pala 2010, 201-3.

51 Most of the statuettes of Eros alone or with Aphrodite may be dated to the 3rd century BC. See Broneer 1935, 109-39.

52 Though Hurwit 2004, 35 suggests it is far older.

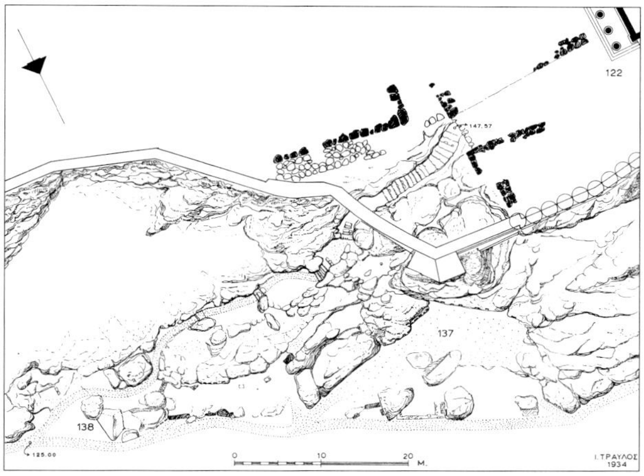

Fig. 3. Terrace of Aphrodite and Eros. North Slope. Acropolis (after Travlos 1971, 229, Abb. 293).

female genitals.[53] A small marble plaque depicting a nude youth, probably Eros. There were also excavated several fragments of Pentelic marble, showing a procession of nine Erotes carrying cult paraphernalia (*philalai*, thymiateria, and pitchers). They have been dated to the second half of the 4th century BC.[54] Due to the absence of ash or other traces of burning, Oscar Broneer suggested that several small benches constructed of rubble or packed earth and covered with stucco set at a certain distance by the rock niches were used not as altars, but as surfaces on which to place further dedications of flowers, fruits, or other bloodless sacrifices.[55] Two inscriptions (450-430 BC) were found cut into the rock at the southwest corner of the sanctuary. One of them can be reconstructed as a dedication to Aphrodite, and the other mentions a spring festival on the fourth day of the month of Mounichion (late April), which was sacred to Eros.[56] Most of the archaeological material found in the sanctuary connects Aphrodite and Eros to a vegetal and fertility cult.[57] In addition, the goddess also played a role in wedding rituals. A marble thesaurus from the 4th century BC was found 100 metres downslope from the sanctuary. It bears the inscription "Treasury for prenuptial offerings to Aphrodite Ourania" and the symbol of a silver drachme, which was to be deposited in the thesaurus before or after a wedding ceremony.[58] Both rituals were rather individual in nature and the sanctuary of Aphrodite and Eros was probably seldom the venue of a communal festival or ritual, though there might have been exceptions. Oscar Broneer first connected this sanctuary with the festival of the "Arrephoria" mentioned by Pausanias: "There is an enclosure in the city (acropolis?) not far from the so-called Aphrodite in the Gardens and through it a natural underground passage downwards. The maidens descend by this."[59] Apparently during the night of the festival, two young aristocratic girls would descend from their house near the temple of Athena Polias on the Acropolis through a secret, subterranean corridor with a basket filled with mystical objects.[60]

53 As well as the pebbles found on some of the stone benches, these votives were offered to the gods as fertility symbols. Broneer, 1935, 133.

54 Athens National Archaeological Museum 1451 and 1452. Broneer 1935, 143-7; Travlos 1971, 228 fig. 292.

55 Broneer 1935, 130-2, dating most of them to the Hellenistic period.

56 Broneer 1932, 43 fig. 10, 44 fig. 11. Dedicated to Aphrodite, *IG* I³, 1382b, and Eros, *IG* I³, 1382a. Two other inscriptions found on the terrace (one with a decree by the archon Nikokles from the year 302/301 BC) were, according to Broneer, originally set up on the Acropolis and were washed down with the earth. Broneer 1932, 43-4, figs 9-10.

57 Since the fourth day of each month was sacred to Aphrodite. See Pala 2010, 202.

58 4th century BC. Π 66-7, Kazamiakis 1991. There was also a sanctuary for Aphrodite Ourania in the agora: see Pirenne-Delforge 1994, 15-9.

59 Paus. 1.27.3 (trans. Parker 2005, 221). However, no ancient source explicitly explains the ritual by reference to the Erechtheus myth. See Brulé 1987, 28-79; Rosenzweig 2004, 46; Parker 2005, 222.

60 According to a scholion on Lucian, these objects – imitations of snakes and male genitals – were made from dough: Lucian 276, 15-7. See also Robertson, 1983, 255-7.

The ritual might reflect a central Athenian myth, which tells how Athena gave the daughters of Kekrops a basket to keep secret. Only one of Kekrops' three daughters was able to suppress her curiosity. The two others looked into the basket and saw the little baby Erechtheus, half-human and half-snake. Struck with madness, they jumped of the Acropolis and died on the spot.[61] Oscar Broneer suggested that the girls descended through an old Mycenaean well, which was accessible only from the summit of the Acropolis and ended right behind the open-air temenos of Aphrodite and Eros.[62] Some of the holes used to support the wooden construction for a long staircase down to the well have been preserved. However, Pausanias' ambiguous passage has been the subject of much speculation since Oscar Broneer first raised this subject.[63]

The function of the small area next to the Aphrodite/Eros temenos, the so-called Skyphoi sanctuary, is also ambiguous. Here, in 1939, Oscar Broneer excavated about 200 miniature vessels from the beginning of the 3rd century BC, deposited on an artificially made terrace (10 m x 4 m), which might have already been erected in Archaic times.[64] While Oscar Broneer suggested that this area was a part of the sanctuary of Aphrodite and Eros, Kevin T. Glowacki refers it to a different unknown deity.[65]

The Aglaurion of the East Slope

Aglauros was one of the daughters of King Kekrops, and according to myth, she jumped to her death from the steepest part of the Acropolis to save the city from a long siege, as prescribed by a Delphic oracle.[66] According to Herodotus, during the Persian occupation of the Acropolis in 480 BC, the invaders climbed up the Acropolis from a part of the rock that had been left unguarded "near the sacred precinct of Kekrops' daughter Aglauros".[67] Pausanias, on his tour of the lower city, described the Aglaurion as being above the sanctuary of the Dioskurai and near the Prytaneum.[68] These two sources led to various theories, which usually located the Aglaurion on the north or west slope of the Acropolis.[69] However, in 1980 a stele (0.96 m x 0.4 m) dating to the 3rd century BC was found *in situ* in front of the large cave on the eastern side of the Acropolis (Fig. 4).[70] The inscription mentions the Aglauros priestess Timokrite, who instructed that the stele should be erected in the Aglaurion.[71] The stele was obviously part of the peribolos of the sanctuary, which must have extended to the east and probably included the cave above. The extent of the temenos cannot have been small. While Bion of Prokonnesos stated that the cult of Aglauros was mainly practised by women, the Athenian sanctuary was also the place where the ephebes, in commemoration of Aglauros' patriotism, went once a year for a festival called the Aglauria, at which they collected their weapons and had to swear an oath of loyalty to their polis.[72] This was an important and certainly very public ritual, watched by many citizens and relatives. According to the inscription, a *pannychis* must have been part

61 Paus 1.18.2; Apollod. 3.14.6
62 Broneer 1932; Burkert 1983, 150-4. See contra discussing the location of the "Aphrodite in the Gardens" precinct Pirenne-Delforge 1994, 54-9; Parker 2005, 221.
63 Discussed in Parker 2005, 221; Pala 2010, 201-11 with older bibliography.
64 Broneer 1935; Greco 2010, 156.
65 Glowacki 1991, 67-73.
66 Philochorus *FGrH* 328 F 105. On Aglauros, see Merkelbach 1972, 277-83; Kearns 2010, 23-7, 57-63.
67 Hdt. 8.52-53.
68 Paus. 1.18.2-3.
69 See discussion in Dontas 1983, 58-63.
70 Acropolis Museum 13371. SEG XXXIII, 115; Dontas 1983, 48-63; Greco 2010, 159.
71 Priestesses of Aglauros also mentioned in *IG* II^2, 3458, 3459. 4th/3rd century BC.
72 *FGrH* IIIb 166. The ephebes also swore allegiance to many other gods, but Aglauros was the first: SEG XXXIII, 115; cf. 36, 169; Parker 2005, 434.

Fig. 4. Aglaurion. East Slope. Acropolis (WikiMedia Commons).

of the festival, and George Dontas suggested that it had a mystic character.[73] Unfortunately, to this day no further material has been excavated to prove the existence of a cult of Aglauros at this place.

The Sanctuaries of the South Slope

On the south slope of the Acropolis, the Pelasgian ground included a relatively large area which was easily accessible from the *hodos tripodes* in the south and the peripatos from the east and west. Though the slope was rocky and perhaps covered with park-like vegetation, it was visible from the densely inhabited area in the south. The Dionysos sanctuary and theatre in particular as well as the Asklepieion are extensively discussed in Classical scholarship, which is why this paper will not give a full account of their topography and development.

The Dionysos Sanctuary

Among the various cult places of Dionysos in Athens, the sanctuary of Dionysos Eleuthereus at the bottom of the Acropolis was the most important (Fig. 5).[74] It was founded in the second half of the 6th century BC by the tyrant Peisistratos or his sons and has been excavated by the DAI of Athens, beginning with A.

73 Line 29; Dontas 1983, 56.

74 Paus. 1.2.5. On the cult places of Dionysos in Athens, see Parker 2005, 290-326.

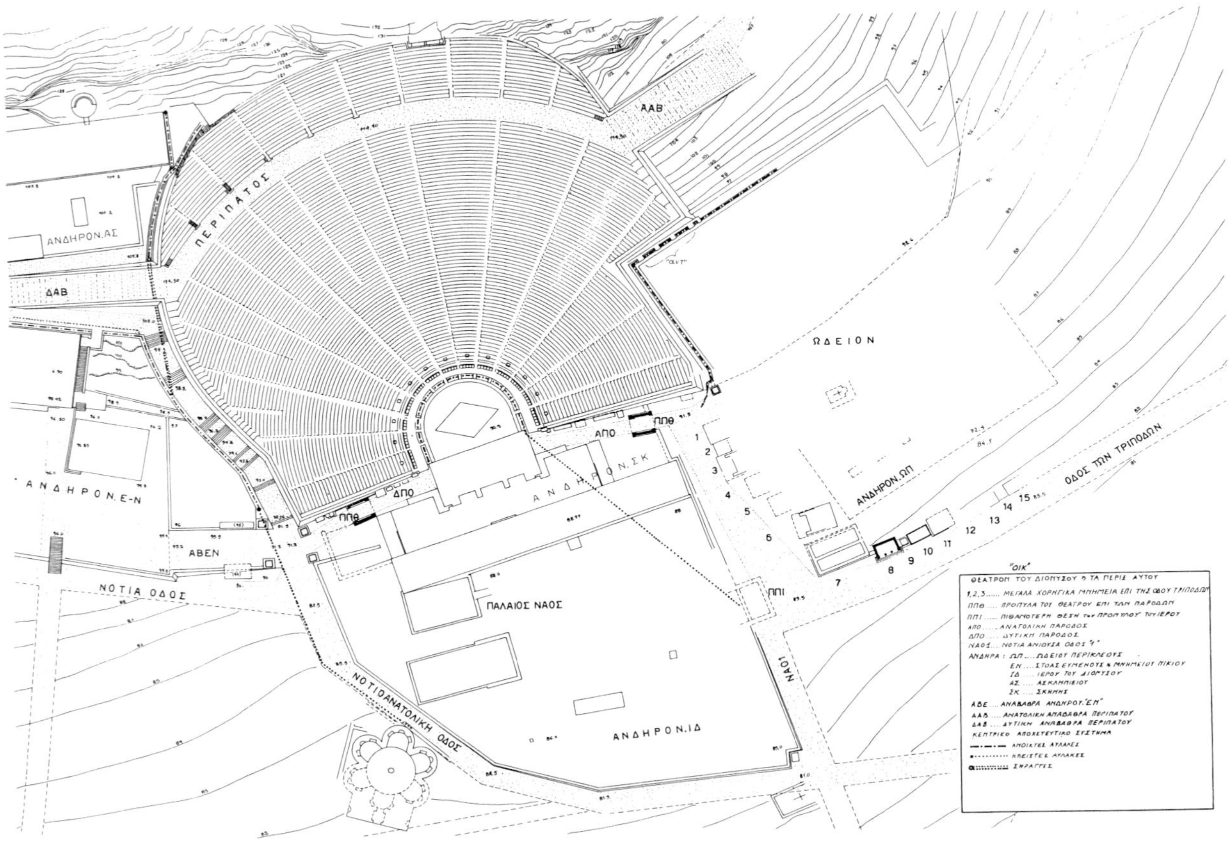

Fig. 5. Dionysos Sanctuary. South Slope, Acropolis (after Korres 1980).

Dörpfeld in the late 19th century. In the first phase, a temple (8 m x 13.5 m) was erected with a circular area (orchestra) above.[75] The worshippers could sit on the slope of the hill to watch the sacred performances (dance, songs, and mime) in honour of the god. With the establishment of organized dramatic and theatrical contests, the orchestra acquired first wooden and later stone seats and a stage. The seats were accessible through the *paradoi* and from the peripatos above. After the middle of the 4th century BC, a second temple (21 m x 9 m) was constructed south of the first one.[76] At the same time, the *koilon* was enlarged, so that the peripatos was incorporated in the upper diazoma.[77] While the seats of the theatre were accessible from the upper part of the Acropolis slope via the peripatos, the main entrance to the temple and the altar were in the south. The lower peribolos was surrounded by walls with a propylon in the east. From here, the *hodos tripodon* (street of the tripods) began, leading around the east and northeast side of the Acropolis. On both sides of the road, various monuments topped by prize tripods were erected, mostly by the victorious choregoi of dramatic contests, who sponsored these monuments as part of their civic and religious duty.[78] It was also used as a processional road during the annual festival of the City Dionysia. In its course, a procession start-

75 For the older theatre, see Dörpfeld & Reisch 1896; Moretti 2001.

76 Paus. 1.29.16; Hintzen-Bohlen 1997; Greco 2010, 160.

77 Korres 2009, 79-81.

78 e.g. a skyphos, early 5th century BC. Bologna. Museo Civico Archeologica. See Parker 2005, 302-3, fig. 19.

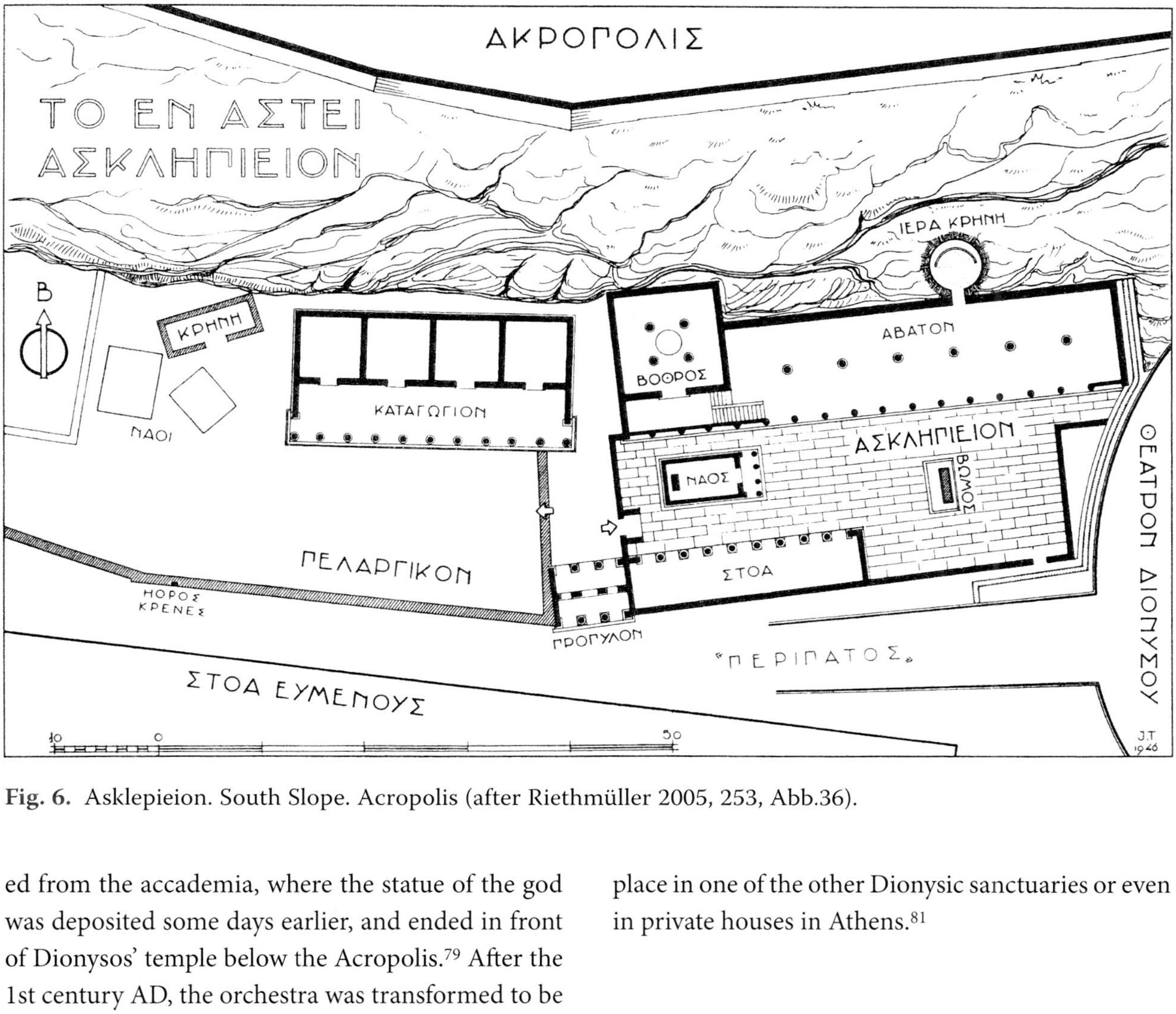

Fig. 6. Asklepieion. South Slope. Acropolis (after Riethmüller 2005, 253, Abb.36).

ed from the accademia, where the statue of the god was deposited some days earlier, and ended in front of Dionysos' temple below the Acropolis.[79] After the 1st century AD, the orchestra was transformed to be used for gladiator contests, animal fights, and naumachiae. Around the end of the 5th century AD, a Christian basilica was built upon the east entrance of the temenos.[80] Throughout antiquity, the area within and around the Dionysos sanctuary was a very public place of festivals for Dionysos and displays of wealth and power addressing the whole polis. Individual dedications to Dionysos were rare and probably took place in one of the other Dionysic sanctuaries or even in private houses in Athens.[81]

The Asklepios Sanctuary

After traversing the Dionysos theatre, the peripatos passes the sanctuary of Asklepios to the south (Fig. 6).[82] The cult of the healing god was introduced to Athens during the Peloponnesian Wars, some 10 years after the destructive plague (420 BC).[83] It was not introduced by the boule or demos, but

79 It was the greatest procession in the ancient Athenian festival year after the Panathenaea. See Xen. *Hipparchikós* 3.2; Parker 2005, 317; Pickard-Cambridge 1968, 61-2.

80 Baldini Lippolis 1995.

81 For informal Bacchic rites e.g. Ar. *Lys* 1-3, see Parker 2005, 325, 373.

82 See also Paus. 1.22.1.

83 Aleshire 1989, 7-9. See also Travlos 1971, 127-37; Riethmüller 2005, 241-78; Melfi 2007, 313-433; Lefantzis & Jensen 2009; Greco 2010, 182-3.

by a private man, Telemachos, from the northern deme of Acharnai, who brought the cult from the sanctuary in Epidauros to Athens.[84] The temenos was excavated by the Greek Archeological Society in 1876-1877. The earliest sanctuary occupied only the eastern terrace and had wooden buildings.[85] Shortly afterwards, a small stone temple (10.4 m x 6 m) which housed the cult statue, a large altar (6 m x 3.5 m), and a doric stoa (50 m x 10 m) in two storeys (possibly the incubation room or abaton) in the north and a rectangular room with a pit (*bothros*) were built. Behind the stoa was a grotto with a sacred well. In Roman times, a second ionic portico was built south of the temple, while a third with four small rooms (4 m x 4 m) was built west of the large portico, possibly another infirmary or a building to house guests and banquets (*hestiatorion*). The sanctuary was surrounded by a temenos wall and was accessible through a monumental entrance.[86]

Inside and around the sanctuary, many dedications were found. Most of them were publically displayed inside the temenos and listed in an inventory list which was kept throughout the life of the sanctuary, from 400 BC to 250 AD.[87] The dedications can be sub-divided into three aspects: ex-votos (replications of healed body parts), coins, and "typoi" (other specific dedications, such as relief representations of worshipers approaching the god and his family).[88] Like the tripods along the road to the Dionysos sanctuary, they were both individual dedications and public representation. While the god of health was certainly frequented concerning the individual health problems of the Athenian citizens, the intra-urban Asklepieion was neither a place of "personal piety" nor for long-lasting health cures nor a target for foreign pilgrims (for these purposes, the sanctuary of Epidauros was the place to go). It was more a place of citizen representation, as well as for informal and formal gatherings, especially during the god's festival. As Asklepios was seen to arrive in the city during the celebration of the Eleusian Mysteries, his festival, the Epidauria, fell on a formerly empty day during the larger Eleusinian festival, the 18th Boedromion, and was celebrated by citizens and foreigners together. [89]

The Smaller Sanctuaries West of the Asklepieion

The terrace west of the Asklepieion was occupied by several smaller cults.[90] Since Mycenaean times, the spring at the base of the Acropolis rock had been incorporated into the defensive outwork. Enclosed by a spring house fronted by a stone porch in the Archaic period, it had been the centre of a cult for Pan, the Nymphs, and probably Hermes since at least the 5th century BC. Its boundary was marked by an inscribed stone built into the east-west wall that closed the southern edge of the terrace to the peripatos.[91] Susan Walker identified the cult as a polis or state cult.[92] In the 4th century BC, however, the porch was demolished. In the same area, a large

84 *IG* II², 4960. The inscription only mentions that the god was brought from Epidauros with Hygieia and a sacred snake. It does not mention the iconographical form of the god. It was found on a foundation stele in front of the sanctuary on the south slope. The stork on the tree trunk depicted on the back face of the plaque might indicate the situation of the sanctuary within the more vegetated area within the city, the *pelasgikon*. 420/410 BC. Athens National Archaeological Museum 2490. See Wickkiser 2008.

85 Lefantzis & Jensen 2009.

86 Probably also depicted on the back of the foundation stele. National Archaeological Museum 2490.

87 Aleshire 1989. Categories after Scott 2011.

88 Aleshire 1989; Melfi 2007, 333-40; Scott 2011.

89 Parker 2005, 462.

90 See Walker 1979, 245, fig. 1.

91 Travlos 1971, 61. A relief with these deities was found in this area. National Archaeological Museum 1966, 2nd century BC.

92 Walker 1979, 246.

marble block (altar?) from the 1st century BC was found, mentioning Hermes, Aphrodite, Pan and the Nymphs, and Isis.[93] The size of the sanctuary could speak for an individual foundation.[94]

The small temple in antis (7.45 m x 5.4 m) facing south to the peripatos is usually identified as a sanctuary of Isis and dated to the 2nd century AD.[95] According to an inscription, both the temple and the cult statue were restored by a private person (probably a woman) in 120 AD, who also donated a statue of Aphrodite to the Egyptian goddess.[96] In the 2nd or 3rd century AD, the cult of Sarapis and Osiris may have joined Isis in her sanctuary.[97]

After passing the Asklepieion, Pausanias further mentions a temple of Themis, right behind a monument for the hero Hippolytos.[98] Several inscriptions from the Roman period mention Themis as the *epiclesis* of different goddesses.[99] Ulrich Köhler identified her hieron with a small rectangular foundation probably built in the 4th century BC opposite the ionic stoa of the Asklepieion (5.1 m x 4.28 m).[100]

Another sanctuary of Aphrodite might have been situated nearby.[101] Just west of the Asklepieion, several votive niches were carved into the bedrock, probably indicating a sacred precinct similar to that of Aphrodite and Eros at the north slope.[102] Elisabetta Pala suggested a prehistoric grave, just down the slope from these niches, as the site of a cult for the hero Hippolytos.[103] Two inscriptions from the same area and from the second half of the 5th century BC also identify a cult of "Aphrodite at/by Hippolytos".[104]

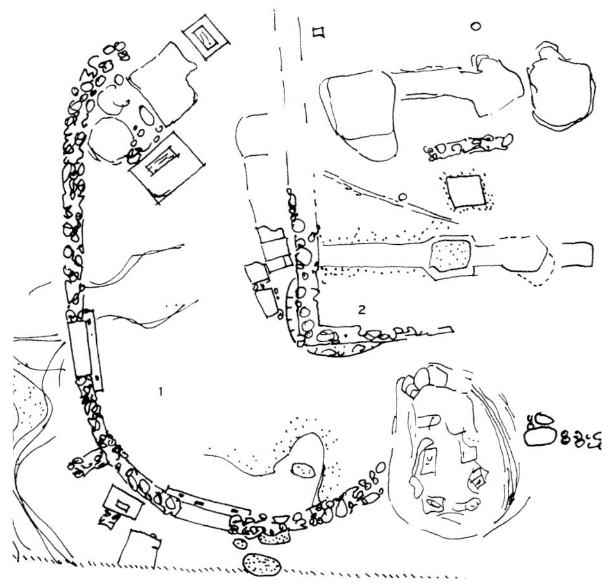

Fig. 7. Nymph Sanctuary. South Slope. Acropolis (after Chr. Lempesi. Photographic Archives of the Acropolis Museum).

The Nymph Sanctuary

One of the earliest sanctuaries on the south slope was a small open-air sanctuary, discovered south of the later Herodeion. It was not directly accessible from the peripatos, but rather from the residential area, which stretched along the busy north-south road coming from the South Gate and leading to the Acropolis. Northwest of the temenos, some Archaic houses have been excavated, and some Classical houses were located right next to it.[105] In the Archaic period, an altar of polygonal blocks was built in an

93 *IG* II^2, 4994. Bricault 2005, 15.
94 Walker 1979, 246.
95 Köhler 1878, 256; Walker 1979; Aleshire 1989, 22-3; Pirenne-Delforge 1994, 43-4; Melfi 2007, 347-8; Greco 2010, 187-8.
96 *IG* II^2, 4771; Bricault 2005. For the cult statue, see Brouskari 2002, 137-9.
97 *IG* II^2, 4815; *IG* II^2, 3564; Bricault 2005, 15-8.
98 Paus. 1.22.1.
99 Chloe Themis: *IG* II^2, 5098; Athena Themis: *IG* II^2, 5130; Ge Themis: *IG* II^2, 5130.
100 Köhler 1878, 238; Greco 2010, 186-7.
101 Eur. *Hipp.* 30-4.
102 Pirenne-Delforge 1994, 44-5.
103 Pala 2010, 201.
104 *IG* I^3 col. II frg. IX.233-4.
105 The temenos was excavated in 1955-1960. See Brouskari 2002, 33-7, 195-6.

open-air precinct, which was surrounded by an oval peribolos wall made of limestone and mud brick (12.5 m x 10.5 m). Two entrances were located on the southern and western sides, opening directly onto the road, but closed with doors. An apsidal structure was built around the altar (Fig. 7).[106]

As proven by several inscriptions, including the marble *horos* inscribed with "boundary of the sanctuary of the nymph" mentioned earlier, it was dedicated to a nymph.[107] A large variety of loutrophoroi found here indicate that the nymph was predominantly worshipped as a protectress of marriage and wedding ceremonies.[108] On the day before a wedding took place, friends of the bride used these vessels to carry water from the Kallirrhoe spring near the Illissos river for the prenuptial bath.[109] The procession was called the loutrophoria and is frequently depicted on the vessels.[110] It ended at the bride's house, but might have passed the nymph's sanctuary. The size of the temenos could accommodate a group of that size. After the wedding, the dedication of the loutrophoroi to the sanctuary took place under less pompous and more individual circumstances. As the peribolos walls were at least over 1.1 metres high,[111] the inside of the sanctuary was probably not visible from the street below, and the ceremony was therefore more private. The large variety of vessels, ranging from products of the best Attic workshops to those of less prosperous citizens as well as the many other objects associated with women, men, and nuptial rituals[112] reflects the popularity of the ritual and sanctuary until the 1st century BC, when the precinct was destroyed. In Roman times, a house was built upon the remains of the sanctuary, which was probably replaced by the Aphrodite sanctuaries on the north and south slopes and the nymph cult place next to the Asklepieion. An inscription on a seat in the theatre of Dionysos indicates that a priestess served the cult of Aphrodite Pandemos as well as the Nymphs and another deity.[113]

The Smaller Sanctuaries above the Odeion

According to Nicander, Solon founded the cult of Aphrodite Pandemos "from the profits taken in by the women in charge of the houses".[114] It is still controversial whether the south slope of the Acropolis hosted one or two sanctuaries of Aphrodite. While Apollodorus, and, following him, also the *Suda*, place a cult of Aphrodite Pandemos, protectress of the Attic demes, in the neighborhood of the old Agora,[115] Pausanias mentions a sanctuary of Aphrodite Pandemos and Peitho, goddess of Persuasion, west of the Asklepieion and in the vicinity of a heroon to Hippolytus.[116] Travlos and Pala located her temenos in the area on the eastern extremity of the south slope, just below the bastion of the Temple of Athena Nike.[117] In this part of the Acropolis, Aphrodite was closely connected to the cults of

106 Korres 2009, 84; Greco 2010, 202; Best 2015, 100-2.

107 *IG* I³, 1064.

108 Brouskari 2002, 36-7; Greco 2010, 200.

109 See also Salta, this volume. Brouskari argues that there was a source close to the sanctuary before, but that it dried up and forced the women to collect the water in the fountains near the Illissos River. See Brouskari 2002.

110 e.g. loutrophoria, 470-450 BC. Acropolis Museum Showcase 5 no.10.

111 This is the height the walls could be reconstructed to, but they were probably higher.

112 e.g. containers for oil and perfume, tableware, jewellery, and spindle whorls. All in Acropolis Museum Showcase 6. Mostly 6th/5th century BC.

113 Whose name is not preserved on the stone. *IG* II², 5149.

114 Nicander of Colophon quoted by Ath. 13.569 d-e.

115 Apollod. *Harp*. 233.13-234.3; *Suda* s.v. Αφροδιτης Πανδημος.

116 Paus. 1.22.1-3; Pirenne-Delforge 1994, 44-5; Greco 2010; Pala 2010, 201.

117 Travlos, 1971; Pala 2010, 199-201. See also Rosenzweig 2004, 14-6.

Demeter and Ge Kourotrophos, as shown below.[118] Here, a pottery fragment with a dedication to Aphrodite was found, as well as several figurines of the goddess and some red-figured loutrophoros fragments decorated with scenes concerning the goddess.[119] Earlier excavations also revealed a Hellenistic Pentelic marble architrave with a dedication to Aphrodite, which was reconstructed to an aedicule for Aphrodite Pandemos.[120] The building was dedicated by Archinos, son of Alypetos from Skambonidai, and his mother, Menekrateia, daughter of Dexikrates from Ikaria, priestess of Aphrodite. It contained a cult statue of the goddess, probably the larger-than-life-size statue whose Parian marble head was found during excavations in 1857 inside the Odeion of Herodes Atticus.[121]

According to Pausanias, in the same area there was a small shrine dedicated to Ge Kourotrophos, Demeter Chloe, and Blaute.[122] However, its exact location is not certain. Greco suggests a *naiskos* (2.95 m x 3.4 m) east of the so-called Temple of Aphrodite as the place where the deities were worshipped. A fragment of an architrave with a dedication to Demeter and Kore from the middle of the 4th century BC might have belonged to this place.[123] There was also a festival for Demeter Chloe, the *Chloia*.[124] After the construction of the Odeion, the accessibility and visibility of this area became significantly less important.

Conclusion

Apart from the gods worshipped there, ancient sanctuaries were dynamic places, continuously restored and remodelled, modified and enlarged. The archaeological and literary material found in the Acropolis slope sanctuaries indicates that these cults cannot simply be described as "rustic" and reserved for the families and individual concerns of the residents of the surrounding areas, as has been suggested by the majority of scholars working on this subject. To a certain extent, some of them also served the communal interests of the polis. Interestingly, a cult's relevance for the community seems to coincide with its topography within the ancient Athenian road network around and up to the Acropolis. The better a sanctuary was visible and accessible from the main access roads, the more a cult was incorporated in the communal religious system. The best examples might be the cults in the caves on the terrace east of the Klepsydra spring: Zeus, Apollon, and Pan. Due to their location right above the *hiera odos*, they were engaged in many communal rituals, representations, and movements: The terrace itself was used as a depositing place for the sacred ship, but also as a tribune for the Panathenaean festival; the cave of Apollon was a place of representation for the Athenian archons, as well as the starting point for the Pythaistai procession to Delphi; and the sanctuary of the cult of Pan, introduced to this place by the polis in the 5th century BC, was the venue for an annual festival and a torch race. Particularly important for the safety and continuity of the polis was the annual oath of the ephebes in the Aglaurion on the east slope of the Acropolis. The size of the temenos indicates a large audience for this ritual. Though the cave was only accessible via the peripatos, it was

118 Paus. 1.22.3. *IG* II², 5183, 5131; Beschi 1967/1968, 518.

119 Dontas 1960.

120 *IG* II², 4596. Beschi, 1967/68, 518 and fig. 9.

121 National Archeological Museum Γ177. Rosenzweig 2004, fig. 4.

122 Paus. 1.22.3. Also for Ge Kourotrophos, see Ar. *Thesm.* 295. For Demeter, see also Ar. *Lys. 835*; Pirenne-Delforge 1994, 26-7; Greco 2010, 192; Pala 2010, 199-200.

123 Greco 2010, 192; *IG* II², 4640. See also other inscriptions from the 5th century BC to the 2nd century AD mentioning the hieron of Ge Kourotrophos: *IG* I³, 1060; *IG* II², 4778, 5152, 15183. For Demeter Chloe specifically, see *IG* II², 1472, 4777, 4750, 4778, 5006.

124 Eup. 183.

easily visible from the site of the older Agora down the hill. However, the sanctuary was never a place of constant individual worship, as no individual dedications were found in this area.

The south slope sanctuaries had a more ambivalent function. All of them were easily accessible and visible from the residential areas south of the Acropolis and were well frequented throughout the year. However, the most monumental precincts in this area, the Dionysos sanctuary and the Asklepieion, were not only the location for communal festivals. Instead, both sanctuaries, donated by wealthy families, were also places of prestige and representation as well as being used for private banquets.

In contrast, the archaeological material of the Aphrodite and nymph cults around the acropolis shows a different picture. On the north slope, Aphrodite was worshipped as a *kourotrophic* fertility goddess with her son Eros, probably linked to rites of passage and status. Her temenos was more remote and less monumental than the other slope sanctuaries. As the terrace was only accessible by a ramp from the peripatos and was not directly visible from the *hiera odos* or the Agora, the place was less attractive for the installation of a representative or "public" cult. Nevertheless, the number of votives and dedications indicates its high popularity among individual worshippers. The same aspects apply to the sanctuaries of Aphrodite Hippolytos, Aphrodite Pandemos, and the nymphs on the south slope. All of these sanctuaries were places of wedding rituals. Pala suggests that prior to their wedding, a couple would first ask Aphrodite Pandemos, in her south slope shrine, to aid in the smooth unification of bride and groom and then continue to the goddess's north slope sanctuary, where Aphrodite and her powers of fertility were worshipped.[125] For that reason, they used the peripatos as a "sacred road" for their private "pilgrimage", either taking the west path below the propylon or the east path passing the Aglaurion. A similar character can be detected for the early nymphs' sanctuary on the south slope, where the nymphs addressed the very private needs and fears of the local women, but were also were venerated as part of the communal wedding celebration and the creation of new citizens.[126] However, Aphrodites' and the nymphs' role as goddesses of marriage always includes a political aspect. As Pala points out, the increase in votive material is due to the social and political dynamics of the late 5th century, namely the development of democracy in Athens, which gave more importance to marriage since legitimate citizenship was restricted to children born to Athenians.[127] As Aphrodite Pandemos presided over both the individual union of the bride and groom and the union of families and clans within the demos, a wedding was not only a private affair, but also the reaffirmation of the *synoikismos*.[128] The fact that Solon was the founder of this cult underlines the social and political dimension of this argument.

The archaeological material of the Acropolis slope sanctuaries could suggest that the topography, visibility, and accessibility of a cult was of high importance, not only for the selection of a cult place, but also for the integration in the religious system of the polis. However, a simple binary division between "individual" and "communal" cult is, as always, not possible.

125 Pala 2010, 195-201.

126 Best 2015, 103.

127 Pala 2010, 214.

128 Similarly Pirenne-Delforge 1994, 81; Rosenzweig 2004, 25, 103.

Abbreviations

IG = *Inscriptiones Graecae* (1873-).

Bibliography

ALESHIRE, S.B. 1989
The Athenian Asklepieion. The People, Their Dedications, and the Inventories, Amsterdam.

BALDINI LIPPOLIS, I. 1995
'La monumentalizzazione tardoantica di Atene', *Ostraka* 4, 169-90.

BESCHI, L. 1967/1968
'Contributi di topografia ateniese', *AsAtene* 29/30, 511-36.

BEST, J. 2015
'Roadside Assistance: Religious Spaces and Personal Experience in Athens', in *Autopsy in Athens: Recent Archaeological Research in Athens and Attica*, M. Miles (ed.), Oxford, 100-7.

BREASTED J.H. 1912
Development of Religion and Thought in Ancient Egypt, London.

BREMMER, J. 2014
Initiation into the Mysteries of the Ancient World, Berlin and Boston.

BRICAULT, L. 2005
Recueil des inscriptions concernant les cultes isiaques, 3 vols, Paris.

BROMMER, F. 1938
'Panbilder des fünften Jahrhunderts', *AA*, 376-81.

BRONEER, O. 1932
'Eros and Aphrodite on the North Slope of the Acropolis in Athens', *Hesperia* 1, 31-55.

BRONEER, O. 1935
'Excavations on the North Slope of the Acropolis 1933-1934', *Hesperia* 4, 109-39.

BROUSKARI, M.S. 2002
'Οι ανασκαφες νοτιως της Ακροπολεως. Τα γλυπτα', *ArchEph* 141, 1-204.

BRULÉ, P. 1987
La fille d'Athènes: La religion des filles à Athènes à l'époque classique. Mythes, cultes et société, Paris.

BURKERT, W. 1983
Homo necans: The Anthropology of Ancient Greek Sacrificial Ritual and Myth, Berkeley.

BURKERT, W. 1985
Greek Religion, Oxford.

CAMP, J.M. 2001
The Archaeology of Athens, New Haven and London.

DONTAS, G. 1960
'Αρχαιστητες Αθννων καινΑττικης ερευνα νοτιως της Ακροπολεως κατα το 1960', *ArchEph* 16, 14-5.

DONTAS, G. 1983
'The True Aglaurion', *Hesperia* 52, 48-63.

DÖRPFELD, W. & E. REISCH 1896
Das griechische Theater, Athens.

DÖRPFELD, W. 1937
Alt-Athen und seine Agora, vol. 1, Berlin.

ECKERT, M. 2012
'Die Aphrodite der Seefahrer', in *Persönliche Frömmigkeit. Funktion und Bedeutung individueller Gotteskontakte im interdisziplinären Dialog* (Hephaistos 28), W. Friese, A. Greve, K. Kleibl, K. Lahn, I. Nielsen (eds.), Münster, 99-124.

EIDINOW, E. 2007
Oracles, Curses and Risk among the Ancient Greeks, Oxford.

ERMAN, A. 1911
'Denksteine aus der thebanischen Gräberstadt' in *Sitzungsberichte der königlich-preußischen Akademie der Wissenschaften, Philosophische Klasse, Jahrgang 1911*, Berlin, 1086-111.

FICUCIELLO, L. 2008
Le strade di Atene, Athens and Paestum.

FRIESE, W., A. GREVE, K. KLEIBL, K. LAHN & I. NIELSEN (EDS.) 2012
Persönliche Frömmigkeit. Funktion und Bedeutung individueller Gotteskontakte im interdisziplinären Dialog (Hephaistos 28), Münster.

GAWLINSKI, L. 2007
'The Athenian Calendar of Sacrifices. A New Fragment from the Athenian Agora', *Hesperia* 76, 37-55.

GEBHARD, E.R. 1998
'Small Dedications in the Archaic Temple of Poseidon at Isthmia', in *Ancient Greek Cult Practice from the Archaeological Evidence. Proceedings of the 4th International Seminar on Ancient Greek Cult*, R. Hägg (ed.), Stockholm, 91-115.

GLOWACKI, K.T. 1991
Topics Concerning the North Slope of the Acropolis at Athens, Bryn Mar.

GOETTE, H.R. (ED.) 2002
Ancient Roads in Greece, Hamburg.

GRAF, F. 1992
'Heiligtum und Ritual. Das Beispiel der griechisch-römischen Asklepieia', in *Le sanctuaire grec*, A. Schachter (ed.), Geneva, 159-204.

GRAF, F. 1997
Magic in the Ancient World, Cambridge, MA.

GRECO, E. 2010
Topografia di Atene: sviluppo urbano e monumenti dalle origini al III secolo d.C., Athens and Paestum.

HINTZEN-BOHLEN, B. 1997
Die Kulturpolitik des Eubolos und des Lykurg. Die Denkmäler- und Bauprojekte in Athen zwischen 355 und 322 v.Chr., Berlin.

HORSTER, M. 2010
'Religious Landscape and Sacred Ground: Relationships between Space and Cult in the Greek World', *RHR* 227, 435-58.

HURWIT, J.M. 2004
The Acropolis in the Age of Pericles, Cambridge.

INSTONE, S. 2009
Greek Personal Religion: A Reader, Oxford.

IOSSIF, P. 2005
'La dimension publique des dédicaces "privées" du culte royal ptolémaique', in *Idia kai demosia. Les cadres 'privés' et 'publis' de la religion grecque antique. Actes du IXe colloque du CIERGA, tenu à Fribourg du 8 au 10 septembre 2003* (Kernos Suppl. 15), V. Dasen & M. Piérart (eds.), Liège, 235-57.

KAVVADIAS, P. 1897
'Τοπογραφικα Αθηνων κατα τας περι την Ακροπολιναnασκαφας', *ArchEph*, 1-32.

KAZAMIAKIS, K.M. 1991
'Θησαυρος Αφροδιτης Ουρανιας η κατασκευη', *Horos* 8-9, 29-44.

KEARNS, E. 2010
Ancient Greek Religion. A Sourcebook, Chichester, West Sussex.

KEESLING, C. 2003
The Votive Statues of the Athenian Acropolis, Cambridge.

KERAMOPOULLOS, A.D. 1929
'Υπο τα προπυλαια της Ακροπολεως', *ArchDelt,* 73-101.

KINDT, J. 2015
'Personal Religion: A Productive Category for the Study of Ancient Greek Religion?', *JHS* 135, 35-50.

KÖHLER, U. 1878
'Hallenanlagen am Südfusse der Akropolis zu Athen', *AM 3,* 147-54.

KORRES, M. 1980
'Εργασιεξ στα νημεια. ιονυσι εατρο. Συντηρηση – αποχατασταη μνημειων', *ADelt* 35, 1980, 9-21.

KORRES, M. 2009
Αττικης οδοι. Αρχαισι δρομοι της Αττικης, Athens.

KRON, U. 1998
'Sickles in Greek Sanctuaries: Votives and Cultic Instruments', in *Ancient Greek Cult Practice from the Archaeological Evidence. Proceedings of the 4th International Seminar on Ancient Greek Cult,* R. Hägg (ed.), Stockholm, 187-216.

LANG, B. 2012
'Persönliche Frömmigkeit. Vier Zugänge zu einer elementaren Form des religiösen Lebens', in *Persönliche Frömmigkeit. Funktion und Bedeutung individueller Gotteskontakte im interdisziplinären Dialog* (Hephaistos 28), W. Friese, A. Greve, K. Kleibl, K. Lahn, I. Nielsen (eds.), Münster, 19-36.

LEFANTZIS, M. & J.T. JENSEN 2009
'The Athenian Asklepieion on the South Slope of the Akropolis: Early Development, ca. 420-360 B.C.', in *Aspects of Ancient Greek Cult. Context – Ritual – Iconography,* J.T Jensen, G. Hinge, P. Schultz & B. Wickkiser (eds.), Aarhus, 91-124.

MELFI, M. 2007
I santuari di Asclepio in Grecia, Roma.

MERKELBACH, R. 1972
'Aglauros: die Religion der Epheben', *ZPE* 9, 277-83.

MORETTI, J.-C. 2001
Théatre et société dans la Grèce antique, Paris.

MORGAN, E.E. 2006
'Einige Bemerkungen zur Thematik der Persönlichen Frömmigkeit', *Studien zur Altägyptischen Kultur* 34, 333-52.

NULTON, P.E. 2003
The Sanctuary of Apollo Hypoakraios and Imperial Athens, Providence.

OGDEN, D. 2007
A Companion to Greek Religion, London.

PALA, E. 2010
'Aphrodite on the Acropolis', in *Brill's Companion to Aphrodite,* A.C. Smith & S. Pickup (eds.), Leiden and Boston, 195-216.

PARKER, R. 2005
Polytheism and Society at Athens, Oxford.

PETSALIS-DIOMIDES, A. 2017
'Palimpsest and Virtual Presence: A Reading of Space and Dedications at the Amphiareion at Oropos in the Hellenistic Period', in *Excavating Pilgrimage. Archaeological Approaches to Sacred Travel and Movement in the Ancient Mediterranean World,* T. M. Kristensen & W. Friese (eds.), Abingdon and New York, 106-29.

PICKARD-CAMBRIDGE, A.W. 1968
The Dramatic Festivals of Athens, Oxford.

PIRENNE-DELFORGE, V. 1994
L'Aphrodite grecque (Kernos Suppl. 4), Liège.

PRICE, S. 1999
Religions of the Ancient Greek, Cambridge.

RAJA, R. & J. RÜPKE (EDS.) 2015
Companion to the Archaeology of Religion in the Ancient World, Malden, MA.

RHODES, R.F. 1995
Architecture and Meaning on the Athenian Acropolis, Cambridge.

RIETHMÜLLER, J. 2005
Asclepius. Heiligtümer und Kulte, Heidelberg.

ROBERTSON, N. 1983
'Arrhephoria', *HSCP* 87, 255-7.

ROSENZWEIG, R. 2004
Worshipping Aphrodite: Art and Cult in Classical Athens, Ann Arbor.

RÜPKE, J. 2013
'Individualization and Individuation as Concepts for Historical Research', in *The Individual in the Religions of the Ancient Mediterranean,* J. Rüpke (ed.), Oxford, 3-40.

RÜPKE, J. & E. REBILLARD (EDS.) 2015
Group Identity and Religious Individuality in Late Antiquity, Washington.

SCOTT, M. 2011
'Displaying Lists of What Is (Not) on Display: The Uses of Inventories in Greek Sanctuaries', in *Current Approaches to Greek Religion,* M. Haysom & J. Wallensten (eds.), Stockholm, 239-52.

SCOTT, M. 2017
'*Mapping the Religious Landscape: The Case of Pan in Athens*', in *Theoretical Approaches to the Archaeology of Ancient Greece: Manipulating Material Culture,* L. Nevett (ed.), Ann Arbor, 212-29.

SOURVINOU-INWOOD, C. 2000A
'What is Polis Religion?', in *Oxford Readings in Greek Religion,* R. Buxton (ed.), Oxford, 13-37.

SOURVINOU-INWOOD, C. 2000B
'Further Aspects of Polis Religion', in *Oxford Readings in Greek Religion,* R. Buxton (ed.), Oxford, 38-55.

TRAVLOS, J. 1971
Bildlexikon zur Topographie des antiken Athen, Tübingen.

WALKER, S. 1979
'A Sanctuary of Isis on the South Slope of the Athenian Acropolis', *Annual of the British School at Athens* 74, 243-58.

WESCOAT, B. 2017
'The Pilgrim's Passage into the Sanctuary of the Great Gods, Samothrace', in *Excavating Pilgrimage. Archaeological Approaches to Sacred Travel and Movement in the Ancient World,* T. Myrup Kristensen & W. Friese (eds.), Abingdon and New York, 67-86.

WICKKISER, B. 2008
Asclepius. Medicine, and the Politics of Healing in Fifth-Century Greece: Between Craft and Cult, Baltimore.

Under the Care of Daemons: From the Athenian Acropolis to Kallirrhoe on the Ilissos*

Maria Salta

> *"καὶ γὰρ ὁ τοῦδε (Φοίβου) γεγὼς Ἀσκληπιός ἐστίν ἰητήρ σώματος, ὡς ψυχῆς ἀθανάτοιο Πλάτων."*
> Diog. Laert. 3.45

In this late epigram dedicated to Plato, who, in his *Phaedrus*, set up a perpetual monument to the land of Ilissos, we find clearly formulated the idea of an extension from the healing of the body to the spirit. The care of the body principally belonged to the cult of Asclepios, housed in the city, whereas the care of the spirit in its metaphysical dimension, and by extension, that of the soul, belonged mainly to the daemons of the afterlife, who were venerated in the *proasteion*, the suburbs of the city, on the banks of the Ilissos River.

Fig. 1. View of the Ilissos River, the Olympieion, and the Acropolis from the so-called Frog-Island (Vatrachonisi) to the north of Kallirrhoe in 1864. To the right is the area of the Zappeion Garden (after Ritter 1999, 30. Photographer: Dimitrios Konstantinou).

In this chapter, I will trace the sacred itinerary from the Acropolis to the Kallirrhoe spring on the Ilissos, which follows a very ancient way that joined the Acropolis of Athens and the settlement beneath with the well-known Gardens to the southeast (Fig. 1). This was really "a land full of gods" related to several periods of the history of the city, but also a place with many graves, some of them belonging to prehistoric times.

Benevolent Ancestors

In the ancient Greek world, life and afterlife were connected by dreams. Around 400 BC, Hippocrates stated in his treatise "Περί διαίτης ὀξέων ἀσθενειῶν" (Regimen in Acute Diseases, Hippoc. *Acut.* 4.92) that it was a good sign to receive something "pure" from the dead. Such a dream indicated good health, because from the dead came nourishment, growth, and seed.[1] This (indeed strange) explanation provided by the famous physician is based on a very

* I am deeply obliged to Dr. Katia Manteli, archaeologist, for her outstanding contribution to the English rendering of the text.

1 Farnell 1921, 356; Gagné 2007, 1. For Asclepios as a chthonian deity and his ability to bring the dead back to life, see Apollod. *Bibl.* 3.10.3; Papachatzis 2006, 120 n. 1.

ancient belief about an interaction between the two worlds of the living and the dead, which is even nowadays accepted in Greek popular culture.

The ancestor cult of the *Tritopatores* or *Tritopatreis* was very important in ancient Athens, and possibly reaches back to the Mycenaean *ti-ri-se-ro-e* or *trisheros*, mentioned in Linear B tablets from Pylos.[2] These genuine ancestors or forefathers were linked to death and the underworld and were honoured in cemeteries. They were variously perceived as "pure" or "impure" and their shrines were "ἄβατα", inaccessible.[3]

The Tritopatores had purifying properties and received sacrifices and libations together with other deities at ceremonies related to birth and marriage, like the Kourotrophos, because they were honoured as protectors of the new life.[4] According to the Orphics, the *Tritopatores* were regarded as keepers and guardians of the winds, like the Homeric Aiolos,[5] and counted among the powers of the weather, which also received chthonian worship.[6]

A well-known sanctuary of the *Tritopatores* was found during the excavations in the Kerameikos necropolis.[7] Their temenos, which already existed by the 6th century BC, probably belonged to the large tumulus of a contemporary noble family. A boundary stone from a *Tritopatores* sanctuary, maintained by the Zakyadai family, was found south of the Zappeion area on the Ilissos (Fig. 2).[8] Unfortunately, the exact circumstances of the find have not been reported.

Fig. 2. View of the Olympieion, the Zappeion area, the Ardettos hill and the Stadium from the Acropolis (postcard from around 1900. Private collection).

Plato's *Phaedrus* and the Ancient Cults on the Ilissos

During excavations conducted by John Travlos in 1956-1967 in connection with landscaping works in the area of the Olympieion, the covering up of the Ilissos River, and the construction of the Ardettos highway, prehistoric sherds were found all over the north side of the Olympieion (Fig. 3).[9] Near Hadrian's Arch, vast quantities of Middle Helladic and Late Helladic pottery were found in stratified deposits. In addition, a large number of Geometric sherds and many graves lining both sides of a very old road leading to a gate in the Themistoklean

2 Farnell 1896-1909, 5:354; Farnell 1921, 355-7; Deubner 1956, 44; Simon 1983, 76; Bravo 2010, esp. 11-3, fig. 1.

3 Robertson 2009, 169-72; Stroszeck 2010, 60. For the impure and pure *Tritopatores* as two versions of the same deities, see Ekroth 2002, 222 (with bibliography). For the existence of another *ἄβατον* on the Ilissos dedicated to Zeus Polieus, see a boundary inscription from the 5th century BC, Iliopoulos 2001-2004b, 209.

4 Dow 1965, 180-213, esp. 189-91, 200-5; Verbanck-Pièrard 1998, 109-27; Larson 2001, 111-2; Ekroth 2002, 156, 225; Stroszeck 2010, 79-80; Vikela 2011, 150 with n. 94. After the Atthidograph Phanodemos, *FHG* I, 367, "μόνοι Ἀθηναῖοι θύουσι καὶ εὔχονται αὐτοῖς ὑπέρ γενέσεως παίδων, "ὅταν γαμεῖν μέλλουσιν". Pearson 1981, 70, 75. For the sacrifices to the impure *Tritopatores*, see Jameson 1994, 43-4; Ekroth 2002, 220-1.

5 Svoronos 1916-1917, 140-1.

6 Ekroth 2002, 225.

7 Goette 2001, 66; Stroszeck 2010, 55-83.

8 Lippold 1911, 106; Judeich 1931, 410; *IG* II^2, 2615, 4th century BC; Gagné 2007, 2. See n. 5 above.

9 Travlos 1971, 289-91, fig. 379.

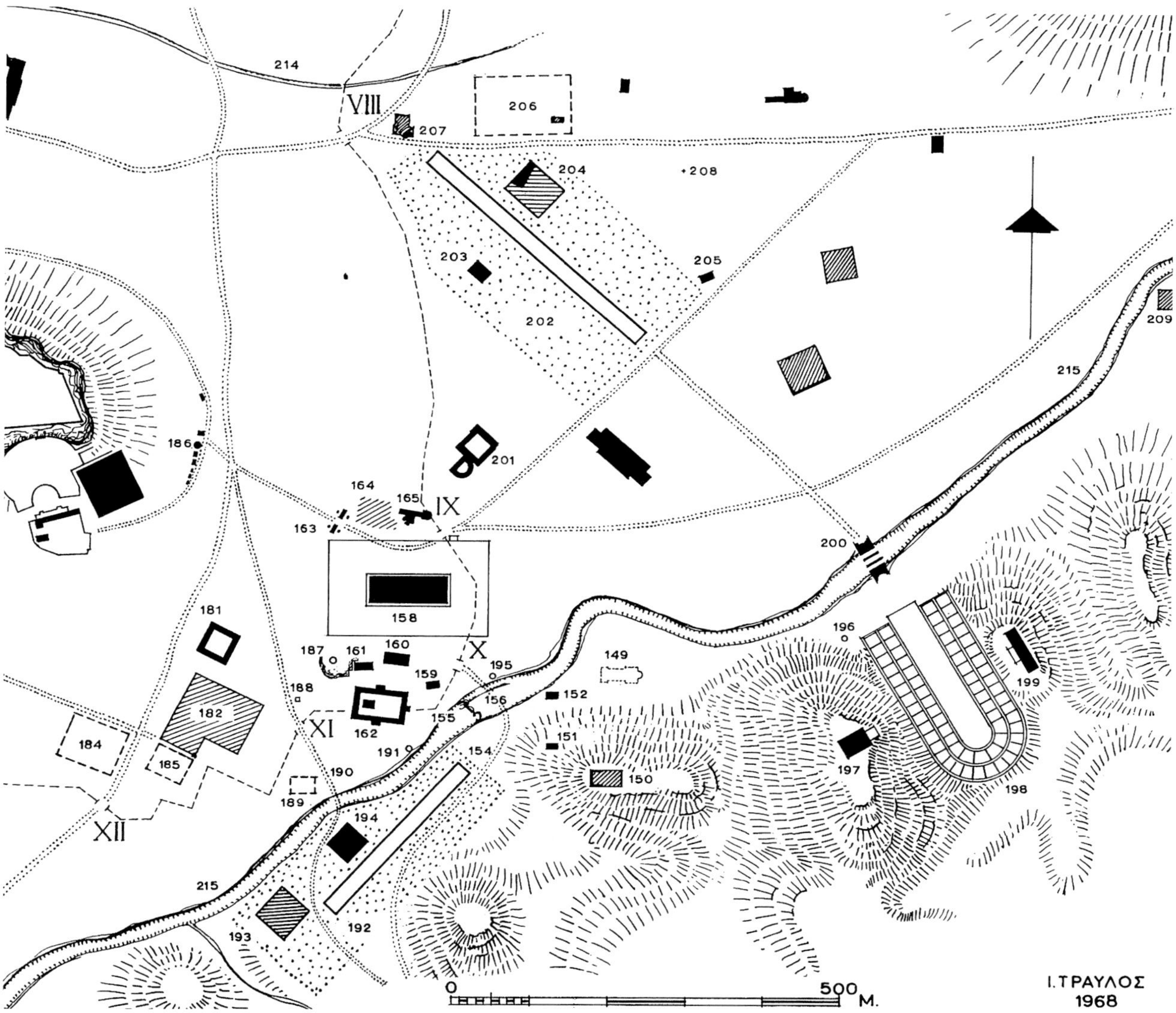

Fig. 3. Plan of the Ilissos area. VIII-XII: Gates in the Themistoklean Wall, demolished in 86 B.C. 150: Shrine of Poseidon Helikonios.151: Artemis Agrotera. 152: Metroon in Agrai. 154: Relief of Pan. 155: Kallirrhoe. 156: Ilissos crossing. 158: Olympieion. 159: Kronos and Rhea. 160: Apollo Delphinios. 161: Lawcourt at the Delphinion. 162: Panhellenion. 163: Arch of Hadrian. 164: Houses. 165: Roman Baths I. 182: Shrine of Kodros. 184: Dionysion in Limnai. 185: Palaistra of Taureas.186: Lysikrates Monument. 187: Shrine of Olympian Ge. 188. Amazon stele. 189: Pythion. 190: Aphrodite in the Gardens. 191: Altar of the Ilissian Muses. 192: Kynosarges. 193: Gymnasium building. 194: Gymnasium building. 195: Shrine of Boreas. 196: Shrine of Pan, Acheloos and the Nymphs. 198: Stadium. 200: Ilissos bridge of Roman date. 202: Lykeion. 209: Herakles Pankrates. 214: Eridanos. 215: Ilissos (after Travlos 1971, fig. 379).

city wall were also found.[10] All along the road and to the north of it, there were houses from the 5th and 4th centuries BC. One of the excavated houses could, according to John Travlos, have been the house of Morychos cited by Plato in *Phaedrus* (Pl. *Phdr.* 227c).

This place, which lies outside a city gate (the "Hippades Gate", according to John Travlos' final attribution),[11] about 500 metres upstream from the Kallirrhoe and northeast of the temple of Zeus Olympios, has been identified by a number of scholars as the Ilissos location described in Plato's *Phaedrus* (Pl. *Phdr.* 230b). This was a spot shaded by a large plane tree and a willow. John Travlos believed that Sokrates and Phaidros strolled along this very old road on the north side of the Olympieion when they were going for a walk outside the city walls.[12] As they left the town, they turned off the road, crossed the Ilissos River, and reached its east bank at the foot of the Ardettos Hill. There was a spring of cool water flowing beneath the plane tree and a shrine to the nymphs and Acheloos, identified in *Phaedrus* by the presence of ornaments and images: "Νυμφῶν τε τινων καὶ Ἀχελώου ἱερόν ἀπό τῶν κορῶν τε καὶ ἀγαλμάτων ἔοικεν εἶναι" (Pl. *Phdr.* 230c).[13] According to Jennifer Larson, the *korai* mentioned in the text were probably doll-like figures placed in or near the spring, while the *agalmata* could be stone reliefs fitted to bases or other objects pleasing to the resident gods.[14] Rhetoric is the chief theme of the Platonic dialogue, but not the only one. In the bright light of the Athenian summer, Sokrates converses with young Phaedrus about love and the nature of the soul, justly rewarded or punished for its conduct in this life.

Connected with the land and with the various aspects of nature, the nymphs promoted the fertility of animals and the soil, and due to their healing and divinatory abilities, they protected human offspring.[15] A well-known votive relief in Berlin, found in the area of the Stadium by the Ilissos riverbank,[16] is thought to have come from the shrine mentioned in the *Phaedrus*, which was possibly located at the foot of the Ardettos Hill.[17] It was dedicated to the nymphs and "all the gods" by an association of launderers who worked in and beside the river, "οἱ πλυνῆς Νύμφαις εὐξάμενοι ἀνέθεσαν καὶ θεοῖς πᾶσιν".[18] The relief depicts two goddesses who are approached by a bearded hero, possibly Demophon, leading a horse.[19] A seated goddess can be identified as Demeter or Meter, while the standing one with the torches could be Kore or Artemis-Hekate.[20] Above, in the votive inscription, we read the names of the dedicators, probably

10 Travlos 1971, 160, 168-9, figs 219 (IX), 222; Theocharaki 2011, 108.

11 Travlos 1971, 160, 168-9, figs 219 (IX), 222; Garland 1982, 155.

12 Travlos 1971, 289.

13 "And it seems to be a sacred place of some nymphs and of Achelous, judging by the figurines and statues" (trans. Fowler 1917).

14 van Straten 1995, 90; Larson 2001, 101-7, 128; Kaltsas & Shapiro 2008, 291.

15 van Straten 1995, 90; Forsén 1996, 140-2.

16 Berlin, Staatl. Mus. Inv. no. 709; Milchhöfer 1880, 217-8; Rodenwaldt 1912, 146-8, fig. 4; Feubel 1935, 12, no. 23, 39; Blümel 1966, 77-8, no. 90, K 87, fig. 123-4; Möbius 1935-1936, 244; Edwards 1985, 529, no. 30; Güntner 1994, 23-5, 128, A 53, pl. 12, 1; Vikela 1997, 213-4; Larson 2001, 128-9, fig. 4.1; Dillon 2002, 206; Comella 2002, 116-7, 203, Atene 156, fig. 117.

17 Travlos 1971, 289, fig. 382; Salta 2015, 319.

18 *IG* II², 2934. See also a base for a ritual basin from the Acropolis dedicated by the washerwoman Smikythe, *IG* I², 473; Kaltsas & Shapiro 2008, 51, no. 10. These washers probably worked nearby, as shown by paintings from the 18th and 19th centuries, such as in an 1835 sketch by the Danish painter Martinus Rørbye, see Papanikolaou-Kristensen 2003, 50 fig. 29.

19 Möbius 1935-1936, 244; Möbius 1967, 115. Concerning Demophon and his brother Akamas, see Kron 1976, 141-70. See also Pearson 1981, 66, 74; Larson 2001, 128.

20 See Güntner 1994, 23-4; Vikela 1997, 214.

Fig. 4 a-b. Marble statuettes from the sanctuary of Eileithyia on Ilissos. National Archaeological Museum, Athens, inv. nos. 693 and 695 (courtesy of The National Archaeological Museum, Athens. © Hellenic Ministry of Culture/Archaeological Receipts Fund. Photographer: George Fafalis).

foreigners,[21] but not slaves, as some scholars have supposed.[22] The top of the relief shows an abbreviated version of the dance of the nymphs in a cave, apparently a shrine to Pan. Hermes leads the dance while the goat-footed Pan[23] and Acheloos, in the form of a protome,[24] are in attendance. These small figures in the upper zone are probably the Ilissian deities who had their shrine near the sanctuary of the two main goddesses. In this way, the cult of the nymphs is related to the Metroon of Agrai, and to the goddesses of the Lesser Mysteries, whose initiates bathed in the Ilissos.[25]

21 Neumann 1979, 74, pl. 47b; Güntner 1994, 24; Löhr 2000, 98-100, no. 116. The dedicants are Ζωαγόρας Ζωκύπρου, Ζώκυπρος Ζωαγόρου, Θάλλος, Λεύκη, Σωκράτης Πολυκράτους, Ἀπολλοφάνης Εὐπορίωνος, Σωσίστρατος, Μάνης, Μυρρίνη, Σωσίας, Σωσιγένης, and Μίδας.

22 The quality of the votive relief as well as the mention of four patronymics speaks against a slave status of the dedicators.

23 A similar statuette of Pan, sitting and playing the syrinx (Panpipes), was found in the Olympieion in 1861 (NM 683, 668). Rhousopoulos 1862, 49, no. 1, pl. 13, 1; Sybel 1881, no. 401; Stais 1916, 83-4, fig. 15; Kaltsas 2002, 264, cat. no. 252; Salta 2015, 319-20, fig. 101.

24 Isler 1970, 37-8, 125 cat. no. 16; Güntner, 1994, 23; *LIMC* I (1981) s.v. Acheloos, 22-4, esp. no. 202. See also Larson 2001, 98-100; 2007, 64-6.

25 Möbius 1935-1936, 234-68; Deubner 1956, 70-1; Larson 2001, 128. For the Metroon ἐν Ἄγρᾳ, see Wycherley 1957, 153, no. 472; Travlos 1971, 112. The Metroon was situated near the Basilica of Ilissos. See also Vermaseren 1982, 113, fig. 8.

A sanctuary dedicated to Eileithyia, a secondary childbirth deity responsible for the protection of young children, especially newborn infants, and, as believed by many, the mother of Eros, must have existed near the Ilissos next to the shrines of the ancestors and the chthonian deities.[26] A place on the northwestern bank of the river yielded four marble statuettes of girls (Fig. 4a-b)[27] and a votive in the form of an inscribed column dedicated to the goddess Eileithyia by a woman named Philoumene.[28]

Fig. 5. The Roman bridge to the Stadium and the Ardettos Hill from the North. At the back, in the middle, the small temple of Artemis Agrotera, transformed to the Orthodox church of Παναγιά στην Πέτρα (after Stuart & Revett 1794, pl. I).

Additional evidence for the existence of a sanctuary of Eileithyia comes from an inscription found in the Theatre of Dionysos[29] and a fragment of Kleidemos' lost work *Atthis*,[30] which probably dealt with the topography of early Athens. The fragment, which is cited by the old grammarian Pausanias in a corrupt and difficult-to-translate passage, refers to Helicon as the old name of "the hill now called Agra" and the "altar of Apollo of Helicon" as well as to the Metroon in Agrai. It is possible that Kleidemos is referring to another sanctuary of Eileithyia and not to the sanctuary of the goddess in the Agora mentioned by Pausanias (Paus. 1.18.5).[31]

Eileithyia was closely associated with Artemis, a kourotrophos deity, who was worshipped as a virgin but also as a fertility goddess who protected women, childbirth, and childhood.[32] The small ionic temple of Artemis Agrotera (Artemis in the Fields or the

26 Baur 1902; Pigniatoglou 1981; Forsén 1996, 134-7 (especially Eileithyia and Artemis). See also Papachatzis 1978. For kneeling statues and statuettes of Eileithyia, see Kabus-Preisshofen 1988. Pindar (Pind. *Ol.* 6.42) calls Eileithyia πραΰμητιν, "gentle", because she gently helps women in labour, see Romilly 2007, 74-5.

27 Furtwängler 1878, 196-8; Milchhöfer 1880, 218 n. 1; Sybel 1881, 110, nos. 591-4; Hadaczek 1901, 209-12, figs 227-9; Svoronos 1917, 87-93; Vorster 1983, 68, 72-3, 330, 351, cat. nos. 1 (NM 693), 2 (NM 694), 59 (NM 695), 60 (NM 696); Kaltsas 2002, 268, 270-1, cat. nos. 559, 560, 565, 566. See also Kaltsas & Shapiro 2008, 300-3, nos. 132, 133; Salta 2015, 317, fig. 98; cf. Couilloud 1968, 72-5.

28 Furtwängler 1878, 197. EM 9037; *IG* II², 4682. Found „unterhalb des obigen Fundorts (nur wenig über dem Ilissos beim sog. Römischen Bade) am Ilissos bei den neuen Theatern". One of those theatres, named "Paradeisos", was situated to the north of Kallirrhoe. See Skias 1897, pl. A. For the Roman baths near the Olympieion, see Gardner 1923, 504 with fig. See also Curtius & Kaupert 1883, Blatt I; cf. Billot 1992, figs 2-3; Greco *et al.* 2011, 454-8.

29 Farnell 1896-1909, 2:608-14, 2:615 n. 2. "At Agrae in Attica: *IG* II² 5099 (III 319) ἐρσηφόροις β' Εἰλιθυίας ἐν Ἄγραις. Bekker's Anecd., 236. 30". See also Deubner 1956, 13 with n. 2.

30 Farnell 1896-1909, 2:615 n. 2; Pearson 1981, 63 with n. 33, fig. 1. The text as given by Bekker, *Anecdota Graeca* 1.326, is as follows: Κλείδημος (sic) ἐν πρώτῳ Ἀτθίδος "Τὰ μὲν οὖν τὰ τοῦ Ἰλισοῦ πρὸς ἀγορὰν Εἰληθυῖα. Τῷ δ' ὄχθῳ πάλαι ὄνομα τούτῳ, ὅς νῦν Ἄγρα καλεῖται, Ἑλικών, καὶ ἡ ἐσχάρα τοῦ Ποσειδῶνος τοῦ Ἑλικωνίου ἐπ' ἄκρου." καὶ ἐν τῷ τετάρτῳ, "Εἰς τὸ ἱερόν τὸ μητρῷον τὸ ἐν Ἄγραις." For the topography of Agrae or Helicon and the eschara of Poseidon, see Judeich 1931, 45, n. 2, 176. For the sanctuary of Eileithyia, see Judeich 1931, 380, 460.

31 Papachatzis 1974, 270. See also Travlos 1971, 28; Greco *et al.* 2011, 534-5. For the ancient city centre, see Robertson 1998, 283-302; Korres 2001, 5. See also Schnurr 1995; Greco *et al.* 2014, 776-7.

32 Vikela 2006, 47; Kaltsas & Shapiro 2008, 80, 289-91. For the kourotrophoi deities, see Hatzisteliou-Price 1978.

Fig. 6. Revetment from a pedestal or altar, probably from the Metroon. National Archaeological Museum, Athens, inv. no. 2668 (courtesy of The National Archaeological Museum, Athens. © Hellenic Ministry of Culture/Archaeological Receipts Fund. Photographer: Eleftherios Galanopoulos).

Huntress) stood on the far bank of the Ilissos River (Fig. 5).[33]

The Metroon is generally located on an islet in the Ilissos[34] by the Basilica of Bishop Leonides,[35] at the foot of the hill of Poseidon Helikonios.[36] According to John Travlos, the shrine where Boreas seized Oreithyia, daughter of Erechtheus, as mentioned in Plato's *Phaedrus* (Pl. *Phdr.* 229b) and Pausanias' *Attika* (Paus. 1.19.5), was located on the west bank of the river opposite the Artemis Agrotera temple.[37] The cult of Boreas was established on the banks of the Ilissos in thanks for his intervention on the Athenians' behalf soon after the victory over the Persians, as recounted by Herodotus (Hdt. 7.189).

According to Karl Kerényi, the rape of a virgin near the Ilissos River is identical to death,[38] and it may be significant that the rape of the Athenian women by the Pelasgians of Lemnos is depicted on

33 Travlos 1971, 112-20; Greco *et al.* 2011, 490-4, figs 270, 271. For the oath of the ephebes in the sanctuary of Agrotera before they entered military service, see Deubner 1956, 209; Beschi 2002, 33 with n. 80; Kaltsas & Shapiro 2008, 87.

34 Travlos 1971, 112, 114, fig. 154, 291, fig. 379; Vermaseren 1982, 113, fig. 8; Greco *et al.* 2011, 486-9.

35 Preuner 1921, 1-2; Sotiriou 1919; Möbius 1935-1936, 243; Bouras 2010, 185, 187, fig. 154, 257 n. 37 (with bibliography).

36 Travlos 1971, 114, figs 154, 379; Greco *et al.* 2011, 486, 494-5. For the cult of Poseidon Helikonios, see Farnell 1896-1909, 4:75.10 and 88 b; Svoronos 1916-1917, 6-8.

37 Travlos 1971, 291, fig. 379 no. 195; Papachatzis 1974, 285; Kaltsas & Shapiro 2008, 172-3. *LIMC* III (1986) s.v. Boreas, 138-42; *LIMC* VII (1994) s.v. Oreithyia I, 64-8. For the winds as elemental forces considered animate, see Larson 2007, 68-70. For the *Tritopatores* worshipped as the fertilizing winds, see Farnell 1921, 356.

38 Kerényi 1961, 24. See also Nagy 1990.

the frieze of the Ilissos Ionic temple in Agrai.[39] The temple is usually attributed to Artemis Agrotera, but some earlier scholars identified it with the Metroon in Agrai or a temple to Demeter, where the Lesser Eleusinian Mysteries were held.[40]

A heavy plaque with five relief figures (Fig. 6) was found in 1893 by Andreas Skias in cistern A in the Ilissos riverbed,[41] together with a corner block (NM 3941) from the Ilissos temple frieze.[42] The badly from river deteriorated plaque belonged to the revetment of a pedestal or altar, probably from the Metroon. Walking in a procession from left to right are a man in a himation carrying a torch or a mystic staff, possibly representing Herakles,[43] Nike with a phiale and another vase, Athena carrying her shield and helmet,[44] a *peplophoros* in a himation holding a sceptre identified as Demeter or Meter, and finally another man or god, possibly Meilichios.[45]

Some scholars have ascribed a headless statue of a female deity identified as Kore (Persephone) found near the Olympieion (Fig. 7)[46] to the same sanctuary, the Metroon, but the figure is also thought to be a statue of Aphrodite, another central deity, worshipped on the Ilissos, by the Olympieion.[47]

A large fragmentary votive relief from the Pankrati district dated to around 420 BC preserves the bodies of two female figures, Demeter and Persephone (Fig. 8).[48] Persephone is seated with her mother standing behind her. The scene was probably a *sacra conversazione*, such as is also seen on the large well-known Eleusinian Relief (NM 126).[49] The figures of the two goddesses in their grandeur recall a "Kultbild", and Evgenia Vikela ascribes the votive relief to the Metroon at Agrai.[50] Demeter, together with her daughter Persephone, suggests a connection between mortal humans, earth, and death.

39 Beschi 2002; McNeill 2005; Palagia 2005. For the Hyakinthids, the dead daughters of Erechtheus, in this area, see Kerényi 1961, 23-4. For their cult, see also Farnell 1921, 22; Larson 1995, 153-4; Ekroth 2002, 176, 186-91, 258, 261.

40 Möbius 1935-1936, 234-68; Travlos 1971, 112, 335; Salta 2015, 307, 309, fig. 95.

41 National Archaeological Museum, inv. no. 2668. Marbles of the Archaeological Society, inv. no. 5017 (July 1893). Skias 1894a, coll. 139-40. pl. 8A; Svoronos 1908-1937, 3,682, pl. 256: Möbius 1935-1936, 251, pl. 91; *LIMC* IV (1988) s.v. Demeter, 881, no. 449; *LIMC* VI (1992) s.v. Nike 871, no. 236; Kaltsas 2002, 209, no. 422; Salta 2015, 321, 325, fig. 105.

42 Marbles of the Archaeological Society, inv. no. 5024 (July 1893). Skias 1894a, 140-2. pl. 8 B. Γ; Möbius 1928, 1-6. pl. I-III; Möbius 1935-1936, 234, 250-1; Krug 1979, 15-7, G, pl. 9a-b; Felten 1984, 71ff, pl. 21, 2a-b; Kaltsas 2002, 118-9, no. 214; Salta 2015, 321, 323 fig. 103.

43 *LIMC* IV (1988) s.v. Demeter, 881, no. 449. For the admission of Herakles into the Eleusinian mysteries, see Farnell 1921, 108, 153. For the political reasons for his initiation, see also Simon 1983, 28.

44 It is known that Athena herself sought purification after witnessing Tydeus' savage act of cannibalism against Melanippos by running to the "mystic torch" and the "pure waters" of the Ilissos at Agrai, which were used for purification in the Lesser Mysteries. Möbius 1935-1936, 250-1; *LIMC* II (1984) s.v. Athanasia, 953-5.

45 Möbius 1935-1936, 251-3. For Herakles and Meilichios in Agrai, see Vikela 1994, 71-74 and 144f.

46 National Archaeological Museum, inv. no. 4762 (Θ 254). Kaltsas 2002, 125, no. 234. In the Inventory of the Theseion Collection of the National Museum, Θ 254 is written "εὑρέθη ἐν τῇ περιοχῇ Ὀλυμπιείου ὅπου καὶ ἡ κεφαλὴ τοῦ Διός" (Θ 234), cf. Salta 2015, 317, fig. 9.

47 Delivorrias 1969; 1974, 168f., pl. 60; *LIMC* II (1984), s.v. Aphrodite 25 no. 152; Kaltsas & Shapiro 2008, 107-13. For Roman statuettes depicting Aphrodite found in the area of the Olympieion, see Vlizos 2008, esp. 413-22.

48 National Archaeological Museum, inv. no. 3572 (BE 155/1923). Karusos 1929, 1-5, pl. 1; Karouzou 1968, 60; Peschlow-Bindokat 1972, 115 n. 215; Mitropoulou 1977a, no. 92, fig. 140; Reeder 1995, 296-7, no. 86; *LIMC* III (1986) s.v. Demeter, 867-8, no. 273, pl. 580; Vikela 1997, 211-2, pl. 27, 3; Kaltsas 2002, 132 no. 252; Comella 2002, 202, Atene 147. On the pilaster at the side are preserved letters from the engraved name of Demeter.

49 Kaltsas 2002, 100-2, no. 180.

50 Vikela 1997, 212. For the cult of Meter and Demeter on the Ilissos, see Greco *et al.* 2011, 486-9.

Fig. 7. Statue of Persephone or Aphrodite from near the Olympieion. National Archaeological Museum, Athens, inv. no. 4762 (courtesy of The National Archaeological Museum, Athens. © Hellenic Ministry of Culture/Archaeological Receipts Fund. Photographer: Tasos Vrettos).

Fig. 8. Votive relief with depiction of Demeter and Persephone. National Archaeological Museum, Athens, inv. no. 3572 (courtesy of The National Archaeological Museum, Athens. © Hellenic Ministry of Culture/Archaeological Receipts Fund. Photographer: Tasos Vrettos).

Certainly, the collection of sacred objects in this area from the earliest times, including some natural locales, is linked with water, a primaeval symbolic element of life and strength.[51] Beliefs about the magical power of the Kallirrhoe and Ilissos River, the latter often represented by the generalized river god Acheloos, were associated with numerous rituals aimed at fulfilling certain wishes or eliminating

51 On the cults on the Ilissos, see Greco *et al.* 2011, 480-3.

an invisible or visible evil, especially in transitional phases of the life cycle.

Prehistoric pottery found everywhere about the Olympieion precinct as well as below the temple provides evidence for an important prehistoric settlement near the Kallirrhoe and the north bank of the Ilissos being a very early place of worship in the area south of Acropolis. In the southwest corner of the hill, on the spot where, according to legend, King Aigeus lived when Theseus first came to Athens, a sanctuary dedicated to Apollo Delphinios was established.[52] The Law Court at the Delphinion was a very ancient precinct. This was the place where Aigeus threw the poison from Theseus' kylix to the earth, probably a sign of a very old chthonian cult.[53] It is possible that this area was the seat of a leading family in prehistoric times, which could explain the long-lasting use of an early grave on this site.[54]

East or south of the Delphinion lay the site of the *Kepoi* ("Gardens"), which included the sanctuary of Aphrodite Ourania, the oriental Queen of Heaven, a deity protecting the rebirth of nature and human fertility and related to Eileithyia. According to myth, Aigeus had established the cult in Athens because the royal house was troubled by a lack of children (Paus. 1.17.7).[55]

As a gift to a chthonian daemon can be explained by the following rite practiced in the area of the Olympieion. Every year, cakes of wheaten meal kneaded with honey were thrown into the cleft by which the waters of Deucalion's flood were said to have been swallowed, in a small precinct dedicated to Ge (Earth) (Paus. 1.18.7).[56] The tomb of Deucalion was located in this neighbourhood.

Fig. 9. Votive relief dedicated to Zeus Meilichios by Kratesion. National Archaeological Museum, Athens, inv. no. 12124 (courtesy of The National Archaeological Museum, Athens. © Hellenic Ministry of Culture/Archaeological Receipts Fund).

The cult of Meilichios on the Ilissos probably served the same function. More than one divinity is known under this name.[57] The euphemistic

52 Deubner 1956, 201; Travlos 1971, 83; Kyriakou 2007, 20-1 (Temple of Olympian Zeus, Precinct Wall); Greco *et al.* 2011, 471-2.

53 Greco *et al.* 2011, 466, 467-8.

54 Pantelidou-Gofa 1975, 80-92, 235 with n. 1 (Grave 13), but see also 113-5 (Grave 23), 141-53, 160, 233-40 and English summary, 241-63; Pantelidou-Gofa 1977, 64-5.

55 Simon 1983, 43-4.

56 Möbius 1935-1936, 246-7; Deubner 1956, 113; Simon 1983, 99. For the "χάσματα" and other chthonian cults, see Vikela 1994, 63-4.

57 Meilichios means the Easy to be entreated, the Gracious. According to Jaqueline de Romilly, it is possible to interpret the flourishing of the ideal of mildness in Athens, especially from the end of the 5th century BC onwards, as an immediate response to the violence, physical and moral, of the Peloponnesian war, described by Thucydides. The virtues aspired to by this ideal soon became the symbol of civilization and a hallmark of Hellenicity as opposed to barbarism, see de Romilly 2007, 15-16, 18.

Fig. 10. Votive relief dedicated to Zeus Meilichios by Aristomenes. National Archaeological Museum, Athens, inv. no. 3329 (courtesy of The National Archaeological Museum, Athens. © Hellenic Ministry of Culture/Archaeological Receipts Fund. Photographer: Kostas Xenikakis).

term "Meilichios" usually connotes the character of a nether-god or daemon and the cult record of Μειλίχιος is like ο Θεός alone.[58] The name "Meilichios" was an epithet of Zeus and often used alone to denote the deity.[59] It refers to a fertility god associated in cult with the nymphs,[60] who had a special affection towards children. Meilichios was often represented in the form of a snake, which was meant to symbolize the qualities of the earth.[61]

58 Farnell 1896-1909, 1: 64-66. cf. Vikela 1994, 65-6.

59 Farnell 1921, 86-7; Cook 1914-1940, 2, 1115-21. For the autonomous use of the *epiklesis* instead of the God's name, see also Vikela 1994, 70, 153-4.

60 Simon 1983, 15 with fig. 2; Larson 2001, 112, 128, 131, 208.

61 Mitropoulou 1977b, 28.

A small fragmentary votive relief (NM 12124) with the inscription "Κρατήσ[ιο]ν Μειλιχί[ῳ]" was found south of the Olympieion in 1938 during an exploratory investigation by Markellos Mitsos (Fig. 9).[62] Two worshippers, a woman wearing a chiton and draped in a long himation drawn up over the back of her head, and a second figure, possibly a man in a himation, approach in adoration gesture a large bearded snake to the right.

On another votive relief (NM 3329) found at "Vatrachonisi" on the Ilissos,[63] is depicted a large snake with a goat-like beard, coiled and facing to the left, as a symbolic representation of Zeus Meilichios (Fig. 10).[64] Three worshippers, members of a family (father, mother, and their little daughter), stand on a higher level than the snake. At the bottom, there is an inscription on the plinth: "Ἀριστομένης [Δ]ιί Μειλιχίῳ" (Aristomenes to Zeus Meilichios).

A shrine to Zeus Meilichios near the site of the Lesser Mysteries in the suburb of Agrai is mentioned by Thucydides (Thuc. 1.26.6) and Aristophanes in the comedy *Clouds* (Ar. *Nub*. 864.408).[65] The foundations of another ancient building in this place were identified in the excavation carried out in the area of the so-called temple of Artemis Agrotera in summer 2014. Especially important for this identification is an inscription that reads "ΔΙΙ ΜΕΙ [ΛΙΧΙΩΙ]" on a votive *kioniskos*, as well as

62 Walter 1940, 168; Lemerle 1939, 294; van Straten 1974, 180 n. 164a; Mitropoulou 1977b, 115, no. 5; Vikela 1997, 213 n. 182; Edelmann 1999, 224, no. G 40. For a votive relief dedicated to Meilichios recently found in this area, see Kyriakou 2001-2004, 281, fig. 80.

63 For the so-called "Vatrachonisi" on the Ilissos, see Biris 2005, 22-3, Λ-14.

64 Karouzou 1968, 147; Mitropoulou 1975a, 121, 122, no. 4, fig. 4; Mitropoulou 1977b, 112-3, no. 1, fig. 48a; Kaltsas 2002, 224, no. 469; Vikela 1994, 233 n. 52; Edelmann 1999, 204, cat. no. D 28; Greco *et al.* 2011, 488-9 fig. 269.

65 Ar. *Nub*. 864, 408 with Schol.; Nilsson 1955, 412; Parke 1987, 186-7; Larson 1995, 71; Greco *et al.* 2011, 486-9, esp. 489.

Fig. 11. Votive relief dedicated to Zeus Meilichios, Athens. National Archaeological Museum, Athens, inv. no. 1779 (courtesy of The National Archaeological Museum, Athens. © Hellenic Ministry of Culture/Archaeological Receipts Fund).

other fragments of votive reliefs. These also suggest that the foundations belong to the temple of Zeus Meilichios known from ancient texts.[66]

Zeus Meilichios can also be represented as a seated god holding a sceptre and a phiale.[67] Most scholars identify the seated deity in front of an archaic altar of stones on another votive relief from Kallirrhoe found in 1893 by Andreas Skias in the bed of Ilissos as that of Meilichios (Fig. 11).[68] Two worshippers, a woman and presumably her daughter, approach from the right. In the fragmentary inscription (IG II², 4707), we read "ἀ]νέθηκεν" and the beginning of another name,[69] a god's name, Naios Zeus according to some scholars,[70] or most probably the name of the female dedicator, Nannion, like Ninnion, the dedicator's name on the famous tablet from Eleusis.[71]

The votive can be attributed to the sanctuary of Zeus Meilichios, where the annual Diasia were celebrated 10 days after the Anthesteria and before the Lesser Mysteries or Mysteries ἐν Ἄγραις.[72] The Diasia was the greatest Athenian festival accorded to Zeus, (Thuc. 1.126), a popular celebration, combined with ancient propitiatory rituals appropriate to a chthonian daemon. Sacrificial cakes in the form of animals,[73] and sometimes burnt sacrifices of real animals, were offered at the Diasia.[74]

66 An announcement in the Καθημερινή newspaper 23rd July 2014 (cf. Charbis 2014). The excavated area is situated between Ardettou, Thomopoulou, Kephalou and Koutoula Streets. See also Travlos, 1971, 114, fig. 154. For Meilichios and the Μειλίχιοι θεοί, see Farnell 1896-1909, 1:64-6, 171-2 n. 138; Deubner 1956, 156-7, esp. n. 2; Larson 1995, 71. The results of the recent investigations of the 3rd Ephorate of Antiquities in the area of the so-called Temple of Artemis Agrotera are still to be published.

67 National Archaeological Museum, inv. no. 2356; Mitropoulou 1977b, 122-3, no. 13, fig. 55; Vikela 1994, 178 n. 36, 233 n. 52.

68 National Archaeological Museum, inv. no. 1779. Marbles of the Archaeological Society, inv. no. 5007 (July 1893); Skias 1894, 133, 136; Svoronos 1908-1937, 3.632, no. 329, pl. 130, 2; Cook 1914-1940, 2:2, 2:1116, fig. 947; Möbius 1967, 117; van Straten 1974, 189 no. 28; Mitropoulou 1977b, 114, no. 3; Vikela 1994, 73-4, 177, 180, 187, pl. 35.2; Vikela 1997, 213 n. 182; Edelmann 1999, 209, E 4; Vlizos 1999, 125-6, WR.4, pl. 7,1; *ThesCRA* VI (2011), 28, pl. 19.3.

69 *IG* II² 4707. «...ἀν]έθηκεν Ναι[". The relief is dated after the middle of the 4th century BC, see Mitropoulou 1977b (350-325 BC).

70 See Palagia 2002, 171-80, esp. 173 with fig. 8 on page 175. For Zeus Νάϊος, see Farnell 1896-1909, 1:38-9.

71 Kaltsas & Shapiro 2008, 150-1. For the representation of mystai in a typically Dionysiac manner on the Ninnion Tablet, see Simon 1983, 34 n. 66, 35-7.

72 Farnell 1896-1909, 1:171 no. 138; Möbius 1935-1936, 256f; Deubner 1956, 155-7; Jameson 1965, 159-66; Simon 1983, 12-5; Parke 1987, 183-7; Greco *et al.* 2011, 489 (Marchiandi). For the Lesser Mysteries and the Metroon in Agrai, see Travlos 1971, 112-3, with fig. 154. See also Simon 1983, 26-7.

73 Deubner 1956, 156; Parke 1987, 184-5, 191, 286. See also Pearson 1981, 62.

74 There were also gifts for children, cf. Ar. *Nub.* 864; Simon 1983, 14-5.

Fig. 12. Votive relief depicting Zeus Meilichios, Acheloos, Hermes, Herakles and Kallirrhoe or Meter. National Archaeological Museum, Athens, inv. no. 1778 (courtesy of The National Archaeological Museum, Athens. © Hellenic Ministry of Culture/ Archaeological Receipts Fund).

Chthonian Zeus appears in votives as Zeus Meilichios, Zeus Pankrates, or Zeus Philios.[75] The purifying function of water, which at a symbolic level was related to the belief in a blessed afterlife, was very important in the rituals of the chthonian cults of the area.

A relation to the Lesser Mysteries is visible in another votive relief found by the spring of Kallirrhoe during the excavations by Andreas Skias in 1893 (Fig. 12).[76] The relief depicts Zeus Meilichios seated to the right on a solid stool and holding a vase.[77] On the side of the seat is a relief head of Acheloos as a representant of the Ilissos River,[78] or as the son of Ge and deity of the fertilizing and generative water,[79] with his name engraved beneath. In the background, behind Zeus, a female figure holding a horn of abundance and a bowl has been identified as Kallirrhoe, the daughter of Acheloos, or Meter, the Mother of Gods.[80] In front of Zeus Meilichios stands Hermes, holding an oinochoe and a *kerykeion*. Herakles on the right, with a lion's pelt on his head and fastened on his chest, holds his club in his left hand and probably a vase in his right.[81] The relief bears witness to the relation of Zeus Meilichios, Hermes, and Herakles to the Lesser Mysteries.

75 Vikela 1994, 72, but also 62; See also Farnell 1896-1909, 1:103, 1:117-9.

76 National Archaeological Museum, inv. no. 1778. Marbles of the Archaeological Society, inv. no. 5006 (July 1893). Skias 1893a, 137 no. 1; 1894a, 137-9, pl. 7; 1894b, 12 with n. 2; Maass 1895, 354-6.; Svoronos 1908-1937, 3.632-3, no. 336, pl. 131; Cook 1914-1940, 2:2, 2:1116, fig. 948; Möbius 1935-36, 247, pl. 90; Hausmann 1960, 80, fig. 47; Linfert 1967, 154; Muthmann 1968, 25 pl. 11.3; Isler 1970, 38-9, 128, no. 35; Travlos 1971, 297, fig. 388; Kater-Sibbes 1973, 85 no. 474 bis; Mitropoulou 1975c, 70-1, no. 51 with fig. ; Mitropoulou 1977b, 114, no. 4. *LIMC* I (1981) s.v. Acheloos, 24 no. 204; Wegener 1985, 113; Reeder 1987, 432-3, fig. 8; Weiss 1984, 162-3; Boardman *et al.* 1990, 168 no. 3376; *LIMC* V (1990), s.v. Hermes, 347, no. 728; *LIMC* V (1990), s.v. Kallirrhoe II, 938, no.3. pl. 604; Tagalidou 1993, 211-3, no. 19 (W), pl. 9; Güntner 1994, 159, no. F6; Vikela 1994, 71 n. 110, 72-4, 156, 203 n. 61, 220 n. 188, pl. 34.1; 1997, 212-3, n. 178, pl. 27,1; Kaltsas 2002, 278 no. 583; Vikela 2011, 173 with n. 296; Tsangari 2011, 148, no. 314; Salta 2015, 321, 323, fig. 102.

77 For the interpretation of the figure, see Tagalidou 1993, 64 with n. 301.

78 Vikela 1997, 212-3.

79 Tagalidou 1993, 130.

80 Vikela 1994, 71-2, esp. n. 110.

81 Mitropoulou 1975c, 70-1. no. 51 with fig.; Vikela 1994, 71-2, 156.

Fig. 13. View of the waterfall of Ilissos by the Olympieion (after Dodwell 1821).

From Kallirrhoe on the Ilissos to the Sanctuary of the Nymphe on the South Slope of the Acropolis

The spring of Kallirrhoe, having until 1962 a considerable flow of water at the foot of a steep slope, is situated southeast of the Olympieion in the Ilissos riverbed opposite the Church of St Photini.[82] In a painting by Edward Dodwell, we see the rocky landscape of the Ilissos with its waterfalls and the spring of Kallirrhoe southeast of the Temple of Olympian Zeus (Fig. 13).[83] The small cubic building to the right could be an old chapel of St Photini.[84] The name Kallirrhoe survived in this place through the Middle Ages to modern times. Thucydides (Thuc. 2.15.4-5) mentions that in his time the fountain, which was constructed by the Tyrants, was called Enneakrounos, "the Nine Spouts", but before this time, the open spring was named Kallirrhoe, "the Fair-Flowing".[85] This spring was used by the Athenians for the most important purposes, and it was still customary, from old habit, to use the water for the prenuptial bath and for other sacred purposes.[86]

On early Attic vases, we see maidens bringing water from a fountain that pours down from spouts fashioned as lions' mouths labelled "Καλλιρρόη κρήνη".[87] The Enneakrounos fountain house built by the tyrants should be located on the west bank of the Ilissos very near the spring. Thucydides made no exact statement as to the position of the spring, which has been disputed mainly due to the difficulty of reconciling Pausanias' description

82 Nikolaidis 1893; Dörpfeld 1894; Harrison 1906, 111-31; Judeich 1931, 193-7; Wycherley 1957, 137-42; Travlos 1971, 204-6, fig. 268. See also Travelos 1971, 289; Tölle-Kastenbein 1986; Greco *et al.* 2011, 476-9, figs 261-3; Salta 2015, 321. For the rock and the spring of Kallirrhoe, and the so-called "tou Vounou" aqueduct, see Biris 2005, 44-5.

83 Bouras 2001,153-5, fig. 8; Lagogianni-Georgakarakos & Koutsogiannis 2015, 16-7; Salta 2015, 313.

84 Salta 2015, 313 n. 53. The new church of St Photini was founded in 1872. Skias 1894b, 16 mentions an old chapel of St Photini in a cave just beneath the modern church.

85 Wycherley 1957, 141-2, no. 455.

86 Gardner 1923, 18; Wycherley 1957, 141-2, no. 455; Larson 2001, 111-2.

87 Travlos 1971, 204-5, fig. 26; Tölle-Kastenbein 1986, 69-70, figs 6, 7. See also the fragment of a black-figure hydria from the Acropolis in Athens, depicting a fountain and three female figures with hydrias in front of it, National Archaeological Museum, inv. no., Ακρ. 732, Kaltsas & Shapiro 2008, 310-1, cat. no. 138. Between the spout and the columned front of the fountain is the inscription KALIPOE.

of the Enneakrounos with other indications, but, Pausanias apart, there is overwhelming evidence that the Kallirrhoe lay in the bed of the Ilissos. According to John Travlos, the Enneakrounos was possibly located in a place where a stone parapet block, certainly coming from the draw basin of a fountain house, was found in 1962, not far away from the bridge on Anapafseos Street.[88]

The performance of a special act of devotion to the river-god, as the source of life and fertility, by youths upon attaining manhood and by maidens at their marriage, is a common rite that we meet through the ages in many places. On the wedding day, the bride washed herself with water from the spring of Kallirrhoe.[89] A boy or girl from among the near relatives of the pair brought the spring's water for the marital bath in a loutrophoros, usually depicting wedding scenes. After the ceremony, the bride offered the loutrophoros, together with other vases, at the special shrine of the Nymphe a divinity of marriage, worshipped on the south slope of the Acropolis.[90] There, south of the Odeion of Herodes Atticus, a votive relief of a woman with a snake was found. The stele carries an inscription, "Ηδέα Διί Μειλιχίῳ", which shows the chthonian character of the cult at this place as well.[91]

The remains of the shrine are dated to the period from the middle of the 7th century BC to the capture of Athens by Sulla's forces in 86 BC. This custom of the loutrophoria is another testimony of an internal bond that linked the Ilissian cults at the spring of Kallirrhoe with the sanctuaries beneath the Acropolis, where also a settlement existed in prehistorie times and numerous Protogeometric and Geometric burials were found. At that time there existed a particularly lively worship of ancestors and heroes of the past. The absence of contemporary burials in a classical peribolos of the 4th cent. BC in Erechtheion Street and the presence of clay piping, possibly intended for blood sacrifices, led Maria Brouskari to the conclusion that the peribolos could be interpreted as a "heroon" erected around the graves of the ancient Geometric dead.[92] It is worth pointing out that the heroon lay south of the Sanctuary of the Nymphe, near the city wall.

The spring of Kallirrhoe trickled from the ridge of the rock that crosses the Ilissos just below the Olympieion. Jacob Spon and George Wheler attest that the abundant spring was still known by the name Kallirrhoe in 1676, but by the first decades of the 20th century, its flow was scanty, possibly due to earthquakes.[93]

Gerhard Rodenwaldt attempted to identify Phaidros' shrine to Pan with the one by the church of St Photini, across the Ilissos River from Kallirrhoe, where a relief of Pan from the 5th century BC or later has been carved on the artificial scarp, now almost weathered away.[94] According to John Travlos, this is the site of another shrine to Pan and the Nymphs near the spring of Kallirrhoe, because, in his own words, "had Sokrates and Phaidros indeed gone there, it would follow that the district of Agrai must be about 500-600 metres further downstream, according to the figures given by Sokrates (Plato Phaedrus 229c), but this view is not supported by the evidence".[95]

88 Travlos 1971, 204.

89 Kaltsas & Shapiro 2008, 291-4.

90 Travlos 1971, 361, figs 464-7; Brouskari 2004, esp. 32-7. See also *LIMC* VIII (1997), s.v. Nymphe I, 902; Kyrkou 2000; Kyrkou 2011. For the prenuptial bath (Thuc. 2.15.3-6) and the Sanctuary of the Nymphe, see Larson 2001, 111-2.

91 Brouskari 2004, 36-7, fig. 38.

92 Brouskari 1980, 13-31; 2004, 29-31. See also Brouskari 1979, esp. 74-82 (Aus dem Athener Kerameikos des 8. Jhs. v. Chr.).

93 Gardner 1923, 21.

94 Rodenwaldt 1912; Travlos 1971, 289; Goette 2001, 101-2, fig. 32.

95 Travlos 1971, 289.

Fig. 14a. Marble cult head of Herakles: **b.** Right side; **c.** Left side. National Archaeological Museum, Athens, inv. no. 367 (courtesy of The National Archaeological Museum, Athens. © Hellenic Ministry of Culture/ Archaeological Receipts Fund. Photographer: Eleftherios Galanopoulos).

Herakles and the Afterlife

In 1893, Andreas Skias excavated at Kallirrhoe and discovered two large cisterns, A and B, in the riverbed and a system of rock-cut tunnels to collect the water and convey it to Piraeus by the so-called "tou Vounou" aqueduct.[96] There, in the Ilissos riverbed, a number of round sculptures and reliefs were found. A colossal head of Herakles found by Andreas Skias in cistern B, lay many years unidentified in the storerooms of the National Museum in Athens. In February 2011 the author was able to define again its provenance and to present it for the first time to the public in the course of the Museum's temporary exhibition "Myth and Coinage" (Fig. 14a-c).[97] The hero is represented as bearded and of mature age, with a lion's head covering his head and tied on the chest with a reef knot, known as the Herakles Knot. His convex forehead bulges slightly in the middle, which is defined by the developed set of teeth in the lion's mouth; the deep eye-sockets and the pronounced dimples on the lean cheeks are in marked contrast to the smooth treatment of the lower part of the face and the beard. The figure turns slightly to the right. The back of the sculpture was not visible, while the lower part was intended to be inserted in the ground.[98] Similar cult heads are known from another neighbouring site on the Ilissos, namely the

96 Skias 1893a; 1893b;1894a; 1894b; 1897; Travlos 1971, 204.

97 National Archaeological Museum, inv. no. 367. (height: 0,67 metres, date: 350-325 BC). In the inventory of the sculpture collection, where it had been recorded, there was no mention of its provenance or its bibliography. The description in the Archaeological Society at Athens' Inventory had also not been correlated with the actual sculpture. Marbles of the Archaeological Society, inv. no. 5016 (July 1893); Tsangari 2011, 124, no. 253. Mentioned Skias 1894a, esp. col. 135; Skias 1894b, 12 with n. 2; Kavvadias 1890-1892, 252, no. 367; Svoronos 1901, 294 with n. 1; Kastriotis 1908, 74, no. 367; Möbius 1928, 4; Kalogeropoulou 1988, esp. 130.

98 The late Professor G. Despinis was of the same opinion.

sanctuary of Pankrates not far from the Lykeion.[99] After 330 BC, they also appear in votive reliefs from the same sanctuary.[100]

The singular sculptural rendering of the hero is associated with the chthonic character of his cult beside the Ilissos, where he had been initiated into the Lesser Mysteries.[101] The work may be attributed to the circle of Skopas, to whose workshop other sculptures from the Ilissos area have been attributed.[102] An interesting parallel is the Skopaic life-size head of Herakles from the Athena sanctuary in Tegea, which possibly originates from a free-standing statue, perhaps a group of Herakles and Telephos.[103]

A chthonian Herakles named Charops was worshipped in Boeotia in the temenos of Zeus Laphystios (Paus. 9.34.5),[104] a personification of Hades.[105] Pausanias (6.23.5) mentions that in the city of Elis, where also a temenos of Hades is attested,[106] in a corner of the so-called Gymnasium Maltho, there was a "πρόσωπον Ἡρακλέους ἄχρι ἐς τοὺς ὤμους",[107] possibly referring to a simple hermaic stele[108] or to a round sculpture of similar function to the hero's head from Ilissos.

In this connection, it is worth mentioning the existence of 4th-century BC grave monuments of people from Elis in the region of Kynosarges. These are mentioned in inscriptions[109] or are known from the literary tradition, as in the case of the family plot of the orator Isokrates from Erchia, situated, according to Pseudo-Plutarch (Decem Oratorum Vitae,

99 Travlos 1971, 278-80, with fig. 379; Kalogeropoulou 1987, 300; 1988, 129-31; Vikela 1994, 163-5; *LIMC* VII (1994), s.v. Pankrates I, 167, nos. 3-4; Vikela 1997, 214-5. For the Lykeion and its connection to the political ideology of Lykurgos, see Schröder 1986. For the Lycurgian proposals in the later 330s, see Humphreys 2004, 77-129; Pritchard 2013, 92-5. For the Lykeion as a meeting-place of philosophers, Socrates being one of them as mentioned in Plato's *Lysis* (Pl. *Lysis* 203a), see Jones 1999, 232; Greco *et al.* 2014, 698-702. For the excavation in the Gymnasion area by E. Lygouri-Tolia, see Greco *et al.* 2014, 703-5, with bibliography.

100 Kalogeropoulou 1987; 1988, 128-9; Vikela 1994, 36-7, B10, pl. 22.2, 39-40, B 13, pl. 24.1, 43, B 18, pl. 26.1, and 163; *LIMC* VII (1994) s.v. Pankrates I, 167, no. 2; Vikela 1997, 214-5, pl. 28.1.

101 Schol. Ar.; *Plut.* 1013; Diod. Sic. 4.14.5; Harrison 1906, 146-7; Brommer 1984, 18-9, with n. 54, 102, with n. 49; Billot 1992, 121 with n. 6; Vikela 1994, 151-3. For the Lesser Mysteries, see Clinton 2008, 2:23.

102 Stele NM 869; Stewart 1977, 117-8, pl. 49a; Kaltsas 2002, 193, no. 382.

103 Delivorrias 1973, 131-5, fig. 9; Stewart 1977, 54, 115, no. 40, pl. 47a; Boardman *et al.* 1988, 790, no. 1313. Stavridi 1996, 58-9, inv. no. 48.

104 Farnell 1921, 153ª; Papachatzis 1981; Tagalidou 1993, 139-42; Papachatzis 2006, 120-1; Kalogeropoulou 1987, 303-4; Vikela 1994, 155-6. For the meaning of Χάροψ and χαροπός, see Skiadas 1967, 14-6. Cf. the votive relief from Pyri depicting Herakles, Plouton, Persephone, and Demeter: Karouzos 1934, 26-7, no. 48, fig. 23.

105 Farnell 1896-1909, 1:50, 1:93-5, 1:110, 1:152 n. 68; 1921, 153a. For the cult of Charops in Thespiai and the possibility that it is identical to that of Herakles Charops of Koroneia, see Schachter 1981-1994, 2:5, 2:34; Vikela 1994, 155 with n. 108. According to Pausanias (9.34.5), a location on Mount Laphystion was believed to be the place where Herakles brought Kerberos up from the Underworld, see Stafford 2012, 184.

106 Paus. 25.2-4; Farnell 1896-1909, 3:281; Papachatzis 1998, 404-6, esp. 406 with n. 1; *LIMC* IV (1988) s.v. Hades, 369 & Anhang, Hades in Elis, 388.

107 "A bust of Heracles as far as the shoulders", (trans. Jones 1965). See also von Heintze 1965, 24 with n. 47; Papachatzis 1998, 400-1; Boardman *et al.* 1988, 786 no. 1218.

108 Cf. Karouzos 1934, 47 no. 160, fig. 36.

109 NM 995. C. 908/179; IG II²,8528 from Brachami; Salta 1991, 184-5. For the alliance of Athens with Elis in the second quarter of the 4th century BC, see Lawton 1995, 9, 94 A 24, pl. 13.

Βίοι τῶν δέκα ρητόρων 838b), next to the Diomeian Gate.[110]

This particular head found near the Kallirrhoe was a cult object in and of itself, a bodyless figure of a chthonian divinity as appears in sanctuaries of Demeter, Kore, Aphrodite, and Dionysos, not only in Boeotia,[111] but also in southern Italy and Sicily.[112] In Attica, in addition to Herakles Pankrates, there are some other parallels in clay and stone, such as the protome-masks of the Nymphe from the open-air sanctuary on the south slope of the Acropolis, excavated by Ioannis Miliadis,[113] along with similar representations of Acheloos, known from many sanctuaries in Attica.[114] The large Acheloos head, appearing from the rocky ground of a cave on the votive relief (NM 1880), could, according to Konstantinos Rhomaios' description, be an independent cult head.[115] The relief dates to before 350 BC and was found in the Pan sanctuary of Phyle on Mount Parnes. The Acheloos head on the votive relief (NM 2012) from the cave of Vari on Hymettos is characterized only by human features and belongs to the last quarter of the 4th century BC.[116] Life-size heads of male and female daemons may also occur in a sepulchral context, such as the 26 clay heads used around 480 BC for the funeral of a queen in the region of Aegae, the ancestral centre of the kingdom of the Macedonians.[117] Being thrown into the tomb, they show the queen's special relationship with the world of gods and daemons and underline her connection to the Great Goddess.[118]

In Attica, Herakles was variously worshipped as a hero and as a god, and the ways in which he is depicted confirm his dual nature.[119] The colossal

110 For the magnificent grave peribolos of Isokrates' family in this region and his relatives from Elis, such as his wife Plathane, possibly Hippias' daughter from Elis and her son Aphareus, probably named after a Messenian king, see Garland 1982, 156, no. G1; Salta 1991, 67 with n. 594, 185 with n. 1884; Scholl 1994, 240-52. Concerning Isokrates' family, see Davies 1971, 245-8, no. 7716. For Hippias, Aphareus, and Plathane, see also Zoumbaki 2005, 200-3, no. 9, 122-3, no. 142, 295-6, no. 16. For the topography of the place, see Judeich 1931, 142, 423; Travlos 1970, 6-8, plan 1. According to Plutarch (*Mor.* 849c), another orator, Hypereides of Kollytos, who died in 322 BC, was buried "with his parents in front of the Hippadic Gate", see also Garland 1982, 155.

111 Vikela 1994, 163-5. For the abbreviation of female figures to simple heads or bust in the western colonies, especially in the worship of Persephone, see Larson 2001, 254-5.

112 Vikela 1994, 163 n. 175. For marble protomes from Nisyros and Rhodes, see Bairami 2013. For a possibly similar Herakles cult on the island of Kos, cf. the marble head of a bearded Herakles covered with a lion's head and found in Halasarna, see Aspetaki-Kyritsi & Toulanta-Parisidi 1998, 103 with fig. ; Stafford 2012, 185-7.

113 *Ergon* 1957, 5-12, esp. 10-1, fig. 7; Miliadis 1957, 26, pl. 3a.

114 For Acheloos protomes and masks, see Isler 1970, 37, no. 51, 113-5. See also Gais 1978, 357 and *LIMC* I (1981) s.v. Acheloos, 12-36.

115 Rhomaios 1905, 110-7, no. 3, fig. 3; Svoronos 1908-1937, 3,577, no. 230, pl. 96; Isler 1970, 30, 36, 123 no. 3; *LIMC* I (1981) s.v. Acheloos 23, no. 168; Edwards 1985, 465, no. 21; Güntner 1994, 13, 119 (A12). For the cult activity in this cave, see Larson 2001, 245-6; Goette 2001, 266-7. For the raised hand holding the upper edge of a mantle or veil of the female figure, cf. EM 2795, Lawton 1995, 122-3, no. 85, pl. 45 (Hebe with Herakles, both worshipped at Kynosarges).

116 Dunham 1903, 291 no. 6; Thallon 1903, 309, pl. 8; Svoronos 1908-1937, 3,581, no. 235, pl. 98; Isler 1970, 125, no. 13; *LIMC* I (1981) s.v. Acheloos 23, no. 179; Edwards 1985, 519, no. 29; Güntner 1994, 121 (A 21); Vikela 1997, 224 with n. 233-6; Kaltsas 2002, 218, no. 452; Schörner & Goette 2004, 71-4, pl. 42, 1.2. For the cult, see also Larson 2001, 242-5; Goette 2001, 192-5; Schörner & Goette 2004, 111-9.

117 Kottaridi 2011b, 156-7, figs 173-4. According to Kottaridi, all the heads would have originally been placed on wooden poles, thus forming statues (xoana). After the burial of the queen, they were deliberately destroyed and thrown into her tomb (cat. nos. 173-4, 178-80).

118 Kottaridi 2011a, esp. 101, figs 90-1.

119 Lawton 1995, 51-2. For general affinities between the Herakles and Asclepios cults in Athens, see Farnell 1921, 19; Riethmüller 1999, esp. 135-43; Ekroth 2012, 331; Stafford 2012, 171-5. Herakles was the first for-

cult head, probably originating from a temenos of his own or with other chthonian deities near the spring of Kallirrhoe, certainly confirms his divine status in this place, which is also supported by other ancient testimonies. There are references to the cult and festival of Herakles at Diomeia, "Ηράκλεια τἀν Διομείοις" (Ar. *Ran.* 651), as well as the post-sacrifice feasting at the Kynosarges sanctuary introduced by Diomos, the eponymous hero of the deme of Diomeia (Paus. 1.19.3).[120] Diomeia, located near the Diomeian gate to the southeast of the city, was a deme of the Aigeis tribe.[121] Herakles is depicted on the Roman calendar frieze from the Hagios Eleutherios church in Athens in connection with the Herakleia "ἐν Κυνοσάργει" mentioned by Harpokration.[122] The nude hero, with a lion-skin on his left arm, holds a club in his left hand, resting on the ground.

The precinct of Herakles, in whose honour the Gymnasium of Kynosarges was founded, should, according to John Travlos, be located near the Ilissos bank by the spring of Kallirrhoe.[123] A decree of 440-430 BC forbids the tanners to soften hides in the river above the precinct of Herakles and specifies that two stelai with the decree should be set up on either side of the Ilissos.[124] It is worth pointing out that until modern times, the tanners

Fig. 15. Votive relief depicting Herakles and kneeling worshipper. National Archaeological Museum, Athens, inv. no. 12126. (Courtesy of The National Archaeological Museum, Athens. © Hellenic Ministry of Culture/Archaeological Receipts Fund).

were installed along this section of the Ilissos because of its unfailing supply of water.[125] One inscription referring to the Dromos towards Agrai (*IG* II², 2119.128) could relate to a race-track at the Gymnasium, where the young men exercised, and should be found in the only level place in the area along the south bank of the Ilissos by the spring of Kallirrhoe, probably beginning at a point near the church of St Panteleimon and ending in the district of Agrai.[126]

The road to Kynosarges, on its way south to the coast, passed through the Diomeian Gate known to us from Diogenes Laertius (Diog. Laert. 6.13) and Plutarch (Plut. *Vit. Them.* 1). John Travlos tentatively

eigner admitted to the Eleusinian Mysteries and the Athenians were the first to worship him as a god. See Larson 2010, 36.

120 Deubner 1956, 226; Stafford 2012, 109, 178-9.

121 Traill 1986, 126-8.

122 Deubner 1956, 248-54, esp. 253, no. 37, pl. 40.

123 Travlos 1970, 8; Kokkou 1970, 165-7 (Hadrian's Gymnasium); Travlos 1971, 340-1, 579, figs 219, 379, nos. 192-4, and 579 (Kynosarges Gymnasium); Travlos 1993, 91-2, pl. IV; Billot 1992; Tagalidou 1993, 57-8; Iliopoulos 2001-2004a; 2010. Cf. also "templum Herculis" by Livius, Skias 1894b, 13. For the attachment of the Nothoi of Attica to Herakles in his shrine of Kynosarges, see Farnell 1921, 164-5; Humphreys 1974.

124 EM 12453; Karouzos 1923, 96-8 fig. 5; *IG* I³, 257, 8-9; Travlos 1970, 8; 1971, 340-1, fig. 442; Billot 1992, esp. 155-6; Tagalidou 1993, 1993, 57-8; Greco *et al.* 2011, 508-9.

125 Skias 1893a, 113; Travlos 1970, 8; 1971, 340. For an installation of tanners by the ruins of the ancient bridge in front of the Panathenaic Stadion, shown in a lithography by Ludwig Lange, see Papanikolaou-Kristensen 2003, 50 fig. 28.

126 EM 10348; Travlos 1970, 8. See also Billot 1992, 140-1; Tagalidou 1993, 58. For an archaic votive inscription referring to the dromos of Kynosarges, see Raubitschek 1949, 341, no. 318; Travlos 1971, 340; 1993, 92.

located it between the Olympieion and the Ilissos River on Athanasiou Diakou Street.[127]

A votive relief to Herakles was found between the south terrace wall of the Olympieion and A. Diakos Street during the excavations of Markellos Mitsos in 1939 (Fig. 15).[128] The bearded Herakles, wearing a lion-skin and holding his club and a horn of plenty, is worshipped by an old bearded man kneeling with arms extended towards him.[129] A kneeling worshipper alone or in front of a deity does not appear in Greek art except in votive and base reliefs after the middle of the 4th century BC.[130] This votive relief recalls the subject of the Pseudo-Platonic dialogue *Axiochos* or *Περὶ θανάτου* concerning Axiochos, a friend of Sokrates, who was scared by a near-death experience.[131] At the beginning of the dialogue, Sokrates is outside the city walls on the way to Kynosarges when he sees Kleinias, the son of Axiochos, running towards Kallirrhoe with his friends.[132] The same text refers to the Itonian Gate (Pl. *[Ax.]* 364D-365A), situated, according to John Travlos, south of the Olympieion on Ioseph ton Rogon Street, where the city wall turns a corner and stops.[133] The gate's name was possibly associated with an unknown sanctuary by the Ilissos River, dedicated to Itonian Athena, a deity connected with the underworld and worshipped as an assessor of Hades and protector of flora.[134] According to tradition, the Thessalian deity Itonia was a descendant of Deukalion, whose sanctuary in Athens was situated south of the Olympieion, near the Ilissos.[135]

The gates in the southern part of the city cannot be identified with certainty, but it is highly likely that at least three gates existed here. These are, from east to west, the Itonian, the Halade, and a third whose name is unknown.[136]

This depiction of Herakles, who is represented as bearded and of mature age, with a lion's head covering his head and tied on the chest with a reef knot, recalls the colossal cult head from the Kallirrhoe (Fig. 14). It is very different from the young unbearded Herakles known from the decree and votive reliefs

127 Travlos 1970, 6 plan 1; 1971, 160; Garland 1982, 156. For Diomeia, Kynosarges, and the Herakles cult in the region, see also Vikela 1997, 215.

128 National Archaeological Museum, inv. no. 12126. Lemerle 1939, 294; Walter 1940, 168; van Straten 1974, 170 no. 13; Mitropoulou 1975b, 46 no. 20; Boardman *et al.* 1988, 804 no. 1389; Vikela 1994, 166 with n. 193, 197-8, n. 28; Edelmann 1999, 241, no. U 115.

129 For Herakles, the horn of plenty, and Pluton on the relief from Pyri, see n. 104 above and Schauenburg 1953, 45, 56. A bearded Herakles wearing a lion skin and holding his club and the horn of plenty is represented on an unpublished Roman herm in the National Museum of Athens, inv. no. 15709.

130 Mitropoulou 1975b, 58. For kneeling down, προσκύνησις, see also Pakkanen 1996, 119-21.

131 For Orphic ideas in *Axiochos*, see Farnell 1921, 390-1.

132 Wycherley 1957, 140-1, no. 449: c. 300 BC?

133 Travlos 1970, 6 plan 1; 1971, 160, fig. 219, XI; Garland 1982, 156-7. See also Woodhead 1997, 171-4, no, 109, col. III, l. 122; Theocharaki 2011, 83, 104, fig. 10.

134 Vaiopoulou 2012 with fig. 4 (The City Wall of Athens and the Itonian Gate). See also *IG* I^2, 310.216 (Ἀθηναία Ἰτωνία).

135 Vaiopoulou 2012, 154. According to Thukydides (1.12), Strabo (9.28.411), and Pausanias (9.34.1), Athena Itonia was also worshipped in a temple of the city of Koroneia, being the meeting-place of the Boeotian League. She was not only a war-goddess, but a protector of arts, especially poetry. As a goddess who fostered the earth's growth, she had some affinity with the cthonian deities. Farnell 1896-1909, 1:300-1 with notes on 1:402-3, and 1:327-8 with pl. XIII.b; Farnell 1921, 356; Rakatsianos & Tziaphalias 1997, 16-7; Vaiopoulou 2012, 156-60. For Hades and Athena in Koroneia, see also Farnell 1896-1909, 3:286 and Athena, R 61.

136 See Garland 1982, 156-7; Salta 1991, 31.

attributed to Kynosarges,[137] such as NM 3491[138] and NM 3952 (formerly Agora S 1249).[139] In the first relief, Herakles is related to the hero Antiochos as his father. Antiochos is also presented on another decree of the Phyle Antiochis (NM 3492), found in the same area.[140] The Heroon of Antiochos was apparently associated with the Herakles sanctuary.

The eschatological aspect of the cults by Kallirrhoe on the Ilissos is more distinct than in other places of the city. This is also attested in the literary tradition, especially from the 5th century BC onwards.

Healing Deities and Medicine

The healing Herakles Menytes seen on another small votive relief (Akrop. Mus. No. 7232 (4901)) belongs to a different context south of the Acropolis, in the Asclepieion.[141] Herakles stands in a short chiton and lion-skin holding a club in his right hand and a horn of plenty in his left. A kneeling female worshipper, the dedicator, extends her arms towards him with open palms facing up. Behind her is an image of a nude woman, represented in four sections: a) head with upper part of the body, b) lower part of the body with thighs, c) arms, and d) lower legs. These

---

137 After Karouzos 1923, 85-6, the decrees of the Antiochis, mentioned in the article, were found in 1922, not *in situ*, namely in house foundations south of the Ilissos and of the Fix brewery, in the neighbourhood of Dourgouti. The find-spot of two of them, inv. nos. NM 3491 and 3492, is, according to the inventory of the Sculpture Collection of the National Museum, not Dourgouti, but the district of Pankrati, situated near the Stadion. The decrees might originally have been erected in the region of Alopeke, a deme of Antiochis, located at Katsipodi, southeast of the Ilissos, and not in the Diomeia, belonging to the Aigeis, and situated by the homonymous gate, close to Kallirrhoe. For both demes, see Traill 1986, 128 (Diomeia), 139 (Alopeke).

138 A document relief of the Phyle Antiochis honouring the taxiarch (commander of the military contigent) Prokleides. The nude Herakles, with a lion-skin draped over his left forearm, holds the top of his club with his right hand, while the lower end of it rests on a rock. Opposite him is a bearded figure wearing a himation, probably his son Antiochos, the Hero of the phyle. Karouzos 1923, 89-96, no. 2, fig. 2; *SEG* 3, 1927, 26, no. 116; Kron 1976, 191-3, 239, 279 no. An 5, pl. 28.1; Pemberton 1981, 319, pl. 55d; *LIMC* I (1981), s.v. Antiochos, 852, no. 6; Boardman *et al.* 1988, 745, no. 275; Vollkommer 1988, 53. no. 393; Meyer 1989, 25, 27, 69, 119-21, 304-5 A 139; Boardman *et al.* 1990, 172, no. 3413; Tagalidou 1993, 100-2, 219-21, no. 22, pl. 11; Vikela 1994, 185, 197, 202, 214; Lawton 1995, 8, 15, 34, 51-2, 150, no. 157, pl. 83; Kaltsas 2002, 238, no. 501; Albersmeier 2010, 248-9, no. 63. See also Woodford 1971, 215-6.

139 Young beardless Herakles, in a variant of the Lenbach type, stands nude, with a lion-skin on his left arm and his club, resting on the ground, in his right hand. In the middle a servant leading a bull, followed by the family of dedicators (man, woman, child) and a maid carrying a kiste on the head. On the epistyle, there is a dedicatory inscription, probably of foreigners: Πάνις Αἰγίριος Ἡρ[α] κλεῖ. Cf. Παννό, Koumanoudis 1979,164, no. 1573. Aigeiros or Aigiros is known as a nymph's name. Cf. also the aigeiros (poplar tree), the sacred tree of Herakles. *Liddell-Scott* 34, v. αἴγειρος; Baumann 1982, 50, colour fig. 76. Boiotia was called "aegerophoros", poplar-bearing, *Max. Tyr.* 29.7. See Demetrakos 1949, 108, v. αἰγειροφόρος. Robinson 1948, with pl. 34, 1; Boardman *et al.* 1988, 747-8, no. 330 (= 803-4, no. 1388); Billot 1992, 137f. fig. 4; Tagalidou 1993, 221-3, no. 23, pl. 13; van Straten 1995, 88, 297, R 90. fig. 93; Edelmann 1999, 102, 151-2, 204, no. D 30; Comella 2002, 122-3, Atene 148, 202, fig. 123; Dillon 2002, 240; *ThesCRA* I (2004) 17 no. 108.

140 Karouzos 1923, 93-4, fig. 3; Laskaris 1923, 106, n. 1, 110. Kastriotis *ArchDelt* 1924/25, Par/ma 24, no. 9; Kron 1976, 192ff, 239, 280, n. 6, pl. 28,2; *LIMC* I (1981), s.v. Antiochos, 852, no. 7; Mantis 1990, 86, no. 10, pl. 39b; Meyer 1989, 212, 289, A 86; Lawton 1995, 143f. no. 145, pl.77.

141 Walter 1923, 60-1, Nr. 108; van Straten 1974, 168, no. 11 fig. 18; Mitropoulou 1975b, 39 fig. 4; van Straten 1981, 106, no. 1.1; *LIMC* IV (1988) s.v. Herakles no. 1386; Tagalidou 1993, 191-2, no. 8, pl. 3; Vikela 1994, 118, pl. 37, 1, 197-8 no. 28; Forsén 1996, 149 with n. 117; Edelmann 1999, 60, 186 B4; Comella 2002, 193, Atene 46. *ThesCRA* III (2005), III Veneration 84, Hikesia 50, Consecration 179, pl. 65 no. 179; Vikela 2006, 51 fig. 6; Salta 2012, 29, 106-7, fig. 22; 2013, 41-2, fig. 22; Stampolidis & Tassoulas 2014, 215-6, no 82.

Fig. 16. Banquet relief. National Archaeological Museum, Athens, inv. no. 3873, now in the New Acropolis Museum (courtesy of The National Archaeological Museum, Athens. © Hellenic Ministry of Culture/Archaeological Receipts Fund. Photographer: Kostas Xenikakis).

four parts presumably make up the image of the worshipping woman.

In Plato's Phaedrus (Pl. *Phdr.* 270b), the scientific method of healing is compared with that of rhetoric, because in both cases a nature is the object of analysis, that of the body and that of the soul. Furthermore, it is noted (Pl. *Phdr.* 270c) that nobody can acquire any appreciable knowledge of the nature of the soul without knowing the nature of the whole man, and according to Hippocrates the Asclepiad, one cannot know the nature of the body either, except in this way.

Several other minor chthonian deities were worshipped in the area, some of them connected with healing and Asclepios. Reliefs with representations of the Agathodaemon (Good Daemon) and Tyche as well as inscriptions bearing their names have been found on the Acropolis slope and in the region of the Asclepieion. Apart from the philological tradition, evidence for the existence of a shrine and the worship of the two gods in Athens is found in the epigraphical record from the 4th century BC until the Roman period.[142] Agathodaemon also held an important position in private worship, although he was more frequently worshipped with other deities, primarily at the Asclepieia, as a god who fostered healing.

During excavations for the Acropolis metro station, a Late Hellenistic marble statuette of a long-haired male figure holding a cornucopia came to light. The figure can be identified as the Agathodaemon, a benevolent deity, which expressed the Ἀγαθόν Πνεῦμα (Good Grace) and endowed happiness.[143]

On a votive relief of the "funeral banquet" type from the same area (NM 3873), a *theoxenia* scene is depicted (Fig. 16).[144] A bearded god or hero wearing a polos and a himation reclines on a couch behind a table laden with food. With his right hand, he holds a rhyton, and with his left, a bowl. His female consort sits at the end of the couch having just taken incense from a box in her left hand to place it in the censer. In front of the table, a snake rears its head, while at the right edge a nude servant holds a bowl. On the left is a family of worshippers.[145] In the top left corner in the background, the protome of a horse is depicted in a border.

Many round sculptures of Eubouleus (the Good Counsellor), a cult figure of the inner Eleusinian circle, were found in the district of Makrygianni

142 For Agathos Daimon and Agathe Tyche on a Classical base found on the Acropolis, Acropolis Museum, inv. no. 4069, see Walter 1923, 184-6, no. 391; Kosmopoulou 2002, 71, 189-90, no. 26, fig. 45. For "Agathodaimon", see also *LIMC* I (1981) 277-82; Bemmann 1994; Machaira 2014.

143 Parlama & Stampolidis 2003, 67-8, no.40.

144 Kaltsas 2002, 231, no. 487; Kaltsas & Despinis 2007, 157, no. 45. Found in Vyronos Street, in Makrigianni, in 1940. Last quarter of the 4th century BC. For the dedication of banquet reliefs in the Asclepieia of Athens and Piraeus, see Hausmann 1948, 111-24. For ritual banquets as a kind of communion, a connection with the divine, see Lambrinoudakis 2014, 20-2.

145 Man, wife, and two children, with slaves and offerings.

Fig. 17. Marble head of a hero, probably Eubouleus. National Archaeological Museum, Athens, inv. no. 2650 (courtesy of The National Archaeological Museum, Athens. © Hellenic Ministry of Culture/ Archaeological Receipts Fund).

and Acropolis.[146] His name, elsewhere associated with the nether Zeus, points to the oracular powers of the chthonian deity who sends up "good counsel" through dreams.[147] According to the Orphic myth, Dionysos Eubouleus, a god of the Nether World, is a son of Zeus and Persephone.[148]

The marble head NM 2650 (Fig. 17), possibly once belonging to a herm, was found near the military hospital in the Makrygianni district.[149] The head depicts Eubouleus, who is regarded as the brother of Triptolemos.[150] The luxuriant hair, restrained by a cylindrical circlet and coiffed in heavy wavy tresses which hang on the forehead and down to the nape, is characteristic of chthonian deities. The sculpture, dated to the 2nd century AD, is a Roman copy of an earlier Late Classical or Hellenistic bust from Eleusis representing the same hero (NM 181).[151]

All the sculptures representing Eubouleus possibly come from the sanctuaries of Asclepios and Dionysos south of the Acropolis. It is interesting to point out that dreaming was an essential part of the healing process during *enkoimesis* in the sanctuaries of healing deities, especially those of Asclepios.[152]

Asclepios, originally a chthonios daemon from Thessaly, a hero and a son of Apollo, developed into the pre-eminent healing god of antiquity, who could experience death, yet had the power of immortality.[153] His appeal to people was obviously the main reason behind the spread of his cult across Attica during the devastating years of the Pelopon-

146 Alexandri 1968, 63, pl. 33b (Kallisperi Street); Brouskari 2011, 68, no. 36, pl. 32 (Acropolis Museum, inv. no. 2934), 69, no. 37, pl. 33 (Acropolis Museum, inv. no. 7285). See also *LIMC* IV (1988), Eubouleus, 44 no.3 c-d. For another Eubouleus from Athens (Athenian Agora, inv. no. Agora S 2089), see Harrison 1960, 382-9.; *LIMC* IV, 44, no. 3e.

147 Farnell 1921, 22. For Zeus Ευβουλεύς see Farnell 1896-1909, 3:280, 3:282, 3:285.

148 30th Orphic hymn, Nilsson 1957, 42.

149 Svoronos 1911, 39f., pl. 3, 4; *LIMC* IV, 44, Eubouleus no. 3b; Clinton 1992, 135 no. 6; Kaltsas 2002, 265, no. 554; Kaltsas & Despinis 2007, 185, no. 59.

150 The figure has been regarded at various times as Triptolemos, Iakkhos, the son of Demeter, or even Alexander.

151 Svoronos 1911, 39f., pl. 3.1-2; *LIMC* IV, 44, Eubouleus no. 3; Clinton 1992, 135 no. 4; Kaltsas 2002, 265, no. 555. National Museum, inv. no. 1839 is also from Eleusis, see Svoronos 1911, 39f., pl. 3.3; *LIMC* IV, 44, no. 3a; Clinton 1992, 135, no. 5; Kaltsas 2002, 266, no. 556.

152 According to Lambrinoudakis (2014, 22-7), sleep healing was a magical imitation of decay, death, and the production of new life, of rebirth.

153 Lambrinoudakis 2014, 17.

Fig. 18. Votive relief depicting Asclepios, Demeter and Kore (Persephone), who receive doctors as worshippers. National Archaeological Museum, Athens, inv. no. 1332, now in the New Acropolis Museum (courtesy of The National Archaeological Museum, Athens. © Hellenic Ministry of Culture/ Archaeological Receipts Fund).

Fig. 19. Heavy plaque, probably from the base of a Dionysos' statue. National Archaeological Museum, Athens, inv. no. 1489, now in the New Acropolis Museum (courtesy of The National Archaeological Museum, Athens. © Hellenic Ministry of Culture/ Archaeological Receipts Fund).

nesian War.[154] One of the particularly recognisable virtues of Asclepios as a god, along with mildness, was philanthropy, which increases the closer we get to Christian times.[155]

Asclepios features in votive reliefs alongside the Eleusinian deities, who were first to offer hospitality to his cult in the City Eleusinion.[156] In a votive relief from the Asclepieion, Asclepios, Demeter, and Kore (Persephone) are depicted receiving worshippers (Fig. 18).[157] Below them are five olive wreaths and the names of the dedicators, famous doctors honoured by the city of Athens.[158]

Dionysos in the Underworld

A heavy plaque, probably from the base of a Dionysos statue, was found in the Theatre of Dionysos in 1937 (Fig. 19).[159] On the right stands Dionysos with a short-sleeved chiton, fawn-skin, cloak, and high boots, holding an amphora and a kantharos. On the left, a woman places incense in a high censer.

154 See Farnell 1921, 259; Neumann 1979, 49. Also Salta 1991, 12.

155 Farnell 1921, 276-7.; Romilly 2007, 88-9, 483 with n. 71. For Asclepios' reputation as Σωτήρ (saviour god), see Clinton 1994, 32f.

156 See Benedum 1986, 154-5.; Clinton 1994, esp. 28ff. On page 26, n. 29, Clinton points out that Asclepios had no need of a μυσταγωγός, nor did any of the other gods who went to Eleusis for the Mysteries, i.e. Dionysos, Herakles, and the Dioskouroi. According to Farnell 1921, 244, Asclepios was admitted to the Eleusinian Mysteries as a new denizen of Athens.

157 New Acropolis Museum, ex National Archaeological Museum, inv. no. 1332; Kaltsas 2002, 224-5, no. 472; Comella 2002, 110-1, fig. 110, 196, Atene 77, fig. 110. See also *LIMC* II (1984) Asklepios 886, no. 313; *LIMC* IV (1988) Demeter, 881, no. 444; Benedum 1986, 154-5. Second half of 4th century BC.

158 *IG* II^2, 4359; Güntner 1994, 45, 145, cat. no. C 51, pl. 24, 2.

159 New Acropolis Museum, ex National Archaeological Museum, inv. no. 1489; Kaltsas 2002, 143, no. 275. See also *LIMC* III (1986) Dionysos, 494, no. 853. Beginning of 4th century BC.

Dionysos, an important Mycenaean deity mentioned in Linear B tablets, was not only the god of fertility and vegetation, but was also an old patron of the city relevant to all Athenian people, including women,[160] men, and children, as the religious calendar shows.[161]

Dionysos also had an obvious chthonian character, since care for the afterlife and worship of the dead were aspects associated with his cult. He was worshipped in Athens as Lenaios, Eleuthereus, and Limnaios in his three homonymous sanctuaries lying east, south, and southeast of the Acropolis.[162] According to Giorgos Despinis, the arrival of Dionysos from the city of Eleutherai to Athens is possibly depicted on the fragmentary double-faced relief of Würzburg-Athens, in which he would have been received by the deities worshipped in the wider region of his sanctuary.[163] These deities characteristically appear divided into two groups, which Giorgos Despinis believes symbolizes the two particularly important localities of the city's cult: on one side, gods of the south slope of the Acropolis are represented; on the other, the gods of the Olympieion and the Ilissos district.[164] It is likely that the dedication of the relief was connected to the major building works that were carried out in the sanctuary of Dionysos Eleuthereus during the last quarter of the 5th century BC.[165] It is also possible that Dionysos and his sanctuaries formed the connecting link between the two sacred areas of Athens, the south-southeastern sector of the city under the Acropolis, and the adjacent suburb on the banks of the Ilissos.

Aristophanes presented his well-known comedy *Frogs* at the celebration of the Lenaia in 405 BC, just before the end of the disastrous Peloponnesian War.[166] This theatrical performance had Dionysos himself as protagonist, who dressed up as Herakles descended to the Underworld in order to bring back the recently deceased Euripides. The comedy ends with the ascension of Aischylos from Hades.

G.T.W. Hooker (1960) attempted to show that Dionysos in the *Frogs* "was actually represented as following a route perfectly familiar to the audience, visiting places well known to them and indeed even in view to them as they sat in the theatre".[167] Dionysos reaches the house of Herakles, situated outside the Diomeian Gate (Travlos X), apparently in a place between the city wall and the Ilissos, and asks the hero what route he had followed when he went down to the underworld to fetch Kerberos. It is possible that the great λίμνη, immediately on leaving the Herakleion and the temenos of the singing frogs, can be identified as the sanctuary of Dionysos ἐν Λίμναις. The name of the sanctuary can be explained from the formation of a marsh in its low-lying ground area, where the Ilissos' water could not readily drain away.

The Dionysion as it is mentioned in the inscription *IG* I³, 84, which came to light in 1884 on the left of the tramway to Phaleron, one house block from the right bank of the Ilissos was in close proximity to the temenos of Kodros, Neleus, and Basile.[168] This temenos was definitely southeast of the Acropolis near the Ilissos. The heroine Basile can be characterized as a kind of personification of sovereignty, connected with the kings of Athens and the birth of Erichthonios. It is possible that she is identical to

160 Isler-Kerényi 1999.

161 Kolb 1977, esp. 120-5; Kaltsas & Shapiro 2008, 267-75, 290.

162 Kaltsas & Shapiro 2008, 267-72. For the festivals of Dionysos, see Simon 1983, 89-105.

163 Despinis 2013, 164-5, fig. 117-8.

164 On the contrary, Angelos Delivorrias has argued that on this double-faced relief the central figure is Asclepios, welcomed to Athens by Apollo leading the other gods, see Delivorrias 1997, esp. 204-7, fig. 13-6.

165 Despinis 2013, 165. However, it was in the same period that the cult of Asclepios was established on the south slope of the Acropolis.

166 For the Lenaia, see Simon 1983, 100-1.

167 Hooker 1960, 112; Guarducci 1982.

168 Koumanoudis 1884, 161-4; Travlos 1971, 332-4.

Iasile, a nymph represented on a well-known votive relief from Neon Phaliron (NM 1783).[169]

The sanctuary of Dionysos ἐν Λίμναις was possibly placed to the north of the Haladai Gate (Travlos XII), at the intersection of the Chatzichristou, Makrygianni, and Veikou Streets.[170] In the *Frogs*, Dionysos entered the underworld after having crossed the λίμνη. There, he met the chorus of initiates, who were singing joyful hymns. It is possible that the marshy flowery meadow towards which they were moving was also located near the Ilissos and that the Mysteries alluded to were the Lesser Mysteries performed at Agrai.[171] The Mysteries at Agrai, concerned with τὰ περί Διόνυσον, were at least partly Dionysiac, and they occurred in Anthesterion, towards the end of February, at the same time of year and in the same area as the Dionysiac ceremonies in the sanctuary ἐν Λίμναις.[172] The cleansing rites, which must have been an integral part of the ritual performance, were particularly used for the preliminary selection of people wishing to undergo the initiation (*mystai*).

G.T.W. Hooker concludes that in depicting the journey of Dionysos, Aristophanes kept close to the facts of Athenian topography and that there was a reputed way down to the underworld in Athens in the sanctuary of Dionysos ἐν Λίμναις, the same one that Herakles had once used when he went down to steal Kerberos.[173]

There is a 5th-century BC fragmentary red-figured loutrophoros-hydria from the Sanctuary of the Nymphe, depicting the wedded couple Herakles and Hebe with Ganymedes, Hermes, and Apollo in attendance, while the secondary register shows the rape of a young woman, possibly Thetis, by Peleus.[174] The vase, a work of the renowned Persephone Painter, symbolically ties together once again the cult of the Nymphe as a deity of marriage, as well as "χθόνιος δαίμων"[175] with the Kallirrhoe spring and the chthonian cults on the Ilissos.[176]

Abbreviations

IG = *Inscriptiones Graecae* (1873-).
LIMC = *Lexicon Iconographicum Mythologiae Classicae* (1981-2009).
Liddell-Scott = *A Greek-English Lexicon.*
ThesCRA = *Thesaurus cultus et rituum antiquorum* (2004-2005).

Bibliography

ALBERSMEIER, S. (ED.) 2010
Heroes. Mortals and Myths in Ancient Greece, Baltimore.

ALEXANDRI, O. 1968
'42. Καλλισπέρη, έργα Δήμου', *ArchDelt* 23, Chronika B1, 63-5.

ASPETAKI-KYRITSI, O. & M. TOULANTA-PARISIDI 1998
Αρχαία Ιστορία της Κώ. Από τα προϊστορικά μέχρι τα ρωμαϊκά χρόνια, Kos.

BAIRAMI, K. 2013
'Νισυρία Κόρη: λίθινη προτομή από το Παλαιόκαστρο Νισύρου', in *Όλβιος Άνερ. Μελέτες στη Μνήμη του*

169 Kaltsas 2002, 135, no. 258; Despinis 2013, 155-67.
170 Travlos 1971, 333, fig. 435; Neumann 1980, 615-7.
171 Hooker 1960, 116.
172 For the character of the Anthesteria, a vegetation cult already celebrated in the Late Bronze Age and one of the oldest Greek festivals, see Simon 1983, 92-9.
173 Hooker 1960, 117.
174 New Acropolis Museum, inv. no. NA -57-Aa 1154; Tsoni-Kyrkou 1988, 225-30, pl. 41-3.
175 Brouskari 2004, 36.
176 For the cult of Herakles and Hebe in the Kynosarges, see Paus. 1.19.3. For his connection with weddings on the island of Kos, see Stafford, 2012, 185-7.

Γρηγόρη Κωνσταντινόπουλου (Ρόδος IV), A. Giannikouri (ed.), Athens, 287-300.

BARRINGER, J.M. & J.M. HURWIT (EDS.) 2005
Periklean Athens and Its Legacy: Problems and Perspectives, Austin.

BAUMANN, H. 1982
Die griechische Pflanzenwelt im Mythos, Kunst und Literatur, München.

BAUR, P.V.C. 1902
Eileithyia (The University of Missouri Studies Vol. 1. No. 4), Chicago.

BEMMANN, K. 1994
Füllhörner in klassischer und hellenistischer Zeit, Frankfurt am Main.

BENEDUM, C. 1986
'Asklepios und Demeter', *JdI* 101, 137-57.

BESCHI, L. 2002
'I Tirreni di Lemno a Brauron e il tempietto ionico dell' Ilisso', *RivIstArch* 57, Ser. 25, 7-36.

BILLOT, M.-F. 1992
'Le Cynosarges, Antiochos et les tanneurs. Questions de topographie', *BCH* 116, 119-56.

BIRIS, K. 2005
Αἱ τοπωνυμίαι τῆς πόλεως καὶ τῶν περιχώρων τῶν Ἀθηνῶν (2nd ed.), Athens.

BLÜMEL, C. 1966
Die klassisch griechischen Skulpturen der Staatlichen Museen zu Berlin, Berlin.

BOARDMAN, J., O. PALAGIA & S. WOODFORD 1988
'Herakles', in *LIMC*, 8 vols, Zürich, München and Düsseldorf.

BOARDMAN, J., W. FELTEN, G. KOKKOROU-ALEWRA, S. WOODFORD, L. TODISCO, PH. BRIZE, W. SMALLWOOD & A.-F. LAURENS 1990
'Herakles', in *LIMC*, 8 vols, Zürich, München and Düsseldorf.

BOURAS, C., M.B. SAKELLARIOU, K.S. STAIKOS & E. TOULOUPA (EDS.) 2001
Athens. From the Classical Period to the Present Day (5th Century B.C. – A.D. 2000), Athens.

BOURAS, C. 2001
'Planning and Architecture in Hellenistic Athens', in *Athens. From the Classical Period to the Present Day (5th Century B.C. – A.D. 2000)*, C. Bouras, M.B. Sakellariou, K.S. Staikos & E. Touloupa (eds.), Athens, 144-65.

BOURAS, C. 2010
Βυζαντινή Αθήνα. 10ος-12ος αι., (Μουσείο Μπενάκη, Παράρτημα 6), Athens.

BRAVO, J.J., III 2010
'Recovering the Past. The Origins of Greek Heroes and Hero Cult', in *Heroes. Mortals and Myths in Ancient Greece*, S. Albersmeier (ed.), Baltimore, 10-29.

BROMMER, F. 1984
Herakles II. Die unkanonischen Taten des Helden, Darmstadt.

BROUSKARI, M.S. 1979
Ἀπό τὸν Ἀθηναϊκό Κεραμεικό του 8ου π.Χ. αἰ., Athens.

BROUSKARI, M.S. 1980
'A Dark Age Cemetery in Erechtheion Street, Athens', *BSA* 75, 13-31.

BROUSKARI, M.S. 2004
'Οἱ ἀνασκαφές νοτίως τῆς Ἀκροπόλεως. Τὰ Γλυπτά', *ArchEph* 141, 2002.

BROUSKARI, M.S. 2011
'Ἰδεαλιστικά κεφάλια ρωμαϊκῶν χρόνων, ἀντίγραφα κλασικῶν ἔργων ἀπό το Μουσεῖο τῆς Ἀκροπόλεως', *ArchEph* 150, 1-119.

CHARBIS, A. 2014
'Ναός του Διός Μειλιχίου στο Μετς', Kathemerini, 23.07.2014. Available online: http://www.Kathimerini.gr/777262/article/politismos/polh/naos-toy-dios-meilixioy-sto-mets.

CLINTON, K. 1992
Myth and Cult. The Iconography of the Eleusinian Mysteries. The Martin P. Nilsson Lectures on Greek Religion, Delivered 19-21 November 1990 at the Swedish Institute at Athens (ActaAth 8.11), Stockholm.

CLINTON, K. 1994
'The Epidauria and the Arrival of Asclepius in Athens', in *Ancient Greek Cult Practice from the Epigraphical Evidence. Proceedings of the Second International Seminar on Ancient Greek Cult, Organized by the Swedish Institute at Athens (1994)*, R. Hägg (ed.), Stockholm, 17-34.

CLINTON, K. 2008
Eleusis. The Inscriptions on Stone. Documents of the Sanctuary of the Two Goddesses and Public Documents of the Deme, Athens.

COMELLA, A. 2002
I rilievi votivi greci di periodo arcaico e classico. Diffusione, ideologia, committenza, Bari.

COOK, A.B. 1914-1940
Zeus. A Study in Ancient Religion, 3 vols, Cambridge.

COUILLOUD, T. 1968
'Nouvelle dédicace attique aux Ilithyes', *BCH* 92, 72-5.

CURTIUS, E. & J.A. KAUPERT 1883
Karten von Attika, Berlin.

DAVIES, J.K. 1971
Athenian Propertied Families 600-300 B.C., Oxford.

DELIVORRIAS, A. 1969
'Eine klassische Kora-Statue vom Metroon am Ilissos', *AntP* IX, 7-14, Pl. 1-5.

DELIVORRIAS, A. 1973
'Σκοπαδικά (I)', *BCH* 97, 111-35.

DELIVORRIAS, A. 1974
Attische Giebelskulpturen und Akrotere des 5. Jh., Tübingen.

DELIVORRIAS, A. 1997
'Συνανήκοντα θραύσματα: Συγκλίνουσες ἐνδείξεις καὶ ἀποκλίνοντες συσχετισμοί', in *Ἔπαινος Ἰωάννου Κ. Παπαδημητρίου*, B. Petrakos (ed.), Athens, 183-215.

DEMETRAKOS, D. 1949
Μέγα Λεξικόν τῆς Ἑλληνικῆς Γλώσσης, Athens.

DESPINIS, G. 2013
Μικρές μελέτες για ανάγλυφα. Συγκολλήσεις και συσχετισμοί θραυσμάτων. Νέες παρατηρήσεις και ερμηνείες, Athens.

DEUBNER, L. 1956
Attische Feste, Berlin.

DILLON, M. 2002
Girls and Women in Classical Religion, London.

DÖRPFELD, W. 1894
'Ἡ Ἐννεάκρουνος καὶ ἡ Καλλιρρόη', *ArchEph*, 1-10.

DODWELL, E. 1821
Views in Greece from Drawings by Edward Dodwell, London.

DOW, S. 1965
'The Greater Demarkhia of Erkhia', *BCH* 89, 180-213.

DUNHAM, M.E. 1903
'The Cave at Vari: The Inscriptions', *AJA* 7.3, 289-300.

EDELMANN, M. 1999
Menschen auf griechischen Weihreliefs, Munich.

EDWARDS, C.M. 1985
'Greek Votive Reliefs to Pan and the Nymphs', PhD diss., New York University, Ann Arbor.

VON EICKSTEDT, K.-V. 1994
'Bemerkungen zur Ikonographie des Frieses von Ilissos-Tempel', in *The Archaeology of Athens and Attica under the Democracy. Proceedings of an International Conference Celebrating 2500 Years Since the Birth of Democracy in Greece, Held at the American School of Classical Studies at Athens, December 4-6, 1992,* W.D.E. Coulson, O. Palagia, T.L. Shear, Jr., H.A. Shapiro & F.J. Frost (eds.), Oxford, 106-8.

EKROTH, G. 2002
The Sacrificial Rituals of Greek Hero-Cults, Liège.

FARNELL, L.R. 1896-1909
Cults of the Greek States, 5 vols, Oxford.

FARNELL, L.R. 1921
Greek Hero Cults and Ideas of Immortality, Oxford.

FELTEN, F. 1984
Griechische tektonische Friese archaischer und klassischer Zeit, Waldsassen, Bavaria.

FEUBEL, R. 1935
Die attischen Nymphenreliefs und ihre Vorbilder, Heidelberg.

FORSÉN, B. 1996
Griechische Gliederweihungen, Helsinki.

FOWLER, H.N. 1914
Plato. Euthyphro. Apology. Crito. Phaedo. Phaedrus (Loeb Classical Library 36), Cambridge.

FRAZER, J.G. 1913
Pausanias Description of Greece, 6 vols, London.

FRIELINGHAUS, H. & J. STROSZECK (EDS.) 2010
Neue Forschungen in griechischen Städten und Heiligtümern. Festschrift für Burkhard Wesenberg zum 65. Geburtstag (Beiträge zur Archäologie Griechenlands), Möhnesee.

FURTWÄNGLER, A. 1878
'Die Chariten der Akropolis', *AM* 3, 181-202.

GAIS, R.M. 1978
'Some Problems of River-God Iconography', *AJA* 82, 355-70.

GAGNÉ, R. 2007
'Winds and Ancestors. The Physika of Orpheus', *HSCP* 103, 1-23.

GARDNER, E.A. 1923
Ancient Athens, New York.

GARLAND, A. 1982
'A First Catalogue of Attic Peribolos Tombs', *BSA* 77, 125-76.

GOETTE, H.R. 2001
Athens, Attica and the Megarid. An Archaeological Guide, London and New York.

GRECO, E., F. LONGO, D. MARCHIANDI, M.C. MONACO, R. DI CESARE & G. MARGINESU 2011
Topografia di Atene. Sviluppo urbano e monumenti dalle origini al III secolo d.C. Tomo 2: Colline sud-occidentali -Valle dell' Ilisso, Athens and Paestum.

GRECO, E., R. DI CESARE, F. LONGO & D. MARCHIANDI 2014
Topografia di Atene. Sviluppo urbano e monumenti dalle origini al III secolo d.C. Tomo 3: Quartieri a nord e a nord-est dell' Acropoli e Agora del Ceramico, Athens and Paestum.

GUARDUCCI, M. 1982
'Le *Rane* di Aristofane e la topografia ateniese', in *Studi in onore di Aristide Colonna*, Università di Perugia, Instituto di filologia classica (ed.), Perugia, 167-9.

GÜNTNER, G. 1994
Göttervereine und Götterversammlungen auf attischen Weihreliefs. Untersuchungen zur Typologie und Bedeutung, Würzburg.

HADACZEK, C. 1901
'Mädchenstatuette mit Vogel im Vatican', *ÖJh* 4, 209-12.

HARRISON, E.B. 1960
'New Sculpture from the Athenian Agora, 1959', *Hesperia* 29.4, 369-92.

HARRISON, J.H. 1906
Primitive Athens as Described by Thucydides, Cambridge.

HATZISTELIOU-PRICE, T. 1978
Kourotrophos. Cults and Representation of the Greek Nursing Deities, Leiden.

HAUSMANN, U. 1948
Kunst und Heiltum, Potsdam.

HAUSMANN, U. 1960
Griechische Weihreliefs, Berlin.

VON HEINTZE, H. 1965
'Herakles Alexikakos', *RM* 72, 14-40.

HOOKER, G.T.W. 1960
'The Topography of the *Frogs*', *JHS* 80, 112-7.

HUMPHREYS, S.C. 1974
'The Nothoi of Kynosarges', *JHS* 94, 88-95.

HUMPHREYS 2004
The Strangeness of Gods. Historical Perspectives on the Interpretation of Athenian Religion, Oxford,

ILIOPOULOS, T. 2001-2004A
'Οδός Διαμαντοπούλου 1, Αδριάνειο Γυμνάσιο', *ArchDelt* 56-59, Chronika. 206-8.

ILIOPOULOS, T. 2001-2004B
'Οδός Διαμαντοπούλου 10 (οικόπεδο Ντινόπουλου)', *ArchDelt* 56, Chronika B1, 208-14

ILIOPOULOS, T. 2010
'News from the Kynosarges Site', in *Neue Forschungen zu griechischen Städten und Heiligtümern*, H. Frieling-haus & J. Stroszeck (eds.), Möhnesee, 85-91.

ISLER, H.P. 1970
Acheloos, Bern.

ISLER-KERÉNYI, C. 1999
'Frauen um Dionysos vom 7. Jahrhundert bis um 540 v.Chr.', *AA*, 553-66.

JAMESON, M.H. 1965
'Notes on the Sacrificial Calendar from Erchia', *BCH* 89, 154-72.

JAMESON, M.H. 1994
'Theoxeneia', in *Ancient Greek Cult Practice from the Epigraphical Evidence. Proceedings of the Second International Seminar on Ancient Greek Cult, Organized by the Swedish Institute at Athens, 22-24 November 1991,* R. Hägg (ed.), Stockholm and Göteborg, 35-57.

JONES, N.E. 1999
The Associations of Classical Athens. The Response to Democracy, New York and Oxford.

JONES, W.H.S. 1965
Pausanias. Description of Greece, Volume III: Books 6-8.21 (Elis 2, Achaia, Arcadia) (Loeb Classical Library 272), Cambridge.

JUDEICH, W. 1931
Topographie von Athen (2nd ed.) (Handbuch der Altertumswissenschaft 3.2.2), Munich.

KABUS-PREISSHOFEN, R. 1988
'Die Statuette eines knienden Mädchens klassischer Zeit', *AntPl* 19, 11-20.

KALOGEROPOULOU, A.G. 1987
'Ἀπό τὸ ἱερό τοῦ Παγκράτους στὴν Ἀθήνα', in *Πρακτικά τοῦ Η΄ Διεθνοῦς Συνεδρίου Ἑλληνικῆς καὶ Λατινικῆς Ἐπιγραφικῆς, Athens, 3-9 October 1982*, vol. 2, Athens, 298-304.

KALOGEROPOULOU, A.G. 1988
'Πλαστικές παραστάσεις τοῦ Παγκράτους', in *Πρακτικά τοῦ XII Διεθνοῦς Συνεδρίου Κλασικῆς Ἀρχαιολογίας, Athens, 4-10 September 1983,* vol. 3, Athens, 127-31.

KALTSAS, N. 2002
Sculpture in the National Archaeological Museum, Athens, Los Angeles.

KALTSAS, N. & G. DESPINIS (EDS.) 2007
Πραξιτέλης, Εθνικό Αρχαιολογικό Μουσείο 25 Ιουλίου-31 Οκτωβρίου 2007, Athens.

KALTSAS, N. & A. SHAPIRO (EDS.) 2008
Worshiping Women. Ritual and Reality in Classical Athens, New York.

KAROUZOS, C. 1923
'Ἀπό τὸ Ἡράκλειον τοῦ Κυνοσάργους', *ArchDelt* 8, 85-102.

KAROUZOS, C. 1934
Τὸ Μουσείο τῆς Θήβας, Athens.

KAROUZOU, S. 1968
National Archaeological Museum, Collection of Sculpture: A Catalogue, Athens.

KARUSOS, C. 1929
'Ein attisches Weihrelief', *AM* 54, 1-5, Pl.1.

KASTRIOTIS, P. 1902
Μνημεῖα τῶν Ἀθηνῶν, ἤτοι περιγραφή ἱστορική, ἀρχαιολογική καὶ τοπογραφική τῆς τε πόλεως καὶ τῶν μνημείων αὐτῆς, Athens.

KASTRIOTIS, P. 1908
Γλυπτά τοῦ Ἐθνικοῦ Μουσείου, Athens.

KATER-SIBBES, G.J.F. 1973
Preliminary Catalogue of Sarapis Monuments, Leiden.

KAVVADIAS, P. 1890-1892
Γλυπτά τοῦ Ἐθνικοῦ Μουσείου, Athens.

KERÉNYI, K. 1961
'Zum Fries des Ilissostempels', *AM* 76, 22-4.

KÖHLER, U. 1879
'Horosstein der Zakyaden', *AM* 4, 287.

KOKKOU, A. 1970
'Ἀδριάνεια ἔργα εἰς τὰς Ἀθήνας', *ArchDelt* 25, Mel. 150-73.

KOLB, F. 1977
'Die Bau-, Religions- und Kulturpolitik der Peisistratiden', *JdI* 92, 99-138.

KORRES, M. 2001
'Athenian Classical Architecture', in *Athens. From the Classical Period to the Present Day (5th Century B.C.-A.D. 2000),* C. Bouras, M.B. Sakellariou, K.S. Staikos & E. Touloupa (eds.), Athens, 1-45.

KOSMOPOULOU, A. 2002
The Iconography of Sculptured Statue Bases in the Archaic and Classical Periods, Madison.

KOTTARIDI, A. 2011A
'Queens, Princesses and High Priestesses: The Role of Women at the Macedonian Court', in *Heracles to Alexander the Great. Treasures from the Royal Capital of Macedon, a Hellenic Kingdom in the Age of Democracy,* A. Kottaridi& S. Walker (eds.), Oxford, 93-126.

KOTTARIDI, A. 2011B
'Aegae: The Macedonian Metropolis', in *Heracles to Alexander the Great. Treasures from the Royal Capital of Macedon, a Hellenic Kingdom in the Age of Democracy,* A. Kottaridi & S. Walker (eds.), Oxford, 153-66.

KOUMANOUDIS, S.A. 1884
'Ἀττικὸν ψήφισμα', *ArchEph*, 161-6.

KOUMANOUDIS, S.N. 1979
Θηβαϊκὴ προσωπογραφία, Athens.

KRON, U. 1976
Die zehn attischen Phylenheroen. Geschichte, Mythos, Kult und Darstellungen (*AM* Suppl. 5), Berlin.

KRUG, A. 1979
'Der Fries des Tempels am Ilissos', *AntPl.* 18, 7-21.

KYRIAKOU, D. 2007
The Olympieion and the Surrounding Area, Athens.

KYRIAKOU, T. 2001-2004
'Συνολική ανάδειξη Αρχαιολογικού Χώρου Ολυμπιείου', *ArchDelt* 56-59, Chronika B1, 278-82.

KYRKOU, M. 2000
'Réalité iconographique et tradition littéraire. Noces d'Admète', in *Ἀγαθὸς δαίμων. Études en l' Honeur de Lilly Kahil* (BCH Suppl. 38), P. Linant de Bellefonds (ed.), 287-95.

KYRKOU, M. 2011
'Πρωτοπορία και τέχνη στον αττικό Κεραμεικό', in *ΕΠΑΙΝΟΣ Luigi Beschi,* A. Delevorrais, G. Despines & A. Zarkadas (eds.), Athens, 201-11.

LAGOGIANNI-GEORGAKARAKOS, M. & T. KOUTSOGIANNIS (EDS) 2015
"a dream among splendid ruins…." Strolling through the Athens of Travelers 17th-19th Century, Athens.

LAMBRINOUDAKIS, V.K. 2014
'Theurgic Medicine', in *Hygieia. Health, Illness, Treatment from Homer to Galen*, N.C. Stampolidis & Y. Tassoulas (eds.), Athens, 17-31.

LARSON, J. 1995
Greek Heroine Cults, Madison.

LARSON, J. 2001
Greek Nymphs. Myth, Cult, Lore, Oxford.

LARSON, J. 2007
'A Land Full of Gods: Natural Deities in Greek Religion', in *A Companion to Greek Religion,* D. Ogdan (ed.), Oxford, 56-70.

LARSON, J. 2010
'The Singularity of Herakles', in *Heroes, Mortals and Myths in Ancient Greece. The Walters Art Museum*, S. Albersmeier (ed.), Baltimore, 31-8.

LASKARIS, N. 1923
'Μορφαί ἱερέων ἐπί ἀρχαίων μνημείων', *ArchDelt* 8, 103-16.

LAWTON, C.L. 1995
Attic Document Reliefs: Art and Politics in Ancient Athens, Oxford.

LEMERLE P. 1939
'Chronique des fouilles et découvertes archéologiques en Grèce en 1939', *BCH* 63, 285-324.

LIPPOLD, G. 1911
'Τριτοπατρεῖς', *AM* 36, 105-9.

LINFERT, A. 1967
'Die Deutung des Xenokrateiareliefs', *AM* 82, 149-57.

LÖHR, C. 2000
Griechische Familienweihungen. Untersuchungen einer Repräsentationsform von ihren Anfängen bis zum Ende des 4. Jhs. v.Chr., Rahden Westf.

MAASS, E. 1895
'Zu den Ilissosreliefs', *AM* 20, 352-6.

MACHAIRA, B. 2014
'Ηρωϊκές λατρείες στην πόλη της Ρόδου', in *σοφία ἄδολος. Τιμητικός τόμος για τον Ιωάννη Χρ. Παπαχριστοδούλου*, "*σοφία ἄδολος*". *Τιμητικός τόμος για τον Ιωάννη Χρ. Παπαχριστοδούλου*, P. Triantaphyllidis (ed.), Rhodes, 271-88.

MCNEILL, R.L.B. 2005
'Notes on the Subject of the Ilissos Temple Frieze', in *Periklean Athens and Its Legacy: Problems and Perspectives. In Honor of J. J. Pollitt,* J.M. Barringer & J.M. Hurwit (eds.), Austin, 103-10.

MANTIS, A. 1990
Προβλήματα της εικονογραφίας των ιερειών και των ιερέων στην αρχαία Ελληνική τέχνη, Athens.

MEYER, M. 1989
Die griechischen Urkundenreliefs (AM Suppl. 13), Berlin.

MILCHHÖFER, A. 1880
'Nymphenrelief aus Athen', *AM* 5, 206-23.

MILIADIS, I. 1957
'Ἀνασκαφὴ νοτίως τῆς Ἀκροπόλεως', *Prakt*, 23-6.

MITROPOULOU, E. 1975A
'Attic Workshops', *AAA* 8, Symmeikta 118-23.

MITROPOULOU, E. 1975B
Kneeling Worshippers in Greek and Oriental Literature and Art, Athens.

MITROPOULOU, E. 1975C
Libation Scenes with Oinochoe in Votive Reliefs, Athens.

MITROPOULOU, E. 1977A
Corpus I. Attic Votive Reliefs of the 6th and 5th Centuries B.C., Athens.

MITROPOULOU, E. 1977B
Deities and Heroes in the Form of Snakes, Athens.

MUTHMANN, F. 1968
'Weihrelief an Acheloos und Naturgottheiten', *AntK* 11, 24-44.

MÖBIUS, H. 1928
'Zu Ilissosfries und Nikebalustrade', *AM* 53, 1-8.

MÖBIUS, H. 1935-1936
'Das Metroon in Agrai und sein Fries', *AM* 60-61, 234-68.

MÖBIUS, H. 1967
Studia Varia, Wiesbaden.

NAGY, G. 1990
Greek Mythology and Poetics, Ithaca.

NEUMANN, G. 1979
Probleme des griechischen Weihreliefs, Tübingen.

NEUMANN, G. 1980
'Dionysos ἐν Λίμναις', in *Στήλη, Τόμος εἰς μνήμην Ν. Κοντολέοντος*, Athens, 615-7.

NIKOLAIDIS, G. 1893
'Περί Καλλιρρόης τῆς καὶ Ἐννεακρούνου', *ArchEph*, 177-86.

NILSSON, M.P. 1955
Geschichte der griechischen Religion I (2nd ed.), Munich.

NILSSON, M.P. 1957
The Dionysiac Mysteries of the Hellenistic and Roman Age, Lund.

PAKKANEN, P. 1996
Interpreting Early Hellenistic Religion, Helsinki.

PALAGIA, O. 2002
'Ζευς Νάιος και Διώνη στην Ακρόπολη τῶν Αθηνῶν', in *Αφιέρωμα στη μνήμη του γλύπτη Στέλιου Τριάντη, Μουσεΐο Μπενάκη* (*Παράρτημα* 1), D. Damaskos (ed.), Athens, 171-80.

PALAGIA, O. 2005
'Interpretations of Two Athenian Friezes: The Temple on the Ilissos and the Temple of Athena Nike', in *Periklean Athens and Its Legacy: Problems and Perspectives. In Honor of J. J. Pollitt*, J.M. Barringer & J.M. Hurwit (eds.), Austin, 177-92.

PANTELIDOU-GOFA, M. 1975
Αἱ Προϊστορικαί Ἀθῆναι, Athens.

PANTELIDOU-GOFA, M. 1977
Ἡ Νεολιθική Ἀττική, Athens.

PAPACHATZIS, N.D. 1974
Παυσανίου Ἑλλάδος Περιήγησις, Ἀττικά, Athens.

PAPACHATZIS, N.D. 1978
'Μογοστόκοι Εἰλειθυίαι καὶ κουροτρόφοι θεότητες', *ArchDelt* 33, Mel. 1-23.

PAPACHATZIS, N.D. 1981
'Ὁ βοιωτικός Χάροψ Ἡρακλῆς', *ArchEph* 120, 38-51.

PAPACHATZIS, N.D. 1992
'Ἡ φύση καὶ ἡ καταγωγή τῆς Θεσσαλικῆς Ἰτωνίας καὶ τῆς Πανελλήνιας Ἀθηνᾶς', in *Διεθνές Συμπόσιο για την Αρχαία Θεσσαλία, στη μνήμη Δ. Ρ. Θεοχάρη*, E. Kypraiou (ed.), Athens, 321-5.

PAPACHATZIS, N.D. 1998
Παυσανίου Ἑλλάδος Περιήγησις, Βιβλία 4, 5 και 6. Μεσσηνιακά και Ἠλιακά, Athens.

PAPACHATZIS, N.D. 2006
Ἡ θρησκεία στὴν ἀρχαία Ἑλλάδα, Athens.

PAPANIKOLAOU-KRISTENSEN, A. 2003.
The Panathenaic Stadium: The History through the Centuries, (eds.) Athens.

PARKE, H.W. 1987
Athenische Feste, Mainz am Rhein.

PARLAMA, L. & N. STAMPOLIDIS (EDS.) 2003
The City beneath the City. Antiquities from the Metropolitan Railway Excavations, Athens.

PEARSON, L. 1981
The Local Historians of Attica (2nd ed.), Ann Arbor.

PEMBERTON, E.G. 1981
'Dedications by Alkibiades and Thrasyboulos', *BSA* 76, 309-21.

PESCHLOW-BINDOKAT, A. 1972
'Demeter und Persephone in der attischen Kunst des 6. bis 4. Jahrhunderts', *JdI* 87, 60-157.

PIGNIATOGLOU, S. 1981
'Eileithyia', PhD diss., Julius Maximilians-Universität Würzburg.

PIRENNE-DELFORGE, V. (ED.) 1998
Les panthéons des cités, des origines à la Periégese de Pausanias (Kernos Suppl. 8), Athens and Liège.

PREUNER, E. 1921
'Aus Alten Papieren', *AM* 46, 1-26.

PRITCHARD, D.M. 2013
Sport, Democracy and War in Classical Athens, Cambridge.

RAKATSIANOS, K. & A. TZIAPHALIAS 1997
Λατρείες και ιερά στην Αρχαία Θεσσαλία, Ioannina.

RAUBITSCHEK, A. 1949
Dedications from the Athenian Acropolis, Cambridge, MA.

REEDER, E.D. 1987
'The Mother of the Gods and a Hellenistic Bronze Matrix', *AJA* 91, 423-40.

REEDER, E.D. (ED.) 1995
Pandora. Women in Classical Greece, Baltimore.

RHOMAIOS, K. 1905
'Εὑρήματα ἀνασκαφῆς τοῦ ἐπί τῆς Πάρνηθος ἄντρου', *ArchEph*, coll. 99-158.

RHOUSOPOULOS, A.S. 1862
'Ἐπιγραφαί Ἑλληνικαί καὶ ὅσα ἄλλα ἀρχαῖα εὑρέθησαν ἐν ταῖς περί τὸ Ὀλύμπιον ἀνασκαφαῖς', *ArchEph* 2, 42-53.

RIETHMÜLLER, J.W. 1999
'*Bothros* and Tetrastyle: The *Heroon* of Asclepios in Athens', in *Ancient Greek Hero Cult. Proceedings of the Fifth International Seminar on Ancient Greek Cult, Organized by the Department of Classical Archaeology and Ancient History, Göteborg University, 21-23 April 1995*, R. Hägg (ed.), Stockholm, 123-43.

RITTER, D. 1999
Im Lichte des Helios. Griechenland in frühen Photographien aus der Sammlung Siegert, München.

ROBERTSON, N. 1998
'The City Center of Archaic Athens', *Hesperia* 67, 283-302.

ROBERTSON, N. 2009
Religion and Reconciliation in Greek Cities: The Sacred Laws of Selinus and Cirene, Oxford.

ROBINSON, D.M. 1948
'A New Heracles Relief', *Hesperia* 17, 137-40.

RODENWALDT, G. 1912
'Pan am Ilissos', *AM* 37, 141-50.

ROMILLY, J. DE 2007
Η ηπιότητα στην αρχαία ελληνική σκέψη, Athens.

SALTA, M. 1991
'Attische Grabstelen mit Inschriften. Beiträge zur Topographie und Prosopographie der Nekropolen von Athen, Attika und Salamis vom Peloponnesischen Krieg bis zur Mitte des 4. Jhs. v. Chr.', PhD diss., Eberhard Karls Universität Tübingen.

SALTA, M. 2012
'Gliederweihungen in attischen Heiligtümern: Die Weihung des Praxias im Athener Asklepeion', *Hephaistos* 29, 87-120.

SALTA, M. 2013
TAMA. Die Votivgabe, Athens.

SALTA, M. 2015
'Strolling East of the Acropolis: Olympieion, Hadrian's Gate, Sanctuaries on the Banks of Ilissos, Stadium Area', in *"a dream among splendid ruins…" Strolling Through the Athens of Travelers 17th-19th Century*, M. Lagogianni-Georgakarakos & T. Koutsogiannis (eds.), Athens, 294-331.

SCHACHTER, A. 1981-1994
Cults of Boiotia, 4 vols, (*Bulletin of the Institute of Classical Studies* Suppl. 38), London.

SCHAUENBURG, K. 1953
'Pluton und Dionysos', *JdI* 68, 38-72.

SCHNURR, C. 1995
'Zur Topographie der Theaterstätten und der Tripodenstrasse in Athen', *ZPE* 105, 139-53.

SCHÖRNER, G. & H.R. GOETTE 2004
Die Pan – Grotte von Vari. Mit epigraphischen Anmerkungen von K. Hallof, Mainz.

SCHOLL, A. 1994
'Πολυτάλαντα μνημεῖα. Zur Literarischen und Monumentalen Überlieferung aufwendiger Grabmäler im spätklassischen Athen', *JdI* 109, 239-71.

SCHRÖDER, S.F. 1986
'Der Apollon Lykeios und die attische Ephebie des 4. Jhs.', *AM* 101, 167-84.

SIMON, E. 1983
Festivals of Attica: An Archaeological Commentary, Madison.

SKIADAS, A. 1967
Ἐπὶ Τύμβῳ. Συμβολή εἰς τὴν ἑρμηνείαν τῶν ἑλληνικῶν ἐπιτυμβίων ἐμμέτρων ἐπιγραφῶν, Athens.

SKIAS, A.N. 1893A
'Ἡ κοίτη τοῦ Ἰλισοῦ παρά τὸ Ὀλυμπιεῖον', *ArchEph*, Σύμμικτα 103-4.

SKIAS, A.N. 1893B
'Περί τῆς ἐν τῇ κοίτῃ τοῦ Ἰλισοῦ ἀνασκαφῆς', *Prakt*, 111-36.

SKIAS, A.N. 1894A
'Ἀνάγλυφα ἐκ τῆς ἐν τῇ κοίτῃ τοῦ Ἰλισοῦ ἀνασκαφῆς', *ArchEph*, coll. 133-42.

SKIAS, A.N. 1894B
Συμβολαί εἰς τὴν ἀθηναϊκήν τοπογραφίαν, Ἐρνέστῳ Κουρτίῳ ἐπί τῇ ὀγδοηκοστῇ γενεθλίῳ, Athens.

SKIAS, A.N. 1897
'Ἀνασκαφαί παρά τὸν Ἰλισόν', *Prakt*, 73-85.

SOTIRIOU, G.A. 1919
Παλαιά Χριϐτιανική Βαϐιλιή Ἰλιϐοῦ, *Arch Ephem* 1919, 1-31.

STAFFORD, E. 2012
Herakles, London and New York.

STAIS, V. 1916
'Εργασίαι έν τοίς Μουσείοις', *ArchDelt* 2, Παρ ρ ημα 77-84.

STAMPOLIDIS, N. & Y. TASSOULAS (EDS.) 2014
Hygieia. Health, Illness, Treatment from Homer to Galen, Athens.

STAVRIDI, A.A. 1996
Τα Γλυπτά του Μουσείου Τεγέας. Περιγραφικός Κατάλογος, Athens.

STEWART, A.F. 1977
Skopas of Paros, New Jersey.

STRATEN, F.T. VAN 1974
'Did the Greeks Kneel Before their Gods?', *BABesch*, 159-89.

STRATEN, F.T. VAN 1981
'Gifts for the Gods', in *Faith, Hope and Worship. Aspects of Religious Mentality in the Ancient World,* H.S. Versnel (ed.), Leiden, 65-151.

STRATEN, F.T. VAN 1995
Hiera Kala. Images of Animal Sacrifice in Archaic and Classical Greece, Leiden, New York and Cologne.

STROSZECK, J. 2010
'Das Heiligtum der Tritopatores im Kerameikos von Athen', in *Neue Forschungen in griechischen Städten und Heiligtümern. Festschrift für Burkhard Wesenberg zum 65. Geburtstag* (Beiträge zur Archäologie Griechenlands), H. Frielinghaus & J. Stroszeck (eds.), Möhnesee, 55-83.

STUART, J. & N. REVETT 1794
The Antiquities of Athens, London.

SVORONOS, J.N. 1901
'Ἑρμηνεία τῶν μνημείων τοῦ Ἐλευσινιακοῦ μυστικοῦ κύκλου καὶ τοπογραφικὰ Ἀθηνῶν καὶ Ἐλευσῖνος', *JIAN* 4, 233-515.

SVORONOS, J.N. 1908-1937
Das Athener National Museum, 3 vols, Athens.

SVORONOS, J.N. 1911
'Πραξιτέλους: Δημήτηρ, Κόρη καὶ Ἴακχος ἐν Ἀθήναις', *ArchEph*, 39-52.

SVORONOS, J.N. 1916-1917
'Τὸ Μητρῷον τοῦ Ιλισοῦ καὶ ἡ ζῳφόρος αὐτοῦ', *JIAN* 18, 1-156.

SVORONOS, J.N. 1917
'Ἀσκληπιακὰ μνημεῖα καὶ κιονολατρεία ἐν Ἀθήναις', *ArchEph* 56, 78-104.

VON SYBEL, L. 1881
Katalog der Skulpturen zu Athen, Marburg.

TAGALIDOU, E. 1993
Weihreliefs an Herakles aus klassischer Zeit (SIMA PB 99), Jonsered.

THALLON, I.C. 1903
'The Cave at Vari: The Marble Reliefs', *AJA* 7, 301-19.

THEOCHARAKI, A.-M. 2011
'The Ancient Circuit Wall of Athens. Its Changing Course and the Phases of Construction', *Hesperia* 80, 71-156.

TÖLLE-KASTENBEIN, R. 1986
'Kallirrhoe und Enneakrunos', *JdI* 101, 55-73.

TRAILL, J.S. 1986
Demos and Trittys. Epigraphical and Topographical Studies in the Organization of Attica, Toronto.

TRAVLOS, J. 1970
'Τὸ γυμνάσιον τοῦ Κυνοσάργους', *AAA* 3, 6-14.

TRAVLOS, J. 1971
Pictorial Dictionary of Ancient Athens, London.

TRAVLOS, J. 1993
Πολεοδομικὴ ἐξέλιξις τῶν Ἀθηνῶν (2nd ed.), Athens.

TSANGARI, D. 2011
Myth and Coinage. Representations, Symbolisms and Interpretations from the Greek Mythology, Athens.

TSONI-KYRKOU, M. 1988
'Λουτροφόρος ἐρυθρόμορφη. Εἰκονογραφικὲς παρατηρήσεις', in *Πρακτικά τοῦ XII Διεθνοῦς Συνεδρίου*

Κλασικῆς Ἀρχαιολογίας, Athens, 4-10 September 1983, vol. 2, Athens, 225-30, Pl. 41-3.

VAIOPOULOU, M.I. 2012
'Η Λατρεία τῆς Ἰτωνίας Ἀθηνᾶς στὴν Ἠπειρωτική καὶ Νησιωτική Ἑλλάδα, μέσα ἀπό τὰ Ἱερά της, τὰ Γραπτά Κείμενα καὶ τους Μύθους', in *Athanasia. The Earthly, the Celestial and the Underworld in the Mediterranean from the Late Bronze and the Early Iron Age. International Archaeological Conference, Rhodes 28-31 May 2009*, N.C. Stampolidis, A. Kanta & A. Giannikouri (eds.), Iraklio, 153-60.

VERBANCK-PIÈRARD, A. 1998
'Héros attiques au jour le jour: les calendriers des dèmes', in *Les panthéons des cités, des origines à la Periégese de Pausanias* (Kernos Suppl. 8), V. Pirenne-Delforge (ed.), Athens and Liège, 109-27.

VERMASEREN, M.J. 1982
Corpus Cultus Cybelae Attidisque (CCCA) II. Graecia atque Insulae, Leiden.

VIKELA, E. 1994
Die Weihreliefs aus dem Athener Pankrates-Heiligtum am Ilissos. Religionsgeschichtliche Bedeutung und Typologie (AM Suppl. 16), Berlin.

VIKELA, E. 1995
'Η ἐπιβίωση τῆς Μινωικῆς ἀνδρικῆς θεότητας στους ἱστορικούς χρόνους', *Archaiognosia* 8 (1993-1994), 199-209.

VIKELA, E. 1997
'Attische Weihreliefs und die Kult-Topographie Attikas', *AM* 112, 167-246.

VIKELA, E. 2006
'Healer Gods and Healing Sanctuaries in Attica. Similarities and Differences', *ArchRW* 8, 41-62, pls. I-IX.

VIKELA, E. 2011
'Τὰ μικρά ἱερά τῆς Ἀθήνας', *ArchEph* 150, 133-96.

VLIZOS, S. 1999
Der thronende Zeus. Eine Untersuchung zur statuarischen Ikonographie des Gottes in der spätklassischen und hellenistischen Kunst, Rahden Westf.

VLIZOS, S. 2008
'Sculptures from the Area South of the Olympieion', in *Athens During the Roman Period. Recent Discoveries, New Evidence,* S. Vlizos (ed.), Athens, 411-23.

VOLLKOMMER, R. 1988
Herakles in the Art of Classical Greece, Oxford.

VORSTER, C. 1983
'Griechische Kinderstatuen', PhD diss., University of Bonn.

WALTER, O. 1923
Beschreibung der Reliefs im Kleinen Akropolismuseum in Athen, Vienna.

WALTER, O. 1940
'Archäologische Funde in Grienchenland von Frühjahr 1939 bis Frühjahr 1940', *AA* 1940, 121-308.

WEGENER, S. 1985
Funktion und Bedeutung landschaftlicher Elemente in der griechischen Reliefkunst archaischer bis hellenistischer Zeit, Frankfurt am Main, Bern and New York.

WEISS, C. 1984
Griechische Flussgottheiten in vorhellenistischer Zeit, Würzburg.

WOODFORD, S. 1971
'Cults of Herakles in Attica', in *Studies Presented to George M.A. Hanfmann*, D.G. Mitten, J.G. Pedley & J.A. Scott (eds.), Cambridge, MA., 211-25.

WOODHEAD, A.G. 1997
Inscriptions: The Decrees, The Athenian Agora XVI, Princeton.

WYCHERLEY, R.E. 1957
Literary and Epigraphical Testimonia. The Athenian Agora III, Princeton.

WYCHERLEY, R.E. 1978
The Stones of Athens, Princeton.

ZOUMBAKI, S.B. 2005
Prosopographie der Eleer bis zum 1. Jh. v. Chr., Institut für Griechische und Römische Antike (Μελετήματα 40), Nationales Hellenisches Zentrum, Athens.

Pausanias and the Intellectual Travellers of the Roman Imperial Period: The Acropolis and the Historical Imagination*

Maria Pretzler

Anybody thinking about ascending and descending the Acropolis in antiquity will soon be confronted with Pausanias' report of doing exactly that, with a good deal of sightseeing in the process. But does Pausanias' visit qualify as "sacred travel"? This chapter was always going to test the boundaries of the definition of "sacred travel" or "pilgrimage", and this is how it turned out at the workshop. This paper will therefore begin with a discussion of Pausanias as a "sacred traveller" and an investigation of the blurred boundaries between the sacred and the precious memories which defined the identity of educated Greeks in the context of the Second Sophistic. The second part of the chapter investigates these themes in Pausanias' description of the Athenian Acropolis, focusing on the selection and preferences his account implies. Finally, I discuss the clash between the Panhellenic ideal of the Roman imperial period and the Classical literary tradition, and how this affected visitors in the Roman imperial period who came to experience Athens as the focus of their Greek identity.

Pausanias' *Periegesis* is the most extensive example of ancient travel literature that survives. Written between c. 160 and 180 AD, the work is based on extensive research and travelling,[1] and covers central and southern Greece in ten books. Hundreds of sites and individual monuments are described in some detail, and many more are mentioned. While we know of a number of ancient works called *Periegesis*, we have no evidence that there was an actual genre of *Periegesis* texts, or that texts with this title took an approach similar to that of Pausanias: he seems to have been unique in covering a large area while still offering detailed descriptions of many sites.[2] There were apparently whole books (now lost) which offered detailed descriptions of particular places, giving a tour with discussions of individual buildings, monuments, and artworks while discussing traditions attached to specific objects. Three authors, all probably Hellenistic, are credited with detailed treatises on parts of Athens, namely descriptions of monuments and demes by a Diodoros,[3] a work on the Acropolis by Heliodoros of Athens,[4] and a number of works by Polemon of Ilion, including at least one, in four books, on the monuments of the Acropolis.[5]

* I would like to thank Wiebke Friese and Søren Handberg for organizing a fascinating workshop, and I am grateful to the other participants for a stimulating discussion which has influenced this chapter. The anonymous reader also made many helpful suggestions which helped making this a better chapter. All errors are of course mine.

1 Pretzler 2004; 2007, 24-7.

2 Hutton 2005a, 241-72; see also Bischoff 1938, 726-8.

3 *FGrH* 372; Bischoff 1938, 728; Plut. *Them.* 32; Steph. Byz. s.v. Trikorython, Trinemeis, Cholargos.

4 *FGrH* 373; Bischoff 1938, 728; [Plut.] *X orat.* 849C.

5 Bischoff 1938, 729; Strabo 9.1.16; Ath. 11.472B-C, 11.486D, 13.587C.

Despite the *Periegesis*' importance for Classical studies ever since its rediscovery in the Renaissance, it was assumed for a long time that these ten books on Greece did not find a readership in antiquity.[6] This assumption has been challenged in recent years, particularly as potential references have been re-assessed and some new ones have recently been suggested.[7] In any case, it is clear that Pausanias' work, though eccentric in some ways, caters to the preoccupations of the educated Greek-speaking elite of the Roman Empire. The *Periegesis* responds to attitudes to ancient sites and historical landscapes which we can also observe in other Greek texts of the period,[8] as we shall see later in this chapter. It is therefore a crucial source for ways in which educated travellers in the Roman imperial period used literary and historical knowledge to enhance their experience of the famous sites of Greece.

The subject of Pausanias and sacred travel burst onto the scene in 1992, with Jaś Elsner's *Past & Present* article entitled "Pausanias: a Greek Pilgrim in the Roman World".[9] This proposition provoked strong criticism,[10] demonstrating in particular that the term "pilgrimage" invites associations with Christian practices and consequently objections based on the obvious differences between Pausanias' project and pilgrimage, narrowly defined. This was a connection Jaś Elsner himself invited by stressing similarities between Pausanias' work and early Christian texts.[11] The article also emphasizes Pausanias' focus on religious sites and customs, but without addressing the question of how much personal investment we should imagine in the many descriptions of cults and sanctuaries which seem focused on fairly detached antiquarian concerns.

There is no question that Pausanias personally took religion very seriously,[12] but in his text, most descriptions of sacred sites, cults, and rituals emphasize cultural interest rather than spiritual involvement. This is, however, not the only mode of interaction documented in the *Periegesis*: in some places, Pausanias did get involved, identifying a personal religious relevance. For example, a few times he stops himself from divulging divine secrets, demonstrating that he is an initiate of the Eleusinian Mysteries, and he shows himself to be an informed and discreet insider of other cults as well.[13] Sacrificing at sanctuaries he visited was apparently a fairly routine process, because he finds it worth noting when he was *not* able to make his own offering.[14] Pausanias' visit to the oracle of Trophonios in Lebadeia perhaps comes closest to what we would expect of a pilgrim's account. He took part in the ritual of consulting the oracle and reports the process with palpable awe, although even here, the description is couched in general terms.[15]

Jaś Elsner's claim that the *Periegesis* "recounts the process of pilgrimage as a personal journey"[16] is very difficult to reconcile with the usually impersonal nature of the text; the argument heavily depends on a single passage where Pausanias suggests that he has changed his mind about the interpretation of certain local myths, which Elsner and others interpret as a kind of pilgrim's revelation.[17] I feel reluctant to read the *Periegesis* as a report of a "pilgrim's progress": the work is a complex synthesis of many visits carried

6 Habicht 1985, 22-6; Diller 1956, 84-5.

7 Pretzler 2007, 27 n. 73, 74; e.g. Bowie 2001, 29-32 (Aelian, Longus).

8 Pretzler 2007, 37-9, 102-3, 107-9.

9 Elsner 1992.

10 Arafat 1996, 10-1; Swain 1996, 334, 342 n. 50.

11 Elsner 1992, 3.

12 For discussion of Pausanias' religious beliefs, see Frazer 1898, I:l-lv; Heer 1979, 127-307; Habicht 1985, 151-9; Pirenne-Delforge 1998; Pretzler 2007, 19-21.

13 Paus. 1.14.3; 1.37.5; 1.38.7; 2.3.4; 2.17.4; 2.37.6; 4.33.5; 5.15.11; 8.37.9; 9.25.5-6.

14 Paus. 8.42.11. See also 2.30.4; 9.39.5-14.

15 Paus. 9.39.5-14.

16 Elsner 1992, 20.

17 Elsner 1992, 20-5. See also Oliver 1972; Veyne 1988, 95-102; Ellinger 2005, 182-6; Hutton 2005a, 273-324; 2005b, 295. The discussion especially focuses on Paus. 8.8.3 as a kind of moment of "revelation".

out over several years or decades, and there is no indication that the route it charts through Greece is intended to be read as the report of one epic journey rather than as a merely organisational device.[18]

While the debate about Jaś Elsner's article demonstrated that defining Pausanias' project as pilgrimage is not a straightforward matter, it also pointed towards a different interpretation. Elsner glances at pilgrimage outside a Christian context and finds it to be "a journey into one's identity in its topographic, cultural and spiritual resonances",[19] which seems more compatible with the central concerns of Pausanias' project. In a postscript, written some ten years later, Elsner clarifies his rejection of narrow definitions of pilgrimage as having a primarily religious objective.[20] In their edited volume on pilgrimage, Elsner and Ian Rutherford then offered a typology of pilgrimage including a wide variety of practices,[21] which, we have to assume, would combine in various ways to create unique experiences and approaches to landscapes for each traveller.

Ultimately, one defining aspect of pilgrimage is an encounter with places which are, and often have been since childhood, central to the imagination, thinking, and identity of the visitor. Every educated Greek visiting mainland Greece in the Roman imperial period would encounter places which were intimately connected with traditions and texts that had been central to their thinking for most of their lives. Such encounters might involve visits to places where mythical historical events had taken place, seeing important buildings and monuments, hearing stories where famous history crossed over into local oral tradition, and observing or participating in local cults so closely linked with the deep roots of Greek religion that they could take on a personal significance for visitors from far away. Pausanias' *Periegesis* gathers literally thousands of such memorable details, and demonstrates throughout that encountering all those significant memories in the landscape meant a lot more than just a purely scholarly exercise.

The area covered in Pausanias' *Periegesis*, the south of mainland Greece, was particularly relevant to Greek identity because so many of the pivotal events which had taken place there – both historical and mythical – had had a lasting impact on Greek identity, for example the Persian Wars or the struggle of the Greek poleis against Macedonia. These events loomed large in the literary canon which defined Greek culture and education in the Roman imperial period.[22] Despite looting and destruction over the centuries, Greece also offered a chance to see perhaps the greatest number of celebrated works of art and architecture by the revered old masters. Pausanias demonstrates that in Greece, you could still discover new details to complement traditional learning: visitors came to find the past they knew from their reading, and local informants were ready to point out the landmarks and offer local insights to enhance the canonical version of the tradition, turning collective memory into an experience of new discovery. These surprise additions to traditional learning were clearly a crucial motivation for Pausanias' efforts.[23]

This is what the term "intellectual travellers" in the title refers to: much of what we may call the "spiritual" experience of discovering mainland Greece was connected to intellectual rather than religious pursuits.[24] However, such a distinction be-

18 Hutton 2005a, 25-8; Pretzler 2007, 4-13, cf. 32; Akujärvi 2005, 60-4.
19 Elsner 1992, 10.
20 Elsner 2004, 284, quoting Arafat 1996, 10.
21 Elsner & Rutherford 2005, 9-30, see esp. 12-4.
22 For a list, see Dio Chrys. 18.6-17.
23 Pretzler 2007, 37-40, 113-4.
24 Note Elsner & Rutherford 2005, 25-6: they include (16) intellectual pilgrimage and (17) pilgrimage and cultural nostalgia in their typology, and with special reference to the Roman imperial period. See particularly Galli 2005 (in the same volume).

tween "intellectual/secular" and "religious" does not do Pausanias' approach justice. Today's concept of a separation between the sacred and the secular does not conform with ancient thinking and practice: just as most public civic buildings contained shrines or sacred images, the functions of sanctuaries included some activities we would define as non-religious. In the Greek imagination, human beings could become heroes and the divine influenced historical events; the difference between myths and history always remained blurred. Greek sacred landscapes were defined by myths and traditions that rooted them firmly in the community's past and defined local identities. This became increasingly important in the Hellenistic and Roman periods, and by Pausanias' time, traditions about the local past and the sanctuaries, monuments, and customs which placed them in the landscape were essential markers of Greek polis culture.[25] The spiritual impact of the Greek landscape is, therefore, not purely "religious" as we would understand it today, since it contained memorials which were central to what it meant to be Greek. But my distinction between "intellectual" and "sacred" travel can only be artificial, catering to today's categories and introducing distinctions which would have baffled Pausanias.

These blurred lines between sacred and intellectual interests are relevant to understanding Pausanias' visit to the Athenian Acropolis. There were few places which evoked as many poignant memories in connection with the literary and cultural canon of the Greek world as Athens did.[26] Pausanias' educated readers would expect references to historical events, famous individuals, widely known myths, and Classical texts. It is impossible to recreate the emotional force of encountering the city which so dominated Greek culture and identity at the time: in Pausanias' Athens, a strict definition of the term "sacred travel" as purely related to religious practice (defined in modern terms) makes little sense, since he is looking at the deep roots of every Greek's cultural identity. While Pausanias' Acropolis does not feature many religious activities (narrowly defined), we should see it as a guide to a potentially spiritual Hellenic experience.

In this context, we also have to consider the relevance of local cults to outside visitors: many places in Pausanias' *Periegesis* do not have a distinctive Panhellenic significance. In fact, Pausanias' insistence on dividing his Greece by polis territories emphasizes crucial tensions between a universal Geek identity and the polis with its local religion and cultural traditions. One important aspect of Pausanias' project is his attention to the sheer diversity of cults and traditions: the polis and its distinct cultural identity are a hallmark of what it means to be Greek – indeed, in the *Periegesis*, Greece is defined by its great diversity. In the context of the old motherland, traditions which seemed alien could be interpreted as relics of the earliest times, more Greek, so to speak, than what might seem more familiar.[27] But if the distinctiveness of local Greek religions (plural!) matters so much, how could travellers, even Greek travellers, from outside relate to them in a personally spiritual way? There were places where Pausanias found local cults which appealed to his personal religious sensibilities, particularly when he encountered cults of Demeter,[28] but more often his reports of local sanctuaries, cults, and myths seem to reflect no more than "mere" anthropological or antiquarian interest. Pausanias' usual mode of description reports local customs

25 Mellor 2008, 113-21; Burstein 2008, 66-7; Salmeri 2011, esp. 206-8; in relation to Pausanias specifically, see Pretzler 2013.

26 Krumeich & Witschel 2010, esp. 28-9.

27 E.g. Paus. 8.42.1-13 reports a very unusual interpretation of Demeter at Phigalia, which he treats with special interest and a certain reverence, cf. Paus. 8.25.4-10, 8.37.1-10.

28 Heer 1979, 127-88; see especially Paus. 1.14.3, 1.37.4, 1.38.7, 4.33.5, 8.37.9.

and stories without suggesting that he is personally invested in, or spiritually affected by, his material.[29]

Polis religion had long been complemented by regional and Panhellenic sanctuaries and festivals. Ian Rutherford has recently traced the development of Panhellenism in relation to such supraregional cults.[30] Ever since the Classical period, and perhaps a good deal earlier, certain festivals, for example at Olympia, were central to defining and re-affirming what it meant to be Greek, although here, too, official links between states and the great sanctuaries maintained the principle that the polis was central to the quintessentially Greek way of life.[31] Later on, Hellenistic kings and Roman conquerors used Panhellenic festivals to emphasise their Philhellenic credentials, and in the Roman imperial period we see the revival (or invention?) of cults and festivals celebrating Greekness.[32] Hadrian's Panhellenion brought together many cities around the central sanctuary in Athens, and membership was explicitly reserved for communities which could prove (however tenuously at times) Greek ancestry.[33] The role of sanctuaries and sacred travel in re-affirming and defining a common Greek identity was therefore established early on, and continued to gain importance after the Classical period. In the Hellenistic period, Athens began to play a particularly important role in Greek cultural traditions, when the focus increasingly turned from conflicts and differences between individual cities to a Panhellenic agenda.

Pausanias lived in a period commonly defined as the Second Sophistic, a term coined in Philostratos' *Lives of the Sophists*.[34] Initially, this term referred to the activities of high-profile intellectuals, the Sophists, whose output dominates the surviving Greek literature from the Roman imperial period. Greek *paideia* is central to the preoccupations of these authors, particularly the recreation of an "authentic" but also highly artificial form of Attic Greek, based on Classical Greek literature.[35] High-profile sophists were exceptional, but they represent the pinnacle of a wider cultural phenomenon. The educational ideals reflected in their texts were widely shared, particularly the focus on Classical Greek literature, rhetoric, and philosophy.[36] This Greek *paideia* went hand-in-hand with wealth and status in the Greek East of the Roman Empire, but many wealthy native Latin speakers in the West also shared these aspirations.[37] Pausanias himself was a *pepaideumenos*, an educated man who was steeped in this tradition, and he writes for readers who shared this *paideia*, not merely education, but a Hellenic culture and identity.

The canon of texts which served as the basis for a thorough Greek education looks familiar even today: the Homeric epics were important above all other texts, followed by Herodotus, Thucydides, the three famous Attic tragedians, Aristophanes, philosophy – particularly Plato and Xenophon (appreciated as a philosopher more than a historian) – and the Attic orators. These were the crucial basics, and thus, for years while they were growing up, Classical Athens would have been uppermost on the minds of those seeking *paideia*.

This view is forcefully expressed in Aelius Aristeides' *Panathenaikos*, a speech praising Athens in the most extravagant terms. Aristeides was a close contemporary of Pausanias, another Greek from Asia Minor looking at Athens from overseas. The *Panathenaikos* is a highly artificial literary construct

29 Pretzler 2007, 102-3.
30 Rutherford 2013, 264-80.
31 Rutherford 2013, 280.
32 Spawforth 2012, 130-8; Thériault 1996, 112-30; Jones 1996, 45; on the wider context, see Spawforth 1994.
33 Spawforth & Walker 1985; 1986; Romeo 2002.
34 Philostr. *V S* 507; Anderson 1986, 11-21.
35 Anderson 1993, 86-94; Swain 1996, 17-64; Schmitz 1997, 67-90; cf. Lucian, *Rhetorum Praecentor* 16-7.
36 Heer 1979, 92-108; Anderson 1993, 47-53, 135; Schmitz 1997, 39-66; Conolly 2001. For the canon of texts, see Dio Chrys. 18.6-17.
37 Whitmarsh 2001, 96-108.

which would have taken hours to perform. The deliberately excessive praise it employs was part and parcel of the epideictic genre, but the "Athenocentric" worldview it presents reflects the special cultural status Athens had attained by this period. While everything in this text is wildly overstated, the arguments still demonstrate how much Athens was able to claim centre stage in the Greek imagination. After explaining why Attica should be seen as the centre of the Greek world, with Athens as the centre of Attica, Aristeides declares the Acropolis the centre of Greek civilisation:

> And as a third centrality after these [Attica, Athens], there rises clear aloft through the midst of the city, what was the old city and is now the present Acropolis, like a mountain peak, not to be the last part of the city, but so that all the remaining body of the city encloses it, where the high and central point coincide, an adornment in the midst of all, and the final boundary marker of the good position of the land. For as if on a shield layers have been set on one another, in fifth place, the fairest among all fills the area up to the boss: if Greece is the centre of the whole earth, and Attica is the centre of Greece, and the city lies in the centre of its territory, and again its namesake is the centre of the city (Aelius Aristeides, *Panathenaikos* 16).[38]

Towards the end of the speech, he goes further and declares that the Acropolis of Athens has the status of an acropolis for all Greeks.

> Therefore, o men of Greece, it is reasonable that you neither are envious of the city nor feel shame in giving precedence to it, but that you aid in its increase as far as you can and feel pride therein. For when the Athenians prevail, the victory is yours. It would be impossible for all men to be the best of mankind. But just as whenever a general is superior, his city shares his glory, so when the leading city is properly honoured, all men participate in its sense of pride. But I think that the Athenians themselves are not ashamed, if somebody prefers their Acropolis. It is fitting that you, too, honour the city in deed and word, in the belief that it is as if it were a sort of Acropolis or summit of Greece, and its kindred people, and with the view that while you participate in its glory, you are not deprived of your own.
>
> (Aelius Aristeides, *Panathenaikos* 402-3).[39]

This reminds us of the dominant position of Athens in the Greek imagination: the role of the Acropolis in this image of cultural centrality is particularly striking. Athens takes on the role of a kind of antidote to the divisions between Greeks, which, as many thought in this period, had led to their downfall.[40] At the same time, Athens, with its glorious Classical monuments, served as a reminder of the greatness of the Greek past. Plutarch, writing

38 Translation Behr 1986: "τρίτη δὲ ἀκόλουθος τούτων ἀνέχει, περιφανὴς ἄνω διὰ μέσης τῆς πόλεως, ἡ πάλαι μὲν πόλις, νῦν δὲ ἀκρόπολις, κορυφῇ παραπλησίως, οὐχ ὡς ὕστατον εἶναι τῆς πόλεως, ἀλλ᾽ ὡς περὶ αὐτὴν πᾶν τὸ λοιπὸν σῶμα τῆς πόλεως, ἄκρου καὶ μέσου ταυτοῦ συμπεπτωκότος, τὸ διὰ πάντων ἤδη τοῦτο κάλλος καὶ ὁ τελευταῖος ὅρος τῆς περὶ γῆν εὐκαιρίας. ὥσπερ γὰρ ἐπ᾽ ἀσπίδος κύκλων εἰς ἀλλήλους ἐμβεβηκότων πέμπτος εἰς ὀμφαλὸν πληροῖ διὰ πάντων ὁ κάλλιστος, εἴπερ ἡ μὲν Ἑλλὰς ἐν μέσῳ τῆς πάσης γῆς, ἡ δ᾽ Ἀττικὴ τῆς Ἑλλάδος, τῆς δὲ χώρας ἡ πόλις, τῆς δ᾽ αὖ πόλεως ἡ ὁμώνυμος.»

39 Translation Behr 1986: "Ἀνθ᾽ ὧν, ὦ ἄνδρες Ἕλληνες, οὔτε φθόνον εἰκὸς ἔχειν τῇ πόλει οὔθ᾽ ὑποχωροῦντας αἰσχύνεσθαι, ἀλλὰ συναύξειν ἐκ τῶν ἐνόντων καὶ φιλοτιμεῖσθαι. τῶν γὰρ Ἀθηναίων νικώντων, παρ᾽ ὑμῖν ἐστι τὸ νικᾶν. Πάντας μὲν γὰρ ἁπάντων εἶναι ἀρίστους ἀδύνατον. ὥσπερ δὲ ὅταν στρατηγὸς προέχῃ, μετέχει τῆς δόξης ἡ πόλις, οὕτω τῆς ἡγουμένης πόλεως τὰ εἰκότα τιμωμένης ἅπασι μέτεστι τῆς φιλοτιμίας. οἶμαι δὲ οὐδ᾽ αὐτοῖς Ἀθηναίοις φέρειν αἰσχύνην, ἄν τις αὐτοῖς πρεσβεύῃ τὴν ἀκρόπολιν. χρὴ τοίνυν καὶ ὑμᾶς, ὥσπερ ἀκρόπολίν τινα ἢ κορυφὴν νομίσαντας τῆς Ἑλλάδος καὶ τῶν ὁμοφύλων τὴν πόλιν καὶ ἔργῳ καὶ λόγῳ κοσμεῖν, καὶ μετέχειν τῆς δόξης, ἀλλ᾽ οὐκ ἀποστερεῖσθαι νομίζοντας."

40 Pausanias' views on the matter are most clearly expressed in his lists of benefactors of Greece (8.52.1-5) and of traitors to the Greek cause (7.10.1-5).

a few decades before Pausanias and Aristeides, puts it most poignantly, referring to Perikles' buildings on the Acropolis:

> That which brought most delightful adornment to Athens, and the greatest amazement to the rest of mankind; that which alone now testifies for Hellas that her ancient power and splendour, of which so much is told, was no idle fiction (Plut. *Vit. Per.* 12.1).[41]

Go to Athens, Plutarch seems to say, and you can find the proof that all you have read about Greece's great past was indeed true. Despite defeat in war, the Roman conquest, and ancient places that have become ruins, visit Athens and you can become a true believer. This aim to experience the great Greek cultural tradition through its tangible relics lies at the centre of an "intellectual pilgrimage" to Athens in this period.

The Acropolis also represented one of the best collections of architecture, sculpture, and paintings by famous artists. Art connoisseurship was important to the self-respecting *pepaideumenos*. While it was probably possible to get to know the works of famous old masters through copies,[42] this was a world without easily transmittable images, and it would have been difficult to get a sense of the Parthenon, the Propylaia, or the Erechtheion without actually visiting them in person. Even now, the remains of these buildings make an impression, and it is difficult to imagine what it would have been like back then to see these famous monuments for the first time after imagining them for a lifetime. Aristeides praises the monuments of the Athenian Acropolis as the greatest achievements in art and architecture.[43] He also emphasises the quasi-religious significance of these famous artworks and their importance within the context of the whole Greek world.

> It [Athens] adorned the Acropolis with monuments of its deeds, and added to its natural beauty the rival beauty of wealth and art, so that the whole Acropolis was like a dedication, or rather like a statue. And again, it conferred the other honours due to the gods in a way beyond the power of all of Greece, some at home and some abroad (Aelius Aristeides, *Panathenaikos* 191).[44]

Pausanias responds to the preoccupations, expectations, and interests of his potential readers, *pepaideumenoi* with an interest in the minutiae of mainland Greece. Each of the thousands of details gathered in the *Periegesis* is part of a cultural project to get to the bottom of what it really means to be Greek within the Roman Empire.

Athens had to play a central role in such a work, and so it may be surprising that it sits rather uneasily within Pausanias' Greece. He was apparently still experimenting when he wrote his first book on Attica and the Megarid: the description lacks the distinctive structure of the remaining nine books, and the combination of descriptions and historical digressions is not yet fully developed.[45] Moreover, Pausanias seems to be reluctant to confirm Athens' dominant role in Greek tradition. He clearly thought that many of the glories of Greece lay outside Athens, and spent years of research attempting to prove it. Pausanias also chose to write in a version of Greek which deliberately avoids many typically

41 Translation Perrin 1916: "ὃ δὲ πλείστην μὲν ἡδονὴν ταῖς Ἀθήναις καὶ κόσμον ἤνεγκε, μεγίστην δὲ τοῖς ἄλλοις ἔκπληξιν ἀνθρώποις, μόνον δὲ τῇ Ἑλλάδι μαρτυρεῖ μὴ ψεύδεσθαι τὴν λεγομένην δύναμιν αὐτῆς"

42 Pretzler 2007, 107-9.

43 Aristid. *Panathenaikos* 354.

44 Translation Behr 1986: "τοῦτο μὲν γὰρ τὴν ἀκρόπολιν κατεκόσμησε τοῖς τῶν ἔργων ὑπομνήμασι, καὶ τῷ τῆς φύσεως κάλλει τὸ παρὰ τοῦ πλούτου καὶ τῆς τέχνης ἐφάμιλλον προσέθηκεν, ὥστ' εἶναι πᾶσαν ἀντ' ἀναθήματος, μᾶλλον δὲ ἀντ' ἀγάλματος· τοῦτο δὲ τὰς ἄλλας τιμὰς τοῖς θεοῖς ἀνῆψε, κρεῖττον ἁπάσης Ἑλληνικῆς δυνάμεως, τὰ μὲν οἴκοι, τὰ δ' ἐν τῇ ὑπερορίᾳ."

45 Hutton 2005a, 295-303.

Attic features,[46] a strikingly eccentric choice in this Attic-obsessed period, but in line with the aims of a writer who made such efforts to describe Greece beyond Attica. In fact, during his description of the Athenian Acropolis, Pausanias reminds himself that he cannot let himself be distracted, since he has to describe "all of Greece":[47] Athens cannot take up too much of his time when there are hundreds more sites to visit.

Pausanias' Visit to the Acropolis

This section will begin with an overview of Pausanias' description (Paus. 1.22-8), followed by a discussion of how history and famous Athenians were linked to monuments and an appraisal of Pausanias' approach to local stories in comparison with the literary tradition. Athens was so dominant in Classical Greek literature that most of its monuments were well documented in the major texts known to all educated Greeks in the 2nd century AD, and many of the sights were very famous indeed. This caused difficulties for an author who was eager to find information and objects that his well-educated readers might find surprising. There was a long tradition of writing Attic local history and descriptions of its famous sites, which in turn informed authors writing in other genres. For example, Diodoros' late 4th-century work on Athenian monuments or Polemon of Troy's periegetic works of the 2nd century BC were, as far as we can tell, more detailed in scope than Pausanias' description.[48] Thus, Pausanias would have come across many objects and stories which "everybody, even a barbarian who has learned Greek" would know about,[49] as he puts it when discussing a detail of the story of Phaidra. Avoiding well-trodden paths was difficult in Athens. Pausanias' description often seems to be going out of its way to avoid over-emphasizing the obvious: this guide for educated visitors to Athens is challenging readers to look beyond the details they expect to find. Pausanias was also challenged, and in turn challenges his readers, to test observations of the contemporary memorial landscape against the literary evidence. This is an important theme in the whole of the *Periegesis*, but nowhere was this kind of enquiry more poignant than in Athens.

Despite his refusal to take Athens' status as the centre of the Greek world for granted, Attica still stands at the beginning of Pausanias' tour and takes up 39 of the 44 chapters of the first book. Sailing from the east around Sounion, Pausanias arrives at the Piraeus and enters the city at the Kerameikos. He proceeds to the Agora and from there climbs up to the Acropolis, but rather than taking the traditional Panathenaic procession route, he walks around the Acropolis clockwise, from the Agora along the road of the Tripods, around the east end of the hill and then along the south slope, past the theatre, to the western end with the monumental gateway. The Areiopagos is discussed when Pausanias is on the way back down to the Agora.[50]

Enough landmarks on the Acropolis are identified to get a rough sense of Pausanias' tour among the monuments, although the location of many individual objects is subject to conjecture. Inevitably, the tour starts with the Propylaia (1.22.4), including the temple of Nike (1.22.4-5) and the collection of paintings held in its north wing, some by famous artists, others mentioned because Pausanias was interested in their content (1.22.6-7).

The next major landmark is the sanctuary of Artemis Brauronia (1.23.7), mentioned only in passing; the rest of the description between the Propylaia and the Parthenon deals with over twenty

46 Hutton 2005a, 175-240; see also Strid 1976; Habicht 1985, 137; Auberger 1994; Arafat 1996, 30.

47 Paus. 1.26.4.

48 Bischoff 1938; see also Hutton 2005a, 247-63.

49 Paus. 1.22.1; note Paus. 1.23.2, a detail never before recorded in writing.

50 Paus. 1.28.5.

individual monuments, mostly statues. Pausanias' description of the Parthenon is short (1.24.5-7). The pediment sculptures are mentioned (famously, the frieze is not), and the main focus is on the gold and ivory statue of Athena, with a particular attention to specific details such as the griffins on Athena's helmet. There is also a statue of Hadrian (1.24.7) reminding us that while Pausanias often ignores Roman buildings or artefacts, this description reflects the Athens of his own time, not some fantasy version of the city in an idealized past. Neither Perikles nor Pheidias is mentioned in the context of the Parthenon, but just after leaving the temple, Pausanias mentions a bronze Apollo by Pheidias (1.24.8), followed by "on the Acropolis, there is also a statue of Perikles" (1.25.1). Their connection to the Parthenon is not made explicit, and Pausanias merely nods to the history he expects everybody to know.

After a few more statues, Pausanias deals with a dedication by the Attalids, which he locates by the south fortification wall close to the Parthenon (1.25.2), followed by yet more statues and a summary of the history of Athens from Chaironeia to the early 3rd century, attached to the statue of the Athenian general Olympiodoros (1.25.2-26.3).[51] Pausanias then moves on to the Erechtheion (1.26.5), with a list of items inside, and a description of sacred places in the vicinity of the building. The Erechtheion offered a whole collection of awe-inspiringly ancient sights, many connected to Athens' earliest mythical history. Pausanias seems astonishingly blasé in the presence of the mark of Poseidon's trident and the salt-water spring, which he compares to another one in Aphrodisias, suggesting that it was not particularly special (1.26.5). The sacred olive tree (1.27.2) at least has a short history attached to it, and a number of other objects are listed. Superlatives are reserved for the ancient statue of Athena Polias (1.26.6), the holiest image in the whole city, dating back to a time before the city was unified. After the Erechtheion, we get a chapter's worth of more statues and dedications, finishing with yet another portrait of Perikles and Pheidias' most celebrated work, the Athena Lemnia (1.28.3). Yet again, Pausanias, while not talking about the two men's role in shaping the Acropolis, signals to the informed reader that he is well aware of their importance.

It is difficult to define Pausanias' approach to any big city or topic: the *Periegesis* is a work of many small details which may or may not provide a coherent general picture. Pausanias' selection and preferences shape the reader's overall impression,[52] but the many pieces hardly ever fit together neatly to form one coherent picture. This means that we have to try to identify general trends and themes while accepting a good deal of inconsistency. Pausanias' description of the Acropolis is no different in this respect.

In Athens, and particularly on the Acropolis, Pausanias' selection from the past is striking. He was always impressed by the stories about the earliest times when gods interacted with human beings, and Athens had a lot to offer in this respect. On the Acropolis, the most important story was the contest between Zeus and Athena: the traces of Poseidon's trident and Athena's olive tree were outside the Erechtheion and the story was represented in art, not least the Parthenon's pedimental sculptures. Theseus represented another important figure in Athens' mythical history.

Among historical events, the Persian Wars loomed large in Pausanias' imagination, and Athens was the place to commemorate Panhellenic co-operation in defeating the barbarians. There were dedications connected to the event and some statues which had survived the Persian sack with minor damage had

51 Gabbert 1996.

52 Regenbogen 1956, 1090; Habicht 1985, 23-4; Pausanias expresses satisfaction with his selective approach: Paus. 3.11.1.

been set up again.[53] Remarkably, the Classical period hardly features at all: even Perikles and Pheidias are subtly left on the sidelines. If we compare Pausanias' focus with the interests of contemporary writers, which usually concentrate on the periods before Alexander, what is most striking is his particular interest in the Hellenistic history of Athens. This emphasis is less evident in the rest of the *Periegesis*; in fact, Pausanias usually concentrates on earlier history.[54] In Athens, however, Pausanias includes long historical digressions on Alexander's successors and later Hellenistic events among the descriptions of monuments on the Agora.[55] The chapters on the Acropolis contain a summary of Early Hellenistic Athenian history (1.25.2-26.3) and a description of the Attalid monument close to the Parthenon (1.25.2).

Pausanias' Athens offers a number of monuments with connections to famous writers: in the home of Classical Greek literature, it was only to be expected that there would be tangible reminders of that distinction. There were statues of the major dramatists in the theatre (1.21.1-2), but famous writers were commemorated elsewhere as well (e.g. Anakreon on the Acropolis, at 1.25.1). Pausanias reports some rather tenuous connections, as in the case of a statue of a general on the Acropolis who was said to have helped Thucydides to return from exile (1.23.9). Two statues of horsemen in front of the Propylaia (1.22.4) demonstrate how much wishful thinking played a role in discovering references to the most famous literary figures. Parts of both bases of the statues – which were offerings made by Athenian knights after a battle in 446 BC – have been found, which included the name of a general called Xenophon.[56] Pausanias, who was certainly adept at reading inscriptions for himself, even if they were not easy to decipher,[57] appears sceptical, but reports that the statues were identified as the sons of Xenophon. Athenians were perhaps trying too hard to provide objects of memory for eager visitors by forging links between monuments and those famous Athenians visitors would want to commemorate. Pausanias chooses to ignore the fact that one of the statues had since been labelled as Germanicus, although the doubtful phrasing of his comments may be designed to invite visitors to pay special attention to the complex identities and traditions attached to this monument.[58]

Athens' role as the home of Greek philosophy was particularly important: young men came to study in its philosophical schools and visitors enjoyed the places and traditions connected with the history of Greek philosophy.[59] The Acropolis could boast one of the most astonishing philosopher's monuments of all: figures of the three Graces allegedly made by Socrates himself (1.22.8). The philosopher may not have left any legacy in writing, but here a devoted visitor could marvel at an artefact from his own hands: more authentic, one might say, than any copied book could ever have been.

One real strength of Pausanias' research is his attention to local oral tradition and memorials which represented a distinct local version of the past.[60] He provides a valuable insight into contemporary local traditions and gives us a sense of how communi-

53 Paus. 1.27.6; cf. monuments from before the Persian sack of Athens: Paus. 1.23.1-2; 1.26.4; 1.28.2; 1.28.4. See Scholl 2010.

54 Pretzler 2007, 77-8; Hutton 2005a, 63-4, 302-3; Habicht 1985, 105-8; Alcock 1996, 251-60; Swain 1996, 333-8; Bearzot 1992, 17-20. For general views at the time, see Touloumakos 1971, 60-4; Segre 2004, 20-4.

55 Paus. 1.4.1-6 (Gauls, cf. 10.19.5-23.14); 1.6.1-8.1 (Ptolemy I and II, Attalos I); 1.9.1-3 (Ptolemy IV); 1.9.5-10.5 (Lysimachos); 1.11.1-13.9 (Pyrrhos of Epiros); 1.16.1-3 (Seleukos I); cf. Hutton 2005a, 276; Pretzler 2007, 75-6.

56 *IG* I², 400, *SIG*³, 51; Chamoux 1992, 198.

57 Whittaker 1991; Frazer 1898, I:lxxv-vi; Habicht 1984, 1985, 64-5 and passim; Bearzot 1995; Bommelaer 1999; Chamoux 2001; Pretzler 2007, 40-1.

58 Krumeich 2010, 358-60.

59 Habicht 1994, esp. 244-5.

60 Pretzler 2005.

ties wanted to be seen by visitors. In Athens, with its strong literary tradition, this is more difficult to observe, but even here, Pausanias revels in the opportunity to hear things locally which one could not find in books. In one instance, this is made explicit when Pausanias stresses that "what I am about to say has never been committed to writing, but is generally known by the Athenians" (Paus. 1.23.2), followed by a rather far-fetched interpretation of a particular statue. He mentions local informants who provide information about specific religious traditions (1.22.3), and at one point he declares himself amazed by a detail of local cult practice, the tasks of the Arrephoroi (1.27.3), which, he says, were not widely known. Everywhere in the *Periegesis*, one gets the sense that these exclusive discoveries were one of the main incentives for Pausanias' efforts: when you visit the sights you expected to see and then make new discoveries about them, the journey really has been worthwhile. In Athens, such moments were perhaps even more precious than elsewhere, because an educated visitor expected to know so much about it already.

Local traditions were, however, not always trustworthy, and had to be scrutinised carefully.[61] In this period, the Greek past was cultural capital, a kind of political asset, and manipulation of the past was rife.[62] Pausanias was often very suspicious: sometimes he undermines local traditions with relish, even in Athens. He remains doubtful about the "statues of the sons of Xenophon", clearly aware that famous names might be gratuitously attached to monuments which lacked illustrious connections (1.22.4). In some cases, Pausanias does not express a suspicion, but it seems likely that the famous names he is mentioning had been linked to a monument at a late stage: for example, the statue of a lioness with a connection to Hippias (1.23.2), a statue which allegedly represented Kylon, who staged the failed tyrannical coup in the 7th century (1.28.1), and a statue of a young man sacrificing a ram, identified as Phrixos (1.24.2). In one case, Pausanias resists the temptation to speculate about historical connections, something many visitors probably did with great relish, given that they all knew the local history so well (1.24.2).

Pausanias himself was usually not averse to presenting his own theories about monuments or local stories, and sometimes he almost boasts that he knows better than the locals.[63] He does, in fact, dispute some of the Athenian traditions which, in his view, contradict the established literary record: for example, a dedication in the Erechtheion presented as the dagger of Mardonios, the Persian commander at Plataiai, is dismissed with the assertion that this would have been captured by the Spartans (1.27.1); on one occasion, Pausanias corrects the interpretation of a statue group reputedly showing Erechtheus fighting Eumolpos by suggesting that it should be Immarados, son of Eumolpos (1.27.4). Even the hallowed tradition that the image of Athena Polias had fallen from heaven is presented with a wry comment that he is not going to discuss whether this is true or not (1.26.6). Here, we see the testing of local tradition against the literary evidence which was probably a crucial part of an educated man's encounter with Athens: there were few places where literary learning could be so intimately in conversation with the memorial landscape. And if the visitor's knowledge was sometimes able to trump the Athenians' own interpretation, what more thrilling experience could a *pepaideumenos* want from a sight-seeing tour?

61 Pretzler 2004; 2007, 80-1.

62 Swain 1996, 65-89; Spawforth 2012, 100-206. For examples in Pausanias, see Pretzler 2013, 221-37 (Mantinea, Corinth, Patrai).

63 Jones 2001, 33; Pretzler 2005, 241-3; 2007, 36-7, 40-2; e.g. Paus. 1.35.7-8, 2.23.5-6, 7.23.7-8.

Athens as the Centre of Greek Culture: Ideals and Historical Reality

Finally, I would like to return to the question of Athens as the centre of the Greek world, as a symbol of Panhellenism, the admired focus of all Greeks' cultural identity. This was not the case in the Classical period, and, ironically, it was Thucydides, that stalwart of the Attic literary canon, who established Athens as an imperialist power bent on suppressing other Greeks. It was difficult to reconcile this image of imperialist Athens with the much-admired centre of all Greek culture in the minds of later observers. For example, in the *Life of Perikles*, Plutarch grapples with Thucydides' depiction, and he objects to such "slander" in stark tones, although he leaves it to anonymous opponents of Perikles in the assembly to express objections to Athenian imperialism. These dissenting voices point out that the Athenians brought the treasury of the Delian League to Athens and were now insulting Greece by using those war contributions to adorn their own city with lavish buildings.[64] Aristeides fills pages denying all of these claims, and paints Athens as a benign benefactor of other Greek cities.[65] Pausanias simply ignores much of this history when it does not suit him: he has little to say about Athens' role as leader of the Delian League, and Perikles remains on the sidelines. Pausanias abhorred the idea of Greeks fighting Greeks, and celebrates events when Greeks collaborated against outside enemies.[66] In this period, Greeks wanted to see Athens as a cultural centre of their world, and preferred to downplay its actions as an imperial power. The result is an Athens where Classical literature looms large, and Classical history is strangely muted.

Pausanias' Acropolis includes a number of reminders of Athens' war record against the Persians and its noble sacrifice in evacuating the city: Persian War spoils in the Erechtheion (1.27.1), the sacred olive tree which was burned when the city was sacked but which miraculously survived (1.27.2), and ancient statues which showed traces of the fire which destroyed the archaic Acropolis (1.27.6). The Persian Wars generally play an important role in Pausanias' work: whenever there is an opportunity, he returns to this episode in Greek history, and uses it to judge whether a particular community had done the right thing and supported the Greek cause against Persia. The memory of the Persian Wars was important in the Roman period: memorials were restored and traditions concerning Greek collaboration against barbarians revived.[67]

In Athens, however, the Hellenistic period played an important role in turning the city into a symbol of this Panhellenic ideal. Athens built on its historical achievements, particularly its role in defeating the Persians, and Hellenistic rulers, beginning with Alexander, bought into this idea. The Attalids singled Athens out as a place where they could commemorate their victory against the Gauls and juxtapose it with Greek successes in the Persian Wars. At the same time, Athens also became a centre of Greek learning and established itself as the centre of Greek culture.[68]

Pausanias, too, seems to think of Athens as a Panhellenic centre. He describes an image of Ge (Earth) asking Zeus for rain, and matter-of-factly speculates that this may have been set up because the Athenians needed rain, "or maybe all the Greeks were suffering from a drought" (Paus. 1.24.3). The idea that the Athenian Acropolis was a place to set up a dedication on behalf of all the Greeks (whatever that means in this context) would have seemed alien in the Classical period. There was a real tension

64 Plut. *Per.* 12.1-2.

65 Aristid. *Panathenaikos* 195-330.

66 Pretzler 2007, 87.

67 Spawforth 1994.

68 Rathmann 2010.

between the reality of Greek city-states at this time and the ideals of educated Greeks in the Roman Empire who took Panhellenism for granted and bemoaned historical conflicts among the Greeks.[69] Pausanias' selection of monuments and the focus of his commentaries tap into a contradiction which may have been particularly powerful in Athens: the imagined Classical Greece of many Greeks was probably much closer to the Panhellenic ideal than the complex world of city-states which emerges from Thucydides or Xenophon, where Athens does not appear as a city particularly concerned with the unity of the Greeks, except under its own leadership. A more benign, idealised, Panhellenic idea of this period emerged, despite much evidence to the contrary, in the Hellenistic period, when Athens began to assert its role as cultural and perhaps even spiritual centre of Greek life. Pausanias may be responding to the history of Athenian self-presentation, prompted by the memorial landscape, when he skirts around the more complicated aspects of Classical history and focuses, in Athens more than elsewhere, on the Hellenistic period.

In the end, Pausanias' Athens is complex: he seems to challenge his readers to leave the beaten track of their Classicising education and to face new aspects of the Athenian past. At the same time, as we walk along with him, it is easy to imagine what emotional impact Athens would have had on a Greek *pepaideumenos*: this was the place where they could experience much of the tradition that defined their Greek identity. This may not qualify as "sacred travel" in the narrowest sense, but we should probably think of it as a kind of intellectual pilgrimage with high emotional impact.

69 Note the contrast between Pausanias' benefactors of (8.52.1-5) and traitors to (7.10.1-5) Greece.

Abbreviations

IG = *Inscriptiones Graecae* (1873-)

FGrH = F. Jacoby, *Fragmente der griechischen Historiker* (Berlin 1923-)

*SIG*³ = W. Dittenberger (ed.), *Sylloge Inscriptionum Graecarum*, 3rd ed., 4 vols. (Leipzig 1915-1924)

Bibliography

AKUJÄRVI, J. 2005
Researcher, Traveller, Narrator: Studies in Pausanias' Periegesis, Stockholm.

ALCOCK, S.E. 1996
'Landscapes of Memory and the Authority of Pausanias', in *Pausanias Historien* (Entretiens sur l'antiquité classique XLI), D. Musti & J. Bingen (eds.), Geneva, 241-67.

ANDERSON, G. 1986
Philostratus. Biography and Belles Lettres in the Third Century AD, London and Dover, NH.

ANDERSON, G. 1993
The Second Sophistic, London.

ARAFAT, K.W. 1996
Pausanias' Greece. Ancient Artists and Roman Rulers, Cambridge.

AUBERGER, J. 1994
'Les mots de courage chez Pausanias', *RPhil* 68, 7-18.

BEARZOT, C. 1992
Storia e storiografia ellenistica in Pausanias il Periegeta, Venice.

BEARZOT, C. 1995
'L'epigramma come fonte storica in Pausania', in *Studia Classica Iohanni Tarditi oblata*, vol. 1, L. Belloni, G. Milanese & A. Porro (eds.), Milan, 695-710.

BEHR, C.A. 1986
Aelius Aristides: The Complete Works, Orationes I-XVI, Leiden.

BISCHOFF, E. 1938
'Perieget', *RE* XIX, 725-42.

BOMMELAER, J.-F. 1999
'Traces de l'épigraphie Delphique dans le texte de Pausanias', in *Urkunden und Urkundenformulare im klassischen Altertum und in den orientalischen Kulturen*, R.G. Khouri (ed.), Heidelberg, 83-93.

BOWIE, E.L. 2001
'Inspiration and Aspiration: Date, Genre and Readership', in *Pausanias. Travel and Memory in Ancient Greece*, S.E. Alcock, J.F. Cherry & J. Elsner (eds.), Oxford, 21-32.

BURSTEIN, S. 2008
'Greek Identity in the Hellenistic Period', in *Hellenisms. Culture, Identity, and Ethnicity from Antiquity to Modernity*, K. Zacharia (ed.), Aldershot and Burlington, VT, 59-77.

CHAMOUX, F. 1992
'Commentaire', in *Pausanias. Description de la Grèce: Livre I: L'Attique* (Budé), M. Casevitz, J. Pouilloux & F. Chamoux (eds.), Paris, 135-286.

CHAMOUX, F. 2001
'Les épigrammes dans Pausanias', in *Éditer, traduire, commenter Pausanias en l'an 2000*, D. Knoepfler & M. Piérart (eds.), Neuchâtel, 79-91.

CONOLLY, J. 2001
'Problems of the Past in Imperial Greek Education', in *Education in Greek and Roman Antiquity*, Y.L. Too (ed.), Leiden, 289-316.

DILLER, A. 1956
'Pausanias in the Middle Ages', *TAPA* 87, 84-97.

ELLINGER, P. 2005
La fin des maux. D'un Pausanias à l'autre, Paris.

ELSNER, J. 1992
'Pausanias: A Greek Pilgrim in the Roman World', *PastPres* 135, 5-29.

ELSNER, J. 2004
'Pausanias. A Pilgrim in the Roman World. Postscript 2003', in *Studies in Ancient Greek and Roman Society*, R. Osborne (ed.), Cambridge, 282-5.

ELSNER, J. & I. RUTHERFORD (EDS.) 2005
Pilgrimage in Graeco-Roman and Christian Antiquity, Oxford.

FRAZER, J.G. 1898
Pausanias' Description of Greece, 6 vols, London.

GABBERT, J.J. 1996
'The Career of Olympiodorus of Athens (c.340-270 BC)', *AncW* 27, 59-66.

GALLI, M. 2005
'Pilgrimage as Elite *Habitus*. Educated Pilgrims in Sacred Landscape during the Second Sophistic' in *Pilgrimage in Graeco-Roman and Christian Antiquity*, J. Elsner & I. Rutherford (eds.), Oxford, 251-90.

HABICHT, C. 1984
'Pausanias and the Evidence of Inscriptions', *ClAnt* 3, 40-56.

HABICHT, C. 1985
Pausanias' Guide to Ancient Greece, Berkeley.

HABICHT, C. 1994
'Hellenistic Athens and her Philosophers', in *Athen in hellenistischer Zeit*, C. Habicht (ed.), Munich, 231-47.

HEER, J. 1979
La personnalité de Pausanias, Paris.

HUTTON, W.E. 2005A
Describing Greece. Landscape and Literature in the Periegesis *of Pausanias*, Cambridge.

HUTTON, W.E. 2005B
'The Construction of Religious Space in Pausanias', in *Pilgrimage in Graeco-Roman and Christian Antiquity*, J. Elsner & I. Rutherford (eds.), Oxford, 291-317.

JONES, C.P. 1996
'The Panhellenion', *Chiron* 26, 29-56.

JONES, C.P. 2001
'Pausanias and His Guides', in *Pausanias. Travel and Memory in Ancient Greece*, S.E. Alcock, J.F. Cherry & J. Elsner (eds.), Oxford, 33-9.

KRUMEICH, R. 2010
'Vor klassischem Hintergrund. Zum Phänomen der Wiederverwendung älterer Statuen auf der Athener Akropolis als Ehrenstatuen für Römer', in *Die Akropolis von Athen im Hellenismus und in der römischen Kaiserzeit*, R. Krumeich & C. Witschel (eds.), Wiesbaden, 329-97.

KRUMEICH, R. & C. WITSCHEL 2010
'Die Akropolis als zentrales Heiligtum und Ort athenischer Identitätsbildung', in *Die Akropolis von Athen im Hellenismus und in der römischen Kaiserzeit*, R. Krumeich & C. Witschel (eds.), Wiesbaden, 1-53.

MELLOR, R. 2008
'*Graecia Capta*. The Confrontation between Greek and Roman Identity', in *Hellenisms. Culture, Identity, and Ethnicity from Antiquity to Modernity*, K. Zacharia (ed.), Aldershot and Burlington, VT, 79-125.

OLIVER, J.H. 1972
'The Conversion of the Periegete Pausanias', in *Homenaje a Antonio Tovar*, Antonio Tovar (ed.), Madrid, 319-21.

PERRIN, B. 1916
Plutarch's Lives. With an English Translation by Bernadotte Perrin (Loeb Classical Library), Cambridge, MA and London.

PIRENNE-DELFORGE, V. 1998
'La notion de "panthéon" dans la *Périégèse* de Pausanias', in *Les panthéons des cités. Des origines à la* Périégèse *de Pausanias*' (Kernos, suppl. 8), V. Pirenne-Delforge (ed.), Liège, 129-48.

PRETZLER, M. 2004
'Turning Travel into Text. Pausanias at Work', *GaR* 51, 199-216.

PRETZLER, M. 2005
'Pausanias and Oral Tradition', *CQ* 55, 235-49.

PRETZLER, M. 2007
Pausanias. Travel Writing in Ancient Greece, London.

PRETZLER, M. 2013
'Greek Tradition and Roman Innovation. Adapting Cults and Local Identities in Pausanias' Greece', in *Cults, Creeds and Identities in the Greek City after the Classical Age*, R. Alston, O.M. v. Nijf & C.G. Williamson (eds.), Leuven, Paris and Walpole, MA, 215-40.

RATHMANN, M. 2010
'Athen in hellenistischer Zeit. Fremdbestimmng und kulturelle Anziehungskraft', in *Die Akropolis von Athen*

im Hellenismus und in der römischen Kaiserzeit, R. Krumeich & C. Witschel (eds.), Wiesbaden, 55-93.

REGENBOGEN, O. 1956
'Pausanias', *RE* Suppl. VIII, 1008-97.

ROMEO, I. 2002
'The Panhellenion and Ethnic Identity in Hadrianic Greece', *CP* 97, 21-40.

RUTHERFORD, I. 2013
State Pilgrims and Sacred Observers in Ancient Greece: A Study of Theōriā and Theōroi, Cambridge.

SALMERI, G. 2011
'Reconstructing the Political Life and Culture of the Greek Cities of the Roman Empire', in *Political Culture in the Greek City after the Classical Age*, R. Alston, O.M. v. Nijf & C.G. Williamson (eds.), Leuven, Paris and Walpole, MA, 197-214.

SCHOLL, A. 2010
'"Es sind da auch noch alte Athena-Statuen…" Pausanias und die vorpersische Akropolisvotive', in *Die Akropolis von Athen im Hellenismus und in der römischen Kaiserzeit*, R. Krumeich & C. Witschel (eds.), Wiesbaden, 251-69.

SEGRE, M. 2004
Pausania come fonte storica, tesi di laurea of 1926/7, Rome and Milan.

SCHMITZ, T. 1997
Bildung und Macht. Zur sozialen und politischen Funktion der zweiten Sophistik in der griechischen Welt der Kaiserzeit (Zetemata 97), Munich.

SPAWFORTH, A. 1994
'Symbol of Unity? The Persian-Wars Tradition in the Roman Empire', in *Greek Historiography*, S. Hornblower (ed.), Oxford, 233-47.

SPAWFORTH, A.J. 2012
Greece and the Augustan Cultural Revolution. Greek Culture in the Roman World, Cambridge and New York.

SPAWFORTH, A.J. & S. WALKER 1985
'The World of the Panhellenion: I. Athens and Eleusis', *JRS* 75, 78-104.

SPAWFORTH, A.J. & S. WALKER 1986
'The World of the Panhellenion: II. Three Dorian Cities', *JRS* 76, 88-105.

STRID, O. 1976
Über Sprache und Stil des Periegeten Pausanias, Uppsala.

SWAIN, S. 1996
Hellenism and Empire. Language, Classicism, and Power in the Greek World, AD 50-250, Oxford.

THÉRIAULT, G. 1996
Le culte d'Homonoia dans les cités grecques, Lyon and Quebec.

TOULOUMAKOS, J. 1971
Zum Geschichtsbewusstsein der Griechen in der Zeit der römischen Herrschaft, Bonn.

VEYNE, P. 1988
Did the Greeks Believe in Their Myths?, translated by P. Wissing, Chicago.

WHITMARSH, T. 2001
Greek Literature and the Roman Empire. The Politics of Imitation, Oxford.

WHITTAKER, H. 1991
'Pausanias and His Use of Inscriptions', *SymbOslo* 66, 171-86.

PART II

MOVEMENT BEYOND THE CITY

The Beginning of Sacred Travel in Ancient Athens and Its Countryside

Søren Handberg

Introduction

In the Late Geometric period, major changes in social organisation are apparent in the archaeological record of Athens and Attica. Signs of such changes are visible in the increased number of both formal burials and settlements. The first tangible evidence of religious activity on the Athenian Acropolis dates to this period, which coincides with a dramatic rise in the number of visible sanctuaries and shrines in the countryside and an intensification in the use of the few pre-existing religious sites.[1]

The fundamental changes that took place in the Late Geometric period have been related to the emergence of the polis and the beginning of a movement towards a more egalitarian social structure. Athenian aristocrats had traditionally used the funerary sphere as a venue for displaying their elite status, but as more members of the community were offered formal burials, the aristocrats' social superiority was challenged, which led them to transfer the display of their elite status to the sanctuaries as a new venue for maintaining and reifying their social superiority.[2]

The fact that the establishment of a cult on the Acropolis and the intensification of religious activity in the countryside happened simultaneously begs the question of to what extent members of the Athenian aristocracy, for lack of a better word, were involved in, or even responsible for, the intensified worship in the Athenian countryside, and how closely the ruling families in the city were connected to these sites. In the case of Athens and Attica, it is usually thought that the religious sites in the countryside were predominantly, or even exclusively, visited by local farmers and herders throughout the Geometric period, and that there were no close ties to ruling families in Athens. Indeed, as François de Polignac has argued, Athens represents an "anomaly" among the major ancient Greek cities exactly because of the absence of strong ties to an extra-urban sanctuary.[3]

In this chapter, I am going to argue that the ruling families in Athens had a vested interest in rural shrines, and that we might see this as a sort of beginning of sacred travel in Athens and Attica. Through some selected case studies, I will first attempt to trace the travels of Athenian aristocrats to areas outside Attica in the Middle Geometric period, which seem closely connected to a network of guest-friendships (*xenia*). Then, having established that this was likely the case, I am going to argue that one of the primary religious concerns of the members of the ruling families in Athens in the Late Geometric period was the veneration of Zeus in his capacity as a weather deity and that they used the sanctuaries on Mount Hymettos and Mount Parnes, which are among the

1 For burials, see Morris 1987; Snodgrass 1980. For settlements, see Mersch 1997. For sanctuaries, see Langdon 1997.

2 Morris 1987; 1997.

3 Polignac 1995, 83-8. See also Morris 1997, 24-5.

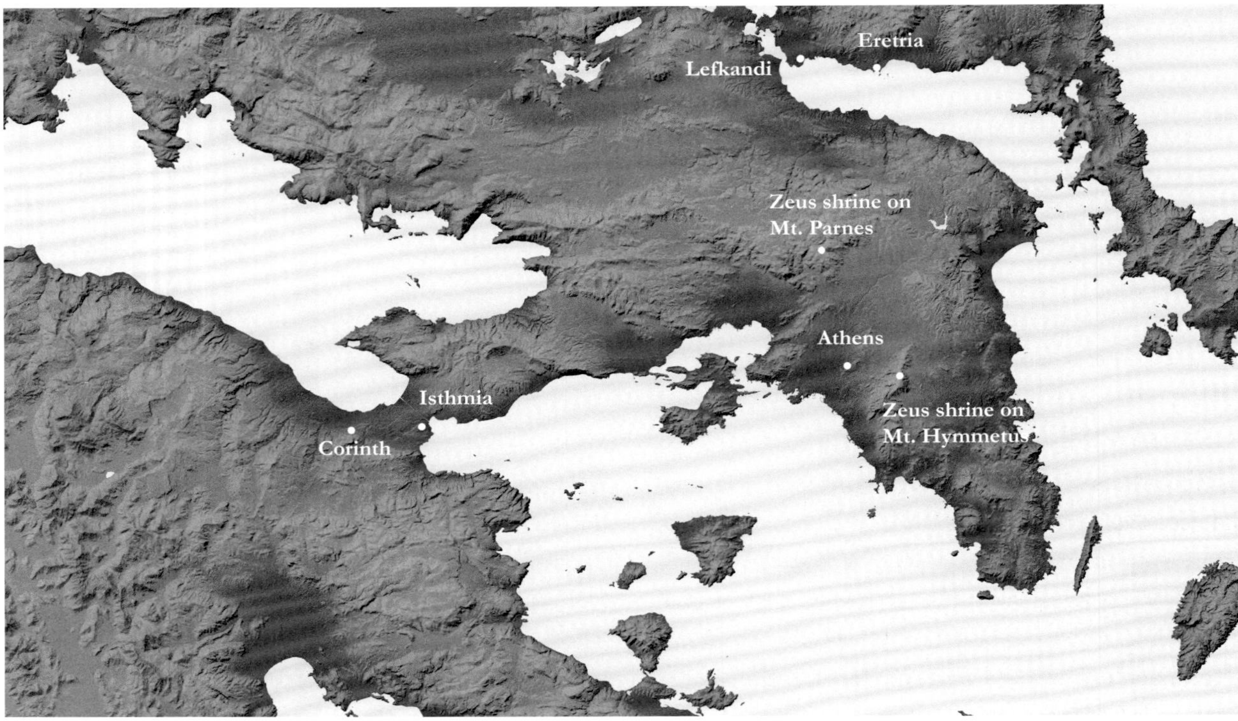

Fig. 1. Map of Attica and surrounding area showing principal sites discussed in the chapter.

earliest post-Bronze Age religious shrines known from Attica, as new venues for aristocratic feasts (Fig. 1).

Sacred Travel in the Greek Early Iron Age

Considering the recent debates regarding sacred mobility and pilgrimage in the ancient world, the use of the term "sacred travel" requires some clarification.[4] Is it at all possible to talk about sacred travel in the Greek Early Iron Age, and if so, what do we mean and how should we approach the archaeological and textual sources in relation to this concept?

The recent theoretical debates show how difficult, if not impossible, it is to define a theoretical framework for the term "pilgrimage" that encompasses and acknowledges the diverse cult practices and historical specificity that characterize sacred mobility.[5] Definitions of sacred travel often stress the subjective religious experience of the traveller, which is most often only identifiable in textual evidence.[6] Given the scarcity of Early Iron Age texts, we cannot really say much about this. Possibly the closest we get to such subjective experiences in early Greece is Hesiod's account of his journey to Mount Helicon to dedicate a tripod to the muses as a thank-offering (Hes. *Op.* 655-60).[7]

The identification of "sacred travel" in the archaeological material therefore depends on heuristic tools and analogies. Jaś Elsner and Ian Rutherford have provided a typology of different types of pil-

4 For recent debates, see e.g. Elsner & Rutherford 2005a; Rutherford 2013; Kristensen & Friese 2017a.

5 Elsner & Rutherford 2005b, esp. 7-8.

6 Elsner 2017, 267.

7 Trans. Most 2006.

grimage in the Classical and Hellenistic periods,[8] but none fit comfortably in the Early Iron Age.

One of the most important points to have emerged from the theoretical debate over the definition of an adequate conceptual framework for "pilgrimage" and "sacred travel" has arguably been the realizations that religious journeys were undertaken for many different reasons and under diverse circumstances.[9] This diversity underlines the methodological importance of recognizing the specific social and cultural context in which the sacred travel is to be understood. In this chapter, I therefore adopt a different approach to sacred travel, one that emphasizes the material traces of sacred travel rather than the concept.

Joy McCorriston has recently addressed this persistent problem of how to identify pilgrimage in the archaeological record and has suggested that the question is best approached by attempting to identify the localities where material traces of pilgrimage are preserved.[10] She proposes that such sites may be identified where there is "a material record of monuments and offerings that indicate episodic gatherings to commemorate earlier socially-constituting rites".[11] A central component in this definition is the mediating role of reaffirming social identities through ritual practices.[12] The advantage of this approach is that it sidelines the conceptual framework and shifts the focus to the specific contextual setting of the archaeological evidence.

Early Religious Activity on the Acropolis of Athens

The first substantial evidence for religious activity on the Athenian Acropolis dates to the Late Geometric period and consists of pottery, terracotta figurines, and bronze votive objects.[13] The clearest expression of the religious character of these finds is found in the bronze votive objects. Most prominent among these are the 70 fragments of bronze tripods, which according to their stylistic particularities seem to have been produced in Athens.[14] Also among the prominent finds are the c. 16 Late Geometric bronze horse and other figurines, which have also been identified as belonging to an Athenian workshop.[15]

The Late Geometric assemblage from the Acropolis also includes several ceramic vessels in a Dipylon style with depictions of *prothesis* and *ekphora* scenes, which could be interpreted as evidence for the existence of Late Geometric burials there.[16] Within this framework, the bronze tripods have been viewed as representing prizes from funeral games that were subsequently put on display on the Acropolis, rather than votives, *sensu stricto*, for the goddess.[17] On the contrary, the almost complete lack of pyxides, which regularly occur in Middle and Late Geometric Athenian graves,[18] has been taken as evidence that the pieces of Geometric pottery on the Acropolis were actually offered as votives.[19] Considering that 19 Mycenaean graves have been identified on the Acropolis, I consider it highly unlikely that no graves of the Geometric period should have been

8 Elsner & Rutherford 2005b, 12-29.

9 Elsner & Rutherford 2005b, 7-8.

10 McCorriston 2017. But see also Kristensen & Friese 2017b, 2-3.

11 McCorriston 2017, 13.

12 McCorriston 2011. For the central role of communality and the maintenance of identities in an ancient Greek setting in Olympia, see also Kowalzig 2005, 42-3 with n. 3.

13 For the early dedications on the Athenian Acropolis, see Graef & Langlotz 1925; Scholl 2006; Gauss & Ruppenstein 1998.

14 Touloupa 1972; Weber 1974.

15 Zimmermann 1989, 269-74; Hurwit 1999, 90, figs 62-3.

16 Gauss & Ruppenstein 1998, 37-40.

17 Langdon 1997, 117-8. This follows Catherine Morgan's (1992, 43-7) suggestion for the bronze tripods from Olympia.

18 *Kerameikos* XIII, 5 n. 17, 8-12.

19 Gauss & Ruppenstein 1998, 31 with n. 107.

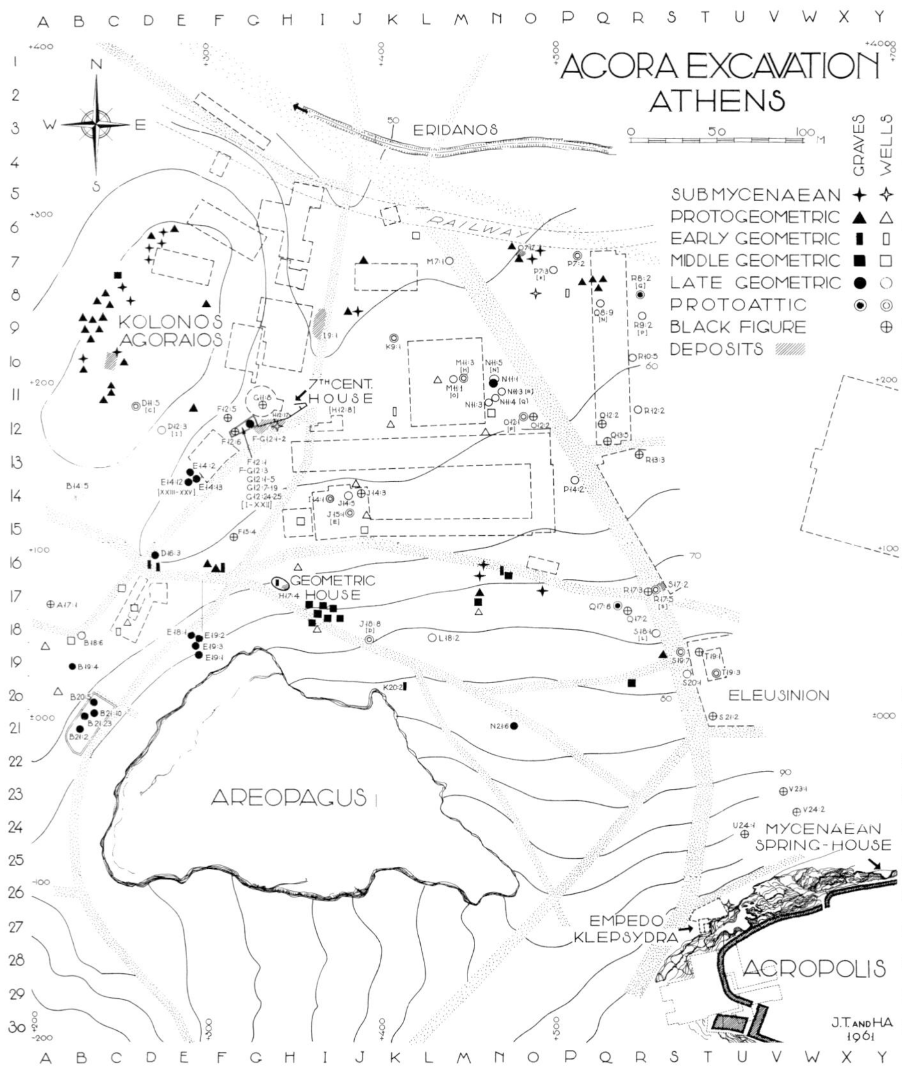

Fig. 2. General plan of the later Classical Agora showing Early Iron Age finds (©American School of Classical Studies at Athens: Agora Excavations).

uncovered, had they been present there.[20] Another explanation for the presence of these vessels has been that they originated from elsewhere in Athens and ended up on the Acropolis as part of the soil used in the fill for the Archaic temple.[21] However, since some of the sherds were found in the Persian destruction debris deposits, this could not have been the case.[22]

The point that I want to emphasise here, as others have already pointed out,[23] is that the cult on the Athenian Acropolis was certainly a local cult closely associated with the Athenian elite, and that the Late Geometric pottery may suggest that aristocratic commensal dinning was practised on the Acropolis. In the next section, I will therefore focus on the contemporary Athenian elite, looking particularly at the aristocratic context that is closest to the Acropolis, the so-called Areopagos Oval House.

20 For a catalogue of the graves, see Gauss & Ruppenstein 1998, 1-26.

21 Graef 1893, 17; Gauss & Ruppenstein 1998, 36.

22 Gauss & Ruppenstein 1998, 36 with n. 134. See also van den Eijde 2010a, 95.

23 e.g. Glowacki 1998, 81.

Fig. 3. Plan of the Areopagos Oval House (© American School of Classical Studies at Athens: Agora Excavations).

Athenian Aristocrats Feasting at Home and Abroad

Aristocratic Feasting in Athens

The Areopagos Oval House situated near the north slope of the Areopagos Hill in Athens immediately southwest of the Classical Agora (Fig. 2-3), is one of the best preserved Geometric buildings in Athens.[24] The building was damaged by later disturbances in the area, but its shape and dimensions can be accurately reconstructed. It is oval in shape with a stone foundation for the walls and measures approximately 11 x 5 m. The walls must have been constructed of mud-bricks and it probably had a thatched roof. A raised stone platform of a depth of more than half a meter running along the interior walls was identified in several places and a burned patch in the centre of the building probably represents the remains of a hearth.

24 For the original publication of the house, see Burr 1933. For subsequent discussions, see most recently van den Eijnde & Laughy 2015.

It has recently been proposed that this building, which was constructed around 850 BC near a preexistent burial plot, should be identified with the type of feasting halls (megara) of rulers or chieftains described by Homer.[25] A comparison of the physical elements of the Oval House and the dining halls of Homer reveals several similar characteristic traits.[26] Homer's feasting halls are described as oblong wooden buildings with a stone foundation for the walls, a clay floor, and an interior hearth.[27] The presence of the built-in platform or bench along the walls is a significant feature of the Oval House that resembles the description of the location of the seats of the leaders of the Phaeacians in King Alcinous' hall:

> Within [the megaron], seats were fixed along the wall on either hand, from the threshold to the innermost

25 Eijnde & Laughy 2015, 238-9.

26 Mazarakis Ainian 1997, 363-7.

27 For a thorough discussion of Homeric descriptions of the feasting halls, see van Wees 1995, 148-54; 1992, 42, 44.

chamber, and on them were thrown robes of soft fabric, cunningly woven, the handiwork of women. On these the leaders of the Phaeacians were wont to sit drinking and eating, for they lived in unfailing abundance (Hom. *Od.* 7.95-9).[28]

Similar built-in benches are known from other slightly later oval or apsidal buildings at other sites in Attica, and one gets the impression that such feasting halls were common at larger and more important sites.[29] The layout of these buildings is mirrored in Late Geometric Athenian iconography. Among the Late Geometric so-called Rattle Group are a number of depictions of elite commensal dining, where participants are seated along the walls of the building on benches (Fig. 4). Homer also describes feasting halls as places where tripods are kept and shields hung on the walls.[30] These elements also recur in the imagery of the Rattle Group, where we see both tripods and shields depicted.[31] No archaeological traces of tripods were reported from the excavations of the Oval House (except for miniatures found in the supposedly votive dump on top of the building),[32] but the dedication of bronze tripods on the Acropolis testifies to the importance of tripods in Athens in this period.

Fig. 4. Pither of the "Rattle Group" with a scene showing two men seated on benches along the interior walls of a building. Late Geometric II. National Archaeological Museum, Athens, inv. no. 17497 (© Hellenic Ministry of Culture and Sports/Archaeological Receipts Fund. Photographer: Stephanos Stournaras).

Commensal feasting was one of the defining characteristics of the ancient Greek aristocracy. The so-called *gerousios oinos* (wine of the elders) is mentioned several times in Homer's epics and refers to a banquet held by the leaders of communities when important political decision-making was necessary. Hosting this feast was the exclusive social prerogative of the kings (*basileis*).[33] The Homeric poems provide ample evidence to show that participation in commensal feasting was intricately connected with the community leaders, and as Hans van Wees has shown, commensal feasting among members of aristocratic families was reciprocal in nature and centred on the principals of hospitality and guest-friendship.[34] A person's social status depended on being inscribed in a circle of inviting and being

28 Trans. Murray 1995.

29 Similar benches are known from other Late Geometric buildings in Attica, e.g. at Tourkovounia and Lathouriza. For a convenient overview of the occurrence of benches in Early Iron Age Greece, see Mazarakis Ainian 1997, 280-1, 292-3. For the Cyclades, see also Christophilopoulou 2007. For a description of the Homeric banquet, see also Węcowski 2014, 206-14.

30 Van Wees 1995, 151.

31 Cook 1946; Buchholz 1987; Mikrakis 2015.

32 Burr 1933, 565, 579, cat. no. 155, 581, fig. 39, 621, cat. no. 329, fig. 87.

33 Węcowski 2014, 199-201. See e.g. Hom. *Il.* 4.258-60 for a reference to the Argive chiefs who meet to mix the "ruddy wine". See also Luke 1994.

34 Van Wees 1995.

invited to feasts by other prominent members of the upper echelon of the society. The social importance of taking part in this cycle of feasting invitations is perhaps best illustrated by a quote from the *Odyssey*, where Odysseus is reassured that his son Telemachos is still considered a member of the social upper class since he is still being invited to "the fair meals with which it is proper for justice-attending man to concern himself" (Hom. *Od.* 11.185-6).

In Athenian society, commensal feasting involving the consumption of wine was probably one of the main ways by which the social elite asserted and reinforced their social position. The central importance of wine consumption in Athens is underlined by the monumental kraters used as grave markers by aristocrats since at least the Middle Geometric period.[35] The Oval House was constructed around 850 BC near a small burial ground on the north slope of the Areiopagos Hill. This cemetery includes the grave of the so-called "Rich Athenian Lady", dating to the same time as the erection of the Oval House, which remains the richest Geometric grave ever discovered in Athens.[36] The existence of the grave, as well as literary tradition that would place the king of Athens on the Areopagos Hill, led Coldstream,[37] among others, to suggest that this was the plot of one of the ruling families in Athens at that time, and it is therefore possible that the Oval House was the ruler's megaron.

Athenian Aristocrats on the Move

In the preceding section, I argued that feasting was important to the ruling aristocrats in Early Iron Age Athens, and that the Oval House might have been the seat of one of the ruling families. In this section, I will attempt to trace these Athenian aristocrats' travels to areas outside the borders of Attica. First, however, some methodological caveats need to be addressed.

Any attempt to trace the movement of people in the archaeological record is faced with serious methodological challenges. This is a particularly acute problem in the Early Iron Age, when literary sources are sparse and the material record is in most cases incomplete.[38] It is abundantly clear that in the Middle Geometric period the export of Attic pottery around the Mediterranean increases dramatically,[39] and Marek Węcowski has recently related this increase to a dissemination of Athenian social values centred on feasting, particularly the consumption of wine, which was so important in Athens.[40] However, despite the wide distribution of Athenian pottery, which reached Spain and Syria, it remains difficult to evaluate to what extent this involved Athenians. This problem resembles the ongoing discussion over the degree of involvement of Euboeans in the distribution of Euboean pottery.[41]

Indeed, a recent survey of the distribution of the early SOS amphoras of the Late Geometric period shows that the SOS amphoras produced in Athens and Euboea, possibly in Chalcis, have a very similar geographical distribution, predominantly covering the central and eastern Mediterranean.[42] Furthermore, it has become clear that this distribution corresponds closely to the distribution of the contemporary Phoenician "torpedo" amphoras, which suggests that Phoenician traders may primarily have been

35 See most recently Coldstream 2011; Węcowski 2014, 261; 2017.
36 Smithson 1968.
37 Coldstream 1995, 393.

38 Discussions on this topic are numerous, but see e.g. Gimatzidis 2011; Kilian-Dirlmeier 1985; Morgan 1992, 61-105.
39 Coldstream 2003, 81; Papadopoulos 2015. See also Węcowski 2017b.
40 Węcowski 2017b.
41 Descœudres 2008, Papadopoulos 1997; 2011; Donnellan 2017.
42 Pratt 2015.

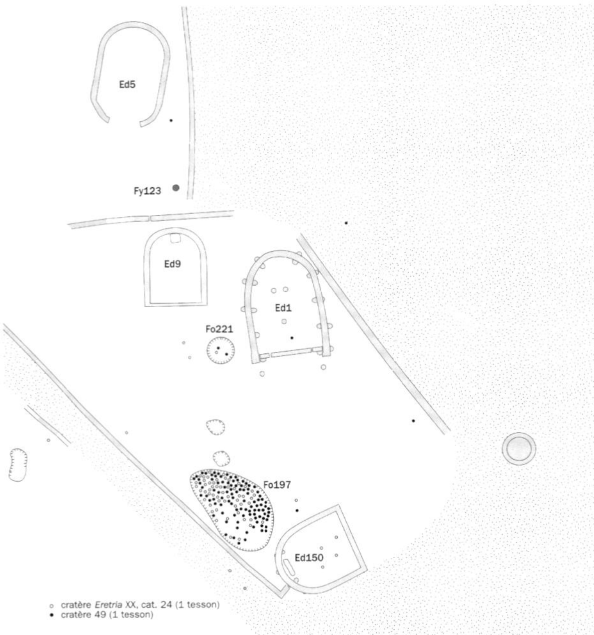

Fig. 5. Topographical plan of the earliest phase of occupation in the Apollo Daphnephoros area in Eretria showing the distribution of krater fragments (courtesy of the Swiss School of Archaeology in Greece).

responsible for transporting these commodities.[43] Since Athenian tablewares were distributed to much the same regions, it may obviously be suspected that Phoenician traders played a part in distributing these wares as well.[44]

However, there appear to be some differences in the scale of distributions of Attic and Euboean pottery. Whereas Attic pottery predominates among the imported pottery on Delos and Crete in the Middle Geometric period, less Euboean pottery has been found on the two islands.[45] Antonis Kotsonas has also recently argued for a direct connection between Euboea/Central Greece and Crete in the Geometric period on the basis of the many Cretan bronzes found in Delphi.[46] Furthermore, in the Middle Geometric period, the Athenian krater was widely distributed, whereas by the Late Geometric period, Euboean kraters had taken over the "market".[47] These patterns do not exclude Phoenician involvement in the distribution of Attic pottery, of course, but they do suggest that different networks were likely to have been involved in the distribution of such wares.

Feasts in Eretria

The Swiss excavations in the central area of the Apollo Daphnephoros sanctuary in Eretria and the subsequent analysis of the remains by several scholars have shown that in the Middle Geometric period before the so-called Hekatompedon temple was constructed, there was in all probability a ruler's habitation complex with an adjacent altar (Fig. 5). One of the earliest houses (Building 1) should most likely be interpreted as a feasting hall.[48] Two facts support this idea. First, evidence for the preparation of meals during the first occupational phase, in the form of traces of hearths and burned bones, has been found in several places outside the buildings.[49] Secondly, fragments of three Attic kraters dating from the Middle Geometric II to the Late Geometric I period have been found in association with the two main early buildings (Buildings 1 and 150).[50] A meticulous reconstruction of the find-spots of sherds belonging to these kraters allows us to form an opinion about their original context of use. Most

43 Pratt 2015, 232.
44 Coldstream 1989; 1995, 399.
45 For the distribution of Eboean pottery, see Descœudres 2006-2007. For Delos, see Morgan 1992, 206-7. For the predominance of Attic pottery on Crete, see Papadopoulos 2015; Coldstream 1996.

46 Kotsonas 2009.
47 Crielaard 1999, 265-71.
48 Verdan 2013, 173-98; 2015, 184-6; Mazarakis Ainian 1987, 20-1; 1997, 58-63, 314, 352-6; 2007, 161; Węcowski 2014, 183-7.
49 Verdan 2013, 184-5.
50 Verdan 2013, cat. nos. 49 and 335. Verdan *et al.* 2008, 118, cat. nos. 24, 143, pl. 9.

of the sherds from two of the kraters were found in Pit 197 just outside Building 150. However, a few fragments belonging to these two kraters were found inside Building 1 and 150, which suggests that they were originally used in the buildings during feasts, such as we see in the previously mentioned scene of the Rattle Group where a krater seems to be standing inside the building.[51] The third krater provides even better evidence for the sympotic function of the early buildings. The lower part of this krater was found imbedded in a clay platform (St210), which was installed in the apsis of the second phase of Building 150.[52] As Węcowski has pointed out, the location of the krater corresponds very well with Homer's description of the location of the krater in Odysseus' dining hall: "Then first arose Leiodes, son of Oenops, who was their soothsayer, and always sat by the beautiful mixing bowl [κρητήρ] in the innermost part of the hall" (Hom. *Od.* 21.144-6).[53]

What is significant in regard to our attempt to trace the movement of members of the Athenian elite is that the three kraters were all produced in Athens. Indeed, the majority of imported pottery found in the area comprises Attic drinking vessels such as skyphoi and kantharoi.[54] What I want to suggest here is that the three Attic kraters, and most likely also many of the drinking cups, may have been brought to Eretria by visiting Athenian aristocrats, who travelled there to participate in feasts. Again from Homer, we know that the krater could be a fitting object in gift exchanges among the elites, since it is the krater that Menelaus gives to Telemachos when he first arrives in Sparta:

> And of all the gifts that lie stored as treasures in my house, I will give you that one which is most beautiful and most precious. I will give you a well-wrought mixing bowl. It is all of silver, and its rims are finished with gold, the work of Hephaestus (Hom. *Od.* 15. 113-17).[55]

Invitations to feasts might have been a good occasion for presenting the local ruler in Eretria with a large and elaborately decorated krater, and judging from the Middle Geometric elite burial plot at Odos Arist. Eratonymou that contained a complete Attic drinking assemblage, it seems that the Eretrian aristocracy favoured Athenian vessels.[56] In fact, it is remarkable how much Attic sympotic pottery has been found in elite burials in Lefkandi, Crete, Cyprus, and the Near East.[57]

The crucial question here is whether the kraters were indeed brought directly by Athenians or whether they ended up in Eretria by any other means, as discussed above. The best evidence for the presence of foreigners in Eretria is the Middle Geometric skyphos with a graffito in Semitic script, which John Papadopoulos has suggested might be evidence of a foreigner in the city.[58] Yet as far as I am aware, there is no comparable evidence for an Athenian presence. However, I believe that the large amount of Attic drinking cups in Eretria supports the idea that the kraters, and the associated drinking vessels, were directly brought to Eretria by Athenian aristocrats. Węcowski has shown that it was important for participants at feasts or symposia to mark the ownership of their drinking cups, at least perhaps on some more official occasions.[59] Several drinking cups with ownership marks have been found in the

51 Verdan 2013, 180 with n. 1023, 182-3, pl. 15a.
52 Verdan 2013, 56, 92, pl. 33c, 34-5, (krater cat. no. 335). For a recent discussion, see Węcowski 2014, 185-7.
53 Trans. Murray 1995.
54 Verdan 2013, 96.
55 Trans. Murray 1995.
56 Blandin 2007, 29-34; Crielaard 2007, 183-4. Węcowski 2014, 258 with note 33. In general, see Crielaard 2007, 183-4. See also Verdan 2015. For the demand for Early Iron Age pottery, see Papadopoulos 2015.
57 Coldstream 1983; 1995, 400-2.
58 Papadopoulos 2011, 116. For the publication of the cup, see Kenzelmann Pfyffer *et al.* 2005, 76-7, cat. no. 66.
59 Węcowski 2014, 135-6.

Fig. 6. Horse-pyxis and body sherd from an amphora(?) from the sanctuary at Isthmia (courtesy of the American School of Classical Studies, Excavations at Isthmia).

Apollo Daphnephoros area in Eretria. One cup in particular bears a dipinto, which was painted onto the cup before firing, with the partially preserved name of an individual who might have been an inhabitant of Chalkis.[60] In my opinion, Węcowski is correct in assuming that this cup was a special commission and that the owner brought his own drinking cup with him when he participated in a feast in Eretria.[61] In this connection, it is also worth mentioning that very little imported pottery is known in Athens in this period, so if foreign traders, and not local Athenian aristocrats, were responsible for shipping the Attic pottery to Eretria, they do not seem to have left any pottery behind in Athens.

Athenian Aristocrats in Isthmia

My second case concerns Athenian connections to Isthmia. Among the Early Iron Age pottery from the site published by Catherine Morgan are a Middle Geometric II-Late Geometric I horse-pyxis and a body sherd of what was presumably a large amphora decorated with a *prothesis* scene (Fig. 6).[62] In this period of time, there is clear evidence of religious activity in Isthmia where, among other votives, bronze tripods and figurines have been found.[63] The presence of both unburned and burned bones in an ash layer in the southeastern part of the temenos, combined with a large number of drinking vessels, suggests, as Morgan has already pointed out, that feasts are likely to have been one aspect of the activities at the site in this period.[64] Based on the fact that the Attic pyxis and large vessels with *prothesis* scenes are almost exclusively used in funerary contexts in Athens and Attica, Morgan thought it more likely that these vessels were brought to the sanctuary by non-Athenians, but the deposition of such vessels on the Athenian Acropolis shows that it is conceivable that Athenian aristocrats actually brought these vessels with them to Isthmia, which Morgan also acknowledges.[65]

We do not have any direct evidence for the presence of Athenians here either, but, as in the case of

60 Kenzelmann Pfyffer *et al.* 2005, 59, cat. no. 1.

61 Węcowski 2017a, 312-3.

62 Morgan 1994, 118. *Isthmia* VIII, 98, cat. no. 264, pl. 35 (pyxis); 123, cat. no. 370, pl. 48 (*prothesis* scene). For a discussion of them, see *Isthmia* VIII, 282-5, 293-4.

63 Morgan 1994, 118-9. *Isthmia* VIII, 159-60, cat. Nos. M14-M19, 326-8 (tripods). See also *Isthmia* VIII, 402-6.

64 Morgan 1994, 113-5. *Isthmia* VIII, 315-6.

65 Morgan 1994, 118. *Isthmia* VIII, 326.

Eretria, some support for this idea exists; in this case in the form of several terracotta boots dating to the Early Geometric Period. Fragments of three terracotta boots were found at Isthmia, all of which were contextually associated with the Early Iron Age ash layer at the East Terrace area.[66] Two pairs of similar terracotta boots were found in an Early Geometric cremation grave south of the Agora area in Athens in 1948.[67] Terracotta boots were also found in another Early Geometric cremation grave in Odos Dimitrios in Athens, and miniature versions of the boots were found in the Early Geometric grave underneath the Oval House.[68] Similar pairs of boots have been found in two later graves in Eleusis, one of which comes from the very rich Late Geometric female "Isis Grave".[69]

As in the case of the connection between Athens and Eretria, it is important to emphasize that in the Geometric period, there was limited exchange of pottery between Athens and Corinth/Isthmia.[70] The boots must therefore certainly represent something special. It is perhaps not possible to directly trace Athenian aristocrats in Isthmia, but we do see a connectivity based on objects that appear to carry with them elite connotations. The fact that these boots appear to be exclusive to female graves is significant, and several scholars see a connection to the *nymphides*, the traditional bridal shoes in ancient Greece. It is likely that these boots symbolise married women who died before childbirth, and that the Attic boots found in Isthmia should be taken as a material sign of elite exogamous alliances.[71]

Summarizing the evidence presented above, there is, in my opinion, good archaeological evidence to suggest that feasting was an important aspect of Athenian aristocratic life throughout the Geometric period, which is supported by the literary sources. Furthermore, the two case studies suggest that members of the Athenian aristocracy had close guest-friendship links, which might have included intermarriages, with rulers in Eretria and Corinth/Isthmia. Such external Athenian relationships might be traced back to the late Protogeometric period.[72] It is particularly interesting that these early contacts seem to focus on contexts of feasting and communal wine consumption in aristocratic settings, which will be important for understanding the development of the religious landscape of Attica, as I will discuss in the next section.

Feasting and Venerating Zeus at the Margins of Athenian Territory

As mentioned above, ritual activity in the landscape surrounding Athens intensified in the Late Geometric period.[73] Activity can be traced back to the Protogeometic period at three sites: the Zeus sanctuaries on Mount Hymettos and Mount Parnes and the Artemis sanctuary at Mounichia. The two Zeus sanctuaries are the only two mountain sanctuaries where Zeus Ombrios was worshipped in his capacity as a weather god, and I believe this constituted a

66 *Isthmia* VIII, 174-5, cat. nos. F36-F38, pl. 74. For a discussion of the interpretation of the boots, see *Isthmia* VIII, 336-8; Morgan 1994, 120-1.

67 Young 1949, 232, 296-97, cat. nos. 22-23, fig. 12, pls. 67, 70.

68 Grave 26 in the Athenian Agora, see Young 1949, 282, 287-8, 296-7, cat. nos. 22-23, fig. 12, pls. 67, 70. For a grave in Odos Dimitrios, see *ArchDelt* 19B, 1964, 54-5, pl. 49g, h.

69 Young 1949, 287, pl. 71; Young & Angel 1939, 234-6.

70 Morgan 1994, 120-1; *Isthmia* VIII, 294.

71 For the idea that the terracotta boots should be viewed in terms of marriage, see *Isthmia* VIII, 337; Morgan 1994, 120-1. For the most recent discussion of these boots, see Haentjens 2002.

72 Coldstream 1995, 401 has proposed that some of the early graves at Lefkandi belong to Attic immigrants.

73 See the recent excellent overviews of Attic shrines in Laughy 2010, 210-53 and van den Eijnde 2010a, 61-298, 306, table 5.

significant factor in the development of sacred travel in the Attic countryside.

In this second part of the chapter, I am going to argue that the increased religious activity observed in the Late Geometric period was intimately connected with the Athenian aristocracy, who used these two sanctuaries as venues for maintaining their elite status, albeit with slightly different purposes. One sanctuary, that on Hymettos, seems to have served primarily local needs, whereas the sanctuary on Mount Parnes was used as a venue for status display in interactions with rulers from neighbouring regions. There is no conclusive evidence which can directly tie members of the Athenian ruling class to either of these two Zeus sanctuaries, but a fair amount of circumstantial evidence suggests that this may very well have been the case.

The sanctuary to Zeus on Mount Hymettos is situated near the summit (1026 metres above sea level) of the mountain range approximately 9 kilometres east-southeast, as the crow flies, of the Athenian Classical Agora. 170 inscriptions on pottery are known from the sanctuary, several of which are dedicatory inscriptions to Zeus, the earliest of which date to the 7th century BC.[74] A few badly preserved architectural remains were found at the site. The largest rectangular structure measures c. 6 x 3.2 m, and judging by the ceramic finds, it was in use throughout the Geometric period. 1,259 pottery sherds spanning the period from the Protogeometric period to the 6th century BC and 120 Roman lamps are noted in Merle Langdon's publication of the material, but the original excavation report mentions 120 baskets of pottery fragments, which certainly must have amounted to much more than the published finds.[75] From the short period c. 750-700 BC there is twice as much pottery as in the period c. 1050-750 BC.[76] The majority of the ceramic vessels consists of pitchers and drinking cups that have been interpreted as signs of feasting, especially wine drinking within the sanctuary.[77]

The cave shrine of Zeus near the summit of Mount Parnes (1412 metres above sea level) was hurriedly excavated by Euthymios Mastrokostas in 1959 and is inaccessible today.[78] The finds from the excavation remain largely unpublished, but from the preliminary reports it seems clear that a huge 2 metre deep ash deposit, presumably from an ash altar, covered the site. Dedicatory inscriptions to Zeus are found on pottery and an iron thunderbolt. The ceramic assemblage spans the period from the Protogeometric period to the 6th century BC, and pouring and drinking vessels, especially oinochoai and kantharoi, predominate among the finds.[79] The most remarkable finds from the shrine are fragments from one or more iron tripods and thousands of iron objects.[80]

The ceramic assemblages at both sanctuaries indicate that feasting, and especially the consumption of wine, was an important activity in both sanctuaries throughout the Geometric period. Numerous drinking cups and a few kraters are present at both sites, although only one krater has been retrieved from Mount Hymettos.[81] The evidence for feasting is most clearly expressed at Mount Parnes, where around 70 iron spits (*obeloi*) for the roasting of meat as well as cooking vessels have been found.[82] In addition, a large number of bones and around 3,000 knives are reported to have been excavated from the ash layer, and it is therefore almost certain that animal sacrifices were performed at the site.[83] The

74 Langdon 1976.
75 Young 1940, 3.
76 Langdon 1976, 75, table 1.
77 Cf. Langdon 1997, 120; Morgan 1990, 29.
78 Mastrokostas 1983; van den Eijnde 2010b; Palaiokrassa-Kopitsa & Vivliodetis 2015, see 155 n. 2 for an extensive bibliography.
79 Palaiokrassa-Kopitsa & Vivliodetis 2015, 157-8.
80 Steinhauer 2001, 95.
81 Langdon 1976, 62, cat. no. 250, pl. 21.
82 For the iron spits, see Fragkopoulou & Zosi 2017, 149.
83 Langdon, 1976, 101.

Fig. 7. Pyxis with granaries from the grave of the "Rich Athenian Lady" (© American School of Classical Studies at Athens: Agora Excavations).

reported traces of walls inside the cave might suggest a space that was specifically organized for feasts.[84]

On Mount Hymettos, the rectangular structure has a recessed platform, which both Alexandros Mazarakis Ainian and Floris van den Eijnde interpret as a bench for participants at feasts similar to those in the Oval House in the Athenian Agora and other buildings from settlements in Attica.[85] Hearths are usually associated with buildings with benches, but no clear evidence for a hearth was found on Mount Hymettos. Its existence might, however, be inferred from the 10-20 cm thick ash layer associated with the structure.[86]

Despite the differences in the find assemblages in the two sanctuaries, we can be almost certain that Zeus was worshipped in his capacity as a weather god at both places. Pausanias states that there was an altar to Zeus Ombrios at both sites (Paus. 1.32.2), and Aristotle (Arist. [*Ath. Pol.*] 16.5-6) relates the story of the tyrant Peisistratos who visited Mount Hymettos, where he conversed with a farmer who complained about the farm taxes. Pausanias also informs us that on Mount Parnes there was an altar to Zeus Semaleos (who gives weather signs)[87] and a statue of Zeus Parnessios, who according to Plutarch (*Mor.* 2.158E) was an important agricultural deity, and whose veneration can be traced in dedicatory inscriptions back into the Early Archaic period.[88] Furthermore, among the dedications at Mount

84 van den Eijnde 2010b, 120-1.

85 Mazarakis Ainian 1988, 117, n. 43 (but see also the comment by Langdon 1997, 121 n. 28); van den Eijnde 2010b, 122, with fig. 6.

86 Young 1940, 3.

87 Parker 1996, 30-2.

88 Palaiokrassa-Kopitsa & Vivliodetis 2015, 159 with n. 49.

Parnes there are numerous iron agricultural tools such as pickaxes and sickles, which show a clear concern for the fertility of the farmland.[89] It thus seems clear that these two sanctuaries primarily served as places for worshippers concerned with the fertility of Attica's farmland.

Farmland and the cultivation of grain played an important part in the subsistence economy of the ruling families in Iron Age Greece. In Homer's *Odyssey* there is ample evidence to show that chieftains, the so-called *polykleroi* (Hom. *Od.* 14.211), owned land estates and large areas of land described as "wheat-bearing ploughland" (Hom. *Od.* 9.577-80 and 20.184-5), which were managed by slaves or dependant landowners.[90] Hesiod specifically connects agriculture to Zeus and Demeter, instructing farmers to make offerings to Zeus before ploughing the fields (Hes. *Op.*, 465-7).

Tangible evidence for the importance of grain cultivation in Early Iron Age Attica comes in the form of terracotta models of granaries in rich female burials in Athens, most famously the pyxis with five granaries from the so-called "Tomb of the Rich Athenian Lady" dating to around 850 BC which was located c. 15 metres north of the Oval House in the Athenian Agora (Fig. 7).[91] Such model granaries are known from several Athenian graves from the Middle and Late Geometric periods and are often found in rich graves.[92] In this connection it is also worth mentioning that three granite querns for the grinding of flour were found both inside and outside the Oval House.[93]

I believe further archaeological evidence ties the Early Iron Age aristocracy even closer to grain cultivation. Another feasting hall has been identified at the site of Lathouriza in southwestern Attica, where a Late Geometric apsidal building (Unit II) is part of an integrated architectural complex consisting of four buildings (Units I-IV).[94] This building, which has been interpreted as a feasting hall, also has built-in benches, and outside the apsidal building is an open-air hearth. Connected to the feasting hall is a small round room (Unit III) that has been interpreted as a granary on the basis of its circular shape.[95] This situation is comparable to the three circular stone foundations for granaries known from the settlement of Xeropolis at Lefkandi, which were found right next to the remains of a contemporary oval house.[96]

The increasing amount of rural sites in the Attic landscape in the Late Geometric period might reflect a growing concern for the cultivation of grain in this period. Langdon has argued that grain was extremely important for the Early Iron Age Athenian community, and that the lack of archaeological finds from the Classical and Hellenistic periods in the Zeus sanctuary on Hymettos should be related to a general shift from grain to olive and wine cultivation in the Athenian territory and the increasing dependency on importation of grain.[97]

89 These are on display in the Archaeological Museum of Piraeus.

90 For an overview, see van Wees 1992, 53, 339 n. 88; Richter 1968. See also van Wees 2013.

91 Smithson 1968; Coldstream 1995; Liston & Papadopoulos 2004, but see also Morris & Papadopoulos 2004.

92 See Cherici 1989 for a list of known examples, although the author interprets them as beehives, which has been refuted by Morris & Papadopoulos 2004.

93 Burr 1933, 547, 549.

94 See Lauter 1985, 14-9. Mazarakis-Ainian 1995.

95 Lauter 1985, 25-6; Mazarakis Ainian 1995, 154; 1997, 238 and 275 with n. 30 for other examples of connections between rulers' complexes and granaries.

96 Popham & Sackett 1980, 8, 23-5, pls. 5-8. I am aware of the controversy regarding the interpretation of the three circular stone platforms and whether they are in fact granaries, but considering Guzzo's (2013) recent study of similar round structures in Sicily, I consider it almost certain that the structures in Xeropolis are in fact foundations for granaries. For a similar stone foundation, although dating to the Hellenistic period, see also Vikatou & Handberg forthcoming.

97 Langdon 1976, 87-95, esp. 92.

Fig. 8. Fragment from a Corinthian skyphos with an incised drawing of a tripod (after Langdon 1976, pl. 15, no. 167. Courtesy of the Trustees of the American School of Classical Studies at Athens).

Against this background, it should not surprise us that the two Zeus sanctuaries are among the earliest sites where ritual activity increases. The find of granary models in rich graves such as that of the "Rich Athenian Lady" and the Homeric reference to the elite ownership of the wheat-bearing fields would therefore naturally seem to connect the ruling families of Athens to the Zeus sanctuaries on Mount Hymettos and Parnes. Indeed, more evidence points in the same direction.

The evidence for feasting at the two sites puts them into an aristocratic context. As described above, feasting was an important venue for maintaining and negotiating social norms, and that this was important to the Athenian elite is illustrated by the Oval House and their likely participation in feasts in Eretria and Isthmia. The best evidence for this is found at Parnes with the *obeloi* for roasting meat. Such roasting spits testify to the importance of aristocratic feasts, as they are most often found in elite settings such as wealthy aristocratic graves.[98]

The presence of iron tripods and swords on Mount Parnes is another indicator of an aristocratic presence. The tripods should certainly be seen as private dedications, most likely made by members of the Athenian aristocracy, just as they had recently started dedicating tripods on the Acropolis.[99] No clear evidence for tripod dedications was recovered from Mount Hymettos, but an image of a tripod was incised on a Corinthian skyphos dating to the late 7th or early 6th century BC (Fig. 8), which might indicate that tripods were originally put up in the sanctuary.[100]

The numerous dedicatory and onomastic graffiti found on Mount Hymettos also carry with them aristocratic connotations. Although Athens and Attica seem to have been a special case, where a more "generalised social literacy"[101] developed through the Archaic period, inscriptions on pots are rare in the Late Geometric and Early Archaic periods, and most often found in aristocratic dining contexts. This has become even clearer from the recent discoveries of the many examples of early writing on drinking sets found at Methone.[102] In this regard, it is perhaps significant that two inscribed sherds were found among the debris associated with the Oval House.[103]

Conclusion

In this chapter, I have argued that we may trace a series of guest-friendship networks of Athenian aristocrats far beyond the borders of Attica in the

98 For a list of contexts with *obeloi*, see Mazarakis Ainian 1988, 118 n. 48.

99 For the argument that the tripods in Olympia were private dedications, see Morgan 1990, 43-7. For the opinion that the only tripod found in an Early Iron Age dwelling at Karphi was the private possession of the owner, see Mazarakis Ainian 1997, 274-5.

100 Langdon 1976, 39, cat. no. 167, 40, fig. 17, pl. 15.

101 Stoddart & Whitley 1988, 771.

102 Besios *et al.* 2012; Clay *et al.* 2017.

103 *Agora* XXI.

Middle Geometric period. In particular, I have addressed the evidence from Eretria and Isthmia, but as briefly mentioned there is evidence that these networks stretched much further to Crete, the eastern Mediterranean, and the Near East. The two cases of Eretria and Isthmia can be distinguished from other examples, because they are habitation and religious contexts whereas other examples originate from funerary contexts. Nevertheless, it seems clear that the networks, or the archaeologically visible traces of the networks, should be inscribed within a framework of aristocratic commensal dining. In the Middle Geometric period then, Athenian aristocrats seemed to travel more to interact with their social peers than for purely religious purposes.

In the Late Geometric period, the practice of marking graves with monumental kraters diminishes,[104] and the export of large Athenian kraters ceases altogether, as far as we can judge from the available evidence. Here we seem to lose track of the postulated aristocratic networks. The disappearance of the long-distance networks is perhaps corroborated by the contraction of the export of Attic pottery, the distribution of which in the Late Geometric period is mostly confined to Attica.[105]

Ian Morris has identified a shift in the area of aristocratic status display from the funerary sphere to the sanctuaries during the Late Geometric period.[106] This shift coincides with the establishment of the cult on the Acropolis in Athens, the intensification of religious activity in sanctuaries in the countryside, and the disappearance of monumental kraters used as grave markers in Athens. This also coincides with the end of the use of the Oval House, where a shrine seems to have been established at the end of the 8th or beginning of the 7th century BC. The old ideal of feasting was, however, still upheld, but elaborate communal dining was now transferred to the sanctuaries rather than the ruler's habitation complex, as exemplified by the two Zeus sanctuaries discussed in this chapter.

Among the evidence that is available from Mount Parnes, there is also that which shows that the sanctuary served as a meeting place for rulers from various regions. Protocorinthian and Euboean pottery and a graffito in the Boiotian dialect suggest that this was an interregional meeting place, perhaps similar to Isthmia and Olympia. Pausanias mentions that in his time boars and bears were still roaming the mountainous region of Parnes (Paus. 1.32.2), which might have been suitable for hunting parties comprising members of ruling houses from adjacent regions. I take this Zeus sanctuary to be a good example of how the aristocracy in Athens transferred aristocratic feasts to the sanctuary arena, which in this case might also explain the disappearance of established social networks. Instead, rulers now dined in the sanctuaries.

The "impoverished" character of the Zeus sanctuary on Mount Hymettos might be explained by the fact that it was closer to Athens and not a natural nodal point in the landscape between various regions. However, the aristocrats still travelled there to venerate Zeus out of concern for their agricultural produce, as well as because it provided a local arena for communal dining. But there was less need for the Athenian aristocrats to display their elite status, which they did to a higher degree on the Acropolis.

The commanding locations at both sanctuaries at the top of the two mountain ranges provided a panoramic view across the Athenian pedion to the Saronic Gulf, which in effect encompasses the entire territorial domain of the local Athenian rulers. The sanctuaries seem to have been strategically located to provide an overview of the full agricultural potential of land held by the rulers, thereby reinforcing the importance of agricultural land and the wealth of the ruling aristocracy.

Following the approach presented at the beginning of the chapter, the archaeological material from

104 Morris 1987, 151-2.
105 Morgan 1992, 87; Coldstream 1983.
106 Morris 1997.

the two Zeus sanctuaries provide "a material record of monuments and offerings that indicate episodic gatherings to commemorate earlier socially-constituting rites",[107] in this case the aristocratic banquet. As such, the transference of the feasting ritual to the sanctuaries exemplifies the aristocrats' wish to maintain a social *status quo* and to regulate power relations between participating groups, which became a hallmark of later polis-theōria and religious gatherings in the Greek world.[108]

The scenario I have presented here provides us with one possible way of understanding the beginning of sacred travels in Athens and Attica. Within this framework, sacred travel in ancient Athens seems to originate from, or at least be tightly connected with, pre-existing social norms and not purely religious concerns. In the future, I hope this aspect of sacred travel will be more critically examined by others, especially in regard to the implications the scenarios outlined here might have for our understanding of later "canonical" pilgrimages to such places as Brauron, Eleusis, and Delphi,[109] and it might help to explain the historical background of the hereditary priesthood of aristocratic families such as, for instance, the Eumolpidae in Eleusis.

Abbreviations

Agora XXI = Lang, M.L. 1976. *Graffiti and Dipinti*, vol. 21 of *The Athenian Agora: Results of Excavations Conducted by the American School of Classical Studies at Athens,* Princeton, NJ.

Isthmia VIII = Morgan, C. 1999. *The Late Bronze Age Settlement and Early Iron Age Sanctuary*, vol. 8 of *Isthmia*, Princeton, NJ.

Kerameikos XIII = Bohen, B. 1988. *Die geometrischen Pyxiden*, vol. 13 of *Kerameikos: Ergebnisse der Ausgrabungen*, Berlin.

107 McCorriston 2017, 13.

108 The Panionia sanctuary on the Mykale peninsula provides a good example of the importance of such sanctuaries in the maintenance of social cohesion of groups and the social order, see Kowalzig 2005, 45-56.

109 See the contributions by Clinton, Angelidis, and Pirisino in this volume.

Bibliography

BESIOS, M., G.Z. TZIFOPOULOS & A. KOTSONAS 2012
Μεθώνη Πιερίας: Επιγραφές, Χαράγματα και Εμπορικά Σύμβολα στη Γεωμετρική και Αρχαϊκή Κεραμική από το Υπόγειο της Μεθώνης Πιερίας στη Μακεδονία, Thessaloniki.

BLANDIN, B. 2007
Les pratiques funéraires d'époque géométrique à Érétrie. Espace des vivants, demeures des morts II, vol. 17 of *Eretria: Fouilles et recherches*, Athens.

BURR, D. 1933
'A Geometric House and a Proto-Attic Votive Deposit', *Hesperia* 2, 542-640.

BUCHHOLZ H.-G. 1987
'Rasseln und Schellen, Reifen, Wippen und Schaukeln', in *Sport und Spiel* (Archaeologia Homerica T), S. Laser (ed.), Göttingen, 100-16, 126-84.

CHERICI, A. 1989
'Granai o Arnie? Considerazioni su una classe fitile Attica tra IX e VIII sec A.C.', *Atti dell'Accademia nazionale dei Lincei: Rendiconti Morali* XLIV, fasc. 7-12, 215-30.

CHRISTOPHILOPOULOU, A. 2007
'Domestic Space in the Geometric Cyclades – a Study of Spatial Arrangements, Function and Household

Activities in Zagora on Andros and Kastro on Siphnos', *Proceedings of the Danish Institute at Athens* 5, 23-33.

CLAY, J.S., I. MALKIN & Y.Z. TZIFOPOULOS (EDS.) 2017
Panhellenes at Methone: Graphê in Late Geometric and Protoarchaic Methone (Trends in Classics – Supplementary Volumes 44), Berlin and Boston.

COLDSTREAM, J.N. 1983
'The Meaning of the Regional Styles in the Eighth Century B.C.', in *The Greek Renaissance of the Eight Century B.C.: Tradition and Innovation. Proceedings of the Second International Symposium at the Swedish Institute at Athens, 1-5 June 1981* (Acta Instituti Atheniensis Regni Sueciae 30), R. Hägg (ed.), Stockholm, 17-25.

COLDSTREAM, J.N. 1989
'Early Greek Visitors to Cyprus and the Eastern Mediterranean,' in *Cyprus and the East Mediterranean in the Iron Age* (Proceedings of the 7th British Museum Classical Colloquium), V. Tratton-Brown (ed.), London, 90-6.

COLDSTREAM, J.N. 1995
'The Rich Lady of the Areiopagos and Her Contemporaries. A Tribute in Memory of Evelyn Lord Smithson', *Hesperia* 64.4, 391-403.

COLDSTREAM, J.N. 1996
'Knossos and Lefkandi: The Attic Connections', in *Minotaur and Centaur. Studies in the Archaeology of Crete and Euboea Presented to Mervyn Popham*, (BAR International Series 638), R.D.G. Evely, I.S. Lemos, S. Sherratt & M.R. Popham (eds.), 133-45.

COLDSTREAM, J.N. 2003
Geometric Greece (2nd ed.), London.

COLDSTREAM, J.N. 2011
'Geometric Elephantiasis', in *The "Dark Ages" Revisited. Acts of an International Symposium of William D.E. Coulson. University of Thessaly, Volos 14-17 June 2007*, A. Mazarakis Ainian (ed.), 801-7.

COOK, J.M. 1946
'A Geometric Graveside Scene', *BCH* 70, 97-101.

CRIELAARD J.P. 1999
'Early Iron Age Greek Pottery in Cyprus and North Syria: A Consumption-Oriented Approach' in *The Complex Past of Pottery. Production, Circulation and Consumption of Mycenaean and Greek Pottery (Sixteenth to Early Fifth Centuries BC). Proceedings of the ARCHON International Conference Held in Amsterdam, 8-9 November 1996*, J. P. Crielaard, V. Stissi & G.J.V. Winjngaarden, Amsterdam, 261-90.

CRIELAARD, J.P. 2007
'Eretria's West Cemetery Revisited: Burial Plots, Social Structure and Settlement Organization during the 8th and 7th Centuries BC', in *Oropos and Euboea in the Early Iron Age: Acts of an International Round Table, University of Thessaly, June 18-20, 2004*, A. Mazarakis Ainian (ed.), Volos, 169-94.

DESCŒUDRES, J.-P. 2006-2007
'Euboean Pottery Overseas (10th to 7th Centuries BC)', *Mediterranean Archaeology* 19/20, 3-24.

DESCŒUDRES, J.-P. 2008
'Central Greece on the Eve of the Colonisation Movement', in *Greek Colonisation. An Account of Greek Colonies and Other Settlements Overseas 2.* (Mnemosyne Bibliotheca Classical Batava), G.R. Tsetskhladze (ed.), Leiden-Boston, 289-382.

DONNELLAN, L. 2017
'The "Euboean" Koine: Reassessing Patterns of Cross-Cultural Interaction and Exchange in the North-Western Aegean Region,' in *Material Koinai in the*

Greek Early Iron Age and Archaic Period. Acts of and International Conference at the Danish Institute at Athens, 30 January – 1 February 2015 (Monographs of the Danish Institute at Athens 22), S. Handberg & A. Gadolou, Aarhus, 43-63.

ELSNER, J. 2017
'Excavating Pilgrimage', in *Excavating Pilgrimage: Archaeological Approaches to Sacred Travel and Movement in the Ancient World*, T.M. Kristensen & W. Friese (eds.), Abingdon and New York, 265-74.

ELSNER, J. & I. RUTHERFORD 2005A (EDS.)
Pilgrimage in Graeco-Roman and Early Christian Antiquity. Seeing the Gods, Oxford.

ELSNER, J. & I. RUTHERFORD 2005B
'Introduction', in *Pilgrimage in Graeco-Roman and Early Christian Antiquity. Seeing the Gods*, J. Elsner & I. Rutherford (eds.), Oxford, 1-38.

FRAGKOPOULOU, F. & E. ZOSI 2017
'Material Koine and the Case of the Phaleron Cups: Conventions and Realities', in *Material Koinai in the Greek Early Iron Age and Archaic Period. Acts of and International Conference at the Danish Institute at Athens, 30 January – 1 February 2015* (Monographs of the Danish Institute at Athens 22), S. Handberg & A. Gadolou, Aarhus, 133-65.

GAUSS, W. & F. RUPPENSTEIN 1998
'Die Athener Akropolis in der frühen Eisenzeit' *AM* 113, 1-60.

GIMATZIDIS, S. 2011
'Feasting and Offering to the Gods in Early Greek Sanctuaries: Monumentalisation and Miniaturisation in pottery', *Pallas* 86, 75-96.

GLOWACKI, K. 1998
'The Acropolis of Athens before 566 B.C.' in *STEPHANOS: Papers in Honor of Brunilde Sismondo Ridgway* (University Museum Monograph 100), K. Hartswick & M. Sturgeon (eds.), Philadelphia, 79-88.

GRAEF, B. 1893
'Allgemeine Ergebnisse der Vasenfunde von der Akropolis zu Athen', *AA* 1893, 13-9.

GRAEF, B. & E. LANGLOTZ 1925
Die Antiken Vasen von der Akropolis zu Athen, Berlin.

GUZZO, P.G. 2013
'Caronda e coloro che si nutrono dallo stesso granaio. Ipotesi sulle strutture circolari di Megara Hyblea, Selinunte e Himera', *RM* 119, 33-42.

HAENTJENS, A.M.E. 2002
'Ritual Shoes in Early Greek Female Graves', *AntCl* 71, 171-84.

HURWIT, J.M. 1999
The Athenian Acropolis: History, Mythology, and Archaeology from the Neolithic Era to the Present, Cambridge.

KENZELMANN PFYFFER, A.K., T. THEURILLAT & S. VERDAN 2005
'Graffiti d'époque géométrique provenant du sanctuaire d'Apollon Daphnéphoros à Erétrie', *ZPE* 151, 51-83.

KILIAN-DIRLMEIER, I. 1985
'Fremde Weihungen in griechischen Heiligtümer vom 8. bis zum Beginn des 7. Jahrhunderts v. Chr.', *JRGZM* 32, 215-54.

KOTSONAS, A. 2009
'Central Greece and Crete in the Early Iron Age', in *Archaiologiko ergo Thessalias kai stereas Helladas 2, 2006: praktika epistemonikes synanteses*, A. Mazarakis Ainian (ed.), Volos, 1051-65.

KOWALZIG, B. 2005
'Mapping out *Communitas*: Performances of *Theōria* in their Sacred and Political Context', in *Pilgrimage in Graeco-Roman and Early Christian Antiquity. Seeing the Gods*, J. Elsner & I. Rutherford (eds.), Oxford, 41-72.

KRISTENSEN, T.M. & W. FRIESE 2017A (EDS.)
Excavating Pilgrimage: Archaeological Approaches to Sacred Travel and Movement in the Ancient World, Abingdon and New York.

KRISTENSEN, T.M. & W. FRIESE 2017B
'Introduction. Archaeologies of Pilgrimage', in *Excavating Pilgrimage: Archaeological Approaches to Sacred Travel and Movement in the Ancient World*, T.M. Kristensen & W. Friese (eds.), Abingdon and New York, 1-10.

LANGDON, M.K. 1976
A Sanctuary of Zeus on Mount Hymettos (Hesperia Supplements 16), Princeton, New Jersey.

LANGDON, M. 1997
'Cult in Iron Age Attica', in *New Light on a Dark Age. Exploring the Culture of Geometric Greece*, S. Langdon (ed.), Columbia, MS, 113-24.

LAUGHY, M.H. 2010
'Ritual and Authority in Early Athens', PhD diss., University of California, Berkeley.

LAUTER, H. 1985
Lathuresa. Beiträge zur Architectur und Siedlungsgeschichte in Spätgeometrischer Zeit (Attische Forschungen II), Mainz am Rhein.

LISTON, M.A. & J.K. PAPADOPOULOS 2004
'The "Rich Athenian Lady" Was Pregnant: The Anthropology of a Geometric Tomb Reconsidered', *AJA* 73.1, 7-39.

LUKE, J. 1994
'The Krater, 'Kratos,' and the 'Polis'', *Greece & Rome* 41.1, 23-32.

MASTROKOSTAS, E. 1983
'Αλάβαστρα του 700 π.Χ. εκ της ανασκαφής του βωμού του Διός επί της κορυφής της Πάρνηθος', *ASAtene* NS 45, 339-345.

MAZARAKIS AINIAN, A.J. 1988
'Early Greek Temples: Their Origin and Function', in *Early Greek Cult Practice. Proceedings of the Fifth International Symposium at the Swedish Institute at Athens, 26-29 June, 1986*, R. Hägg, N. Marinatos & G. C. Nordquist (eds.), Stockholm, 105-19.

MAZARAKIS AINIAN, A. 1987
'Geometric Eretria', *Antike Kunst* 30.1, 3-24.

MAZARAKIS AINIAN, A. 1995
'New Evidence for the Study of the Late Geometric-Archaic Settlement at Lathouriza in Attica', *Bulletin of the Institute of Classical Studies. Supplement, no. 63. Klados: Essays in Honour of J.N. Coldstream*, J.N. Coldstream & C. Morris (eds.), 143-55.

MAZARAKIS AINIAN, A. 1997
From Rulers' Dwellings to Temples. Architecture, Religion and Society in Early Greece (1100-700 B.C.) (Studies in Mediterranean Archaeology CXXI), Jonsered.

MAZARAKIS AINIAN, A. 2007
'Architecture and Social Structure in Early Iron Age Greece', in *Building Communities: House, Settlement and Society in the Aegean and Beyond: Proceedings of a Conference held at Cardiff University, 17-21 April 2001*, (British School at Athens Studies 15), R. Westgate, N.R.E Fisher & J. Whitley (eds.), London, 157-68.

MCCORRISTON, J. 2011
Pilgrimage and Household in the Ancient Near East, Cambridge.

MCCORRISTON, J. 2017
'Inter-Cultural Pilgrimage, Identity, and the Axial Age in the Ancient Near East', in *Excavating Pilgrimage: Archaeological Approaches to Sacred Travel and Movement in the Ancient World*, T.M. Kristensen & W. Friese (eds.), Abingdon and New York, 12-23.

MERSCH, A. 1997
'Urbanization of the Attic Countryside from the Late 8th Century to the 6th Century BC', in *Urbanization in the Mediterranean in the 9th to 6th Centuries BC* (Acta Hyperborea 7), H. Damgaard Andersen, H.W. Horsnæs, S. Houby-Nielsen & A. Rathje (eds.), Copenhagen, 45-62.

MIKRAKIS, M. 2015
'Pots, Early Iron Age Athenian Society and the Near East: The Evidence of the Rattle Group', in *Pots, Workshops and Early Iron Age Society. Function and Role of Ceramics in Early Greece*, (Études d'Archéologie 8), V. Vlachou (ed.), Bruxelles, 277-99.

MORGAN, C. 1992
Athletes and Oracles. The Transformation of Olympia and Delphi in the Eighth Century BC (2nd ed.), Cambridge.

MORGAN, C. 1994
'The Evolution of a Sacred "Landscape": Isthmia, Perachora, and the Early Corinthian State', in *Placing the Gods. Sanctuaries and Sacred Space in Ancient Greece*, S.E. Alcock & R. Osborne (eds.), Oxford, 105-42.

MORRIS, I. 1987
Burial and Ancient Society. The Rise of the Greek City-State, Cambridge.

MORRIS, I. 1997
'The Art of Citizenship', in *New Light on a Dark Age. Exploring the Culture of Geometric Greece*, S. Langdon (ed.), Columbia, MS, 9-43.

MORRIS, S. & J.K. PAPADOPOULOS 2004
'Of Granaries and Games: Egyptian Stowaways in an Athenian Chest', in *ΧΑΡΙΣ: Essays in Honor of Sarah A. Immerwahr* (Hesperia Supplements 33), A.P. Chapin (ed.), Athens, 225-42.

MOST, G.W. 2006
Hesiod. Theogony. Works and Days. Testimonia (Loeb Classical Library 57), Cambridge.

MURRAY, A. T. 1995
Homer, Odyssey (Loeb Classical Library 105) (revised by George E. Dimock), Cambridge.

PALAIOKRASSA-KOPITSA, L. & E. VIVLIODETIS 2015
'The Sanctuaries of Artemis Mounichia and Zeus Parnessios. Their Relation to the Religious and Social Life in the Athenian City-State until the End of the 7th Century B.C.', in *Pots, Workshops and Early Iron Age Society Function and Role of Ceramics in Early Greece. Proceedings of the International Symposium Held at the Université libre de Bruxelles 14-16 November 2013*, V. Vlachou (ed.), Brussels, 155-80.

PAPADOPOULOS, J.K. 1997
'Phantom Euboians', *JMA* 10.2, 191-219.

PAPADOPOULOS, J.K. 2011
'"Phantom Euboians" – A Decade On', in *Euboea and Athens. Proceedings of a Colloquium in Memory of Malcolm B. Wallace, Athens 26-27 June 2009* (Publications of the Canadian Institute in Greece, no. 6), D.W. Rupp & J.E. Tomlinson (eds.), 113-33.

PAPADOPOULOS, J.K. 2015
'Owls to Athens: Imported Pottery in Early Iron Age Athens', in *Pots, Workshops and Early Iron Age Society Function and Role of Ceramics in Early Greece. Proceedings of the International Symposium Held at the Université libre de Bruxelles 14-16 November 2013*, V. Vlachou (ed.), Brussels, 201-15.

PARKER, R. 1996
Athenian religion: a history, Oxford.

POLIGNAC, F. DE 1995
Cults, Territory, and the Origins of the Greek City-State. Chicago and London.

POPHAM, M.R. & L.H. SACKETT 1980 (EDS.)
Lefkandi I. The Iron Age. The Settlement, London.

PRATT, C.E. 2015
'The "SOS" Amphora: An Update', *BSA* 110.1, 213-45.

RICHTER, W. 1968
Die Landwirtschaft im homerischen Zeitalter (Archaeologia Homerica H), Göttingen.

RUTHERFORD, I. 2013
State Pilgrims and Sacred Observers in Ancient Greece. A Study of Theōriā and Theōroi, Cambridge.

SCHOLL, A. 2006
'Αναθήματα των Αρχαίων. Die Akropolisvotive aus dem 8. bis frühen 6. Jhs. v. Chr.', *JdI* 121, 1-173.

SMITHSON, E.L. 1968
'The Tomb of a Rich Athenian Lady, ca. 850 B.C.', *Hesperia* 37, 77-116.

SNODGRASS, A.M. 1980
Archaic Greece: The Age of Experiment, Berkeley.

STEINHAUER, G. 2001
The Archaeological Museum of Piraeus, Athens.

STODDART, S. & J. WHITLEY 1988
'The Social Context of Literacy in Archaic Greece and Etruria', *Antiquity* 62 (237), 761-72.

TOULOUPA, E. 1972
'Bronzebleche von der Akropolis in Athen. Gehämmerte geometrische Dreifüsse', *AM* 87, 57-76.

VAN DEN EIJNDE, F. 2010A
'Cult and Society in Early Athens. Archaeological and Anthropological Approaches to State Formation and Group Participation in Attica 1000-600 BCE', PhD diss., Amsterdam.

VAN DEN EIJNDE, F. 2010B
'The Forgotten Sanctuary of Zeus on Mount Parnes', *Talanta* 42-43 (2010-2011), 113-28.

VAN DEN EIJNDE, F. & M. LAUGHY 2015
'The Areopagos Ocal Building Reconsidered', in *Regional Stories Towards a New Perception of the Early Greek World, Acts of an International Symposium in honour of Professor Jan Bouzek, Volos 18-21 June 2015*, A. Mazarakis Ainian, A. Alexandridou & X. Charalambidou (eds.), Volos, 229-48.

VAN WEES, H. 1992
Status Warriors: War, Violence and Society in Homer and History, Amsterdam.

VAN WEES, H. 1995
'Princes at Dinner: Social Event and Social Structure in Homer', in *Homeric Questions: Essays in Philology, Ancient History, and Archaeology, Including the Papers of a Conference Organized by the Netherlands Institute at Athens (15 May 1993)*, J.P. Crielaard (ed.), Amsterdam, 147-82.

VAN WEES, H. 2013
'Farmers and Hoplites: Models of Historical Development', in *Men of Bronze. Hoplite Warfare in Ancient Greece*, D. Kagan & G.F. Viggiano (eds.), Princeton and Oxford, 222-54.

VERDAN S. 2013
Le Sanctuaire d'Apollon Daphnéphoros à l'Époque Géométrique, vol. 12 of *Eretria: Fouilles et Recherches*, Athens.

VERDAN, S. 2015
'Geometric Eretria: Some Thoughts on Old Data', in *Mediterranean Archaeology 25, Zagora in Context: Settlements and Intercommunal Links in the Geometric Period (900-700 BC). Proceedings of the Conference Held by The Australian Archaeological Institute at Athens and The Archaeological Society at Athens*, J.-P. Descœudres (ed.), Athens, 181-9.

VERDAN, S., A.K. PFYFFER & C. LÉDERRY 2008
Céramique Géométrique D'Érétrie, vol. 20 of *Eretria: Fouilles et Recherches*, Athens.

VIKATOU & HANDBERG FORTHCOMING
'Excavations on the Lower Acropolis Plateau in Kalydon', in *2ο Διεθνές Αρχαιολογικό και Ιστορικό Συνέδριο "Το Αρχαιολογικό Έργο στην Αιτωλοακαρνανία και στη Λευκάδα από τους προϊστορικούς έως τους ρωμαϊκούς χρόνους"*.

WEBER, M. 1974
'Zur frühattischen Gerätfiguren', *AM* 89, 27-46.

WĘCOWSKI, M. 2014
The Rise of the Greek Aristocratic Banquet, Oxford.

WĘCOWSKI, M. 2017
'Wine and the Early History of the Greek Alphabet. Early Greek Vase-Inscriptions and the Symposion', in *Panhellenes at Methone: Graphê in Late Geometric and Protoarchaic Methone*, (Trends in Classics – Supplementary Volumes 44), J.S. Clay, I. Malkin & Y.Z. Tzifopoulos (eds.), Berlin and Boston, 309-358.

WĘCOWSKI, M. 2017
'The "Middle-Geometric Attic Koine" and the Rise of the Aristocratic Symposion', in *Material Koinai in the Greek Early Iron Age and Archaic Period. Acts of and International Conference at the Danish Institute at Athens, 30 January – 1 February 2015* (Monographs of the Danish Institute at Athens 22), S. Handberg & A. Gadolou, Aarhus, 315-22.

YOUNG, R.S. 1940
'Excavations on Mount Hymettos, 1939', *AJA* 44.1, 1-9.

YOUNG, R.S. 1949
'An Early Geometric Grave Near the Athenian Agora', *Hesperia* 18.4, 275-97.

YOUNG, R. & J. ANGEL 1939
Late Geometric Graves and a Seventh Century Well in the Agora. (Hesperia Supplements 2).

ZIMMERMANN J.-L. 1989
Les Chevaux de bronze dans l'art géométrique grec, Mainz and Geneva.

“To the Mountain”: The Ritual Space of Maenadism in the Athenian Imaginary

Ariadne Konstantinou

This article focuses on one of the rituals associated with maenads in ancient Greece, during which the female participants left their homes and the polis to worship the god Dionysus in the mountains in a ceremony that was sometimes called *oreibasia*, literally “mountain climbing.”[1] In recent years, historians of religion and archaeologists have become increasingly aware that the movement of participants towards and within ritual spaces played an important role in their experience.[2] The path towards the sanctuary, the arrangement and orientation of the temple, the altar or other buildings, and how these dictated particular way(s) or perspectives to the worshipers are all factors that are currently being considered in more detail. The study of the ways in which worshipers might have interacted with ritual space will hopefully contribute to a better understanding of their overall experience.

However, scholars are not always fortunate enough to have archaeological finds at their disposal that could aid in reconstructing this experience, since some rituals were not conducted within sanctuaries and have not left behind any identifiable material traces. The early ritual at the mountain is one such ritual. The mountain as the locus of maenadic ritual was an ephemeral ritual space, transformed impromptu every time the participants performed the ritual. It was a rather shifting and permeable space. There are, therefore, no material remains that might attest to its specific location or to the actual rituals that took place. Just as Janett E. Morgan argues regarding domestic rituals in ancient Greece, the boundaries of ritual space in non-monumental sanctuaries seem to be rather blurry.[3] Because of its temporary nature, I speculate that we are unlikely to find “hard” archaeological evidence for ritual maenadism in the Classical period: there appear to be no remains of monumental architecture and, as far as we know, no inscriptions to mark the location or commemorate the gathering.[4]

In addition to the lack of archaeological or architectural evidence for maenadism, the nature of the extant sources is also somewhat challenging, especially for the earlier period on which this article focuses. Two main sources from the 5th century

1 Some representative and influential contributions on Dionysus, maenadism, and Euripides’ *Bacchae* include Dodds 1951, 270-82; 1960; Henrichs 1982; 1984a; 1984b; and 1990; Seaford 1996; 2006; Vernant 1988; Detienne 1989; Versnel 1990; Segal 1997.

2 See the concise discussion in Elsner 2012 and Kristensen & Friese 2017.

3 Morgan 2007.

4 An additional point, perhaps less relevant in the context of this article, concerns the gender of the participants. While the majority of scholars assume that maenadic rituals were female-only, as in Henrichs 1984b, some scholars have recently argued to the contrary, reassessing the extant evidence for male participants. On males mentioned in post-Classical inscriptions see Jaccottet 2003, 1:94-100; Scullion 2013 also argues for male participants based on earlier sources, namely from Euripides.

BC are preserved. One is pottery that depicts scenes with maenads, however problematic the terminology and identification.[5] The second is Euripides' *Bacchae* from the end of the century (c. 406 BC). Generations of scholars have studied both sources and there is a consensus that neither of them reflects a faithful representation of the ritual. Vase paintings are not realistic photographs of antiquity. They have their own language and system of signification.[6] Likewise, the *Bacchae* is, first and foremost, a tragedy of a dramatized myth, and Albert Henrichs is right to consider that we are unlikely to untangle "the intricate web of maenadic myth and cult" that the play presents.[7]

Still, vase paintings and the *Bacchae* should not be discarded altogether, if only because they are the only significant sources we are ever likely to possess from this time period. Even if what they can tell us about the realia of maenadism is rather blurry, we can resort to them in order to consider how an Attic poet or painter might have imagined this ritual space or their assumptions about it. We know from post-Classical sources, namely Pausanias (Paus. 10.4.3), that women from Attica called the Thyiades travelled to Delphi in order to take part in a ritual at Mount Parnassus together with local women.[8] However, it is impossible to determine how far back in time we can take this ritual, or whether rituals of this kind were also performed in Attica.[9] While Pausanias himself seems to think that it is old,[10] scholars have been debating whether maenadic rituals, including the one at the mountain, may be shown to have taken place in Attica during the Classical period.[11] Rather than reiterate the controversy over whether the early sources present aspects of myth or ritual, I propose to proceed with the premise that the literary and pictorial sources on early maenadism form part of the Athenian imaginary; they belong to the realm of representations. After all, the mountain is a noted locus of reversals in the Greek imaginary and maenads are frequently related to the space of the mountain in both early and late textual sources.[12] This imaginary is Athenian in the sense that Attic painters created the vase paintings, regardless of their intended market, about which there is often limited knowledge. Also, Euripides is an Athenian playwright probably writing this play for an Athenian audience, although of course the drama unfolds

5 On maenads in art, see Moraw 1998; Villanueva-Puig 2009; and the shorter essays in Edwards 1960; McNally 1978; Hedreen 1994; Kauskopf *et al.* 1997. On the "Lenaia" vases, see Frontisi-Ducroux 1986; Osborne 1997; Peirce 1998. There is no uniformity among scholars on terminology, nor was there in antiquity. Vernant 1988, 405-6 discusses the interchangeability of *mainas* and *bacchē* in the *Bacchae*. Carpenter 1997, 52-3 uses the term "maenads" to designate mortal women, whereas he uses "nymphs" for the imaginary figures of divine or semi-divine status. At the same time, Peirce 1998 designates the women of the "Lenaia" vases as *bacchae*, while Villanueva-Puig 2009 speaks of "maenads." This article makes use of the term "maenad" throughout.

6 See Bérard *et al.* 1989, especially 23-38.

7 Henrichs 1978, 122.

8 It is also interesting to mention that the Thyiades together with Dionysus were shown in the west pediment of the 4th-century BC temple of Apollo at Delphi.

9 Villanueva-Puig 1986.

10 Villanueva-Puig 1986, 35.

11 See especially Osborne 1997 and Gould 2001.

12 On the mountain in Greek myth, see Buxton 1992. The earliest reference to maenads and the mountain is in *Hom. Hymn Dem.* 385-6, "ἡ δὲ ἰδοῦσα ἤϊξ' ἠΰτε μαινὰς ὄρος κάτα δάσκιον ὕλῃ", "when she saw she darted like a maenad down a mountain with thick-shaded forest". Richardson 1974 thinks that the simile does not refer to a "mad woman" (as in Hom. *Il.* 22.460) but to a maenad, and that the mountain forms part of the simile. See also Alcm. fr. 56 Page and Anac. fr. 357 Page. For a connection of maenads to mountains in post-Classical sources, see the Hellenistic inscription from Miletos in Henrichs 1978, 148 and Jaccottet 2003, 2:no. 149, the inscription from Physcos in Sokolowski 1969, no. 181 (2nd century CE), and Plut. *Mor.* 953d.

in Thebes.[13] In what follows, the question about the historicity of maenadic rites during the Classical period in Attica shall not be addressed further; it seems impossible to prove or disprove it, and thus it may be, in the end, the wrong question to ask.

My discussion on the ritual space of the mountain is based on the so-called "early" literary and visual sources from the 5th century BC. The first part describes the structuring of space in the *Bacchae*, staged during the last years of the 5th century BC. This is certainly not the first attempt to analyse the construing of space in the *Bacchae*, one of the most important and famous sources on maenadism.[14] The second part of the article moves back in time to the first third of the 5th century BC and to a different artistic medium. It is devoted to a rather small group of red-figure cup paintings from the Late Archaic period. Unlike the tendency of Greek vase painters to focus on human figures and disregard the landscape, it seems that the artists who decorated these vases might have been making a rare attempt to represent the space of the mountain. The mountain as a ritual space is hence represented in both textual and pictorial sources from the 5th century BC. Just as the study of archaeological space has proven informative in tracing the worshipers' experience in a sanctuary, studying the representation of this mountain space can also shed some light on the ritual experience of maenads in the Athenian imaginary. The material is presented in a counter-chronological order, beginning with the text and then turning to the vases. It also moves from the more familiar to the less, in the sense that these specific vases have served as sources for the study of landscape depiction in ancient pottery rather than as sources for maenadism.

Before proceeding to the two corpora, a note on this ritual experience of maenads under discussion is in order. At some point during the ritual, the maenads became ecstatic. Ritual ecstasy has had its own history in Greco-Roman antiquity and in modern scholarship, from hypotheses of mass hysteria or trance to more serene pictures of an inspired possession.[15] This article assumes, following Jan N. Bremmer, that the ecstatic dance and *mania* of maenads involved some form of "altered state of consciousness".[16] This altered state also entails a change in the sensory perception of space on the part of the participants. The *Bacchae* portrays how Dionysiac ecstasy may have affected perception, as in Pentheus' hallucinatory vision of two suns and two cities (Eur. *Bacch.* 918-9) or in Agave's delirious misconception of having hunted down a lion's cub while holding her dead son's head (Eur. *Bacch.* 1169-262).[17] As Richard Seaford notes, "Dionysiac ecstasy extends itself to animate and inanimate nature. This is based on the reality that ecstatic movement may alter perception."[18]

Blurred Spaces in Euripides' *Bacchae*

The *Bacchae* depicts a variety of spaces through which the different characters move. The spatial polarities between inside/outside, *oikos*/polis, and polis/mountain have been thoroughly discussed in previous literature and are often related to the ambiguous and "other" nature of Dionysus himself. The stage displays the city of Thebes outside the palace, as Dionysus proclaims at the opening of the play: "I, the son of Zeus, have come to this Theban land"

13 On this point, see Henrichs 1990, 257. On Thebes as a kind of anti-Athens in tragedy, see Zeitlin 1990.

14 Segal 1997; Rehm 2002, 205-12.

15 Osborne 1997, 187-90; Seaford 2006, 105-10; Ustinova 2017.

16 Bremmer 1984, 281. On altered states of consciousness in antiquity, see Ustinova 2009, 13-28; 2017.

17 Devereux 1970.

18 Seaford 1996, 208. See also Dodds 1960, 166, mentioning additional passages in which the "inanimate nature shares in the Dionysiac ecstasy".

(Eur. *Bacch.* 1).[19] Narrations of events that take place elsewhere are reported on stage, as is customary in tragedy; the two messenger speeches are particularly relevant in this respect, since they report the happenings on the mountain (Eur. *Bacch.* 677-774, 1043-152). Overall, the space of the polis is opposed to the space of the mountain. Mount Cithaeron, where the Theban maenads have gone, is outside the city limits and represents "nature" as opposed to the "culture" of the polis.

Furthermore, the characters in the play move through the various spaces in different directions. Dionysus and his escort of Lydian maenads have come from Lydia in the east to Thebes (Eur. *Bacch.* 64-7), and will continue together so that the god may manifest himself in other Greek cities as well (Eur. *Bacch.* 47-50). The punishment inflicted upon the Theban maenads and the daughters of Cadmus for having denied the new god entails moving away from their hearths and looms, leaving the city of Thebes, and being compelled to go "to the mountain".[20] The two messengers enter the city (and the stage) to report what has happened on the mountain. Teiresias and Cadmus, as well as Dionysus and Pentheus, also leave the city, the latter with tragic consequences.[21]

While there is no denying that the Theban homes and city are opposed to the mountain as the space of maenadic *mania*, it is equally interesting to notice that spaces do not remain stable in the course of the play. Instead, they constitute fluid entities that are gradually blurred. As Rush Rehm has noted, "far from a set of spatial oppositions, the play seems to assume the interpenetration of foreign and Theban, of Asian and Greek, suggesting a spatial scheme far broader and more flexible than that of structural polarities or of dyads 'conjoined'".[22] It is possible to take this argument about the flexibility of these famous spatial polarities one step further and relate it to the religious experience of maenads.[23] The idea of a fluid spatial scheme in the play may also be regarded as a gradual transformation of the spaces themselves. Just as the maenads dance and move about in ecstasy, so does their surrounding space, which gradually partakes in this change and motion, possibly reflecting how a ritual space filled with dancing maenads appears to an onlooker. At the same time, such a flux of space in movement may have been part of the maenads' own experience, implying their own blurred sensory perception of space during the ritual. Thus, the general blurring of spaces in the *Bacchae* may be related to Dionysiac ecstasy as well as to the power of Dionysus, if indeed Euripides did have an opportunity to witness this or similar ecstatic rituals, perhaps in Macedonia.

The most notable description of a blurred space takes place during the so-called "miracle" of the palace. While several points of the text and its staging remain unclear,[24] the Lydian maenads proclaim that "soon the house of Pentheus will be shaken to pieces and fall" (Eur. *Bacch.* 586-8). They feel that the architrave is ready to fall (Eur. *Bacch.* 591-2) and are under the impression that "the son of Zeus is coming towards this house, turning it topsy-turvy!" (Eur. *Bacch.* 602-3).[25] Indeed, "Dionysus is in the

19 All translations are my own.

20 The maenads move from the *domoi* (Eur. *Bacch.* 32-3), *domata* (Eur. *Bacch.* 217-20) or *ge* (Eur. *Bacch.* 665-6) of Thebes to the *oros* (Eur. *Bacch.* 32-3, 217-20) or *orgades* (Eur. *Bacch.* 445). Interestingly enough, the first part of the spatial opposition is twice substituted with weaving and the loom, as this was an important domestic female activity: Eur. *Bacch.* 114-19, 1235-7, and cf. 511-4.

21 On Dionysus and Pentheus, see Eur. *Bacch.* 1043-7. Cadmus and Teiresias presumably leave twice, the second time to fetch the corpse of Pentheus (Eur. *Bacch.* 1222-6).

22 Rehm 2002, 211.

23 I am, however, reluctant to go as far as Seaford 1996; 2006 and speak of a change of identity, since the relation of the *Bacchae* to mystic cults is far from certain.

24 On some interpretative attempts, see Castellani 1976 and Fisher 1992.

25 See also *Bacch.* 605-6, 622-3, 633.

house" (Eur. *Bacch.* 589).[26] Spatial boundaries are also blurred during the imprisonment of the Theban maenads. While Pentheus has caught and imprisoned some of them (Eur. *Bacch.* 226-7), it is reported later on that they have been miraculously released (Eur. *Bacch.* 443-50). This is also the case with the imprisonment and miraculous release of Dionysus himself (Eur. *Bacch.* 610-46). The Dionysiac blurring of spatial boundaries reaches the confines of the prison; these incidents may be related to the nature of Dionysus "Lysios", the liberating.[27] The description of the maenads' prison specifically refers to the ceiling or roof (*stegē*),[28] but the term may sometimes suggest any built enclosure. The roof as an architectural element is mentioned in other Dionysiac contexts as well, most famously in a fragment attributed to Aeschylus' *Edonoi* (fr. 58), ἐνθουσιᾶ δὴ δῶμα, βακχεύει στέγη, "Surely the house is in ecstasy, the roof is in Bacchic frenzy". There are additional examples from later sources on the alleged transformation of roofs in a Dionysiac context, such as those in the stories of the Minyads or the Gallic maenads.[29] At the opening of the *Bacchae*, the Theban and Cadmean maenads "sit on roofless (ἀνορόφους) rocks under the green fir trees" (Eur. *Bacch.* 38). While this adjective is virtually a hapax in Classical literature, it seems reasonable to interpret it in the context of maenadism, as signifying a Dionysiac blurring of spatial boundaries.[30]

In addition to the palace and prison, the Dionysiac blurring of spatial boundaries further permeates the whole city of Thebes as well as the mountain. In the prologue, Dionysus describes how all local women have left their houses in a state of *mania* and gone to Mount Cithaeron. This allows for the stage to be literally filled by the rather solemn chorus of Lydian maenads. According to Dionysus, moreover, there is an impression that the city itself has become a maenad:

> πρώτας δὲ Θήβας τάσδε γῆς Ἑλληνίδος
> ἀνωλόλυξα, νεβρίδ' ἐξάψας χροὸς
> θύρσον τε δοὺς ἐς χεῖρα, κίσσινον βέλος·
> And Thebes here was the first of Greek land that I excited with Bacchic cries, clothed it in fawnskin and put the thyrsus into its hand, the ivied missile (Eur. *Bacch.* 23-5).

Whereas Pentheus attempts to shun the new god, the polis of Thebes falls under his spell, and is imagined as wearing a *nebris* and holding a thyrsus – it is garbed in maenadic attire. Interestingly enough, Eric R. Dodds' and Richard Seaford's commentaries do not allude to personification in this context. Nor does it seem that they understand the reference to Thebes in this passage as a collective plural for its

26 This blurring of spatial boundaries in the palace may be compared to the one described in Eur. *HF*. After Heracles, in his madness, murders his sons and wife inside his palace, the palace itself is also said to collapse (see esp. Eur. *HF* 864-65, 905-9, 1055, 1142-3). This image is very different from that of the palace in Eur. *Med.*: while the audience hears the screams of the children being murdered by their own mother inside the palace (Eur. *Med.* 1270-81), no change takes place in the palace itself, perhaps since there is nothing ecstatic about Medea's act.

27 Segal 1997, 100-1.

28 "πανδήμοισι … στέγαις" (226-7), "ἐν δεσμοῖσι πανδήμου στέγης" (444), and Segal 1997, 88.

29 On the Minyads' *oikos*, see Ov. *Met.* 4.389-415: the looms and cloth grow ivy leaves, the ceiling begins to shake, the lamps are ablaze, and fire breaks out. On the Gallic maenads, see Strabo 4.4.6: their main activity has to do with building and destroying the temple's roof. This passage is discussed in Detienne 1989, 42-56.

30 Dodds 1960, 65 and Roux 1972, 255 maintain that the adjective establishes an opposition between rocks and caves. Seaford 1996, 153, on the other hand, argues that it is indicative of the disruption of the household following a woman's departure from her house to the mountain. However, it is not clear to me how this could explain the specific reference to the roof in this unique adjective.

maenads.[31] Yet the Lydian maenads in the *parodos* also pray that "at once the whole land shall dance" (αὐτίκα γᾶ πᾶσα χορεύσει, Eur. *Bacch.* 114). This participation of the city of Thebes in the Dionysiac revelry is repeated towards the end of the play, when Cadmus reveals the sequence of tragic events to Agave just after she comes back to her senses: πᾶσά τ' ἐξεβακχεύθη πόλις ("And the whole city was filled with Bacchic frenzy", Eur. *Bacch.* 1295).

In these famous passages, the surroundings participate in the ritual experience, as if the *gē* or polis, both of which serve as subjects in the respective sentences, were one more dancing participant in motion. This is certainly not a common trope in early Greek literature or art, and some scholars have noted that it may be identified as a "pathetic fallacy" in which the natural world is presented as responsive to human emotion and mood.[32] Indeed, Euripides relocates the ritual experience to the *gē* or polis, which, in its turn, responds by displaying the same ritualistic mood and motion. It is equally possible to assume that Thebes is presented as a maenad rather than as a collective plural for its dancing maenads, since, as part of their altered state of consciousness, the ecstatic maenads are also imagined as conceiving their surrounding ritual space in movement.

The spatial boundaries of palace, prison, and polis are gradually blurred in the course of the play, while the personification of Thebes is a particularly interesting phenomenon. This brings me to discuss the ritual space of the mountain in the *Bacchae*, where it is also possible to trace a similar blurring, almost a transformation of space. In this case, the mountain as a ritual locus seems to become blurred as a consequence of the maenads' presence, partaking in their experience, and this change may, in turn, be reflective of the maenads' own religious experience. At the beginning of the play, Dionysus narrates that the Theban maenads are at the mountain together with the daughters of Cadmus (Eur. *Bacch.* 32-8). The call of the Chorus in the *parodos* εἰς ὄρος εἰς ὄρος, "to the mountain, to the mountain" (Eur. *Bacch.* 116), has even been considered as replicating the cry of the ritual itself.[33] It is, however, in the two messenger speeches that the main information regarding the happenings on the mountain reaches the stage. The first messenger speech (Eur. *Bacch.* 677-774) opens with a serene vision of maenadic experience deeply connected to nature and animals. The maenads lie sleeping on fir branches and oak leaves (Eur. *Bacch.* 684-5). After they awaken, a peak moment ensues when they seem to become one in motion with the mountain and its animals, as if in a perfect harmony.

> πᾶν δὲ συνεβάκχευ' ὄρος
> καὶ θῆρες, οὐδὲν δ' ἦν ἀκίνητον δρόμωι.
> The whole mountain joined in Bacchic revelry,
> and the beasts, and nothing was motionless in the course (Eur. *Bacch.* 726-7).

This idyllic moment rapidly switches to a violent scene upon the maenads' realization that they are being hunted down. After tearing the cattle apart (Eur. *Bacch.* 735-47), the maenads rush down to the plains and attack the nearby villages. The villages themselves seem to be transformed by their presence. The maenads "turned everything topsy-turvy" (Eur. *Bacch.* 753-4), before returning to the place from which they started (Eur. *Bacch.* 765). Dionysiac *mania* has also reached the lowlands.

31 Dodds 1960, 66 notes that Murray suggested a change to "πρώτην δὲ Θήβην τήνδε" in order to provide the verb with a personal object (i.e. the eponymous nymph), without however explaining the incentive for such a change. Roux 1972, 250 does identify this as a personification.

32 On the pathetic fallacy in archaic art and literature, see Copley 1937; Hurwit 1982 (with the critique in Madden 1983) and Jenkyns 1998, 21-72, especially 37-8 for a discussion of the Euripidean passages.

33 Segal 1997, 112; Bremmer 1984, 277; Gould 2001, 275.

A similar transformation also takes place in the second messenger speech (Eur. *Bacch.* 1043-152), when Pentheus, Dionysus, and the attendant "enter the bare rock of Cithaeron" (Eur. *Bacch.* 1045). The report speaks of a calm and primitive landscape: "There was a mountain glen with cliffs all around, moist with waters, shaded from pine trees, where the maenads sat keeping their hands in pleasant tasks" (Eur. *Bacch.* 1051-3). Nature is then put to a standstill together with the maenads (1084-5) so that they may apprehend Pentheus' presence. Soon afterwards, the scene drastically alters to become dangerous and finally murderous. Agave, "throwing foam out of her mouth, rolling her twisted eye pupils and being out of her right senses, is possessed by Bacchus" (Eur. *Bacch.* 1122-4). Conveying an altered state of consciousness and blurred sensory perception, the scene culminates with Agave tearing Pentheus apart as if he were a lion cub. Ritual space becomes a horrible murder scene and Dionysus even turns the motherly instinct upside down.

City and mountain are famously opposed in the *Bacchae*. At the same time, however, the various places also become blurred in the course of the play as a consequence of Dionysiac experience. This change sometimes assumes a particular shape in the text: a composite verb that denotes the *baccheia* (συν-/ἐκ-βακχεύειν) takes an inanimate location as its subject (polis and mountain). This syntax seems to relocate the ritual experience of the maenads to the surrounding space, which, in turn, responds by displaying the same movement and ritualistic maenadic mood. Such a construction also appears in fragment 58 from the *Edonoi* mentioned already, ἐνθουσιᾶ δὴ δῶμα, βακχεύει στέγη, "Surely the house is in ecstasy, the roof is in Bacchic frenzy", where Lycurgus' palace partakes in the *baccheia* of the maenads.[34] Furthermore, this Dionysiac transformation of space is sometimes imagined in its totality, with the repetition of the adjective πᾶς. Spaces seem to move and change because the maenads move, dance, and change as part of the ritual. What is remarkable and has not been addressed until now is the possibility that this description of space is not restricted to literary sources – with the *Bacchae* the most notable among them – but may also be found in the pictorial record.

The Space of Maenadic Ritual on Vases

Vases from the Late Archaic period commonly depict maenads, yet for many of them it is hard to identify the locus of the imagined scene. This is in line with the more general tendency of Greek vase painters to disregard the landscape, at least in comparison to other ancient cultures.[35] Sometimes, however, it is possible to identify whether a scene is interior or exterior, the latter when a rock or a tree is visible.[36] There are numerous depictions of maenads, either together with satyrs or on their own, who sit or lean on rocks employed as props indicating an outdoor location.[37] There are some interesting cases in which the rock is covered with ivy, implying that the spa-

34 Cf. Eur. *El.* 691, "ὀλολύξεται πᾶν δῶμα", "the whole house shall cry with a loud voice", and Eur. *IT* 1242-4.

35 See Hurwit 1991 on the representation of nature in Archaic art in comparison to other ancient cultures, and Cohen 2007, 306; see also Dietrich 2010, for a different interpretation, which argues for the inapplicability of the category of landscape in vases, at least in comparison to modern figurative art.

36 See discussion of interior and exterior spaces in maenadic scenes in Paleothodoros 2008. It should be stressed that even when Greek painters depict aspects of landscape, this is not necessarily a realistic portrayal of space.

37 For example, a cup attributed to Makron: Boston, Museum of Fine Arts 1901.8072, *ARV*² 461.36, *BAPD* 204718.

Fig. 1. Terracotta skyphos attributed to the Brygos Painter. The Metropolitan Museum of Art, 29.131.4 (© The Metropolitan Museum of Art, Fletcher Fund, 1929).

tial element of the rock has a specifically Dionysiac connotation.[38]

I will discuss some scenes with maenads and rocks here by looking into a limited number of rocks drawn on Late Archaic red-figure cups from roughly the first third of the 5th century BC. They are attributed to the Brygos Painter and his circle, among whom are also the Briseis and Dokimasia Painters.[39] As Marie-Christine Villanueva Puig notes, it is very characteristic of this group to represent the landscape in maenadic scenes.[40] My interest lies in large human-sized rocks that are not used as props, and this difference in dimensions and function is significant.

The distinction of whether rocks are used as props or not follows an argument developed by Guy M. Hedreen, who distinguishes between "elements of setting that operate directly in visual narratives" (as props) and a "setting that operates indirectly, by facilitating allusion to moments in a story not shown".[41] Of particular relevance to my discussion is the suggestion by Jeffrey M. Hurwit and Guy M. Hedreen that such rocks in vases might act as a synecdoche for the whole mountain, as *pars pro toto*, presenting nature in a minimalist way.[42] A skyphos in New York attributed to the Brygos Painter depicts a wing-sleeved maenad dancing flanked by two large rocks that are at least as tall as her, while on the other side a maenad is playing the aulos, facing a rock that also matches her height (Fig. 1).[43] The rocks on this skyphos and similar representations are commonly identified by art historians as signifying cave openings, especially when the upper part of the rock bends slightly sideways.[44] Nevertheless, Matthew Dillon brings up the New York skyphos alongside literary and epigraphical sources as one more testimony regarding "maenads on the mountains".[45] To complicate the issue further, in the *Bacchae*, the outdoor activity of maenads is not linked to caves.

38 See Basel, Antikenmuseum und Sammlung Ludwig BS 407, *ARV*² 1688.12, *Paralipomena* 469, *Beazley Addenda*² 354, photo in *BAPD* 275512 and Oxford, Ashmolean Museum G284, *ARV*² 1258.1, photo in *BAPD* 217069 (both attributed to the Eretria Painter; the Ashmolean chous has alternatively been attributed to the Codrus Painter). Cf. London, British Museum E125, *ARV*² 770, photo in *BAPD* 209534 and Ancona, Mus. Arch. Naz. 3258, *ARV*² 764.12, *BAPD* 209469 (attributed to the Sotades Painter).

39 This is the group referred to by Beazley as the "Mild Brygan Group". See *ARV*² 405 with further references to individual painters.

40 Villanueva-Puig 2009, 62.

41 Hedreen 2001, 20.

42 See Hurwit 1991, 43, whose examples have to do with tree(s) standing for a forest, and, more relevant to my discussion, Hedreen 2001, 182 on rocks standing for a mountain, based on a white ground lekythos in Munich (Antikensammlungen S80, *ARV*² 1568, *Paralipomena* 438, *Beazley Addenda*² 312, photo in *BAPD* 213977).

43 New York, Metropolitan Museum 29.131.4, *ARV*² 381.176, *Beazley Addenda*² 227, *BAPD* 204073.

44 On the typology of caves, see Siebert 1990. On this and similar rocks in Dionysiac scenes as depicting cave openings, see Villanueva-Puig 1992, 129 with n. 24 (which appears with slight changes in Villanueva-Puig 2009, 61-2) and Paleothodoros 2008, 231-2 with ns 5 and 7. Cf. Carpenter 1997, 38.

45 Dillon 2002, 143-4.

Fig. 2. Red-figure cup (side A) attributed to the Briseis Painter. New York, Market, *ARV*² 406.4 (drawing: N. Young based on the photo in *BAPD* 204403).

Fig. 3. Red-figure cup (side B) attributed to the Briseis Painter. New York, Market, *ARV*² 406.4 (drawing: N. Young based on the photo in *BAPD* 204403).

On the contrary, it even seems to be contrasted with them.[46]

There seems to be a discrepancy between the art historical interpretation, which maintains that these rocks signify cave openings, and the interpretation of Matthew Dillon, who specializes in the history of religion. This discrepancy invites an investigation of the representation of rocks in scenes with maenads in order to better understand the space in which the maenads are imagined to be during the ritual. It is proposed that rather than interpreting rocks as signifying a generic wilderness or a cave entrance, as is common among art historians, some of the rocks on vases attributed to the Brygos Painter and his circle might actually be an attempt of the vase painters to represent the space of the mountain during the ritual. This is a space in which the maenads are imagined to dance at night to the rhythm of drums and, at some point, to reach some kind of altered state of consciousness. The vases portray how the space of the ritual is construed in the Athenian imaginary, however challenging it may be to determine to what extent this representation draws from the realm of myth, from ritual, or perhaps from both. Viewed in this light, the vases have the potential to reveal an imagined ritual space, yet one that predates the *Bacchae* by two-thirds of a century.

The most telling example of human-sized rocks not used as props is depicted on a cup last seen in New York, attributed to the Briseis Painter, with a maenadic scene represented on both sides, each showing two satyrs alternating with two maenads dressed in animal skins and holding *thyrsoi* in their hands (Figs. 2 & 3).[47] On both sides, a rock as tall as the figures is depicted to the right of the composition, next to the cup's handles, and it is not used as a prop. The non-naturalistic protruding facets and serpentine outline of these rocks are quite exceptional. The uniqueness of this depiction becomes apparent when compared to other human-sized

46 The only cave (*andron*) mentioned in the play is that of the Korybantes (123-5). See above on how *anorophous petras*, "roofless stones", in *Bacch.* 38 opposes the very concept of cave. On caves in Dionysiac cults, see Boyancé 1962 and Ustinova 2009, 234-9.

47 New York market, *ARV*² 406.4, photo in *BAPD* 204403. The whereabouts of this cup are unknown and the Beazley Archive Database does not record the gallery which sold it. It is called the New York cup here for convenience, since this is its last known location.

Fig. 4. Red-figure cup (side B) the Brygos Painter (Negrioli). Ferrara, Musei di Arte Antica 247 (© Civica Fototeca di Palazzo Bonacossi, Ferrara. The author thanks the curator Maria Teresa Gulinelli for the permission to publish the photograph).

Fig. 5. Red-figure cup (interior) attributed to the Briseis Painter. New York, Market, *ARV*[2] 406.4. (drawing: N. Young based on the photo in *BAPD* 204403).

rocks on maenadic scenes attributed to the Brygos Painter and his circle, which are in themselves a rare feature in vases from the period. One such example appears on a cup in Ferrara related to the manner of the Brygos Painter (Fig. 4).[48] While in this case the rock is human-sized and not used as a prop, it is quite rounded and lacks texture compared to the rock on the New York cup. The curved and winding protrusions of the rock on the New York cup seem to infuse it with a certain movement. This may constitute an attempt on the part of the vase painter to show the inanimate rocky landscape in movement, to communicate a "dancing" mountain. Indeed, this rock may stand in lieu of an additional dancing figure in the composition. If so, this would bring this cup close to the image of the maenadic mountain in the *Bacchae*: the rock seems to anticipate Euripides' πᾶν δὲ συνεβάκχευ' ὄρος (Eur. *Bacch.* 726), albeit in a different artistic medium and about two-thirds of a century earlier.

A serpentine-shaped rock is also depicted on the interior of the New York cup (Fig. 5). Rocks such as this, decorating the interior, are of the same conceptualization as the ones on the cup exteriors; in this case, however, the rock rises like a wavy line next to the meander ring that encloses the tondo's composition, presenting the protrusions of the rocks in profile. Since the Brygos Painter is equally capable of drawing a pointy rock next to a maenad in the tondo, the wavy quality of these rocks should not be attributed to the tondo's limited space.[49] Again, this might constitute an attempt to depict the maenadic ritual space in movement and in dancing motion, with the rock standing for the mountain as *pars pro*

48 Ferrara (catalogued as Palazzo Schifanoia 277), *ARV*[2] 387.1, *Beazley Addenda*[2] 229, photo in *BAPD* 204142.

49 See, for example, the cup in Amsterdam, Allard Pierson Museum 2829, *ARV*[2] 390.39, photo in *BAPD* 204185. Compare this to the rock (and tree?) on the tondo of a cup in Athens, National Museum 17869, *ARV*[2] 864.9, drawing in *BAPD* 211370.

Fig. 6. Red-figure cup (side B) attributed to the Briseis Painter. British Museum, 1843.1103.54 (© Trustees of the British Museum).

toto. Furthermore, it should be borne in mind that such cups were primarily used for wine-drinking in the context of the symposium. When the wavy rocks are drawn on the tondo, the rock is practically concealed when the cup is full and becomes gradually revealed as its holder consumes the wine. With every sip and every slight movement of the wine, the waves of the rock become momentarily mixed with the waves of the wine, implying a further blurring of compositional, spatial, and sensory boundaries for the sympotic drinker, which is also Dionysiac in nature, though this blurring is evidently unrelated to the space of the ritual on the mountain.

The Briseis Painter also depicts human-sized rocks in other maenadic scenes. Notable examples are on cups which are now in Oxford and London (Fig. 6).[50] While the rocks in these instances may seem to lack the serpentine outline of the New York cup, they are still rather exceptional. They rise as tall as the maenads, do not function as props, and are visible at the edges of the composition, next to the handles. Most importantly, however, they are not rounded like the rock on the Ferrara cup, but exhibit a texture rimmed with rounded protrusions. While some painters of the Mild Brygan group sometimes depict high rocks in hunting scenes, possibly to denote a generic wilderness, the rocks they portray in those cases seem to lack a serpentine shape.[51] It is the wavy outline of the rocks in the scenes with maenads that suggests an attempt to represent a "dancing" mountain and thus to reflect the ecstatic movement of the maenads. It is also possible that the shape of the rock represents some blurred sensory perception of space or a vision that sprang forth during the mountain ritual. The zigzagged shape of the rock may even be related to phosphenes or entoptic phenomena, which often form part of altered states of consciousness.[52]

Wavy rocks seem to be more common on the interiors of cups. An interesting case occurs on a partially preserved cup in Paris (Fig. 7).[53] There, the rhythm of the wavy rock is repeated in the twists of a snake wrapped around the *thyrsos* held by the dancing maenad, with an additional curve to the right of the maenad, on the tail of the animal skin she is wearing. This repetitive use of the wave transmits the movement from animate to inanimate objects in the composition and appears in addition to the

50 Oxford, Ashmolean Museum 1944.87, *ARV*[2] 406.3, photo in *BAPD* 204402; London, British Museum 1843.1103.54, *ARV*[2] 406.2, *Paralipomena* 371, *Beazley Addenda*[2] 232, *BAPD* 204401. In addition, see a cup fragment in Adria, which might have presented a similar rock among maenads (Museo Archeologico Nazionale 22144, *ARV*[2] 406.5, *Beazley Addenda*[2] 232, photo in *BAPD* 204404).

51 See Copenhagen, National Museum 6327, *ARV*[2]413.16, *Beazley Addenda*[2] 233, photo in *BAPD* 204498 (attributed to the Dokimasia Painter). Cf. the cave opening on New York, Metropolitan Museum 38.11.2, *BAPD* 5968 (attributed to the Brygos Painter) and Berlin, Antikensammlung 3359, *ARV*[2] 407.19, photo in *BAPD* 204418 (attributed to the Briseis Painter).

52 See Horowitz 1964; Lewis-Williams & Dowson 1988; Ustinova 2011.

53 Paris, Louvre G159, *ARV*[2] 413.26, *Beazley Addenda*[2] 233, photo in *BAPD* 204508 (attributed to the Dokimasia Painter). The exterior also seems to depict maenads among tall rocks. See Bérard *et al.* 1989, 30 and Jaccottet 2011, 414 for a short discussion of this cup interior.

Fig. 7. Red-figure cup (interior) attributed to the Dokimasia Painter. Paris, Louvre G159 (Photo © Musée du Louvre, Dist. RNM-Grand Palais).

motion of the dancing maenad, creating the impression that the mountain itself is dancing along with her. Perhaps these waves may also be suggestive of a blurred sensory perception related to the maenad's ecstasy. Wavy rocks on the tondos are found in additional cups attributed to the Brygos Painter and his group.[54] Painters from the Early Classical period also sometimes draw similar rocks, though evidently the rock in those cases is often smaller in size.[55]

The unique shape, size, and positioning of rocks on Late Archaic cups presenting maenadic scenes has led me to argue that the rocks are endowed with a dynamic quality and appear to be responsive to the movement of the maenads, perhaps as a consequence of the altered state of consciousness related to maenadism. This might constitute an attempt to convey the ritual space of the mountain, possibly even a "dancing" mountain, and to show the same blurring and transformation of Dionysiac space found in the *Bacchae* almost two-thirds of a century later.

Conclusion

This article proposed to reconstruct the space of the mountain during the maenadic ritual in the Athenian imaginary, based on literary and pictorial sources from the 5th century BC. This is a ritual for which it seems safe to assume that we are unlikely to find any monumental architectural traces, since it was performed in an ephemeral ritual space. While there is no denying that both clusters of sources communicate a spatial representation that fluctuates between myth and ritual, they still present a relatively consistent picture. The mountain is related to movement, dancing, and blurred spatial boundaries, possibly alluding to the maenads' own religious experience of dancing, movement, and an altered state of consciousness. In the Athenian imaginary, maenadic experience seems to be accompanied by a blurred sensory perception of space, creating the impression of a "dancing" mountain. One could even take this consistent representation in both media as an indication that Athenian vase painters and

54 See Basel, Antikenmuseum und Sammlung Ludwig BS441, *ARV*[2] 378.135, *Paralipomena* 366, *Beazley Addenda*[2] 226, photo in *BAPD* 204032; Cambridge, Fitzwilliam Museum GR2.1896, *ARV*[2] 393.39, photo in *BAPD* 204238; Adria, Museo Archeologico Nazionale BC31, *ARV*[2] 379.152, *Beazley Addenda*[2] 227, photo in *BAPD* 204049; and London market, photo in *BAPD* 8517. It is less clear whether the cup fragment in Würzburg with remainders of a rock also depicted a maenadic scene: Würzburg, University, Martin von Wagner Museum H5402, photo in *BAPD* 6376. Cf. also Germany, Private 81, *BAPD* 19747.

55 See Houston, TX, Museum of Fine Arts 34.135, *ARV*[2] 394.7, *Beazley Addenda*[2] 229, photo in *BAPD* 204257 (attributed to the Painter of Munich 2676); Bologna, Museo Civico Archeologico 415BIS, *ARV*[2] 920.9, photo in *BAPD* 211179 (attributed to the Aberdeen Painter, its exterior presents athletes); Ferrara, Palazzo Schifanoia 266, *ARV*[2] 883.59, *Beazley Addenda*[2] 301, photo in *BAPD* 211624 (attributed to the Penthesilea Painter); Cambridge, MA, Harvard University, A. M. Sackler Museum 1925.30.128, *ARV*[2] 357.68, photo in *BAPD* 203750 (attributed to the Colmar Painter).

poets alike were somehow familiar with maenadic ritual, though the nature of the primary sources precludes a conclusive assessment.[56] After all, we are in the realm of Dionysus, who can blur spatial boundaries, turning reality and imagination topsy-turvy. It should be no surprise that, in such state of consciousness, maenads and mountain seem to dance together during the ritual.

Abbreviations

ARV² = Beazley, J.D. 1963. *Attic Red-figure Vase-painters*, Oxford.

BAPD = Beazley Archive, http://www.beazley.ox.ac.uk

Beazley Addenda² = Carpenter, T.H., with T. Mannack & M. Mendonca 1989. *Beazley Addenda: Additional References to ABV, ARV² & Paralipomena*, Oxford.

Paralipomena = Beazley, J.D. 1971. *Paralipomena: Additions to Attic Black-figure Vase-painters and to Attic Red-figure Vase-painters*, Oxford.

Bibliography

BÉRARD, C., C. BRON, J.-L. DURAND, F. FRONTISI-DUCROUX, F. LISSARAGUE, A. SCHNAPP & J.-P. VERNANT 1989
A City of Images: Iconography and Society in Ancient Greece, translated by D. Lyons, Princeton.

BOYANCÉ, P. 1962
'L'antre dans les mystères de Dionysos', *RendPontAcc* 33, 107-27.

BREMMER, J.M. 1984
'Greek Maenadism Reconsidered', *ZPE* 55, 267-86.

BUXTON, R.G.A. 1992
'Imaginary Greek Mountains', *JHS* 112, 1-15.

CARPENTER, T.H. 1997
Dionysian Imagery in Fifth-Century Athens, Oxford.

CASTELLANI, V. 1976
'That Troubled House of Pentheus in Euripides' *Bacchae*', *TAPA* 106, 61-83.

COHEN, A. 2007
'Mythic Landscapes of Greece', in *The Cambridge Companion to Greek Mythology*, R.D. Woodard (ed.), Cambridge, 305-30.

COPLEY, F.O. 1937
'The Pathetic Fallacy in Early Greek Poetry', *AJP* 58, 194-209.

DETIENNE, M. 1989
Dionysos at Large, translated by A. Goldhammer, Cambridge and London.

DEVEREUX, G. 1970
'The Psychotherapy Scene in Euripides' *Bacchae*', *JHS* 90, 35-48.

DIETRICH, N. 2010
Figur ohne Raum? Bäume und Felsen in der attischen Vasenmalerei des 6. und 5. Jahrhunderts v.Chr., Berlin and New York.

DILLON, M. 2002
Girls and Women in Classical Greek Religion, London and New York.

56 For the development of such a line of argument regarding a different group of vases with maenadic scenes, see Osborne 1997, 196: "Neither literature nor art can claim unique status as purveyors of 'the truth', but … they have complementary strengths as historical documents."

DODDS, E.R. 1951
The Greeks and the Irrational, Berkeley.

DODDS, E.R. 1960
Euripides: Bacchae, Oxford.

EDWARDS, M.N. 1960
'Representation of Maenads on Archaic Red-Figure Vases', *JHS* 80, 78-87.

ELSNER, J. 2012
'Material Culture and Ritual: State of the Question', in *Architecture of the Sacred: Space, Ritual, and Experience from Classical Greece to Byzantium*, B.D. Wescoat & R.G. Ousterhout (eds.), Cambridge, 1-26.

FISHER, R.K. 1992
'The "Palace Miracles" in Euripides' *Bacchae*: A Reconsideration', *AJP* 113, 179-88.

FRONTISI-DUCROUX, F. 1986
'Images du ménadisme feminin: les vases de "Lénéennes"', in *L'association dionysiaque dans les societés anciennes. Actes de la table ronde organisée par l'École française de Rome (24-25 mai 1984)*, Rome, 165-76.

GOULD, J. 2001
'Dionysus and the Hippy Convoy: Ritual, Myth, and Metaphor in the Cult of Dionysus', in *Myth, Ritual Memory, and Exchange: Essays in Greek Literature and Culture*, Oxford, 269-82.

HEDREEN, G.M. 1994
'Silens, Nymphs and Maenads', *JHS* 114, 47-69.

HEDREEN, G.M. 2001
Capturing Troy: The Narrative Functions of Landscape in Archaic and Early Classical Greek Art, Ann Arbor.

HENRICHS, A. 1978
'Greek Maenadism from Olympias to Messalina', *HSCP* 82, 121-60.

HENRICHS, A. 1982
'Changing Dionysiac Identities', in *Self-Definition in the Greco-Roman World*, vol. 3 of *Jewish and Christian Self-Definition,* B.F. Meyer & E.P. Sanders (eds.), Philadelphia, 137-60.

HENRICHS, A. 1984A
'Loss of Self, Suffering, Violence: The Modern View of Dionysus from Nietzsche to Girard', *HSCP* 88, 205-40.

HENRICHS, A. 1984B
'Male Intruders Among the Maenads: The So-Called Male Celebrant', in *Mnemai: Classical Studies in Memory of Karl K. Hulley*, H.D. Evjen (eds.), Chico, CA, 69-92.

HENRICHS, A. 1990
'Between Country and City: Cultic Dimensions of Dionysus in Athens and Attica', in *Cabinet of the Muses: Essays on Classical and Comparative Literature in Honor of Thomas G. Rosenmeyer*, M. Griffith & D.J. Mastronarde (eds.), Atlanta, 257-77.

HOROWITZ, M.J. 1964
'The Imagery of Visual Hallucinations', *Journal of Nervous and Mental Disorder* 138, 513-23.

HURWIT, J.M. 1982
'Palm Trees and the Pathetic Fallacy in Archaic Greek Poetry and Art', *CJ* 77, 193-9.

HURWIT, J.M. 1991
'The Representation of Nature in Early Greek Art', in *New Perspectives in Early Greek Art*, D. Buitron-Oliver (ed.), Hanover, 33-62.

JACCOTTET, A.-F. 2003
Choisir Dionysos: Les associations dionysiaques ou la face cachée du dionysisme, 2 vols, Zurich.

JACCOTTET, A.-F. 2011
'Integrierte Andersartigkeit: Die Rolle der dionysischen Vereine', in *A Different God? Dionysos and Ancient Polytheism*, R. Schlesier (ed.), Berlin, 413-31.

JENKYNS, R. 1998
Virgil's Experience: Nature and History; Times, Names, and Places, Oxford.

KAUSKOPF, I., E. SIMON & B. SIMON 1997
'Mainades', *LIMC* 8.1, 780-803.

KRISTENSEN, T.M. & W. FRIESE (EDS.) 2017
Excavating Pilgrimage: Archaeological Approaches to Sacred Travel and Movement in the Ancient World, London.

LEWIS-WILLIAMS, J.D. & T.A. DOWSON 1988
'The Signs of All Times: Entoptic Phenomena in Upper Palaeolithic Art', *CurrAnthr* 29, 201-45.

MADDEN, J.D. 1983
'The Palms Do Not Weep: A Reply to Professor Hurwit and a Note on the Death of Priam in Greek Art', *CJ* 78, 193-9.

MCNALLY, S. 1978
'The Maenad in Early Greek Art', *Arethusa* 1, 101-35.

MORAW, S. 1998
Die Mänade in der attischen Vasenmalerei des 6. und 5. Jahrhunderts v. Chr.: Rezeptionsästhetische Analyse eines antiken Weiblichkeitsentwurfs, Mainz am Rhein.

MORGAN, J.E. 2007
'Space and the Notion of a Final Frontier: Searching for Ritual Boundaries in the Classical Athenian Home', *Kernos* 20, 113-29.

OSBORNE, R. 1997
'The Ecstasy and the Tragedy: Varieties of Religious Experience in Art, Drama, and Society', in *Greek Tragedy and the Historian*, C. Pelling (ed.), Oxford, 187-211.

PALEOTHODOROS, D. 2008
'Espace public et espace domestique dans l'imagerie attique des rituels dionysiaques du Ve siècle av. J.-C.', in *Image et religion dans l'antiquité gréco-romaine: Actes du colloque de Rome, 11-13 décembre 2003*, S. Estienne, D. Jaillard, N. Lubtchansky & C. Pouzadoux (eds.), Naples, 231-42.

PEIRCE, S. 1998
'Visual Language and Concepts of Cult on the 'Lenaia Vases'', *ClAnt* 17, 59-95.

REHM, R. 2002
The Play of Space: Spatial Transformation in Greek Tragedy, Princeton.

RICHARDSON, N.J. 1974
The Homeric Hymn to Demeter, Oxford.

ROUX, J. 1972
Euripide: Les Bacchantes, Paris.

SCULLION, S. 2013
'Maenads and Men', http://www.classics.ox.ac.uk/tl_files/Downloads/Maenads-and-Men.pdf (accessed 06.07.2014).

SEAFORD, R. 1996
Euripides: Bacchae, Warminster.

SEAFORD, R. 2006
Dionysos, London and New York.

SEGAL, C. 1997
Dionysiac Poetics and Euripides' Bacchae: Expanded Edition, Princeton.

SIEBERT, G. 1990
'Imaginaire et images de la grotte dans la Grèce archaïque et classique', *Ktèma* 15, 151-61.

SOKOLOWSKI, F. 1969
Lois sacrées des cités grecques, Paris.

USTINOVA, Y. 2009
Caves and the Ancient Greek Mind: Descending Underground in the Search for Ultimate Truth, Oxford.

USTINOVA, Y. 2011
'Consciousness Alteration Practices in the West from Prehistory to Late Antiquity', in *Altering Consciousness: Multidisciplinary Perspectives*, E. Cardeña & M. Wilkelman (eds.), Santa Barbara, 45-72.

USTINOVA, Y. 2017
Divine Mania: Alteration of Consciousness in Ancient Greece, London.

VERNANT, J.-P. 1988
'The Masked Dionysus of Euripides' *Bacchae*', in *Myth and Tragedy in Ancient Greece*, J.-P. Vernant & P. Vidal-Naquet, translated by J. Lloyd, New York, 381-412.

VERSNEL, H.S. 1990
Ter Unus: Isis, Dionysos, Hermes: Three Studies in Henotheism, vol. 1 of *Inconsistencies in Greek and Roman Religion*, Leiden.

VILLANUEVA PUIG, M.-C. 1986
'À propos des Thyiades de Delphes', in *L'association dionysiaque dans les societés anciennes. Actes de la table ronde organisée par l'École française de Rome (24-25 mai 1984)*, Rome, 31-51.

VILLANUEVA PUIG, M.-C. 1992
'Les répresentations des ménades dans la céramique attique à figures rouges de la fin de l'archaïsme', *RÉA* 94, 125-54.

VILLANUEVA PUIG, M.-C. 2009
Ménades: Recherches sur la genèse iconographique du thiase féminin de Dionysos des origines à la fin de la période archaïque, Paris.

ZEITLIN, F. 1990
'Thebes: Theater of Self and Society in Athenian Drama', in *Nothing to Do with Dionysus? Athenian Drama in its Social Context*, J. Winkler & F. Zeitlin (eds.), Princeton, 130-67.

Journeys to the Eleusinian Mysteria (with an Appendix on the Procession at the Andanian Mysteria)

Kevin Clinton

The journey of initiates to Attica and their subsequent participation in the procession to Eleusis at the Mysteria is the subject of three sacred laws. The first is an Athenian law dated by letter style to c. 470-460 BC, now in the British Museum – in fact, it is an Elgin Marble. It has the shape of a pillar, broken on top and inscribed on all four sides. The side that is now called Side B contains the information about the initiates' journey; it calls for a truce that will be in effect for foreigners and Athenians:

1. *IEleusis* 19.B (*IG* I^3, 6.B)

[ι· σ]πονδὰς εἶν-
[αι] τοῖσι μύστ-
[εσιν] καὶ το[ῖς]
[ἐπ]όπτεισιν [κ]-
[αὶ τ]οῖς ἀκολ[ο]-
[ύθ]οισιν καὶ [χ]-
[ρέ]μασιν τõν [ὀ]-
[θ]νείον καὶ [Ἀθ]-
[ε]ν[α]ίοισιν [h]ά-
πασιν· ἄρχε[ν] δ-
ὲ τὸν χρόνο[ν] τ-
õν σπονδõν [τ]õ
Μεταγειτνιõ-
νος μενὸς ἀπ[ὸ]
διχομενίας [κ]-
αὶ τὸν Βοεδρ[ο]-
μιõνα καὶ τõ [Π]-
υανοφσιõνος
μέχρι δεκάτε-
ς hισταμένο· τ-
ὰς δὲ σπονδὰς
εἶναι ἐν τε͂ισ-
ι πόλεσιν hό[σ]-
αι χρõνται τõ-
ι hιερõι καὶ Ἀ-
θεναίοισιν ἐ-
κεῖ ἐν τε͂ισιν
αὐτε͂σι πόλεσ-
ιν· τοῖσι δὲ ὀλ-
είζοσι μυστε-
ρίοισιν τὰς [σ]-
πονδὰς εἶνα[ι]
τõ Γαμελιõνο-
ς μενὸς ἀπὸ δ[ι]-
[χ]ομενίας κα[ὶ]
τὸν Ἀνθεστε[ρ]-
[ι]õνα καὶ τõ Ἐλ-
αφεβολιõνος
μέχρι δεκάτε-
ς hισταμένο.
vacat

"Let there be a truce [σπονδαί] for *mystai*, *epoptai*, servants, baggage of the foreigners, and all Athenians."[1] The truce is to be in effect from the middle of Metageitnion, i.e. a month before the start of the Mysteria, until the tenth of Pyanopsion, i.e. about fifteen days after the end of the festival. It is further specified that the truce is to be valid in the cities that make use of the sanctuary and for Athenians in the same cities. Thus it is not necessarily a Panhellenic truce, but those cities "that make use of the sanctuary" would at least include a broad area of central Greece. It seems to imply that there were agreements or understandings between the various cities and Athens concerning use of the sanctuary. Significant here is the control by Athens: first, the sanctuary is at Eleusis, but Athens controls the access to it (this is especially clear in the regulations on Side A, which provide for exclusion of a city from the sanctuary for improper behavior); second, although not mentioned here, the initiates do not go directly to Eleusis, but to central Athens, the asty, from where the procession continues the journey to Eleusis.

Descriptions of processions during the Mysteria are provided by two other sacred laws. These processions include the procession of the sacred objects from Eleusis to the City Eleusinion before the start of the festival and processions to Eleusis during the festival. A decree of the early 3rd century of our era presents a problem concerning the date of the

1 On the spondai, see *IEleusis* 2:19 (Commentary).

procession to Eleusis with the sacred objects, which it declares to be Boedromion 19 (lines 18-22):

2. *IEleusis* 638 (= *IG* II², 1078) c. AD 220

ἔδοξεν τ]ῶι δήμωι· Ἀραβιαν[ὸς ἦρχεν . . c.8 . . . ἐπρυ]-[τάνευε]ν· Εὔτυχος ἐγραμ[μάτευεν . . . c.11 . . . . ἐπε]-[στάτει]· Δρυαντιανὸς ἄρχων [τῶν Εὐμολπιδῶν εἶπεν]· [ἐπει]δὴ καὶ διατελοῦμε[ν ἐν τοῖς νῦν καθάπερ] καὶ [δ]ιὰ τῶν παρῳχημένων [χρόνων τελοῦντες τὰ μυ]στήρι-α, καὶ τὰ πάτρια προστάττ[ει τῶι γένει τῶν Εὐμο]λπιδῶν πεφροντικέναι ὅπως ἂν [ἐν κόσμωι ἀχθ]είη τὰ ἱερὰ δεῦρο τ' ἐκ τῆς Ἐλευσεῖνο[ς καὶ πάλιν ἐκ το]ῦ ἄστεως Ἐ-λευσεῖνάδε, ἀγαθῆι τύχ[ηι δεδόχθαι] τῶι δήμωι προσ-τάξαι τῶι κοσμητῆι τῶν [ἐφήβων κ]ατὰ τὰ ἀρχαῖα νόμι-μα [ἄ]γειν Ἐλευσῖνάδε τοὺ[ς ἐφήβ]ους τῆι τρίτηι ἐπὶ δέ-[κα] τοῦ Βοηδρομιῶνος με[τὰ το]ῦ εἰθισμένου σχήμα-[τος] τῆς ἅμα ἱεροῖς πομπ[ῆς, ἵ]να τῆι τετράδι ἐπὶ δέκα πα-[ραπ]έμψωσιν τὰ ἱερὰ μέχ[ρι] τοῦ Ἐλευσινίου τοῦ ὑπὸ [τῆι π]όλει, ὡς ἂν κόσμο[ς τ]ε πλείων καὶ φρουρὰ μείζων [περὶ] τὰ ἱερὰ ὑπάρχο[ι], ἐπειδὴ καὶ ὁ φαιδυντὴς τοῖν θε-[οῖν] ἀγγέλλει κατὰ τὰ πάτρια τῆι ἱερείαι τῆς Ἀθηνᾶς ὡς [ἥκει τὰ] ἱερὰ κ[αὶ] ἡ παραπέμπουσα στρατιά, κατὰ τὰ αὐτὰ [δὲ τῆι] ἐνάτηι ἐπὶ δέκα τοῦ Βοηδρομιῶνος προσ-[τάξα]ι τῶι κοσμητῆι τῶν ἐφήβων ἄγειν τοὺς ἐφή[βους] [πάλιν Ἐ]λευεῖνάδε μετὰ τοῦ αὐτοῦ σχήματος π[αραπέμ]-[πο]ντας τὰ ἱερά. μέλειν δὲ τούτου τῶι κατ' ἐν[ιαυτὸν] κοσμητῆι, ὅπως μηδέποτε τοῦτο ἐκλε[ιφθείη μη]-δὲ ὀλιγωρηθείη ποτὲ τὰ τῆς εὐσεβείας [τῆς πρὸς τὼ θε]-ώ. παραπέμπειν δὲ τοὺς ἐφήβους π[άντας, ἔχοντας] τὴν πανοπλίαν, ἐστεφανωμέν[ους μυρρίνης στεφά]-νωι, βαδείζοντας ἐν τάξει. ἐπ[εὶ] δ[ὲ προστάττομεν τοῖς ἐ]-φήβοις τὴν τοσαύτην ὁδοιπορῆσαι π̣[ομπὴν, δίκαιον αὐτοὺς] καὶ θυσιῶν καὶ σπονδῶν καὶ παιάνων τῶ[ν κατὰ τὴν] ὁδὸν μεθέξειν, ὡς ἄν τά τε ἱερὰ μετὰ φρουρᾶ[ς ἰσχυρο]-τέρας καὶ πομπῆς μακροτέρας ἄγοιτο, οἵ τε ἔφ[ηβοι] παρακολουθοῦντες τῆι περὶ τὸ θεῖον τῆς πόλεω[ς] θεραπείαι καὶ ἄνδρες εὐσεβέστεροι γείνοιντο. μεθέ-ξουσιν δ[ὲ] καὶ οἱ ἔφηβοι πάντες τῶν τε ἄλλων ὧν ἂν παρέχ[ηι τ]οῖς Εὐμολπίδαις ὁ ἄρχων τοῦ γένους, καὶ τῆ[ς] δι[αν]ομῆς. γενέσθαι δὲ τὴν γνώμην ταύτην φα[νερ]-ὰν καὶ τῆι ἐξ Ἀρείου πάγου βουλῆι καὶ τῆι βουλ[ῆι] τῶν Φ ν καὶ τῶι ἱεροφάντηι καὶ τῶι γένει τῶν Εὐ[μο]λπιδῶν. ἀναγράψαι δὲ τὸ ψήφισμα τοῦτο τὸν [τα]μία[ν τ]οῦ γέ-νους τῶν Εὐμολπιδῶν ἐν τρισὶν [στή]λαις καὶ στῆσαι τὴν μὲν ἐν Ἐλευσινίωι τῶι ὑπὸ [τ]ῆι π̣όλει, τὴν δὲ ἐν τῶι Διογενείωι, τὴν δὲ ἐν Ἐλευσεῖνι ἐν τῶι ἱερῶι πρὸ τοῦ βου[λ]ευτηρίου.

Plutarch, on the other hand, attests that the Athenians "lead out Iakchos", the divine leader of the initiates, on Boedromion 20: "περὶ αὐτὴν τὴν εἰκάδα τοῦ Βοηδρομιῶνος ᾗ τὸν μυστικὸν Ἴακχον ἐξάγουσιν "(*Vit. Cam.* 19.10); "εἰκάδι γὰρ ἡ φρουρὰ Βοηδρομιῶνος εἰσήχθη μυστηρίων ὄντων, ᾗ τὸν Ἴακχον ἐξ ἄστεος Ἐλευσινάδε πέμπουσιν" (*Vit. Phoc.* 28.2-3). Furthermore, the chorus in Euripides' *Ion*, in its lyric description of the great Reception of Iakchos, which took place as the initiates arrived at the sanctuary,[2] alludes to the 20th as the day of the event (Eur. *Ion* 1074-86 [cf. Schol. Ar. *Ran.* 314]).[3] It is clear from Ar. *Ran.* 313-53, Eur. *Ion.*, and especially Hdt. 8.65 that the initiates accompanied Iakchos in this procession while they sang the "Iakchos song".[4] It is surprising, then, that for such a well-known procession we have two contradictory dates, from two authoritative sources, Plutarch and the decree. The key to the solution lies in the fact that in the decree there is not a word about initiates (*mystai*) or Iakchos; this decree describes only an escort (*pompe*) of the sacred objects (*hiera*); it refers to the procession as the *pompe hama hierois.* The solution, as I argued in 1988, following a suggestion by John Mansfield, must be that there were two processions, an Escort with Sacred Objects, which

2 The Epimeletai of the Mysteria were in charge of the reception: "ἐπεμελήθησαν δὲ καὶ τῆς ἅλαδε ἐλάσε[ως] καὶ τῆς Ἐλευσῖνι τοῦ Ἰάκχου ὑποδοχῆς" (*IEleusis* 208.20-1 = *IG* II³, 1.1164).

3 "αἰσχύνομαι τὸν πολύυμνον θεόν, εἰ παρὰ Καλλιχόροισι παγαῖς λαμπάδα θεωρὸς εἰκάδων ἐννύχιον ἄυπνος ὄψεται, ὅτε καὶ Διὸς ἀστερωπὸς ἀνεχόρευσεν αἰθήρ, χορεύει δὲ σελάνα καὶ πεντήκοντα κόραι †Νηρέος αἱ κατὰ πόντον ἀεναῶν τε ποταμῶν† δίνας χορευόμεναι τὰν χρυσοστέφανον κόραν καὶ ματέρα σεμνάν." Schol. Ar. *Ran.* 323a (Chantry): "μία τῶν μυστηρίων ἡ εἰκάς ἐστιν, ἐν ᾗ τὸν Ἴακχον ἐξάγουσι."

4 Hdt. 8.65: "ἰδεῖν δὲ κονιορτὸν χωρέοντα ἀπ' Ἐλευσῖνος ὡς ἀνδρῶν μάλιστά κῃ τρισμυρίων, ἀποθωμάζειν τέ σφεας τὸν κονιορτὸν ὅτεών κοτε εἴη ἀνθρώπων, καὶ πρόκατε φωνῆς ἀκούειν, καί οἱ φαίνεσθαι τὴν φωνὴν εἶναι τὸν μυστικὸν ἴακχον."

set out on the 19th, and a procession leading out Iakchos on the 20th.[5]

Another solution, proposed in the 19th century and followed by many scholars since then, is that the initiates set out on the morning of the 19th, but that their arrival at Eleusis in the evening actually occurred on the 20th, according to the Athenian reckoning of the evening as the start of the new day.[6] However, the evidence that the Athenians began their day in the evening as opposed to the morning is unconvincing. In any case, the literary sources and the sacred law date the procession by its *start*: Plutarch states that they lead out Iakchos on the 20th; the sacred law assigns the *pompe* to the 19th. The time of arrival in Eleusis is irrelevant; each procession starts on a different day. Another possible solution, which I do not believe has been proposed, might be that there was a change in the date of the procession between the Classical period and the early 3rd century AD. However, Plutarch uses the present tense – "the Athenians lead out Iakchos on the 20th of Boedromion" – so is clearly referring to the present time, approximately a hundred years before the decree. Most significantly, there has been no change in the date of the procession with Iakchos between the time of Euripides and that of Plutarch. Given the time-honoured status of this day of procession, it is highly unlikely that the decree from the early 3rd century AD would have changed it, especially in view of the fact that the decree is archaizing and bases its practice on *ta patria*, ancestral tradition (line 7) and "original customs" ("ἀρχαῖα νόμιμα", line 11).[7] Thus the decree should refer to a different procession, the "Escort with the *Hiera*", as it says, and not the leading out of Iakchos.

In accordance with the Athenian practice of assigning each day of the Mysteria its own name, the 19th could have been called "πομπὴ ἅμα ἱεροῖς", whereas the day on which they lead out Iakchos was called "Ἴακχος" according to Hesychius.[8]

Let us look more closely at the text of the decree:

> Dryantianos, archon [of the Eumolpidai proposed]: since we continue celebrating the Mysteria in the present as in past times, and ancestral tradition commands [the *genos* of the Eumolpidai] to see to it that the sacred objects be conducted both hither from Eleusis and again to Eleusis from the asty....

Dryantianos was a member of the *genos* of the Eumolpidai, and so the restoration that he was the archon is highly likely.[9] The fact that the proposer was the archon of this *genos*, that the hierophant and the *genos* were informed of the decision of the decree (line 38), and that the treasurer of the Eumolpidai had the decree inscribed on three *stelai* (lines 39-40) strongly supports the restoration of the *genos* in line 6, and makes clear that this ancestral custom, the Escort with the *Hiera*, was the province of the Eumolpidai and its leader, the hierophant. It is also clear that the *hiera* were normally kept in the sanctuary at Eleusis.[10]

Lines 9-21 present what is to be decreed:

---

5 Clinton 1988, 70.

6 Foucart 1914, 324-5.

7 That there was a procession with Iakchos at its head around this time is confirmed by the existence of the Iakchagogos priest, Flavius Iakchagogos Agryleus, archon at the end of the 2nd century or beginning of the 3rd century AD: *IG* II^2, 3680 (= *Agora* XV, 453), 3732, with Follet 1976, 516. The use of hieronymy suggests an increase in prestige for the priesthood since the time of the last known incumbent in the second quarter of the 2nd century AD (Clinton 1974, 96-7).

8 *s.v.* ""Ἴακχον· τὸν Διόνυσον ASn. ἢ μίαν ἡμέραν τῶν μυστηρίων, ἐν ᾗ τὸν Ἴακχον ἐξάγουσι. καὶ ἡ ᾠδή, ἣν οἱ μεμυημένοι ᾄδουσι· καὶ ἥρως, <οὗ> καὶ ναὸς ἐν τῇ Ἀττικῇ καὶ ἄγαλμα. τινὲς δὲ καὶ αὐτὸν τὸν Διόνυσον οὕτως ἔλεγον."

9 See the stemma in Oliver 1949, 243-58 and the commentary in Aleshire 1991, 72 (with stemma, table 1).

10 This is also clear from the rescue of the *hiera* from the sanctuary as the Costobocs invaded (*IEleusis* 494.515-6).

> For good fortune let it be decreed by the Demos to order the cosmete of the ephebes in accordance with the original customs to conduct the ephebes to Eleusis on Boedromion 13 in the customary formation of the escort with the sacred objects, in order that on Boedromion 14 they escort the sacred objects to the Eleusinion below the Acropolis, so that greater *kosmos* and better protection be available for the sacred objects, when also the Phaidyntes of the Two Goddesses announces to the Priestess of Athena according to ancestral custom that the sacred objects and the military escort have arrived. And in the same way on Boedromion 19 to order the cosmete of the ephebes to conduct the ephebes again to Eleusis in the same formation, as they escort the sacred objects….

On the 14th they escort the *hiera* c. 21 kilometres to the Eleusinion below the Acropolis – an exercise that healthy and disciplined 18- or 19-year-olds should be able to perform as a matter of course. Five days later, on the 19th, they set out again with the *hiera* on the 21 kilometre journey to Eleusis and, after taking part in various festivities along the way (sacrifices, libations, paeans), arrive at the sanctuary by the late afternoon or early evening. If they had to escort yet another procession to Eleusis, this time with Iakchos and the intiates, on the morning of the very next day, they would have to walk 21 kilometres back to central Athens from Eleusis on the evening of the 19th, arriving late at night, then early in the morning, presumably after little sleep, march 21 kilometres again to Eleusis, escorting Iakchos and the initiates. So it is not surprising that the decree says nothing about the ephebes performing an evening march to central Athens and another escort on the 20th for Iakchos and the initiates. Such an inhumane schedule would likely not have been demanded of the ephebes, especially since the decree acknowledges (lines 27-8) that they had already performed an "extensive escort" by the end of Boedromion 19.

The other possibility, adopted by many scholars, is that the procession escorted by the ephebes included Iakchos and the initiates on the 19th along with the *hiera*.[11] The decree, however, offers no support for an ephebic escort on Boedromion 19 which included Iakchos and the initiates. This would involve a change in the traditional date, Boedromion 20, of the Iakchos procession, i.e. the leading out of Iakchos; and surely it would be rather bizarre for such a decree as this one, which emphasizes that it is based on ancestral tradition, to serve as the announcement of such a change. Furthermore, it mentions in lines 27-8 that because of "such an extensive escort" on the 19th, the ephebes deserve certain privileges, namely participation in sacrifices, libations, and paeans along the route as well as privileges that the archon of the Eumolpidai provides, including the "distribution", a sum of money.[12] Since these privileges are based on the ephebes' services as escorts, it is surprising that an ephebic escort of Iakchos and the initiates, if it occurred at the same time, is not mentioned in this document as part of the ephebes' meritorious work ("greater *kosmos* and stronger guard for the *hiera*" [15-6] and "a stronger guard and a more extensive escort" [30-1]).

Finally, a most critical omission concerns the song called the Iakchos song – a major feature of the Iakchos procession – yet the only songs in which the ephebes participate, according to the decree, are paeans. It is hard to imagine any reason why the ephebes would not participate in the Iakchos song if it was being sung, or even why the Iakchos song is not mentioned at all. Thus the absence of any reference at all to Iakchos (or the initiates) is astonishing, especially the absence of Iakchos as the star of this procession, leading the initiates on the way to Eleusis (described below and illustrated in paintings).[13]

11 See recently Parker 2005, 349 n. 91.

12 On the distribution, see Clinton 1974, 23.

13 Paintings: Clinton 1992, 64-75.

In the Late Hellenistic period, the ephebes had escort duties that were significantly less onerous than those required by this decree, as we learn from several Hellenistic decrees honouring ephebes. These decrees state that the ephebes met the *hiera* and escorted them, expressed by the formula "ἐποιήσαντο δὲ καὶ τὴν ὑπάντησιν τοῖς ἱεροῖς καὶ προέπεμψαν αὐτά, καὶ τὸν Ἴακχον ὡσαύτως" (e.g., *IG* II², 1008.7): "they also performed the *hypantesis* of the *hiera* and escorted them onward, and Iakchos likewise". The adverb "likewise" indicates an action parallel to what they did for the *hiera*: they also performed the *hypantesis* for Iakchos and escorted *him* onward.[14] There were two parallel actions; not a single procession, but separate ones.[15] No Hellenistic document reports that the ephebes went all the way to Eleusis to fetch the *hiera*. In fact, the *hypantesis*, a meeting or formal reception, implies that they intercepted the sacred objects or Iakchos before the *hiera* or Iakchos reached a destination. In a common form of *hypantesis*, a group of officials would go out of their city and meet a distinguished guest (or in some cases the entire citizen body would turn out) and escort the guest into the city.[16]

14 "ὡσαύτως" with reference to Iakchos also occurs in *IG* II², 1028.9-10, 1030.6-7 (restored), *SEG* XXII, 111.6-7 (restored), XXIV, 189.5 (restored); alternatively, "ὁμοίως δὲ καί", in *IG* II²,1006.9,74, 1011.8, *SEG* XXI, 476.6 (restored).

15 One decree tells us that these meetings took place at a site called "Echo" (*IG* II², 1011.7-8). A suitable spot would be in the pass through Mt. Aigaleos, where now the sound of automobiles reverberates off the nearby hills, not far from the entry into the Thriasian Plain.

16 See the full description of a formal ὑπάντησις in a decree of Cyzicus when the city welcomed its benefactors, the kings Roimetalkes, Polemon, and Kotys and their mother in AD 39 (*SIG*³, 798.19-25). Another example, closer to the time of the ephebic decrees, is the Athenians' welcome of Athenion (in 88/7) when he came from Mithradates to win the city over to the side of the king: "ὑπήντησαν δ' αὐτῷ καὶ οἱ περὶ τὸν Διόνυσον τεχνῖται, τὸν ἄγγελον τοῦ νέου Διονύσου καλοῦντες ἐπὶ τὴν κοινὴν ἑστίαν καὶ τὰς περὶ ταύτην εὐχάς τε καὶ σπονδάς" (Ath. 5.49, 212D).

Thus the ephebes would have met the *hiera* as the *hiera* were approaching the asty of Athens, and met Iakchos as he was approaching Eleusis. Iakchos did not need to approach Athens in a procession; he was already there, in his temple; the only time that the ephebes could meet him was when he approached Eleusis. The *hiera*, on the other hand, approached Athens on Boedromion 14. The ephebes must have been in central Athens on that day, as there is no mention of an escort from Eleusis in the Hellenistic decrees, and so we can assume that at that time they performed the *hypantesis* and escort onward into the central city. But the question then arises: When did the ephebes go to Eleusis in order to perform the *hypantesis* for Iakchos as he approached the deme? It seems to make the most sense to assume that they escorted the *hiera* on the 19th from Athens to Eleusis; in that case, the ephebes were already in Eleusis as Iakchos approached on the 20th. This also suits the language of the Hellenistic ephebic degrees: the *hypantesis* and escort of the *hiera* always precedes that of Iakchos. Thus the ephebes' *hypantesis* on the 14th and escorts on the 14th and 19th precede their *hypantesis* and escort of Iakchos on the 20th.[17] In mentioning that the ephebes performed the *hypantesis* and escorted the *hiera* onward, the decree assumes that the reader will know that the escort onward had two parts – escorting the *hiera* to the City Eleusinion on the 14th and continuing the escort to Eleusis five days later, on the 19th. On the following day, the 20th, they did the same for Iakchos, coming out from Eleusis to meet him and escort him into Eleusis. The escort of Iakchos into Eleusis on the 20th was a relatively short trip, not a physically demanding one.[18]

17 Usually the decrees then mention that the ephebes lifted the oxen for sacrifice at Eleusis.

18 For further discussion of the two processions, including the interpretation of Graf 1996, 61-4, see *IEleusis* 2:638 (Commentary), 2:407-9.

The decree from the 3rd century AD (*IEleusis* 638) does not mention a *hypantesis* of Iakchos by the ephebes, presumably because their role as escorts of the *hiera* was complete after they had escorted the *hiera* to Eleusis. The Reception of Iakchos in Eleusis, which is attested at the end of the 3rd century BC (*IEleusis* 208 = *IG* II^3, 1164) and which we know was taking place at least from the time of Euripides, may have been felt, in the early 3rd century AD (or even earlier), to be a sufficient welcome for Iakchos, so that a *hypantesis* was no longer necessary. It seems to be a reasonable hypothesis that the ephebic *hypanteseis* of the *hiera* and Iakchos were Hellenistic innovations and did not represent ancestral tradition, hence they were superseded by the scheme described in the archaizing sacred law from the early 3rd century AD. The original ancestral tradition, as I will suggest shortly, was a full military escort for the *hiera*; this was relaxed in Hellenistic times by the introduction of the *hypanteseis*, but was fully reinstated by the late Roman decree (*IEleusis* 638).[19]

3. *IEleusis* 250 (= LSS 15)

This Hellenistic document (Agora Excavations, Inv. No. I 3844, published by James Oliver in 1941), though fragmentary, is our other main sacred law concerning a procession at the Mysteria. It gives us a glimpse of the complexities of organizing the great procession of Iakchos, consisting of thousands of initiates and other participants, as it made its way from the centre of Athens along the Sacred Way to Eleusis.

[- - - - - - - - - - -]Ο̣ΓΙΔΙΣ ὑ̣π̣ά̣ρχ̣οντο̣[ς -]
[- - - - - - - - - - τοῦ δ]ήμο̣υ̣· τ̣ύχη ἀ̣γ̣[αθῆ δεδόχθαι τῆ βουλῆ -]
[- - - - - - - - - - -]ΙΕΙΑ̣Λ[- -]
[- -]Λ̣ΕΙΑ[- - - - - -]ΝΑΠΟ[- -]
[- - - - - - - κατὰ τὰ π]ά̣τ̣ρια̣ τῷ[ν -]
[- - - - -]Ε̣ΙΑ[- κατὰ τὰ] π̣ά̣τρια̣ κα̣ὶ [-]
[- - - - - - - - - - - - - - -]Ι[. . .]Τ̣[-]
[- - - - - - - - - - κατὰ?] φυλὰς π̣ρὸ μ̣υ̣[στηρίων -]
[- - - - - -] ἑκάσ̣τ̣η̣ Ι[. . . 7 . . . .]ΙΛ̣Ι[. .]Σ̣[.]ντ[-]
[- - - - - τ]ῶν μυσ̣τ̣α̣γωγῶ̣ν̣ ἐ[κ]κ̣λησ̣[ία -οἱ πάρε]-
[δροι τοῦ βασ]ιλέως καὶ οἱ ἐπιμελ̣ηταὶ τῶν μ̣υ̣σ̣τ̣ηρίων [-]
[- - - -]ω̣ς̣, λ̣ειτουργείτωσαν δὲ τ̣ο̣ῖ̣ς̣ τελ̣ο̣[υ̣μένοις -]
[. . . . . οἱ ἱερεῖ]ς οἵ τε δημόσιοι πάντ̣ες [κ]α̣ὶ̣ [- -]
[. . . . 9 . . . . . Κ]ηρύκων καὶ Εὐμολπιδῶν [- -]
[- - - - -] τοὺς ἱκανοὺς κα̣ὶ [- -ἐλαύ]-
[νειν δὲ κατὰ] τ̣άξιν καὶ τὴν π̣ορείαν εὐ̣κ̣ό̣[σμως] π̣[οι]ε̣ῖ[ν] ὥ̣στ[ε] Α̣Τ[- - - - - - - - - - - - - - - - -]
[- - - ἐὰ]ν δ̣ὲ ο̣ἱ μυσ̣ταγωγοὶ μὴ σ̣υ̣ν̣π̣[ο]ρ̣ε̣ύ̣ω̣ντ̣α̣ι τ̣ο̣ῖς μ[ύσταις -]
[. . . . πρὸ τοῦ τῆς] μυ̣ή̣σεως κ̣α̣ιρ[ο]ῦ̣ ἐ̣ξ[ηγῶντα]ι τ[ο]ῖς μ̣ύ̣στ̣[αις -]
[- - - - ὅταν] δ̣ὲ̣ ἄ̣γωσι τοὺς μύστας ἐ[πὶ . . . .]¯ ¯Ο[.]α̣ν̣ [- - -] μυστ[- - - - - - - - - - - - - - - - - - -]
[- - - - - -] καὶ οἱ τῶν μυστηρί[ω]ν̣ [ἐπιμε]λ̣ηταὶ κ̣[ύριοι ἔστω]σαν ζ̣ημ[ιῶ]σαι τ̣ο̣ὺ̣[ς . . . .]
[- - - - - -]θ̣αι παραχ[ρ]ῆμα ἐ[ν] τ̣ῷ̣[ι . . . . 7-8 . . . .]ΔΕΤΟΙ[- c.6 -]ς καὶ ἔνδε[ιξις ἔσ]-
[τω πρὸς τὸν βασιλέ]α̣ τῷ βο̣υ̣λομένῳ ο̣ἷ̣ς ἔξ[εστι Ἀθηναίων - -] κ̣α̣[ὶ] το[ῖ]ς ἐπιμεληταῖ[ς . . . 7 . . . .]
[. . . . τῶν μυστηρ]ίων· τὸν δὲ ἐνδε[ιχ]θ̣έ̣[ντα - - - - -]¯ ε̣ἰ̣ς̣ ἕ̣να [καὶ π]εντακοσίους [. . . . . 10 . . . . .]
[κατὰ δὲ τὰς στ]ή̣λ̣α̣[ς] τ̣ε[ι]μάτω αὐτῷ ἢ̣ [ἡ]λ̣ι̣α̣[ία, ἐὰν ἁλῷ], τ[ί χρὴ παθεῖν ἢ ἀ]π̣ο̣τεῖσ[α]ι· τὰς δὲ πε[ρὶ ἀσεβείας]
[μυστηρίων λαγ]χ̣ανο̣μένας δίκας εἰσαγέτωσ[α]ν ο̣ἱ ἐπιμε[ληταὶ] τ̣ῶ̣ν̣ [μυ]σ̣τ̣ηρίων πρώτα̣[ς εἰς πάντα]

19 There may also have been a *hypantesis* by ordinary Athenians if Foucart 1914, 306 is correct in his interpretation of a passage in [Lys.] *Against Andocides* 50.

[τὰ δικαστήρια] ἐ̣ν τῷ ἐ̣π̣ομέν̣ῳ μετὰ τὰ μ[υστήρι]α̣ μερισμῷ̣ κ̣ατ̣ὰ τὰ μ[έρη] δ̣έκ̣[α]· ὅ̣ταν̣ [ἐ]λ̣ά̣σ[ωσιν οἱ μύσ]-
[ται ἐξ ἄστεως, ἀ]γέτωσαν αὐτοὺς οἱ μυσ[ταγωγοὶ . .]κερ[- - - c.16 - - -] ἐ[π]ὶ το̣ῖ̣ς ὀ̣χήμ[ασι . .5. . .]
[. . . .9. . . . . ἐλ]α̣υνέτωσαν ὅταν καὶ ὡς ἂν [ὁ βασιλεὺς καὶ οἱ τῶν μυστηρίων ἐ]π̣ιμε̣λητ̣α̣ὶ τάξω[σιν - - - -]
[- - - - μηδὲ π]ο̣[ρ]ε̣[ύε]σθαι μη̣δ̣ένα μύ[στην, μηδὲ ἐ]λ̣α̣ύν̣ε̣ι[ν ἄλλοθε]ν̣ ἢ ἐ̣κ τοῦ ἀποδεδειγμέ[νου χωρίου]
[- - -] μηδὲ π̣ρ[οπορε]ύ̣εσθαι πρὸ τῆς κο[μιδῆς . . .]II μ[ηδ]ὲ κ̣α̣[τα]β̣αίνε[ι]ν̣ ἀπὸ τῶν ὀ̣[χ]ημάτων [- - - -]
[- - - - ἢ π]ρ[ὸ]ς τὸ ἀ̣πο[δεδε]ι̣γμένον χωρίον ὑπ[ὸ] τ̣[ῶν] π̣ρὸς το[ύτοις] τεταγμένων, [μ]ηδὲ ἄ̣λ[λο]θεν ἐλα̣[ύνειν μη]-
[δὲ κατ' ἄλλας ὁ]δ̣ο̣ὺ̣ς ἢ [τὰς] ἀ̣[π]οδ̣ε̣δειγμένας, μηδ' εἰσιέ̣ναι κ̣α̣τ̣' ἄ̣[λλα]ς πύλας ἢ καθ̣ὼ̣ς πάτριόν ἐστι· [- -]
[- - - - ἐὰ]ν̣ δὲ ἄ[λλως] πο̣ι̣ῇ, ἔ̣νοχος ἔσ̣τ̣ω ὁ μυσταγωγὸς το̣ῖ̣ς ἐ̣π̣ά̣νω γεγραμμένοις ἐ̣π̣ιτε̣ι̣μ[ίοις κα]-
[τὰ τὰ δόξαντα] τάδε· κ[αὶ] ἐν Ἐλ̣[ευσῖνι] τ̣ῷ τε Ἰάκχῳ συνεισ̣ελ̣α̣ύνειν ὡς ἂ̣ν ὁ βασιλεὺς κ̣α̣ὶ οἱ ἐ̣π̣ιμ[εληταὶ τά]-
[ξωσι καὶ - - - -] ν̣ύ̣κτωρ κάθ̣[εσθαι ἐσ]τ̣εφ̣α̣ν̣ω̣μένους ἐ̣π̣άναγ̣κες ἐν τῷ [ἀπο]δ̣ε̣δειγ̣μ̣έ[νῳ χωρίῳ - - - -]
[- -]

It is in fact a decree, as indicated in line 11. In lines 14-5, there is reference to ancestral tradition. Line 19 mentions a gathering of mystagogues ("ἐκκλησία μυσταγογῶν"), apparently before the beginning of the Mysteria (cf. line 17). Various officials are mentioned in lines 19-23, as well as members of the Eumolpidai and Kerykes.[20] Line 25 states the necessity of keeping good order during the procession. Line 26 seems to suggest a penalty for mystagogues if they do not march together with their *mystai.* Line 27 mentions the possibilty of receiving *exegesis* before the time of the preliminary *myesis*, no doubt to deal with issues regarding eligibility for participation. Line 28 refers to people who "conduct" the initiates, presumably the mystagogues and administrative officers, such as the *basileus* and his *epimeletai.* Lines 29-35 concern penalties and judicial actions for improper behaviour at the Mysteries. Lines 35-42 contain precise regulations about the conduct of the procession: the mystagogues are to "guide" the initiates; the *mystai* are to (start) marching only from their designated spot; they are not to advance ("π̣ρ[οπορε]ύ̣εσθαι") in front of something transported; they are not to descend from their vehicles (the latter two provisions perhaps applying to officials); they are to march toward the assigned spot, presumably the stopping point, and along the designated roads; they are not to pass through gates other than the traditional ones; a mystagogue is to be punished if he does not provide proper guidance. Finally (lines 43-4), at Eleusis they are to march in together with Iakchos just as the *basileus* and *epimeletai* order ("κ[αὶ] ἐν Ἐλ[ευσῖνι] τ̣ῷ τε Ἰάκχῳ συνεισ̣ελ̣αύνειν ὡς ἂ̣ν ὁ βασιλεὺς κ̣α̣ὶ οἱ ἐ̣π̣ιμ[εληταὶ τάξωσι"); during the night, they are to sit (presumably by the sanctuary) wearing their crowns in their assigned place. At this critical moment – entrance into Eleusis – the initiates enter with Iakchos; there is no mention of the *hiera.*

Especially interesting is the absence of any mention of the *hiera.* All indications are that this is the procession of the *mystai*, i.e. the Iakchos procession; there is no mention of an ephebic escort. The verb used for the initiates' activity is ἐλαύνειν. Their mystagogues guide, ἄγουσι. Thus the character of the procession is altogether different from the procession on the 19th, a *pompe hama hierois*, an Escort with the *Hiera.* The procession of the initiates on the 20th is an *elasis*, a march. This is also what the initiates do in their other great procession during the Mysteria: on the 16th of Boedromion, the day called *Elasis halade*, March to the Sea, when they march down to Phaleron with their piglets.[21] The decree *IEleusis* 250 presents a picture of initiates prone to disorder as they march; they have to be rigorously regulated. This march obviously lacked the *kosmos*

20 Perhaps all the public priests (line 22, but this restoration may not be correct).

21 See Mylonas 1961, 249; Foucart 1914, 314-6.

of the Escort of the *Hiera*. The Iakchos March was a joyous affair, with the *mystai* shouting "Iakche, Iakche" as they sing the Iakchos song – a march with Dionysiac enthusiasm.

The *mystai* in the *Frogs* generally see Iakchos as a fellow traveler (396), even an escort (408) as he sometimes appears in vase paintings.[22] But they are not his escort. In the actual *elasis*, as Plutarch says, "they [the Athenians] lead out Iakchos", i.e. his statue is on a wagon, at the head of the procession, guided by the sacred official called Iakchagogos.[23] The chorus in the *Frogs* sing (350-2) "Illuminating with torchlight, lead out to flowering meadowland our youthful chorus, blessed one!" Iakchos is the focus and star of this procession of the *mystai*, whereas the focus of the *pompe hama hierois* on the 19th is the *hiera*, the sacred objects, most likely led by the hierophant. The *pompe hama hierois* featured a military escort enhancing the dignity and solemnity of the *hiera* while protecting them against the possibility of impiety (*IEleusis* 638).[24] The decree refers to the ephebes as "an escorting military force", "παραπέμπουσα στρατιά" (line 19). If there is significance in this phrase, used in this archaizing document, which bases itself on ancestral tradition, I suspect that it is the fact that, early on, a military force guarded the *hiera* on the long journeys from Eleusis to the Eleusinion and from the Eleusinion to Eleusis, even before the formal institution of the ephebes, because the *hiera* needed to be protected against impiety, especially during times of hostilities. By the Late Hellenistic period, however, there was much less need for such a military escort from Eleusis to the asty; by then, the *hypantesis* was sufficient to honour the approaching *hiera*.

IEleusis 250 (above, pp. 166-7) mentions some of the officials who accompanied the initiates in the Iakchos procession: the *basileus* and the *epimeletai* of the Mysteria (lines 20, 29, 37, 43). They were administrators of the Mysteria, as we know from the *Athenaion Politeia* and a law of the 4th century BC (*IEleusis* 138).

The only Eleusinian sacred official explicitly mentioned in connection with the *pompe hama hierois* is the *phaidyntes*, but the famous Bridge Decree of 422 BC (*IG* I³, 79 = *IEleusis* 41) concerning the construction of a bridge across the Rheitos mentions priestesses carrying the *hiera*. These should be the two hierophantides, whose sculptural representations appear in the Lesser Propylaea at Eleusis.[25] The other major priestess of the Mysteria, the priestess of Demeter and Kore, surely would not be absent from such a procession, nor would the principal priests – the hierophant, *dadouchos*, and sacred herald. A document of c. AD 170 (*IEleusis* 489 = *IG* II², 1092) lists recipients of shares of an endowment established for the Eleusinian sanctuary:

ἱεροφάντης διπλῆν
δᾳδοῦχος διπλῆν
ἀρχιερεὺς διπλῆν
ἐξηγητὴς διπλῆν
ἐξηγηταὶ τρεῖς διπλᾶς
ἱεροκῆρυξ διπλῆν
ἐπὶ βωμῷ διπλῆν
Ἀθηνᾶς ἱέρεια διπλῆν
Δήμητρος κ Κόρ διπλῆν
ἱεροφάντιδες δύο διπλᾶς
ἱέρεια Κα̣λ̣[...6...ἁπλῆν] 66 ἄρχ[ων] Ε[ὐ]-
ἱέρεια Μοι[ρ...6...ἁπλ]ῆ(ν) μολπιδ(ῶν) ἁπ[λῆν]
καὶ ὅσοι π[αῖδες μυηθέν(τες)] *v* ἀφ᾽ ἑσ[τίας]
φαιδυντὴ̣ς [ἁπλῆν] *vvv* [- - - - - - -]
Διὸς ἱερεὺ[ς ἁπλῆν *vacat?*]
Ἰαχχαγωγὸ[ς ἁπλῆν]

22 See above, n. 13.

23 Clinton 1974, 96-7.

24 The separateness of the two processions is also reflected in *IG* II², 1191 (= *IEleusis* 95.15-9) (1. τὰ ἱερά, 2. ἡ πανήγυρις τῶν Ἑλλήνων): ὅ[πω]ς τ[ὰ] ἱερὰ ἀσφαλῶς καὶ καλῶ[ς π]ορε[ύ]ητα[ι] καὶ ἡ πανήγυρι[ς τῶν] ε[ἰσα]φι[κ]νο[υ]μένων [Ἑ]λλήν[ων Ἐλευ]σ[ῖ]νάδε καὶ εἰς τὸ ἱερόν, [καὶ] οἱ τὸ προάστιον οἰκοῦν[τ]ε[ς καὶ] οἱ γεω[ρ]γοὶ σώιζωνται".

25 Clinton 2004, 85-7.

Βουζύγη[ς   ἀπλῆν   ]
πυρφόρο[ς   ἀπλῆν   ]
παναγὴς ᵛ[ἀπλῆν   ]
ἱερεὺς Θεο[ῦ καὶ Θεᾶς ἀπλῆν   ]
ἱερεὺς Τρ[ιπτολέμου ἀπλῆν]

Here we see in part a hierarchical list of sacred officials that looks very much like the order of a procession, and in this case the procession can only be the *pompe hama hierois*: hierophant, *dadouchos*, high priest (of the imperial cult), exegete (of unstated type), three exegetes (presumably of the Eumolpidai), sacred herald, altar-priest, priestess of Athena, priestess of Demeter and Kore, the two *hierophantides*, two priestesses (whose titles are not completely preserved), initiates from hearth, *phaidyntes*, priest of Zeus, Iakchagogos, Bouzyges, *pyrphoros*, *panages*, priest of the God and the Goddess, priest of Triptolemos, and archon of the Eumolpidai.[26] However, only the list down as far as the *hierophantides* (the first column) could probably represent the order of the procession of the *hiera* (they are in fact the more important priests and they receive a double share of the endowment); the initiates from hearth and the Iakchagogos must of course belong to the March with Iakchos.

A notable exception to these dual processions was the procession organized by Alcibiades in 407 BC, who had the infantry provide an escort in order to put an end, if only temporarily, to the processions by sea, which had been necessitated by the Spartan occupation of Decelea and the passes to Eleusis. These processions by sea, as Plutarch noted (*Alc.* 34.3-7), lacked the "splendour" (*kosmos*) of the traditional ritual (*telete*) and omitted "also sacrifices and dances and many of the rites along the route when they march out Iakchos".[27] Plutarch clearly implies that a single procession took place on a single day because of the presence of hostile forces. It was prompted by Alcibiades' desire to make a grand display, in response to the Athenians' disappointment about the rites omitted during the sea voyages which had replaced the traditional Iakchos processions. Evidently the Athenians had been sending both the *hiera* and the initiates to Eleusis in ships on the same day. Obviously circumstances could dictate flexibility in the arrangement and timing of the processions, and Alcibiades responded by reverting to the land route with the help of the army.

The terms "ἱεροφαντία καὶ μυσταγωγία" (*Alc.* 34.6), used by some observers of this procession, seem to reflect the unusual combination of the processions of the *hiera* and of Iakchos, the term *hierophantia* suggesting that it consisted of the most important priests of the Mysteria led by the hierophant (as in the escort with the *hiera*), the term *mystagogia* suggesting that it included the *mystai* with their mystagogues; that is, it combined both processions. The combination was necessary because it would have been impractical for the infantry, just as we saw in the case of the ephebes, to conduct processions from the asty on two days in a row: from the asty to Eleusis, then in the evening back to the asty, and the next morning back to Eleusis with Iakchos. (The *hiera* in this time of warfare would have been kept in the City Eleusinion, not at Eleusis.) Plutarch's description of the order of the participants – "ἱερεῖς καὶ μύσται καὶ μυσταγωγοί" – would also be consistent with "ἱεροφαντία καὶ μυσταγωγία".[28] The ἱερεῖς would

26 Further discussion in *IEleusis* 2:489 (Commentary).

27 *Alc.* 4: οὐδένα κόσμον εἶχεν ἡ τελετὴ πεμπομένη κατὰ θάλατταν, ἀλλὰ καὶ θυσίαι καὶ χορεῖαι καὶ πολλὰ τῶν δρωμένων καθ' ὁδὸν ἱερῶν, ὅταν ἐξελαύνωσι τὸν Ἴακχον, ὑπ' ἀνάγκης ἐξελείπετο.

28 *Alc.* 6: ἱερεῖς δὲ καὶ μύστας καὶ μυσταγωγοὺς ἀναλαβὼν καὶ τοῖς ὅπλοις περικαλύψας, ἦγεν ἐν κόσμῳ καὶ μετὰ σιωπῆς, θέαμα σεμνὸν καὶ θεοπρεπὲς τὴν στρατηγίαν ἐκείνην ἐπιδεικνύμενος, ὑπὸ τῶν μὴ φθονούντων ἱεροφαντίαν καὶ μυσταγωγίαν προσαγορευομένην.

belong to the Escort of the Hiera (here called *hierophantia*), the μύσται καὶ μυσταγωγοί to the Iakchos March (here called *mystagogia*). Alcibiades led them in good order and silence, Plutarch said. This was a significant change from the style of the Iakchos March, which on this occasion would have lacked much of its Dionysiac character; thus the term *mystagogia* would be more appropriate. If they made the entire journey in silence, one wonders about the sacrifices and dances and other rites that were omitted when the procession had gone by sea, i.e. whether they were now also omitted during Alcibiades' military escort; the silence suggests omission, unless the omission was restricted to a critical point of the journey, namely the march over Mount Aigaleos, where the threat from a hostile force would be most serious.

In conclusion, there were normally two processions from central Athens to Eleusis at the Mysteria, the Escort of the *Hiera* on Boedromion 19 and the Iakchos March on the next day; this satisfies the evidence for the two dates and the implication in Hellenistic decrees that the *hiera* were conveyed in a separate procession, preceding the procession with Iakchos.[29] However, in times of emergency, the processions could take place on the same day, with the *hiera* preceding the initiates and mystagogues. This recognition brings us closer to the religious atmosphere of the festival. The Escort of the *Hiera* was an august affair, an ancestral tradition, conducted with the great dignity that can be bestowed by a military escort; it was accompanied by sacrifices, libations, and paeans, and comprised the hierophant and major priests and priestesses of the Mysteria. The Iakchos March, on the other hand, included the initiates and their mystagogues, led by the initiates' divine spirit, Iakchos, the god of many hymns. It was the *panegyris* of the Hellenes, raising an enormous cloud of dust as they marched, singing the Iakchos song. It too was accompanied by sacrifices, and also by dances, as Plutarch noted. Unlike the solemn *pompe* of the *hiera*, it was a Dionysiac affair.

29 The arrangement made good sense administratively; having each procession on a separate day facilitated organization, considering how difficult it can be to organize a major procession, and it allowed each procession's distinct character to be the focus of the day.

Appendix

The Procession at the Andanian Mysteria

A comparison of the Eleusinian procession with the one at the Andanian Mysteria helps to shed light on the roles of processions in both festivals, especially since the Andanian one is a well-described procession in a mystery cult, in legislation called *diagramma* (*IG* V,1 1390.28-34):[30]

> πομπᾶς. ἐν δὲ τᾶι πομπᾶι ἁγείστω Μνασίστρατος, ἔπειτεν ὁ ἱερεὺς τῶν θεῶν, οἷς /(29) τὰ μυστήρια γίνεται, μετὰ τᾶς ἱερέας, ἔπειτα ἀγωνοθέτας, ἱεροθύται, οἱ αὐληταί· μετὰ δὲ ταῦτα αἱ παρθένοι αἱ ἱεραί, καθὼς ἂν λά/(30)χωντι, ἄγουσαι τὰ ἅρματα ἐπικειμένας κίστας ἐχούσας ἱερὰ μυστικά· εἶτεν ἁ θοιναρμόστρια ἁ εἰς Δάματρος καὶ αἱ ὑποθοιναρ/(31)μόστριαι αἱ ἐμβεβακυῖαι, εἶτεν ἁ ἱέρεα τᾶς Δάματρος τᾶς ἐφ' ἱπποδρόμωι, εἶτεν ἁ τᾶς ἐν Αἰγίλạ· ἔπειτεν αἱ ἱεραὶ κατὰ μίαν, κα/(32)θώς κα λάχωντι, ἔπειτεν οἱ ἱεροί, καθώς κα οἱ δέκα διατάξωντι. ὁ δὲ γυναικονόμος κλαρούτω τάς τε ἱερὰς καὶ παρθένους καὶ ἐπιμέλειαν /(33) ἐχέτω, ὅπως πομπεύωντι, καθώς κα λάχωντι. ἀγέσθω δὲ ἐν τᾶι πομπᾶι καὶ τὰ θύματα, καὶ θυσάντω τᾶι μὲν Δάματρι σῦν ἐπίτοκα, Ἑρμᾶ/(34) νι κριόν, Μεγάλοις Θεοῖς δάμαλιν σῦν, Ἀπόλλωνι Καρνείωι κάπρον, Ἅγναι οἶν.

Concerning the Procession: In the procession Mnasistratos must lead, then the priest of the gods for whom the Mysteries are celebrated in company with

30 The text is that of Gawlinski 2012, 70, 72.

> the priestess, then the *agonothetes*, the *hierothytai*, and the *auletai*. And after those, the sacred virgins, as allotted, leading the chariots with a *kista* set upon them containing the *hiera mystika*. Then the *thoinarmostria* for (the sanctuary) of Demeter, and the assistant *thoinarmostriai* who are mounted (on them), then the priestess of Demeter at the Hippodrome, and then the priestess of Demeter in Aigila. Then the sacred women, one by one, as allotted, then the sacred men, as the Ten Men arrange them. The *gynaikonomos* must allot the places of the sacred women and virgins and is to see that they process as they were allotted. The sacrificial animals are also to be led in the procession, and they must sacrifice a pregnant sow to Demeter, a ram to Hermes, a young pig to the Great Gods, a boar to Apollo Karneios, and a sheep to Hagna.[31]

Laura Gawlinski (and, so far as I know, all other commentators) understood the procession to be the one that escorted the *hiera* from Messene to the sanctuary called Karneiasion in Andania.[32] A different interpretation now seems to me more likely.[33]

Some regulations in the Messenian *diagramma* are similar to those in the fragmentary decree *IEleusis* 250 (above, pp. 166-7). The participants are placed with precision; the sacred women and men are ordered to remain in their allotted positions, with special concern expressed about the behaviour of the sacred women (the *gynaikonomos* is to take care that they process according to their allotted order). There is a hierarchy, as we saw in the (probable) order of the Eleusinian Escort of the *Hiera* (*IEleusis* 489, above, p. 168). In the Andanian law it is precisely stated: 1) Mnasistratos; 2) the priest and priestess of the Mysteria; 3) the officials associated with the sacrifice (*agonothetes, hierothytai, auletai*);[34] 4) the sacred virgins leading the *hiera*; 5) the banquet mistress of Demeter, her assistants, two priestesses of Demeter;[35] 6) sacred women; 7) sacred men. The animals follow, as well as the command to sacrifice them and to which gods.

However, there is no mention of initiates and their mystagogues.[36] Thus the Andanian procession, at first glance, is more like the Eleusinian Escort of the *Hiera* (rather than the march [*elasis*] of the initiates from central Athens to Eleusis as described in *IEleusis* 250, above pp. 166-7). If this is the case, and the procession began in Messene, it is odd that the place from which the *hiera* are fetched is not mentioned, as it is in the Eleusinian document (*IEleusis* 638, above, p. 162).

There is a further major difference between the Eleusinian and Andanian escorts (*pompai*). At the tail end of the Andanian procession, the sacrificial animals are listed (a position that ensures the participants will not be forced to step on the animals' excrement), and the officials in charge of the sacrifice appear in the third section, close to the front of the procession. What is clear about this procession

31 Trans. Gawlinski 2012, 71, 73, except for "αἱ ἐμβεβακυῖαι" (31).

32 Gawlinski 2012, 30; Deshours 2006, 119-20.

33 It occurred to me at this time as I closely studied details of the procession and related ritual (oaths and sacrifices) in preparing this article.

34 The connection of the *agonothetes* with sacrifice is noted by Gawlinski 2012, 138 n. 169, with reference to Winand 1990, 179. See also Wörrle 1988, 190 on the sacrificial functions of the *agonothetes* of the Demostheneia at Oinoanda and *agonothetai* elsewhere.

35 This fifth group consists of sacred officials of Demeter, the first with duties at the banquet, and we can hypothetically assume that all these sacred officials of Demeter had to do with the banquet. Demeter's special status at the festival is reflected in her primary position at the sacrifice preceding the Sacred Meal, noted by Gawlinski 2012, 19. On Demeter and her priestesses at Messene, see Deshours 2006, 124-5, 188-9, 204-5, 226-33; Gawlinski 2012, 19-21, 141-2.

36 At the Eleusinian Mysteria the initiates and mystagogues journeyed in a march (*elasis*) to Eleusis, discussed above, pp. 167-8; such a march could have been described on a missing stele of the *diagramma*. On the existence of a preceding stele, see Gawlinski 2012, 2, 61.

therefore is that it belongs to the category of processions that lead to a sacrifice followed by a meal, in this instance a major sacrifice and a "sacred" meal. It was a "Sacrificial Procession", *Opferzug* in Martin P. Nilsson's terminology.[37] This is confirmed by the section on the Sacred Seal (lines 95-9):[38]

> Concerning the Sacred Meal: The Sacred Men, after removing the customary portions for the gods from each of the sacrificial victims led in the procession, must use the rest of the meat for the sacred meal, with the Sacred Women and Virgins, and they must invite the Priest and the Priestess and the Priestess of Karneios (ἱέρεαν τοῦ Καρνείου) and Mnasistratos and both his wife and his children and those artists who served in the dances and those serving as their helpers. And for the rest of the expenses they must make no greater expenditure than [blank] drachmas.[39]

The fact that it is a procession leading to a sacrifice and meal is not decisive in determining when it took place; however, the aorist participle indicates that the dances have already been performed, and therefore the procession, sacrifice, and sacred meal took place toward the end of the festival. It remains to be determined whether other information in the *diagramma* is in harmony with this inference.

The section entitled "Concerning the Supplying of Sacrificial Animals" states (lines 64-5):

> After their appointment the Sacred Men, having made an announcement in advance, are to contract out the supplying of sacrificial animals, which must be sacrificed and presented in the Mysteries (θύεσθαι καὶ παρίστασθαι ἐν τοῖς μυστηρίοις).

The animals are to be presented twice, as the text goes on to explain (lines 69-72):

> And the contractor, having provided guarantors to the Sacred Men, must take the funds and present very holy, pure, whole animals and show (ἐπιδειξάτω) them to the Sacred Men **ten days** before the Mysteries. The Sacred Men are to put a mark on those approved (τοῖς δοκιμασθέντοις), and the contractor must present (παριστάτω) the marked ones. If he does not present them for the scrutiny (μὴ περιστᾶι ἐπὶ τὰν δοκιμασίαν), the Sacred Men must exact from the guarantors the amount plus half, and they themselves must supply the animals and from the exacted funds recover the resulting expenditure for the animals.[40]

The first presentation of the animals by the contractor was for a *dokimasia*, to take place 10 days before the Mysteria; the second was the presentation of the approved animals at a (second) *dokimasia* "in the Mysteria" (line 65). This raises the question about the start date of the festival.

We have no explicit information about the start date of the Andanian Mysteria, i.e. whether, like the Eleusinian Mysteria, the festival started before the initiates arrived at the sanctuary, where the main ritual took place. However, the very beginning of this stele of the *diagramma* states: "The Secretary of the *Synedroi* must administer the oath written below

37 Nilsson 1916, 311-2. This is his type II (*Götterzug*), 1 (*Zug zum Gott*) a (*Opferzug*). He does not include it under type II, 1, c (*Zug, der die Verbindung zweier Kultstätten* ausdrückt), to which he assigns the "Iakchoszug", presumably because he found no indication in the Andianian *diagramma* for such a connection.

38 To my knowledge, this is the only example of a post-sacrifice meal (δεῖπνον) which is qualified as ἱερόν. This qualification may indicate that the participants of the meal are celebrants of the cult (in the case of the most prestigious celebrant, Mnasistratos, his family is also included). Such a meal seems to be alluded to in *IG* V,2 269:22-4, at Mantinea: "καλεῖν δὲ αὐτὴν κα[ὶ] ἐπὶ τὰ γέρα δι' αἰῶνος καὶ τοὺς ἐκγόνους αὐτῆς, καθ' ὃ ἂν δειπνῶσι οἱ ἱερεῖς".

39 Trans. Gawlinski 2012, 85, 87, except for the phrase in lines 97-8: "τῶν τεχνιτᾶν τοὺς λει[τουργή]σαντας [ἐν τα]ῖς χορείαις".

40 Trans. Gawlinski 2012, 79, 81.

immediately, unless someone is ill, while they pour blood and wine as the sacrifices are burning" ("[ἱερῶ]ν καιομένων", lines 1-2). After these instructions, it goes on to state (line 7): "The Priest and the Sacred Men should administer the same oath to the Sacred Women in the sanctuary of Karneios [ἐν τῶι ἱερῶ⟨ι⟩ τοῦ Καρνείου] *on the day before the Mysteria*."[41] It was especially urgent that the oaths of the men be administered immediately after their selection, obviously because the *diagramma* was issued very close to the start of the Mysteria. In the following year ("the 55th"), i.e. a normal year, the sacred men and women simply swear the oath in the eleventh month, before the Mysteria, for in this next year there will obviously be no special urgency, and nothing is said about the necessity of the women taking the oath in the sanctuary of Karneios (lines 10-1). If the sanctuary of Karneios is the Karneiasion (the term used elsewhere in the document), then the women took this oath, in the current year when the legislation occurred, in the Andanian sanctuary on the day before the Mysteria, not as in the following year, in the eleventh month on some unspecified day before the Mysteria (after the sacred men had sworn) at a venue that did not need to be specified.

We must next consider whether the sanctuary of Karneios (or Karneion) in question was located in Messene. In the current year, "immediately" (upon the selection of the sacred men), the sacred men took the same oath as the women (except for an appendix contained in the women's oath), "as the sacrifices are burning". The precise location is not mentioned; the most convenient one would presumably be somewhere in the city of Messene. As it was a matter of such urgency that immediately upon the allotment of the sacred men the secretary of the *synedroi* had to administer the oath, there seems to be no reason why it could not be administered in the very place where the *synedroi* met, issued the *diagramma*, and conducted the allotment of the sacred men – the *synedrion*, the Messenian Council.[42] Since the oath took place more than 10 days before the start of the festival, that is, before the sacred men had time to advertise and conclude a contract (or contracts) for the animals to be presented at a *dokimasia* on the tenth day before the Mysteria (line 70), we should not expect the sacred men to be in Andania at this early point.

The oath taken by the women (surely also as sacrifices were burning)[43] must be taken "in the sanctuary of Karneios on the day before the Mysteria". If the sanctuary of Karneios were in the city, surely it would also be the appropriate venue for the oath of the sacred men. But since the men were not required to take their oath in this sanctuary, this fact tends to confirm that the venue for the women's oath was not a Karneion in the city, but the sanctuary of Karneios at Andania, also called simply Karneiasion. If a woman failed to take the oath, she was not replaced, like a man who refused, but was fined 1000 drachmas and prohibited from celebrating the rituals at sacrifices (which started even before the festival began) and from taking part in the Mysteria (lines 8-10). Fundamentally, neither the selected sacred men nor the selected sacred women could undertake their official activities before taking their respective oaths, activities that would include the *pompa* leading to the sacrifice. Both the sacred men (administering the oath) and the women (taking the oath) had to be in the sanctuary on the day before the start of the Mysteria. It was therefore impossible for the *pompa* to have taken place before the eve of the Mysteria.

These details concerning the venues and times of the oath-taking of the sacred men and women suggest that the Messenian participants (and others) in the Mysteria arrived at the Karneiasion before

41 Trans. Gawlinski 2012, 67.

42 On the functions of the *synedroi* of Messene and the location of the *Synedrion*, see Deshours 2004, 136-9.

43 Although this is not mentioned, it is implied by the command to take "the same oath," line 8.

the festival began, on the preceding day or, if they wished, even earlier. Since the procession, sacrifice, and sacred meal took place "in the Mysteria", these events had to take place after the start of the festival at the sanctuary, theoretically even on the first day.[44] However, in that case the procession could not have been one that went from Messene to the Andanian sanctuary, because the sacred men and all the sacred women present in Andania on the eve of the festival for the oath would have had to travel c. 17 kilometres back to Messene on the day before the Mysteria and then repeat the same trip of c. 17 kilometres in a procession back to the sanctuary on the following day, the first day of the Mysteria – a total of c. 34 kilometres of travelling over two days. This of course is highly unlikely. However, we cannot exclude the possibility that there was an *elasis* from Messene to the sanctuary before the start of the Mysteria, like the Iakchos march from central Athens to Eleusis; such an *elasis* could have been described on a preceding stele.[45]

At the Eleusinian Mysteria, the main sacrifices at the Eleusinian sanctuary most probably took place on the day after the secret ritual within the sanctuary.[46] At Andania, if there is significance in the rather early placement of the procession and sacrifice on this stele of the *diagramma* (lines 28-34, following some early events and issues), it might suggest that they took place early on. Thus if the position of the description of the procession in the *diagramma* has significance, it could have been one of the opening events of the festival (although any such significance is diminished by the fact that the beginning of the *diagramma* most probably occurred on anothther stele).[47] As an opening event, the procession would have celebrated the introduction of the *hiera* contained in (evidently more than one) *kista*, mounted on chariots led by the sacred maidens, and the presentation of the principal sacred officials of the Mysteria – Mnasistratos, priest and priestess, those in charge of the sacrifice and sacred meal (*agonothetes, hierothytai, auletai, thoinarmostriai,* priestesses of Demeter), sacred women and men, and performing artists. It culminated in a sacred meal for the procession's participants and the priestess of Karneios (invited because it was her sanctuary, but she did not take part in the procession because it was not the festival of Karneios).[48] Thus it could have been a relatively short procession honoring this important group and the *hiera*.

However, what seems to be more significant than the early placement of the description of the procession within the *diagramma* is the chronological order in the delivery of the sacrificial and purificatory animals, which must be "presented in the Mysteria" (lines 67-9):

> ἔστι δὲ ἃ δεῖ παρέχειν, πρὸ τοῦ ἄρχεσθαι τῶν μυστηρίων, ἄρνας δύο λευκούς, ἐπὶ τοῦ καθαρμοῦ κρίον εὔχρουν, καί, ὅταν /(68) ἐν τῶι θεάτρωι καθαίρει, χοιρίσκους τρεῖς, ὑπὲρ τοὺς πρωτομύστας ἄρνας ἑκατόν, ἐν δὲ τᾶι πομπᾶι Δάματρι σῦν ἐπίτοκα, τοῖς δὲ Μεγάλοις /(69) Θεοῖς δάμαλιν διετῆ σῦν, Ἑρμᾶνι κριόν, Ἀπόλλωνι Καρνείωι κάπρον, Ἅγναι οἶν.

This appears to be in chronological order: 1) "before the beginning of the Mysteria", two white lambs; 2) "at the time of [ἐπί] the purification" (which we

44 This would be true of the sacrifice if there were a procession from Messene to the sanctuary, as Gawlinski 2012, 206 logically pointed out.

45 See n. 36 above. The women who had been selected to serve as sacred women presumably would not have to perform official duties during such a march.

46 See Clinton 1988, esp. 70-1.

47 On the question of a missing stele, see n. 36 above.

48 The other participants in the procession – *agonothetes, hierothytai, auletai, thoinarmostriai,* priestesses of Demeter – were not mentioned as participants in the Sacred Meal, presumably because, as they were involved with the sacrifice and the organization and preparation of the Sacred Meal (see p. 172 above), it was understood that they would participate in the meal itself.

would expect at the beginning), a ram of good complexion;[49] 3) "when one purifies in the theatre", three piglets;[50] 4) "on behalf of the first-time initiates", 100 lambs; 5) "in the procession", the animals for the sacrifice and sacred meal (above, p. 18). For each of the first three deliveries, a time is specified. It seems most natural to understand the last two deliveries in the same way: they took place toward the end of the festival, after the completion of the mystic rites. 100 lambs could have fed several hundred people; "ὑπέρ", undoubtedly meaning "on behalf of", need not mean that the sharing of the meat was limited to the initiates themselves.

Finally, as noted earlier (p. 172), in the section on the sacred meal, the last participants listed are the sacred artists and their assistants (lines 97-8): "τῶν τεχνιτᾶν τοὺς λει[τουργή]σαντας [ἐν τα]ῖς χορείαις καὶ τᾶν ὑπηρεσιᾶν τοὺς λειτουργοῦντας αὐτοῖς". Here, the aorist participle indicates antecedent action, as so often in qualifying an already completed office or liturgy in inscriptions: "those artists who served in the dances and those serving as their helpers".[51] The dances have already taken place; the sacred meal occurred at a later point in the festival.

Thus the sacrifices and sacred meal took place after the performance of the artists, which most likely took place at a central point in the festival, and this order, as has been shown, is consistent with all other information in the *diagramma*, including the order of delivering the sacrificial victims, with the 100 lambs "for the sake of the first-time initiates" and those for the sacred meal delivered at the end.[52] Sacrifice towards the end of the festival would parallel the order at Eleusis, with the great sacrifices and sacrificial feasts taking place after the mystic rites.

We could imagine that while the leading sacred officials, including members of Mnasistratos' family, enjoyed a sacred meal, the initiates and their families (and presumably others) participated in the feast provided by 100 lambs sacrificed "for the sake of the initiates", preceded by its own very simple procession. At any rate, the *diagramma* ought to have contained information about this other significant sacrifice (it would have entailed expenditures); it is hard to imagine that it was not described on the missing stele, along with other information concerning first-time initiates and other participants in the festival. As Gawlinski noted, sacrifices formed a major part of the festival, "evidenced by the repeated linking of 'αἱ θυσίαι καὶ τὰ μυστήρια' (lines 9-10, 39, 74, 75, 85-86, 183-184), phrasing which shows that a distinction was seen between the rituals of *thysia* and *mysteria*".[53] Given the prominence of the sacrifices, we are left to assume that there was a further description of the sacrifice for the initiates on the missing stele.

At Eleusis too there must have been a procession at the time of the major sacrifices that provided a meal for the entire festive throng. Though such a procession is not specifically attested, it is to be expected – a local procession leading to the sacrifice, when the ephebes, who took part in this (short) procession, lifted the sacrificial bulls for the slaughter,[54] followed by the participants' meal.

The precise route of the Andanian *pompa* is not specified in the *diagramma*, presumably because it was a traditional one known to all. The presence of the *hiera* would suggest that it terminated near

49 On such a purification ritual at Delos and elsewhere, see Clinton 2005, 172-3.

50 On this type of purification, see Gawlinski 2012, 170; Clinton 2005, 169-70; Parker 1981, 21.

51 Gawlinski 2012, 85 translated the participle with the English present participle ("serving"); Deshours 2006, 39 with the French future perfect ("auront joué"). Neither can be correct here.

52 On the importance of dancing and music during initiations in mystery cult, see Gawlinski 2012, 177-8.

53 Gawlinski 2012, 165.

54 See Clinton 1988. Sometimes the ephebes slaughtered the animals ἐν τῶι περιβόλωι τοῦ ἱεροῦ (*IG* II^2,1028.11), but the altars on which they were sacrificed and the *escharai* on which the meat was cooked were located in front of the sanctuary.

where the *hiera* would be housed until the next festival, perhaps in the Temple of the Great Gods or the Oikos. The procession may have started at the place where the *hiera* were displayed in the ritual.

In conclusion, the following seems to be the general order of the festival:

1) The participants, initiates and others, arrived in the sanctuary by the day before the start of the festival and set up their tents. (There was no formal *pompa* from Messene to the Karnaseion.)[55] Presumably on this day the two white lambs were sacrificed.
2) The festival began on the next day, and the sanctuary was purified with the sacrifice of "a ram of good complexion".
3) A major part of the ritual took place in the theatre, which was purified with three piglets.
4) *Pompa* and sacred meal. In addition, probably at this time 100 lambs were sacrificed "on behalf of the first-time initiates", followed by a meal for the first-time initiates and other participants.

Abbreviations

IEleusis = K. Clinton, *Eleusis. The Inscriptions on Stone. Documents of the Sanctuary of the Two Goddesses and the Public Documents of the Deme* 1 (2005), 2 (2008).
IG = *Inscriptiones Graecae* (1873-)
SEG = *Supplementum epigraphicum Graecum* (1923-)

Bibliography

ALESHIRE, S.B. 1991
Asklepios at Athens: Epigraphic and Prosopographic Essays on the Athenian Healing Cults, Amsterdam.

CLINTON, K. 1974
The Sacred Officials of the Eleusinian Mysteries, Philadelphia.

CLINTON, K. 1988
'Sacrifice at the Eleusinian Mysteries', in *Early Greek Cult Practice*, R. Hägg & N. Marinatos (eds.), Stockholm, 69-79.

CLINTON, K. 1992
Myth and Cult. The Iconography of the Eleusinian Mysteries. The Martin P. Nilsson Lectures on Greek Religion, Delivered 19-21 November 1990 at the Swedish Institute in Athens, Stockholm.

CLINTON, K. 2004
'Epiphany in the Eleusinian Mysteries', *Illinois Classical Studies* 29, 85-109.

CLINTON, K. 2005
'Pigs in Greek Rituals', in *Greek Sacrificial Ritual, Olympian and Chthonian,* R. Hägg & B. Alroth (eds.), Stockholm, 167-79.

DESHOURS, N. 2004
'Les institutions civiques de Messène à l'époque hellénistique tardive', *ZPE* 150, 134-46.

DESHOURS, N. 2006
Les mystères d'Andania: étude d'épigraphie et d'histoire religieuse, Bordeaux.

FOLLET, S. 1976
Athènes au IIe et au IIIe siècle, Paris.

FOUCART, P. 1914
Les Mystères d'Éleusis, Paris.

GAWLINSKI, L. 2012
The Sacred Law of Andania: A New Text with Commentary, Berlin.

55 On the question of an *elasis*, see n. 36 above.

GRAF, F. 1996
'*Pompai* in Greece: Some Considerations about Space and Ritual in the Greek *Polis*', in *The Role of Religion in the Early Greek Polis,* R. Hägg (ed.), Stockholm, 55-65.

MYLONAS, G.E. 1961
Eleusis and the Eleusinian Mysteries, 1961.

NILSSON, M.P. 1916
'Die Prozessionstypen im griechischen Kult', *JdI* 31, 309-39.

OLIVER, J.H. 1949
'Two Athenian Poets', *Hesperia Suppl.* 8, 243-58.

PARKER, R. 1981
Miasma: Pollution and Purification in Early Greek Religion, Oxford.

PARKER, R. 2005
Polytheism and Society at Athens, Oxford.

WINAND, J. 1990
Les hiérothytes: recherche institutionnelle, Brussels.

WÖRRLE, M. 1988
Stadt und Fest im kaiserzeitlichen Kleinasien, Munich.

Individuals and Polis in Cult: The Procession from Athens to Eleusis in Classical Times*

Soi Agelidis

Movement is an essential element of ancient Greek religious practice. The spatial arrangement of sanctuaries and other sacred places and the close political and religious connections among cities or between whole regions required a high degree of mobility from people in order for them to perform their religious duties. This movement had a different quality in various contexts, and in some cases it could even be part of certain rituals. It is a difficult endeavour to classify these different modes of movement and reach a consensus on the application of specific terms for each of them. This becomes obvious, for instance, when we consider the debate on terms such as "pilgrimage" or "sacred travel". The definitions for these phenomena cover a wide spectrum, from very generic to highly specific, and cannot be discussed here *in extenso*.[1] To indicate the differences, I will by way of introduction briefly discuss some of the definitions that have been put forward by scholars.

Matthew Dillon classified every visit by an individual to a religious place outside the borders of its physical environment as a pilgrimage.[2] Ian Rutherford defined it as a journey of considerable length to a sacred place,[3] and stated later that all cases where people visit sanctuaries for a religious reason could qualify as such.[4] Jaś Elsner and Ian Rutherford, who brought together a series of criteria to identify "pilgrimage" and thus outlined the problem rather than offering a definition of the term, give a more differentiated approach.[5] Broad definitions of the term like those of Matthew Dillon and Ian Rutherford allow us to consider a wide range of religious actions in this context, but on the other hand they pose the risk of generalising the label to such a degree that it could become insignificant. To avoid this, we could deal more intensively with two main points of contention in this debate: How important was the individual traveller? And how relevant was the purpose of the travel?

In the present paper, I emphasize these two elements, so I will refer primarily to the criteria of "activity at the sanctuary and motivation" according to Jaś Elsner and Ian Rutherford.[6] My specific interest pertains to the distinction

* I would like to thank Wiebke Friese, Søren Handberg, and Troels Myrup Kristensen for the invitation to present a paper at the conference at the Danish Institute in Athens and to contribute to this volume. For their helpful comments on my talk and the draft of my paper, I also thank the anonymous reviewers and the participants of the conference. Finally, I thank Katharine Handel and Alexander Jacobs for improving my English text.

1 On the definition of "sacred travel", see also the introduction to the present volume.

2 Dillon 1997, xviii.

3 Rutherford 2000.

4 Rutherford 2013, 12-4.

5 Elsner & Rutherford 2005, esp. 1-32. The criteria which they provide (11-2) are very instructive for the creation of a typology of pilgrimage: the spatial relation between sanctuary and clientele; the identity of the pilgrims; timetable; activity at the sanctuary; motivation.

6 See n. 5 above.

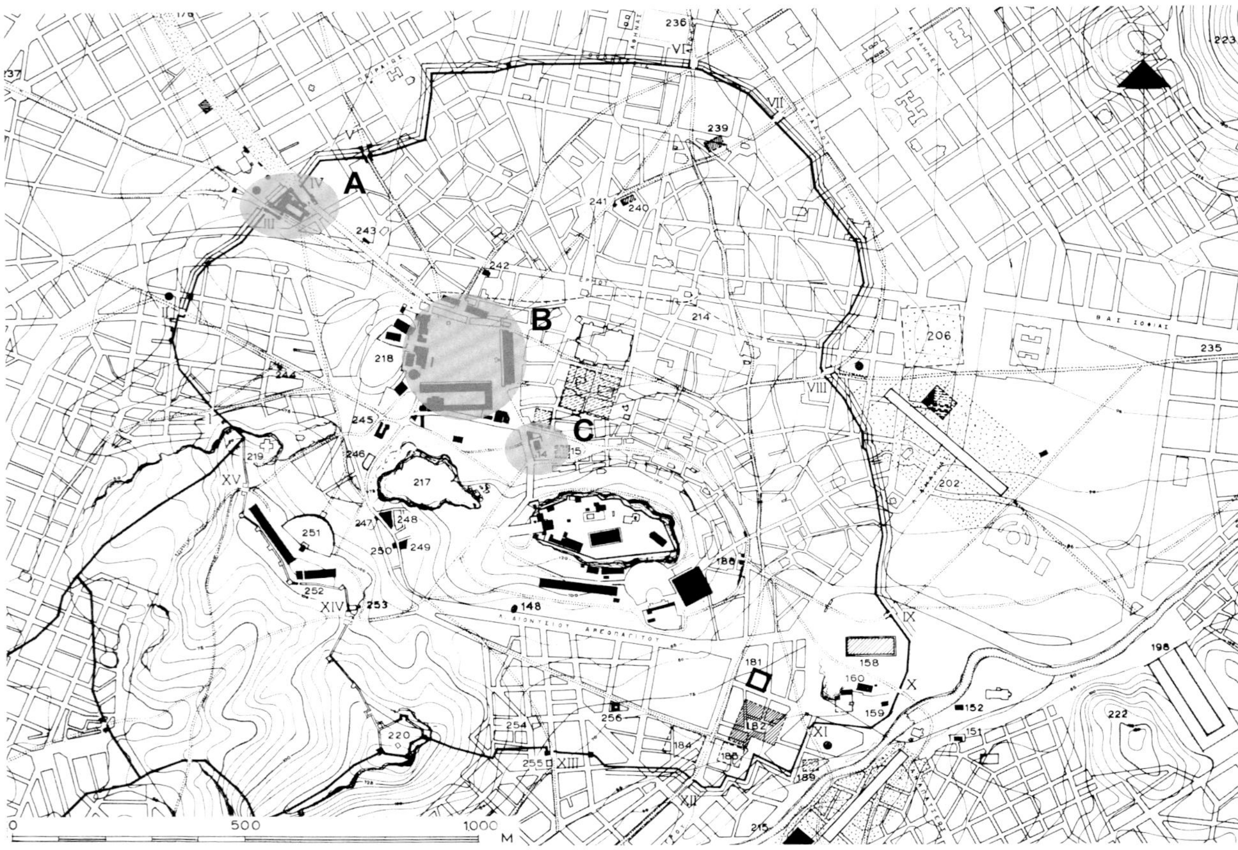

Fig. 1. Plan of the city of Athens. Marked are the venues of events connected with the Eleusinian Mysteria: A. Sacred Gate, B. Agora, C. City Eleusinion (after Travlos 1988, 169 fig. 219).

between "pilgrimage" or "sacred travel" and other forms of religiously motivated movement such as religious processions. In contrast to these *pompai*, I understand "pilgrimage" or "sacred travel" as a journey of one or more individuals to a place of religious importance for the traveller(s) if the journey itself is not conceived primarily as a cultic ritual. Admittedly, this is a working definition, which disregards important aspects of the matter, e.g. the application of the concept to travels with a destination of no religious relevance.[7] My aim though is not to achieve a universally accepted definition of the term, but to discuss some features central to the understanding of the phenomenon. Some references to the categories of "polis religion" and "individual religion" will additionally be important for my perspective on the subject.

The procession leading from Athens to Eleusis before the Eleusinian Mysteries will serve as my case study. In contrast to other *pompai* like the ones during the Great Panathenaia or the City Dionysia, this religious act can be considered in the context of "sacred travel" due to its specific character as a part of the Mysteria cult. To begin with, I will lay out the course, form, and significance of the procession from Athens to Eleusis. After a short description of the participants and of the events preluding the cortege, a detailed analysis of the character of the procession will follow.

The prospective initiates performed the *pompe* from Athens to Eleusis in advance of the mysteries. In preparation for the event, the Eleusinian priests,

7 See n. 52 below.

Fig. 2. Plan of Attica. Marked are venues connected with the Eleusinian Mysteria: Eleusis, city centre of Athens, Phaleron (after Travlos 1988, XVI fig. 1).

escorted by the ephebes, brought the *hiera*, the sacred objects, from Eleusis to Athens on the 14th of Boedromion.[8] These paraphernalia were kept at the Eleusinion, the small sanctuary of the Eleusinian gods and goddesses in the southeast of the Agora (Fig. 1), until the main procession leading back to Eleusis a few days later. The people who intended to be initiated into the mysteries of Eleusis and join the procession also came to Athens ahead of time in order to participate in preliminary acts and rituals.[9] On the 15th of Boedromion, the initiates gathered at the Athenian Agora to attend the proclamation of the festival by the Eleusinian priests, the *hierophantes* and the *dadouchos*.[10] The announcement informed those present that people who did not speak proper Greek – in other words, barbarians – and those polluted by bloodguilt were forbidden either to participate in the festival or to be initiated into the mysteries. The next days were dedicated to purification through various actions. On the 16th of Boedromion, the initiates went to Phaleron to wash themselves in the sea, in order to purify themselves for the upcoming procession and mysteries (Fig. 2). The initiates also carried piglets to the sea and purified them in the waters because the animals would

8 Sourvinou-Inwood 2003, 38; Parker 2005, 346-7.

9 Whether the "pre-initiation" and the participation in the Lesser Mysteria were obligatory for the prospective initiates, and where these acts were performed, is not clearly attested: Parker 2005, 343-5.

10 Isoc. 4.157; Schol. Ar. *Ran.* 369; Clinton 1974, 10-68; Sourvinou-Inwood 2005, 60-2; Parker 2005, 347.

later be sacrificed to the goddesses.[11] The purification of the initiates continued over the next three days of fasting and was thus actually extended to the interior of their bodies. During this period, no actions or events relevant to the mysteries took place, so people were given time to collect their strength and contemplate before the rather stressful following days. The preparation of the initiates for the procession and the mysteries was completed immediately before the beginning of these acts, when they dressed themselves accordingly because it was obligatory to adopt a specific appearance that was appropriate to the occasion. Therefore, they put on old, worn-out garments, placed a wreath of myrtle on their loose hair, and held a branch of myrtle in their hands.[12] Officials of the Athenian polis and the Eleusinian sanctuary escorted the crowd. The Eleusinian priests were also dressed in particular garments and wore crowns of myrtle on their heads like the initiates.[13]

The procession took place on the 19th or 20th of Boedromion, starting in the morning of that day.[14] The prospective initiates of the Mysteria gathered in the *intra muros* area by the Sacred Gate in the demos of Kerameis (Fig. 1).[15] This is where the shrine to Iakchos – the personified cry of the initiates – was located, with his statue in it.[16] The Athenian and Eleusinian priests escorted by the ephebes carried the *hiera* from the Eleusinion on the northern slope of the Acropolis to the Sacred Gate, where they met the initiates. Here the actual procession was formed. The priests walked ahead with the *hiera*, and behind them, the statue of Iakchos was carried, followed by the initiates. This mass of people, a few thousand, moved from the district by the city walls, passed the Sacred Gate, and walked along the Sacred Way to finally reach the sanctuary of Demeter and Kore in Eleusis (Fig. 3). During the *pompe*, the participants sang joyful songs and voiced the cultic cry, the *iakchos*. One can imagine the procession as a merry celebration of the initiates who looked forward to the mysteries.

It would take about 4 hours, at an average velocity of 5 kilometres per hour for normal walking pace, to traverse the approximately 21 kilometres between Athens and Eleusis. The procession needed a whole day to cover that distance – it never arrived at the Eleusinian sanctuary before nightfall – for various reasons.[17] First of all, a mass of people moves more slowly than a single man, even more so when thousands of people are involved as in this case, among them old people and women.[18] Additionally, walking for a religious purpose is a solemn activity and thus requires a measured pace. Carrying ritual devices, like the *hiera* or the statue of Iakchos, as well as the

11 Parker 2005, 332, 347-8. Figure vases in the form of young men holding a piglet dating to the 4th century BC obviously show initiates of the mysteries and were found in Eleusis as well as at the Kerameikos excavation: Stroszeck 2014.

12 Graf 1995, 97; Parker 2005, 361; Bremmer 2012, 379.

13 Istros, FGrH 334 F 29; Clinton 1974, 32-3, 48, 116; Sourvinou-Inwood 2005, 61; Parker 2005, 334.

14 In the following, I refer to the opinion of Graf (1996, 61-3), Parker (2005, 348), and Bremmer (2012, 378-81), among others. Clinton (in this volume, and 1988) and Mansfield (1985 – *non vidi*) favour the possibility of two processions taking place on the 19th and 20th of Boedromion: first priests and ephebes would have escorted the *hiera* back to Eleusis, and on the next day the prospective initiates of the mysteries following the statue of Iakchos would have walked from Athens to the Eleusinian sanctuary.

15 The name "Kerameikos" did not apply to the demos, as it is used often in modern scholarship, but to the street leading to the academy; the demos was actually called "Kerameis" in Classical times: Stroszeck 2003, 54-69 fig. 1-20, 69-73.

16 On the iconography of Iakchos, see Graf 1974, 187-8; Clinton 1992, 64-71.

17 Parker 2005, 350-1.

18 Women from the upper class in particular rode on buggies (see Parker 2005, 349-50), but nevertheless the pace of the procession was kept back by the slowest participants.

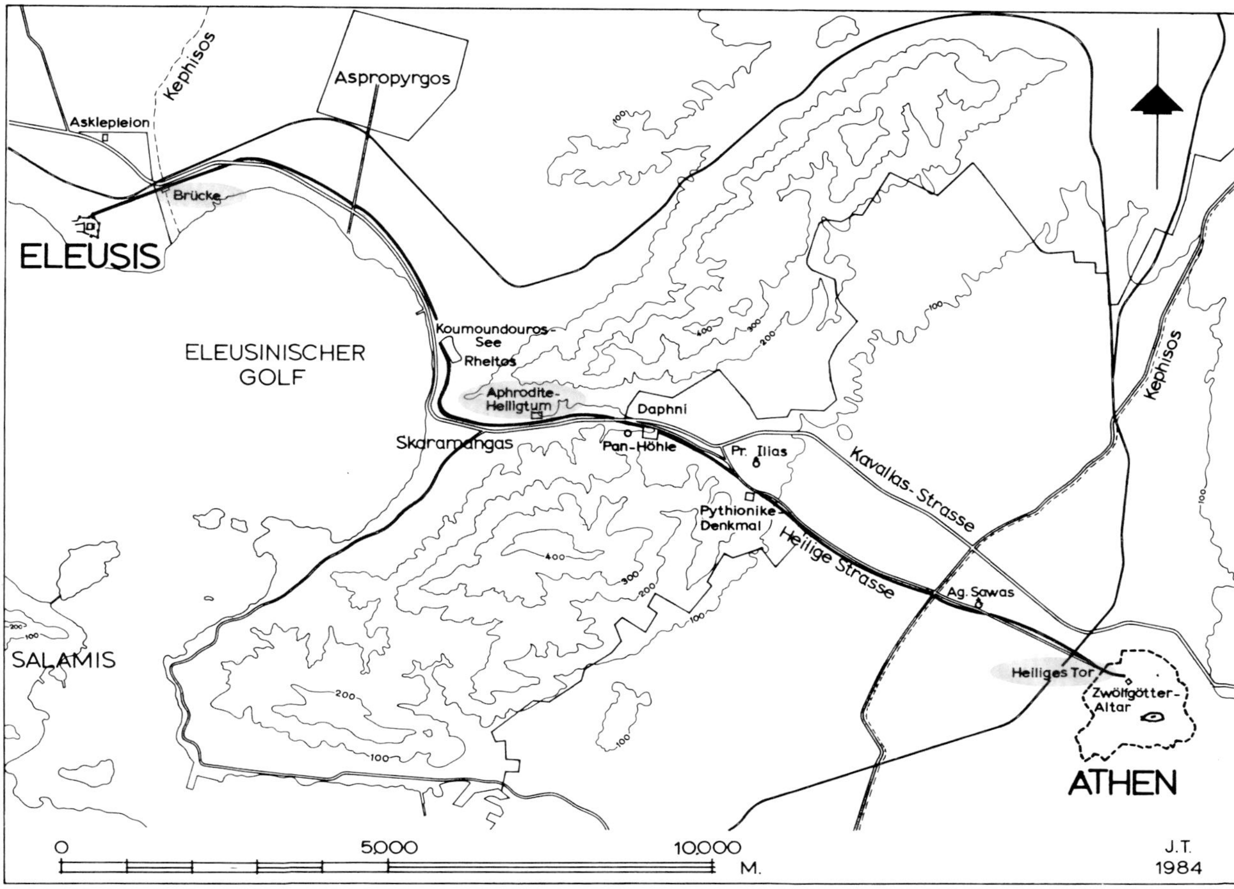

Fig. 3. The route of the procession from Athens to Eleusis. Marked are (possible) venues of some (possible) stops: Sacred Gate (departing point), Rheitos and Bridge (possibly *gephyrismos*) (after Travlos 1988, 181 fig. 228).

equipment for the overnight stay at Eleusis also reduced the speed of the *pompe*, even if donkeys bore much of this load. Most important were the stops at various points on the way, where certain rituals were performed.[19] Our information about these pauses is limited, so we do not know much about the specific places or actions. The sources give clear testimony only for "sacrifices, libations, dances and *paians*" as well as for a purification that took place at the Rheitoi – waters sacred to Demeter.[20] The venues for other rituals could vaguely be reconstructed according to the description by Pausanias.[21] Sanctuaries of Demeter and Kore were certainly among them, such as the one they shared with Athena and Poseidon which also marked the location of the house of Phytalios: According to myth, Demeter met a representative of Athens there and received cult together with the patron deities of the city.[22] The procession ended at the sanctuary of Demeter and Kore south of the Eleusinian Acropolis, where the "reception of Iakchos" took place. What happened next was kept secret.[23]

19 Parker 2005, 347.

20 Plut. *Alc.* 34.4; IG II², 1078:29-30.

21 Paus. 1.36.3-38.7.

22 Graf 1996, 63.

23 Parker 2005, 350.

The special character of the Eleusinian *pompe* and the particular focus of the mysteries on the individual have been connected with the form of ancient religious practice termed "individual religion".[24] I would now like to develop this further by concentrating on the participants. According to the rules concerning the festival, every adult was allowed to participate except people who did not understand Greek properly and those who had committed murder. The reason for the latter restriction is obvious: The immense impurity of these men was contradictory to the requirements of any religious action.[25] The reason for the first restriction could be regarded as a practical one, but it was actually relevant to the essence of the rituals, i.e. the successful initiation of the people into the mysteries. The rites of the festival and especially of the initiation were strongly based on myth, and the means of participating in it was mainly – one could say almost exclusively – the language. Movement and further actions were also important, but in order to perform the rituals properly and reach the required state of mind for a successful initiation, it was crucial to understand the meaning of the words being said during the procedures. The part played by the initiates, their actual performance, was mainly to hear these words and give answers.[26]

The initiates of the mysteries could be men or women, citizens, alien residents or slaves, Athenians or strangers. Various ancient authors indicate that almost every Athenian was initiated.[27] Based on the sources, this notion has frequently been wrongly generalized. One aspect is often overlooked, i.e. the financial burdens the participants had to deal with. In order to obtain the right of participation, a fee had to be paid to the officiates of Eleusis before the festival; moreover, each initiate was obliged to bring a piglet, provided through their own means, to sacrifice to the goddesses.[28] In addition to these expenses, the participants stayed away from their work for an extensive period of time and thus had to deal with a considerable loss of earnings. The festival with all its single acts – including proclamation, purification through bath and fasting, procession, and initiation – lasted about a week in total. People from the rural demes of Attica, and those who came from outside the borders of the polis even more so, needed additional time to travel to the city centre where the preliminaries took place. It is thus obvious that people could only be initiated into the mysteries if they could afford it.[29]

These practical parameters already made the participation into a matter of personal decision. In addition, the Eleusinian mysteries were not the kind of religious events attended by institutionalised groups of people like the *gene* or the phylai, nor was the initiation a civic obligation for the Athenians. Each individual pondered over the significance of the mysteries for themselves and consciously chose to take part. The motivation for this decision was certainly derived from the specific beliefs connected with the Eleusinian cult. The initiation into the mysteries was linked to a promise of a better life in the underworld, which seems to have been one of the main reasons why people strived for it.[30] The exact

24 Rutherford 2013, 13; Kindt 2015, 44; Eidinow 2015, 58-9. Burkert (1990, 19-34) uses the term "personal religion" in this context. See also n. 37 below.

25 On religious impurity, the *miasma*, see Parker 1983.

26 On the mysteries, single acts performed, and the stages of initiation, see Graf 1974, passim; Clinton 1992, passim; 2003; Sourvinou-Inwood 2003; Parker 2005, 343-6, 352-60; Bremmer 2012, 381-91.

27 Parker (2005, 342-3) discusses the ancient sources with the proper skepsis.

28 Bremmer 2012, 377; Parker 2005, 342 n. 65; Sourvinou-Inwood 2005, 61.

29 To estimate the complete expenditure for the initiation, one should additionally take into account the time and money people needed for the pre-initiation and the Lesser Mysteria as well, see Parker 2005, 343-5.

30 On the eschatological aspects of the mysteries, see Graf 1974, 79-94; Burkert 1990, 27, 29; Sourvinou-Inwood 2003, esp. 34, 40-1; Parker 2005, 354-68; Bremmer 2012, 391-3.

content of this promise as well as the actions and ideas connected with the rituals were kept secret, as was required by the officials of the festival and the community of the *mystai*. Only one testimony mentions the island of the blessed as the pleasant alternative way of being in the underworld for the initiates of Eleusis.[31]

Along with these considerations, another aspect reveals how deeply personal this affair was. The eschatological component of the festival addresses the most personal matter of all, that is to say death.[32] Although death was a very important part of social, religious, and political communication in ancient societies, its incidence affected the dying person alone each and every time – even if many people died at the same time under the same circumstances. The effort to ameliorate the perspective of death was consequently a highly personal matter.

The procession to Eleusis and the rituals of initiation at the sanctuary were in accordance with this "lonely" perspective on death. Although these actions took place within a huge crowd, they had a considerable effect on the individual, but did not affect their family, their phyle, or their polis. The procedures over the course of the actual initiation in particular indicate that they were intended as an individual experience: people respectively heard and saw certain actions which gradually revealed to them the secret contents of the mysteries. During these events, the emotional involvement of the initiates was intense, since they dealt with feelings of fear and joy, and thus their perception was effected individually.[33]

The structure and sequence of the preliminary and proper events of the festival intensified this perception. All related actions, in Athens, on the way to Eleusis, and at the sanctuary, gradually detached the people from everyday life, abolished normality to a certain degree, and most importantly, set social conventions aside. The first step in reaching this condition was the purification of the participants through washing in the sea and fasting for three days. Then, on the day of the procession, the initiates dressed themselves, in a manner contrary to everyday life but also to all other festivals: the worn-out garments and loose hair visualised the striking condition of these people and made their intentions recognizable for everyone who saw them and knew of the regulations concerning the mysteries and this particular *pompe*. These procedures allowed the individual to concentrate on themselves, let loose from the social conventions, and detach from their socially determined roles.

The process of detachment reached its highest impact during the *pompe*, when the crowd left the city and walked to Eleusis. From the very beginning of the procession, the participants could physically experience the separation of the group from the city by stepping over its borders at the Sacred Gate.[34] In fact, the *pompe* did not at any time exit the territory of the polis, but only left the fortified *asty*, although the symbolic meaning of leaving the city centre, with all its sanctuaries and seats of the political institutions, could also be attributed to leaving behind the social structures and rules of civic life. The consequence of this general observation for the Eleusinian procession with its peculiar constellation was that the position of people in everyday life due to their gender, social status, or origin was irrelevant while attending the *pompe*. This transitory stage for the participants has been convincingly associated by many scholars with the evaluation of pilgrimage by Victor Turner, who underlines that such religious actions frequently entailed the reversal and confusion of social order.[35] This phenomenon manifested

31 Diog. Laert. 6.39.

32 See Parker 2005, 342-3; Kindt 2015, 44.

33 Burkert 1990, 75-80. See also n. 26 above.

34 On the significance of city walls and gates as transitory places, see Agelidis 2017.

35 Turner 2013, esp. 247-9; Graf 1995, 95-8; Graf 1996, 63-4; Bremmer 2012, 380-1.

itself particularly strikingly in the *gephyrismos*,[36] an act which took place on the bridge of the Athenian Kephisos. Here, people, mostly young men, mocked the passing procession participants, among them respected and prominent citizens of the polis. Although this behaviour was definitely contradictory to social norms and rules, it aroused neither resistance nor complaint during the *pompe* because these social norms and rules did not apply in this special context. The gradual disengagement of people from their socially determined position resulted in a relocation of the focus back on the individual. The participants did not attend the procession as representatives of something or someone, but for their own sake.

The image of the Eleusinian *pompe* which I have drawn so far has not taken into account the role of the procedure for the Athenian polis. On the contrary, I have first tried to show how intensely and in how many ways this event affected the individual.[37] The importance of the event for Athens as a city and state is nevertheless undoubtedly major.[38] Different parts of the city were already involved in the preparatory actions (Fig. 1. 2): The proclamation of the festival took place in the Agora, the washing in the sea took place in Phaleron, and the *hiera* were kept in the Eleusinion, in the north of the Acropolis. The maximum topographic range was then reached during the procession along the c. 21 kilometre long way. The ritual space as it was constituted by the interaction of the participants, their actions, and the venues comprised a significant part of the Athenian territory, thus demonstrating during the celebration the territorial extent of the Athenian state and hence its political influence. The fixed points of this network of sacred places were also physically present through the permanent shrines and in this way perpetuated the presence of the Eleusinian element in the city.[39] In addition, the rituals performed during the procession's pauses at sanctuaries and shrines along the Sacred Way aimed at the welfare of the polis as a community. The operations at the site where Demeter had encountered the first Athenians in the context of the Eleusinian myth are particularly indicative of the importance of the cortege for the entire polis. The participation of Athenian officials and the ephebes further underlined the involvement of the Athenian state in the celebration.

Hence, the *pompe*, due to its spatial disposition, visualized the extent of the Athenian sphere as well as the influence of the polis, and demonstrated through the presence of Athenian institutions and some specific rituals the festival's connection with Athens. Nevertheless, the sequence of actions and the way they were performed as presented above reveal, in my opinion, a strong focus of the feast on the individual.

This evaluation of the Eleusinian *pompe* is in accordance with the way scholars such as Julia Kindt and Esther Eidinow regard the relationship between polis and individual religion.[40] Contrary to the frequently exaggerated concentration on the – undoubtedly important – concept of "polis religion",[41] they focus more intensively on the individual in order to consider religious practices independently of the

36 Hesychios s.v. gephyrismos. Graf 1996, 63; Bremmer 2012, 380-1.

37 This matter has been neglected by the majority of scholarship. As one of the few, Graf (1995, 99-100; 1996, 64) has repeatedly explicitly pointed out that the procession to Eleusis and the Mysteria were a personal affair.

38 Out of the countless works dealing with this subject, I single out the following: Graf 1996, 63-4; Sourvinou-Inwood 1997; 2003, 27-8.

39 On the sanctuaries connected with the Eleusinian across Attica, see Parker 2005, 332-3 with further references. Nevertheless, the mysteries took place only at the original sanctuary in Eleusis: Burkert 1990, 41-2.

40 See Kindt 2012; 2015; Eidinow 2015.

41 For a critical discussion of the concept of "polis religion" and of the overemphasizing of its application to ancient religious practice in general see Kindt 2012, 12-35, 94-5; Eidinow 2015, 55-9. .

polis. In their analysis, they both emphasize that the concept of individual religion is not to be set simply in contrast to the official religion, but forms the idea of another dimension of the ways people acted in the religious contexts of their everyday life and their festivals.[42] The evaluation of a certain practice within the framework of either of the two concepts is thus not exclusive, as has also been shown here for the Eleusinian *pompe*: the event can be regarded as an action performed by an individual for their own sake and as a demonstration of the polis' piety and strength at the same time.

I return now to the main concern of this chapter and would like to prove whether the concept of "sacred travel" can be helpful in the evaluation of the Eleusinian *pompe*. One of the key factors in differentiating "sacred travel" and religious processions seems to be the extent to which the journey to the sanctuary is considered to be a religious ritual. In my understanding, it is not the journey that is of primary religious significance for a "sacred travel", but the destination. The processions, however, are themselves religious rituals of the first rank.[43] Actually, when we try to prove the validity of the working definition, which underlies the present paper, through the example of the procession from Athens to Eleusis, we again come across the ambiguity in the nature of the event, as a part of the individual as well as the polis religion. The prospective initiates walked from Athens to Eleusis with the motivation of reaching the sanctuary of Demeter and Kore and of being let in on the mysteries. For the initiation, the procession was irrelevant,[44] and thus from the perspective of the initiates the *pompe* was most probably simply a group of people wandering with the same destination, not a ritual relevant to their religious interest or to the aims of their journey. Under these circumstances, we could classify the procession as "sacred travel". From the perspective of a non-involved person, however, the group of people who followed the statue of Iakchos along the way from Athens to Eleusis was a proper *pompe*, a part of a religious festival leading from the centre of Athens to a rural sanctuary which belonged to the polis. Here, then, the religious and political role of the event was perceived as formative.[45]

In the case of the Eleusinian *pompe*, its designation as "sacred travel" or as a normal religious procession is therefore mainly a question of perception. The approach of an involved person would focus rather on the first aspect, while a non-actively involved person would recognize the latter. Once again, the relation between individual and polis religion can beneficially be parallelized with the distinction between "sacred travel" and processions: Both aspects of religious practice coexist in a single event, and it is not the action itself that qualifies being one or the other, but the action within its context.[46]

The Eleusinian *pompe* is nevertheless a special case. Other processions, for example those at the Great Panathenaia or the City Dionysia, cannot be seen as "sacred travel" in any terms. The participants of these processions were attending as holders of certain offices or as agents for parts of the citizenship and military, so they only represented particular parts or institutions of the polis. Their individual needs and concerns had no place in this context. Moreover, these *pompai* belonged to a series of rituals related to a particular festival and themselves

42 See especially Kindt 2012, passim; 2015, 37, 43-4; Eidinow 2015, 60-2, 70-1.

43 Here I follow the narrow understanding of the term *pompe* as stated e.g. by Graf 1996, 56.

44 Nevertheless, the mental state the participants reached after a march of more than 20 kilometres would certainly have amplified the effect of the rituals. On the psychological effect of movement, see the contribution by Pretzler in this volume.

45 Elsner & Rutherford (2005, 17-8) also classify the Eleusinian *pompe* as a "pilgrimage", but note that this was not the only function of the procession.

46 See Kindt 2015, 38-9.

had a major religious significance.[47] In contrast, the journey of individuals or groups of people to oracles and healing sanctuaries were themselves not rituals – although they were conducted out of religious motives – but their main intention was to reach their destination and to perform a religious act there. Here, the journey could be classified as "sacred travel".[48]

I would like to conclude with some methodological remarks. The categorization we make, with any further distinction we try to introduce in its details, systematizes differences which the ancient observer possibly perceived, but obviously felt no need to define: Neither "pilgrimage" nor "sacred travel" is a pre-Christian category.[49] By using these concepts, we are trying to define a phenomenon that *we* observe in ancient Greek religious practice, which the Greeks did not need to name. Despite the rejection of the term by various colleagues such as Robert Parker or Scott Scullion,[50] and the problems we are confronted with when we try to reach a clear definition, I think that this categorization can be a useful heuristic tool to describe parts of religious practice more precisely and to gain a deeper understanding of their formation, development, and interweaving. By applying this category to the procession from Athens to Eleusis, we can distinguish the aspects of individual religious practice and polis religion and evaluate their interaction with each other. This is one way in which operating within the concept of "sacred travel" can be beneficial for our analysis. Nevertheless, it is important to emphasize that this model cannot be applied to any kind of journey to a place of religious importance; otherwise the concept would become arbitrary.[51] The term necessarily requires a definition that is both precise and flexible. In order to operate successfully within this concept, the criteria for characterizing the movement of people as "sacred travel" cannot be consistently applied to every piece of evidence documenting such a phenomenon.[52]

47 The author has argued extensively on the political impact of the *pompai* of the Great Panathanaia and the City Dionysia: Agelidis 2017; 2018.

48 See e.g. Elsner & Rutherford 2005, 12-7.

49 See Elsner & Rutherford 2005, 7-8.

50 Scullion 2005 and Parker 2005, 348-9, reject the usage of the term "pilgrimage" for ancient Greek phenomena, similar to the ones we characterize here as "sacred travel". See also Elsner & Rutherford 2005, 2.

51 See Elsner & Rutherford 2005, 5-6; Funke 2010, 225.

52 One problematic feature of the term is the bonding with the sacred, for in some contexts the very personal approach to certain places affects the individual deeply and causes a psychological effect, which is sacred-like, though without concerning a sacred venue, and although the journey is not undertaken out of a religious motivation respectively. On this perspective, see the contribution by Pretzler in this volume. On Pausanias' *periegesis* and its classification (or not) as pilgrimage as a further example for this kind of problems, see Elsner & Rutherford 2005, 4; Funke 2010, 224-5 with further references; Kindt 2012, 40.

Bibliography

Note: The scholarly literature on Eleusis and the Mysteria is vast. Only a fraction could be taken into consideration in my paper and is listed here.

AGELIDIS, S. 2017
'The "Spatial Turn" in Ancient Greek Festival Research: Venues of the Athenian City Dionysia and the Great Panathenaia *Pompai*', in *Theoretical Approaches to the Archaeology of Ancient Greece. Manipulating Material Culture*, L. Nevett (ed.), Ann Arbor.

AGELIDIS, S. 2018
'Connecting Routes within a Polis: Religious Processions as a Reflexion of Identity and Self-Perception in Classical Athens', in *Sacred Landscapes and Connecting Routes* (Caeculus), Chr. Wiliamson & O. van Nijf (eds.), Groningen (forthcoming).

BREMMER, J.N. 2012
'Initiation into the Eleusinian Mysteries: A "Thin" Description', in *Mystery and Secrecy in the Neg Hammadi Collection and Other Ancient Literature: Ideas and Practices*, Ch.H. Bull, L.I. Lied & J.D. Turner (eds.), Leiden, 375-97.

BURKERT, W. 1990
Antike Mysterien. Funktionen und Gehalt, Munich.

CLINTON, K. 1974
The Sacred Officials of the Eleusinian Mysteries (Transactions of the American Philosophical Society N.S. 64), Philadelphia.

CLINTON, K. 1988
'Sacrifice at the Eleusinian Mysteries', in *Early Greek Cult Practice. Proceedings of the Fifth International Symposium at the Swedish Institute at Athens, 26-29 June 1986* (Skrifter Utgivna av Svenska Institutet i Athen = Acta Instituti Atheniensis Regni Sueciae, Series in 4°, 38), R. Hägg, N. Marinatos & G.C. Nordquist (eds.), Stockholm, 69-80.

CLINTON, K. 1992
Myth and Cult. The Iconography of the Eleusinian Mysteries. The Martin P. Nilsson Lectures on Greek Religion, delivered 10-21 November 1990 at the Swedish Institute at Athens (Skrifter Utgivna av Svenska Institutet i Athen = Acta Instituti Atheniensis Regni Sueciae, Series in 8°, 11), Stockholm.

CLINTON, K. 2003
'Stages of Initiation in the Eleusinian and Samothracian Mysteries', in *Greek Mysteries. The Archaeology of Ritual of Ancient Greek Secret Cults*, M.B. Cosmopoulos (ed.), Oxford, 50-78.

DILLON, M. 1997
Pilgrims and Pilgrimage in Ancient Greece, London and New York.

EIDINOW, E. 2015
'φανερὰν ποιήσει τὴν αὑτοῦ διάνοιαν τοῖς θεοῖς: Some Ancient Greek Theories of (Divine and Mortal) Mind', in *Public and Private in Ancient Mediterranean Law and Religion*, C. Ando & J. Rüpke (eds.), Berlin, Munich and Boston, 53-73.

ELSNER, J. & I. RUTHERFORD 2005
'Introduction', in *Pilgrimage in Graeco-Roman & Early Christian Antiquity. Seeing the Gods*, J. Elsner & I. Rutherford (eds.), Oxford and New York, 1-38.

FUNKE, P. 2010
'Pausanias und die griechischen Heiligtümer und Kulte', in *Viajeros, peregrinos y aventureros en el Mundo Antiguo*, F. Marco Simón, F. Pina Polo & J. Remesal Rodríguez (eds.), Barcelona, 219-26.

GRAF, F. 1974
Eleusis und die orphische Dichtung Athens in vorhellenistischer Zeit, Berlin and New York.

GRAF, F. 1995
'Umzüge und Prozessionen. Raum und Religion in der griechisch-römischen Antike', in *Wanderungen*, F. Graf & E. Hornung (eds.), Munich, 85-112.

GRAF, F. 1996
'*Pompai* in Greece. Some Considerations about Space and Ritual in the Greek *Polis*', in *The Role of Religion in the Early Greek Polis* (Skrifter Utgivna av Svenska Institutet i Athen = Acta Instituti Atheniensis Regni Sueciae, Series in 8°, 14), R. Hägg (ed.), Stockholm, 55-65.

KINDT, J. 2012
Rethinking Greek Religion, Cambridge and New York.

KINDT, J. 2015
'Personal Religion: A Productive Category for the Study of Ancient Greek Religion?', *JHS* 135, 35-50.

MANSFIELD, J.M. 1985
'The Robe of Athena and the Panathenaic Procession', PhD diss., University of California, Berkeley.

PARKER, R. 1983
Miasma. Pollution and Purification in Early Greek Religion, Oxford.

PARKER, R. 2005
Polytheism and Society at Athens, Oxford.

RUTHERFORD, I. 2000
'Pilgerschaft', *Der Neue Pauly* 9, 1014-9.

RUTHERFORD, I. 2013
State Pilgrims and Sacred Observers in Ancient Greece. A Study of Theōriā and Theōroi, Cambridge.

SCULLION, S. 2005
'"Pilgrimage" and Greek Religion: Sacred and Secular in the Pagan *Polis*', in *Pilgrimage in Graeco-Roman & Early Christian Antiquity. Seeing the Gods*, J. Elsner & I. Rutherford (eds.), Oxford and New York, 111-30.

SOURVINOU-INWOOD, C. 1997
'Reconstructing Change: Ideology and Ritual at Eleusis', in *Inventing Ancient Culture. Historicism, Periodization and the Ancient World*, M. Golden & P. Toohey (eds.), London, 132-64.

SOURVINOU-INWOOD, C. 2003
'Festival and Mysteries. Aspects of the Eleusinian Cult', in *Greek Mysteries. The Archaeology of Ritual of Ancient Greek Secret Cults,* M.B. Cosmopoulos (ed.), Oxford, 25-49.

SOURVINOU-INWOOD, C. 2005
'The Priesthoods of the Eleusinian Cult of Demeter and Kore', in *Thesaurus Cultus et Rituum Antiquorum* 5, Los Angeles, 60-5.

STROSZECK, J. 2003
'Ὅροσ Κεραμεικοῦ. Zu den Grenzsteinen des Kerameikos in Athen', *Polis 1, Studi interdisciplinari sul mondo antico*, 53-83.

STROSZECK, J. 2014
'Plastic Vases Related to Eleusinian Cult from the Athenian Kerameikos', in *Des vases pour les Athéniens (VIe-IVe siècles avant notre ère)*, M.-Ch. Villanueva-Puig (ed.), (Mètis N.S. 12), Paris, 145-62.

TRAVLOS, J. 1988
Bildlexikon zur Topographie des antiken Athen, Tübingen.

TURNER, V.W. 2013
'Liminalität und Communitas', in *Ritualtheorien. Ein einführendes Handbuch* (5th ed.), A. Belliger & D.J. Krieger (eds.), Wiesbaden, 247-58.

The Route of the Athenian Pythaïs across the City and Its Territory*

Daniele Pirisino

The road system of ancient Athens and its territory was characterized by numerous processional paths, the routes of which reflected the complex religious life of the city in relation to its sacred topography. Among the Athenian processional routes, two in particular are well known to scholarship: that of the Eleusinian Mysteries and that of the Panathenaïa. In this chapter, I will discuss an Athenian processional route that, in spite of its importance in antiquity, has never been fully archaeologically contextualized: the route of the Pythaïs. This paper does not seek to give a definitive ruling on the precise route of the Pythaïs; it rather offers a discussion of long-standing problems and proposes a hypothesis on the course of this pilgrimage in Attica.

The Pythaïs was an Athenian sacred delegation dispatched to Delphi in honour of Apollo Pythios which staged the Athenian version of Apollo's mythical journey from his birthplace in Delos to his main oracular site by way of Athens and Attica. This was an inter-regional pilgrimage route: the Pythaïs crossed Attica, Boiotia, and Phokis along an overland journey of at least 150 kilometres through its shortest possible route (Fig. 1).[1] There is no certainty as to the precise path of the Pythaïs, as literary and archaeological sources regarding the spatial framework of this pilgrimage are scarce and fragmentary. The scholarly literature concerning the route of the Pythaïs has tended to centre the discussion on the possible course of this sacred route through Athens and Attica, while generally devoting less attention to its subsequent path across Boiotia and Phokis.[2] Two factors in particular have determined this tendency: first, most extant information on the ritual context of the Pythaïs concerns Athens and Attica; second, the direction of the pilgrimage through Athens and its territory would have affected the pilgrimage route outside of Attica as well. The present paper follows in the footsteps of this scholarly trend, but it considers the issue in the light of current knowledge of the archaeology of Athens and Attica, and with a more archaeologically oriented discussion of the topic. In short, I will mostly discuss the processional route of the Pythaïs across Athens and Attica, and will address the question of how it related to the topography of the city and the religious landscape of the city's territory.

Much like the physical path of its route, the chronology of the institution of the Pythaïs is not completely clear. This ceremony may have been first celebrated at Athens in the 6th century BC, or in

* I am thankful to the editors for including this paper in the present volume. The route of the Pythaïs was the subject of the author's doctoral thesis, 'The Route of the Pythaïs through Athens and Attica', which includes a more in-depth discussion of the relevant aspects addressed in this paper, see Pirisino 2015.

1 On the "international" character of the sacred road of the Pythaïs, see Daverio Rocchi 2002, 149.

2 For an overview of early scholarly literature on the Pythaïs, see Fachard & Pirisino 2015, 147-8.

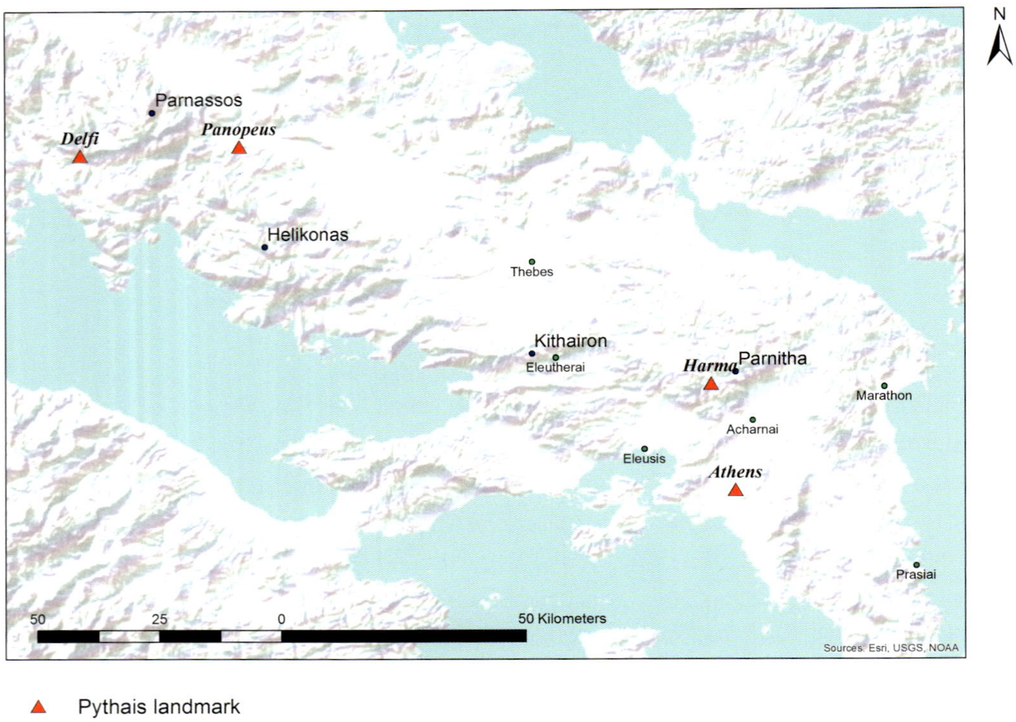

Fig. 1. Map of the regions crossed by the Pythaïs. Red triangles indicate the landmarks of the pilgrimage (map prepared by the author).

the 5th century BC at the latest.[3] I uphold the view of a 6th-century BC establishment of the Athenian Pythaïs on the grounds of textual and archaeological evidence discussed later in the paper. The Pythaïs was conducted from the 6th century BC to around the time of Augustus, when the ceremony was eventually taken over by a Dodekaïs.[4] There is no certainty as to the actual frequency of the Pythaïs during this long period. For most of its duration, the pilgrimage of the Pythaïs was conducted at irregular intervals, as it depended upon the unpredictable appearance of a divine sign (the sighting of a lightning); indeed, the number of documented Pythaïdes is very low.[5] Furthermore, the overland pilgrimage to Delphi may have been suspended for protracted periods of time due to contemporary events that may have put the safety of the pilgrims at risk.[6]

In the words of Aelius Aristides, the Pythaïs was a ceremony native only to the Athenians.[7] However, the Athenian Pythaïdes were not the first or the

3 For evidence of the Athenian Pythaïs in the 6th century BC, see Rutherford 1990, 174-6. According to some scholars, the Athenian Pythaïs was first introduced after the battle of Plataia in 479 BC; see Furley & Bremer 2001, 132-4, with notes. The fundamental work on the chronology and the main aspects of the Pythaïs remains Boëthius 1918.

4 On the Dodekaïs, see in particular *FdD* III[2], 59-67. Athens dispatched regular Dodekaïdes to Delos throughout the first half of the 2nd century AD (*ID* 2535, 2536, 2538); see Rutherford 2013, 311-2.

5 The most eloquent description of the rituals preceding the procession itself is provided by Strabon (9.2.11). The first definite documented Pythaïs is that of 355 BC, as indicated in a speech by Isaeus (Isae. 7.27); see Boëthius 1918, 15; Parke 1939. Between the very end of the 2nd century BC and the beginning of the 1st century BC, the pilgrimage occurred on a more regular basis; see Daux 1936, 557-9.

6 Events such as the Peloponnesian War in the 5th century BC and the Aetolian rule over Delphi in the period from the 3rd century BC to the second half of the 2nd century BC certainly affected the frequency of the Athenian pilgrimage to Delphi.

7 Aelius Aristides, *Panathenaic Oration* 363. On this aspect, see Boëthius 1918, 14.

only ones in Attica. The earliest Pythaïdes were probably those of the Marathonian Tetrapolis, which dispatched its own pilgrimages to Delphi distinct from the Athenian ones until the 2nd century BC, when the two ceremonies merged into one.[8] Philochoros describes rituals that likely concerned the Marathonian Pythaïs: a sacred delegation started from the Pythion at Aiantid Oinoe and possibly headed into Boiotia via Aphidna, or even via another route closer to the coast. From the Delion of Marathon, a further theoria was sent in the opposite direction to Delos.[9] From Marathon, this sacred delegation proceeded southwards and possibly reached Prasiai, from which it sailed towards the island.[10]

The Journey of Apollo: The Athenian Version and Some Notes on Its Mythical Topography

In order to geographically contextualise the route of the pilgrimage from Athens, it is best to begin by reviewing the mythical accounts of Apollo's quest for his major oracular shrine. The purpose of such an analysis is not to find a perfect correspondence between the pilgrimage route and the myth, but rather to bring the myth into play as a background reference for a preliminary hypothetical reconstruction of the pilgrimage route of the Pythaïs. As mentioned above, the Pythaïs re-enacted Apollo's mythical journey from Delos to Delphi via Athens; however, this is in contrast with the mainstream version of the myth. The oldest complete description of the god's journey is illustrated in the third Homeric Hymn, which was probably the best known of the hymns to Apollo in antiquity.[11] The route described in the hymn crosses the territories of Thessaly, Euboea, and Boiotia, and completely bypasses Attica on its way to Phokis. Nevertheless, the local Athenian form of Apollo's journey to Delphi sets the story, or at least part of it, in a different part of Greece: the territories of Attica. It is not possible to determine with certainty when this Athenian tradition developed, but it was certainly recognized from at least the 5th century BC. However, evidence suggests that this local version may have already been well known in the 6th century BC.[12]

This Athenian myth could be the subject of the Alkmaionidai east pediment on the temple of Apollo at Delphi. Some scholars suggest that this sculptural composition may have influenced later literary sources on the Athenian myth, specifically Aischylos' account of the god's journey.[13] Sporadic references to this Athenian version of the myth can be found in three ancient sources: the *Eumenides* by the aforementioned Aischylos, Ephoros, and an inscribed paean which was definitively attributed to Limenios and performed as a προσόδιον (processional song) to accompany the Pythaïs in 128 BC:

8 The *koinon* of the Marathonian Tetrapolis included Marathon, Oinoe, Probalinthus, and Tricorythus. The Athenian and Marathonian ceremonies merged into one in the second half of the 2nd century BC (*FdD* III^2, 7). For more on the Marathonian Pythaïs, see Milchhöfer 1873, 56-7; Töpffer 1888; Daux 1936, 532-40; Bousquet 1942, 127-8.

9 *FGrH* 328 F 75.

10 This pilgrimage route was probably related to the ancestral path of the Hyperborean offerings. According to the version recounted by Pausanias, these offerings were passed down to Prasiai, whence they were taken to Delos by the Athenians (Paus. 1.31.2). Pausanias' account probably refers to an Athenian version of the Hyperborean itinerary (cf. Hdt. 4.33.1-3; see the comment by Corcella 1993, 259-60). The pilgrimage route through northeast Attica was a very ancient one; see Farnell 1907, 106-11.

11 *Homeric Hymn to Apollo* 179-299.

12 I am referring to a paean by Simonides discussed later in this paper and possibly composed for a Pythaïs (*POxy*. 2430 (*PMG* 519 fr.35)).

13 Dörig 1967, 109.

λιπὼν δὲ λίμνην Δηλίαν τε χοιράδα, / κέλσας ἐπ᾽ἀκτὰς ναυπόρους τὰς Παλλάδος, / ἐς τήνδε γαῖαν ἦλθε Παρνησοῦ θ᾽ ἕδρας. / πέμπουσι δ᾽αὐτὸν καὶ σεβίζουσιν μέγα / κελευθοποιοὶ παῖδες Ἡφαίστου, χθόνα / ἀνήμερον τιθέντες ἡμερωμένην (Aesch. *Eum.* 9-14).[14]

(᾽Απόλλωνα) ἐξ ᾽Αθηνῶν δ᾽ ὁρμηθέντα ἐπὶ Δελφοὺς ταύτην ἰέναι τὴν ὁδόν, ᾗι νῦν ᾽Αθηναῖοι τὴν Πυθιάδα πέμπουσι· γενόμενον δὲ κατὰ Πανοπέας Τιτυὸν καταλῦσαι ἔχοντα τὸν τόπον, βίαιον ἄνδρα καὶ παράνομον· ... τί δ᾽ ἂν εἴη μυθωδέστερον ἢ ᾽Απόλλων τοξεύων καὶ κολάζων Τιτυοὺς καὶ Πύθωνας καὶ ὁδεύων ἐξ ᾽Αθηνῶν εἰς Δελφοὺς καὶ γῆν πᾶσαν ἐπιών (Ephoros, *FGrH* 70 F 31 b [12]).[15]

τότε λιπὼγ Κυνθίαν νᾶσον ἐ[πέβα θεὸ]ς / πρω[τό]καρπογ κλυτὰν Ἀτ[θ]ίδ᾽ ἐπὶ γααλ[όφωι / πρῶνι] Τριτωνίδος (Limenios, F*d*D III^2, 138. 12-5).[16]

These sources make direct or indirect reference to the following landmarks in the geography of the myth: Delos, the coasts of Attica, Athens (probably with reference to the Acropolis), Panopeus, and of course, Delphi.[17] These literary *testimonia* emphasise the relationship between Apollo's mythical route and the actual pilgrimage route. It is the pilgrimage road itself that plays an essential role in the context of the myth as much as in the context of the ritual. Indeed, memories of the ceremony and in particular the importance of the pilgrimage road were long-lasting: as late as the 2nd century AD, the road of the Pythaïs from Athens to Delphi was remembered as an *ergon* (work) of Athens.[18]

The mythical and religious relevance of this road was fully reflected in the actual topography of the ritual; indeed, an inscribed 4th-century BC boundary stone indicates that the Pythaïs followed a sacred road in its own right: one that was officially known as a proper *hiera hodos.*[19] This evidence is of the greatest importance for a preliminary understanding of the status of the road. In fact, although scholars of different disciplines often use the expression *hiera hodos* rather loosely as a technical term to indicate any processional road, the specific term *hiera hodos* is very rare in both ancient Greek literary sources and inscriptions. Ancient Greece knew many processional roads, but in the Greek literary tradition, only six roads were specifically defined by the term *hiera hodos*:

14 "Leaving Delo's lake and ridge of rock / he put in at Pallas Athena's shores, haunt of ships, / then came to this land and a place to settle on Parnassus. / He was given escort and shown great reverence / by Hephaestus' sons, builders of roads, / who made tame the savage land" (trans. Podlecki 1989).

15 "And that when he [Apollo] set out from Athens to Delphi he went by the road which the Athenians now take when they conduct the Pythias; and that when he arrived at the land of the Panopeans he destroyed Tityus, a violent and lawless man who ruled there .... But what could be more mythical than Apollo shooting with arrows and punishing Tityuses and Pythons, and travelling from Athens to Delphi and visiting the whole earth?" (trans. Jones 1927, 365, 367).

16 "Leaving the isle of Kynthia the god arrived in Attica, / famous for the first corn, on [Athena] Tritonis' craggy slope" (trans. Furley & Bremer 2001, 137).

17 For more on the possible reference to the Acropolis in Limenios' paean, see Bélis 1992, 134. Outside Attica, Panopeus was most probably one of the stations of the Athenian Pythaïs on its way to Delphi. For the mythical, religious, and political bonds between Athens and Panopeus, see Camp *et al.* 1997.

18 Aelius Aristides, *Panathenaic Oration* 363. The relevance of this religious route and its relationship to the Athenian mythical and religious tradition (especially Theseus) is remarked on by the scholiasts; see Boëthius 1918, 153-4.

19 Agora 19, H 34:῞Ορος ἱερᾶς ὁδõ δι᾽ ἧς πορεύεται ἡ Πυθαὶς ἐς Δελφός ("Marker of the Sacred Road by which the Pythaïs proceeds to Delphi", trans. Parsons 1943, 237).

The road from Athens to Eleusis	Dicaearchus, fr. 21.3 Wehrli; Callisthenes of Olynthus, *FGrH* 124 F 45.2; [Plut.] *X orat.* 832b-852e; Paus. 1.36.3; Ath. 13.67.12
A geographic area in central Ukraine	Hdt. 4.52.14
The road to Delphi through Boiotia and Phokis	Hdt. 6.34.7; Plut. *Quaest. Graec.* 12 (293c)
A road at Abdera in Thrace	Hippoc. *Epid.* 3.7
The road from Mylasa to Labraunda	Strabon 14.2.23
The road from Elis to Olympia	Paus. 5.25.7

The occurrences of this term in the epigraphic record are even fewer. From a quick search, only three roads are mentioned in the inscriptions by the expression *hiera hodos*:

The road from Miletus to Didyma	Didyma, 103 (2nd BC); Didyma, 384 (mid-2nd AD); Didyma, 544 (AD 101/2)[1]
The road to Eleusis	SEG X, 367 (c. 430 BC); *IG* II², 673 (278/7 BC)
The road of the Pythaïs	Agora inventory number I 5476 (4th BC)

To this list, we should add the references in Greek to the Via Sacra in Rome. As shown by Tønnes Bekker-Nielsen, it seems reasonable to observe that ancient sources use the term *hiera hodos* not only to indicate a road's religious relevance, but also as a toponym designating a specific road as a topographically distinct local feature.[20]

Apart from the few landmarks indicated in the textual sources on the myth (Fig. 1), the information on the actual ritual of the Pythaïs is limited; in short, we do not have unmistakable evidence for the precise route of the pilgrimage. Most of the scholars concerned with the archaeology of the Pythaïs generally consider the sacred route from Athens to Delphi as the main spatial parameter for the reconstruction of the ceremony. However, the Pythaïs was probably a particularly complex ritual which may have spatially transcended the primary pilgrimage route alone. The complete ceremony might have involved a number of smaller-scale rituals and processions through secondary routes, incorporating diverse sacred places dedicated to Apollo and even to other deities. For example, as with the Marathonian Pythaïs, the Athenian Pythaïs may have included the sending of a sacred delegation to Delos as well, which may have involved a procession from Athens to Prasiai; this was the place from which the Athenian delegations to the island traditionally departed and where Apollo's first mythical landing in Attica could have found a suitable setting.[21] Indeed, the hypothesis of a Delian sacred delegation as part of the Athenian Pythaïs is perhaps indicated by the much-debated "first fruits" offering inscription (*IG* II², 2336) and by fragmentary information from an Oxyrhynchus Papyrus where the lightning ritual is possibly connected with a Delian theoria rather than a Delphic one.[22] Similar spatial complexity was likely reflected in the procession of the Pythaïs through the city, across the city's territory, and beyond Attica. In a nutshell, the reconstruction of the straightforward route of the Pythaïs to Delphi may only constitute a partial view of the whole ritual.

With these considerations in mind, the following questions should be addressed: How much is known about the ceremony of the Pythaïs, and what public

20 Bekker-Nielsen 2009, 12.

21 Ficuciello 2008, 32.

22 *POxy.* 2086. See Parsons 1943, 237, n. 121. Epigraphic material from Delos dating to the end of the 2nd century BC makes reference to the Delphic Pythaïs, see Roussel 1908, 422-3, nos. 20-1. However, the "first fruits" inscription listing the contributors for the Pythaïs for the years 102/101-95/94 BC (*IG* II², 2336) may not have been related to a Delian theoria, but to a Delphic one; see Tracy 1982.

buildings and spaces were involved in the celebration of the procession?

We can draw a general outline of the ritual events that characterized the Pythaïs. Strabon (9.2.11) recounts that a group of officials called Pythaïstai had to keep watch over the area of Mount Harma – a site in Attika on Mount Parnes (Parnitha in modern Greek) – for a period of three days and nights during three consecutive months. The Pythaïstai had to wait for a lightning flash that propitiated the sending of the pilgrimage. They kept watch from the altar of Zeus Astrapaios, located between the Pythion and the Olympieion.[23] If the Pythaïstai observed lightning over Mount Harma, then the procession could commence. This ritual probably occurred in late spring, possibly starting during or shortly after the Thargelia (in late May).[24] During this time of year, lightning density is rather sparse in this part of Greece. This consideration, in combination with the limited temporal frame of the observation period, determined the rarity of the sighting.[25] Indeed, such a sighting occurred so infrequently as to have become proverbial as early as the time of Perikles.[26] In short, because of the infrequency of the appearance of lightning to trigger the procession, the complete pilgrimage to Delphi was conducted only at irregular intervals, at least initially.

When the full pilgrimage was undertaken, offerings were brought to Delphi by a large crowd, which by the 2nd century BC featured hundreds of pilgrims. Chants and hymns accompanied the journey. Along with the offerings and other rituals, a number of contests were held.[27] Two important rituals were carried out as an integral part of the ceremony: the *tripodephoria* and the *pyrphoria*. A bronze tripod was dedicated at Delphi, while another tripod and the sacred fire were brought back to Athens.[28]

There is no certainty as to the chronology of the ritual described by Strabon. However, the lightning observation rite is probably documented in the Athenian sacrificial calendar of the late 5th century BC, which likely includes earlier religious material dating back to the time of Solon.[29] In fact, the ritual sighting of the lightning over Harma is possibly alluded to in the 6th century BC in a fragmentary paean ascribed to Simonides, which mentions Mount Parnes in relation to Apollo:

23 Strabon 9.2.11.

24 For a recent discussion of the time of year during which the early and Hellenistic Pythaïdes were sent, see Rutherford 2013, 223-4, nn. 53-6.

25 On the frequency of lightning in the Mediterranean coastal areas in late spring, see Anderson & Klugmann 2014, 821, figs 2, 8-10.

26 Boëthius 1918, 1-12, 145-6. Literary contextual reference to the lightning over Harma to indicate an event which occurs only rarely can be found until the 2nd century AD (Plut. *Quaest. conv.* 5.679C.). Later mentions of the proverb occur in lexicographical content as well as that of grammarians and commentators; see Boëthius 1918, 145-6.

27 The majority of information on the Pythaïs and its participants comes from the inscriptions on the south wall of the Athenian treasury at Delphi and dates from the second half of the 2nd century BC and the 1st century BC (*FdD* III[2], 2-70). These texts indicate that athletic, equestrian, theatrical, musical, and literary contests took place during the celebrations, see *FdD* III[2], 34-50. The earliest source for some of the objects carried during the Pythaïs is the Athenian sacrificial calendar dating to the 5th/4th century BC (Lambert 2002, fr. 1 A, column 3, 26-30). As discussed in this paper, the earliest chant which may possibly be associated with a Pythaïs dates to the last quarter of the 6th century BC: a fragmentary paean ascribed to Simonides, *POxy.* 2430 (*PMG* 519 fr.35); see Rutherford 1990, 169-71. Another hymn probably connected with a Pythaïs is Aristonoos' 4th-century BC paean to Hestia (*FdD* III[2], 192; see Furley & Bremer 2001, 118). Further known hymns performed during the ceremony are those by Athenaios and Limenios (*FdD* III[2], 137-8).

28 The tripod dedication at Delphi during the Pythaïs is recorded in *FdD* III[1], 511. For the ritual fetching of the Delphic tripod, see *FdD* III[2], 32-3; the conveyance of the sacred fire is documented in *FdD* III[2], 13, 32.

29 *IG* II[2], 1357; Lambert 2002, fr. 1 A, columns 2-3, 26-30. On the chronology of the calendar, see Parker 1996, 42; Lambert 2002, 354.

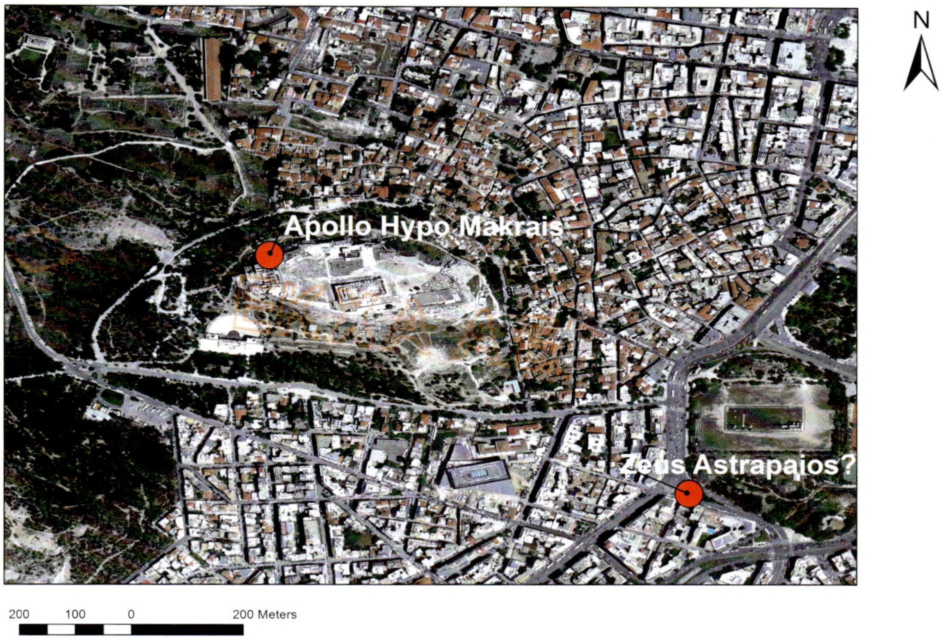

Fig. 2. Location of the Cave of Apollo Hypo Makrais and possible location of the Altar of Zeus Astrapaios (map prepared by the author. Basemap: orthophotograph after Ktimnatologio).

> Π]ά̣ρνηθος [.] πὸ ζα̣[θεοῦ /].΄δοις Ἄπ̣ο̣λλον /] οι ᾿Ἀθάνας / ἐν]θ̣άδ᾿εὐμενεῖ φρεν̣ὶ [/]αίτιον οὐ πάρειτι ἔαρ·. / π]όνον ὑπομίμνομε[ν /]α̣ν ὀριδρόμον Ἄρτεμιν[/ Παρ]θ̣ενικάν καί σε, ἄναξ ἑκαβ[ε- /]λ̣ε̣τ̣α ἱέμενοι ἐνοπὰν ἀγανοῖσιν [/] εὔφαμον ἀπὸ φρενὸς ὁμορρόθο[υ (Simon. *POxy*. 2430 (*PMG* 519 fr.35 b)).[30]

Ian Rutherford suggests that this paean should be connected with a Pythaïs and, among other interpretations, hypothesizes that it was performed at the altar of Zeus Astrapaios during the lightning observation ritual.[31] I also propose that the Parnes-Apollo connection in the context of this Pythaïstic paean may directly or indirectly refer to the Athenian version of the god's journey; this was also the case with the Pythaïs paean by Limenios, in which Apollo's arrival from Delos is described in relation to Attica and possibly the Acropolis.[32] In any case, two elements emerge when we consider Simonides' paean as being associated with the Pythaïs: first, the reference to Mount Parnes pinpoints and confirms the relevance of this area as a focal point in the mythical and ritual context of the Pythaïs, and second, associating this paean with the Pythaïs pushes the first reference to the Athenian version of Apollo's journey, and the chronology of the ceremony, back to the fourth quarter of the 6th century BC.

The Route of the Pythaïs across the City

As we saw in the description of the lightning ritual, the contextualization of the altar of Zeus Astrapaios is key to understanding the course of the procession through the city, as the urban segment of the procession most likely originated from the nearby shrine

30 "From [or under] the sacred Parnes ... / Apollo ... / of Athens ... / here he is gracious ... / spring has not yet passed ... / we do the toil of waiting ... / the Virgin Artemis Oridromos and you, far shooting lord / we honour unanimously uttering gentle words" (trans. Rutherford 1990).

31 Rutherford 1990, 169-76. For an argument against this interpretation, see Poltera 2008, 370-1.

32 *FdD* III², 138.

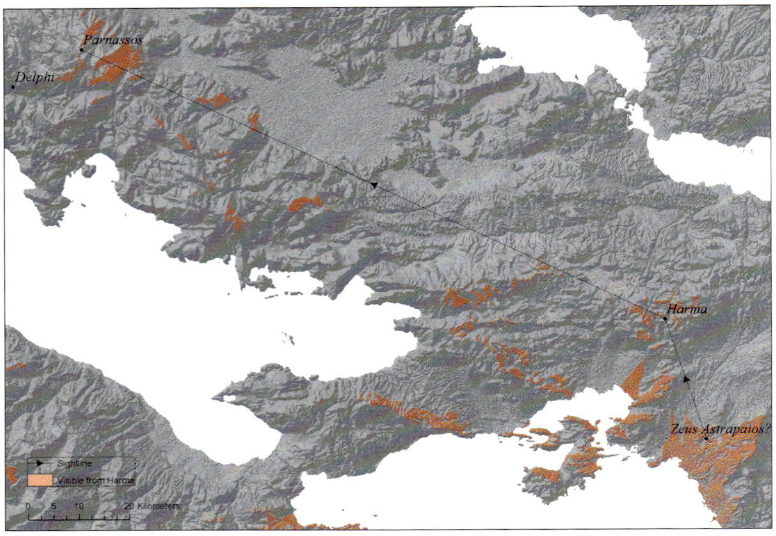

Fig. 3. Viewshed analysis centered on Harma as the observer point, showing sightlines construction (map prepared by the author).

of Apollo. In this regard, the main topographical question is the location of the Pythion referenced by Strabon. On the grounds of a supposed duplication of the Pythian shrines in Athens, scholarship tentatively locates the lightning observation spot near the Cave of Apollo on the northwest slope of the Acropolis, or at the Pythion located by the Ilissos.[33] However, epigraphic records indicate that Apollo was officially worshipped in the cave with the epithet of Hypo Makrais from at least the 5th century BC; hard evidence unmistakably locates the primary (and probably only) Pythion south of the Olympieion in the Ilissos area (Fig. 2).[34]

Although the north slope of the Acropolis offers a favourable view of Parnes, this mountain range, including Harma, was perfectly visible from the Ilissos area as well. In this regard, Lewis Richard Farnell made the following comment in 1900: "When it is a question of observing lightning above a peak some 12 miles away, it is a matter of indifference whether one's standpoint is three hundred yards nearer or further."[35] The development of the modern city makes first-hand observation very difficult, but the experiment was done by the (at that time) director of the British School. With reference to this experiment, Lewis Richard Farnell continues by reporting the words of the director *verbatim*: "From careful experiments … he [the director] concludes that 'from the wall (near the Peisitratid temples), still better from a tower on the wall, the whole of Parnes and Harma was visible.'"[36] Today, this experiment can be done with a GIS-generated visibility map, which proves that Harma is actually visible from the Ilissos area (Fig. 3).

As already mentioned, the Pythaïs featured two important rituals that were fundamental to the ceremony: the *tripodephoria* and the *pyrphoria*. These two rituals are crucial for the spatial contextualization of the Pythaïs as a whole. The *tripodephoria* consisted in the offering of a tripod (or more than one) to Delphi and the conveyance to Athens of the "Delphic" tripod. The *tripodephoria* was a way of re-affirming a connection with Delphi

33 For a recent discussion of the topographical issues pertaining to the cave of Apollo Hypo Makrais in relation to the sanctuary of Apollo Pythion, see Nulton 2003, 15-23.

34 On the 5th-century BC cult of Apollo Hypo Makrais in the cave, see Gawlinski 2007. Evidence for the location of the Pythion in the Ilissos area is provided by the epigraphic record (*IG* I^{3}, 948).

35 Farnell 1900, 372.

36 Farnell 1900, 373.

through the ritual re-establishment of a Delphic cult branch in the city – in the words of Boëthius, a "Kultfiliale".[37] Therefore, the tripod ceremony should be seen as a ritual foundation or re-foundation of the primary Athenian Pythion, that is the shrine of Apollo by the Ilissos.[38] In this respect, textual sources unanimously inform us that the Pythian sanctuary in Athens came into existence under Peisistratos.[39] The connection between this shrine and the Peisitratids is also documented archaeologically. Thucydides writes that Peisistratos the Younger dedicated an altar to Apollo Pythios in the sacred precinct, and records its dedicatory inscription.[40] This inscribed monument (more precisely, the altar's crowning block) has actually been found in the area south of the Olympieion, confirming the approximate location of the shrine.[41] Once in Athens, the Delphic tripod must have been kept in this "Peisistratid" shrine, since its counterpart at Delphi was kept within the temple of the god.[42] The altar of Zeus Astrapaios should be located near the Pythion at the Ilissos; the lightning observation must have taken place here. It was from this shrine that the urban course of the pilgrimage started.

The attention paid by Peisitratos and the Peisistratids to the cult of Apollo Pythios may possibly be related to the introduction of the Pythaïs in Athens in this very period. Ancient literary sources on the Pythaïs emphasise the importance of the pilgrimage road itself and the participation of the Athenians in tracing it.[43] This fits well into the Peisitratid plan involving the maintenance (and possibly the new layout) of the road system across both the city and the countryside.[44] The religious and political policies of the Peisistratids may have found some resonance in the compositions of their artistic entourage. As discussed in this chapter, the earliest document on the ritual of the Pythaïs is a paean ascribed to Simonides, who was probably invited to Athens by Hipparchos himself.[45] This paean may have been written during the posited poet's stay in Athens, possibly before Hipparchos was murdered in 514 BC, sometime between 527 and 514 BC. By this time, the Pythaïs may already have been firmly established.[46]

As already observed, along with the *tripodephoria*, the ritual involved a *pyrphoria*. This was the conveyance of the sacred fire from Delphi (it is not clear whether this was from the temple of Apollo or from the Prytaneion of Delphi). Aside from the purificatory meaning associated with this ritual and with the

37 Boëthius 1918, 74.

38 Boëthius 1918, 77.

39 On the literary tradition surrounding Peisitratos' role in the construction of the Pythion, see Wilson 2007, 153, nn. 13-4. Suda *s.v.* Πύθιον; Phot. *s.v.* Πύθιον vaguely mention the establishment of a sanctuary and not the erection of a temple. An anecdote recounted by Hesychios seems to point to the construction of an actual temple under Peisistratos. However, the Athenians despised it so much that they tried to hinder the construction of this building by excreting on its foundations (Hsch: <ἐν Πυθίῳ χέσαι>).

40 Thuc. 6.54.7. See Camp 2001, 36-7.

41 *IG* I³, 948. The inscription dates to 522/521 BC. Koumanoudis 1877, 149-52 gives the first report on the first discovery. Recent investigations in the area brought to light another fragment of the inscribed crowning block; see Charami & Bardani 2011.

42 Boëthius 1918, 79.

43 See for example Aesch. *Eum.* 12-4, and *scholia ad loc.*

44 See for example Steinhauer 2009, 37.

45 *POxy.* 2430 (*PMG* 519 fr.35); see Rutherford 1990, 169-71. The building programme and the religious fervor of the Peisistratids were matched by their artistic patronage; for example, Hipparchos probably added Homeric recitals to the Panathenaïa and invited the lyric poets Anacreon and possibly Simonides to Athens. The disputed presence of Simonides at the tyrants' house seems confirmed by scholarship. As was customary for court poets, he may have composed works in praise of his patrons and their deeds. On the relationship between Simonides and the Peisistratidai, see Molyneux 1992, 65-79.

46 According to some scholars, the Athenian Pythaïs came to be after the battle of Plataia in 479 BC; see Furley & Bremer 2001, 132-4, with notes.

cult of Apollo in general, the *pyrphoria* could also have had another religious significance in the context of the early Athenian Pythaïdes.[47] The fetching of the sacred fire was a common practice in Greek religion for the founding of shrines and colonies from at least before the end of the 7th century BC.[48] I suggest that along with the purificatory function of the renewal of the fire, the Pythaistic *pyrphoria* strengthened the symbolic re-foundation of the Pythion in Athens conducted with the *tripodephoria*.

The sacred fire is strongly connected with the cult of Hestia. Indeed, the celebration of the goddess was most likely an integral part of the Pythaïs. An inscribed 4th-century BC paean by Aristonoos of Corinth dedicated to Hestia was recovered from the area of the Athenian Thesauros at Delphi; as with many of the inscriptions carved on the Athenian Thesauros – in particular the later paeans by Athenaios and Limenios – it was probably related to a Pythaïs.[49]

As far as the topography of the ritual is concerned, the sacred fire and the cult of Hestia in Athens are at best contextualized in the Prytaneion, which was probably involved in the first phases of the ceremony as well as at the end of the celebration, when the Pythaïs made its way back to Athens. The Pythion has already been mentioned in previous scholarship as a landmark for the Athenian Pythaïs.[50] On the other hand, it has never been comprehensively contextualized in relation to the reconstruction of the processional course of the ceremony through Athens. A new discussion of the relationship between these cult places and the Pythaïs is particularly timely, due to new archaeological discoveries and recent scholarly contributions on the locations of those shrines. A reconstruction of the processional path through Athens must begin with the spatial context of the Pythion.

The Pythion lay somewhere along the right bank of the Ilissos River, within a maximum range of 200 meters southwest of the peribolos of the Olympieion. The approximate location of the sanctuary was identified in the 19th century.[51] However, with regard to the course of the Pythaïs across Athens, it is necessary to expand on the possible physical location of the Pythion in order to understand its relationship with the road system of the city. No architecture in the area south of the Olympieion can be conclusively identified with the Pythion, and the hypothetical location of this shrine was mostly based upon the distribution of the finds associated to the Pythian shrine. In a recent article, Angelos Matthaiou has re-examined all these finds,[52] and I would like to emphasise some of them, in particular:

1. The inscribed crowning block of the altar of Apollo Pythios set in the Pythian precinct by Peisistratos the Younger.[53]
2. The tripod bases dedicated by the choregoi victorious in the dythyrambic contests held during the Thargelia festival. These tripods were set within the Pythian precinct, as clearly indicated by the literary sources.[54]
3. Three inscribed ceramic fragments, probably related to the cult of Apollo Pythios, from a Late Archaic structure (the Law Court at the Delphin-

47 For the cult of Apollo in connection with purification rituals, see Karila-Cohen 2007, 231-5.

48 Malkin 1987, 114-34.

49 *FdD* III^2, 192. See Weil 1893, 569-83; 1894, 345-62. The possibility that Aristonoos' *paean* to Hestia might refer to a Pythaïs is suggested by Furley & Bremer 2001, 118. The hymns by Athenaios and Limenios are in *FdD* III^2, 137-8.

50 See in particular Milchhöfer 1873, 43-57; Curtius 1877; Boëthius 1918, 73-80.

51 Koumanoudis 1877.

52 Matthaiou 2011.

53 Thuc. 6.54.7; *IG* I^3, 948.

54 Matthaiou 2011, 259-61. The fact that the choregic tripods for the Thargelia were dedicated in the Pythion is stated, for example, in Suda *s.v.* Πύθιον; Phot. *s.v.* Πύθιον; Isae. 5.41; Pl. *Grg.* 472.B.1.

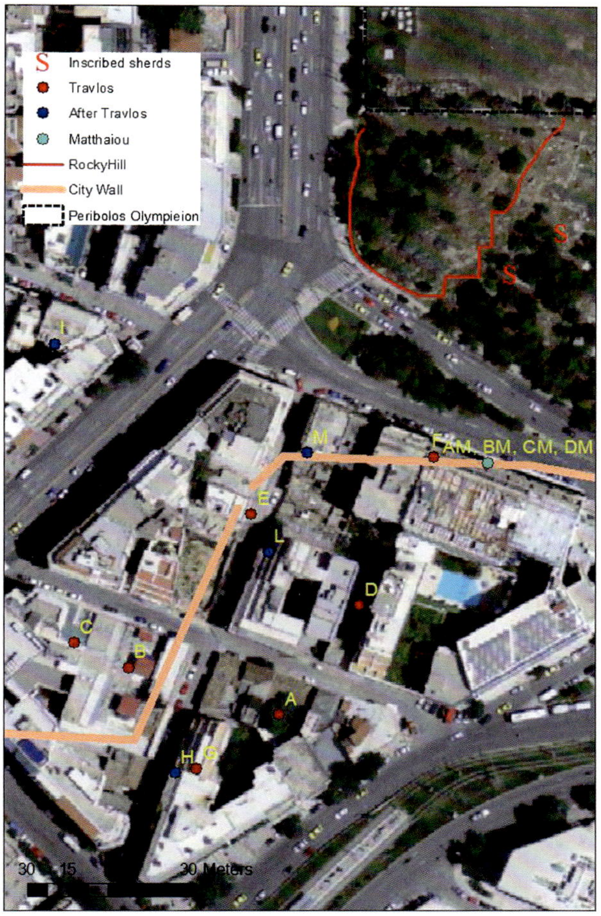

Fig. 4. Distribution map of the finds commonly used for the topographic contextualization of the Pythion (map prepared by the author. Basemap: orthophotograph after Ktimnatologio).

ion?) against the rocky hill to the southwest of the Olympieion (Fig. 4).[55]

However, there is uncertainty about the find-spot of some of those monuments, mostly for those discovered in the 19th century. John Travlos drew a distribution map of the most relevant finds in the area, which has been challenged by Angelos Matthaiou and by new archaeological discoveries.[56] Among those finds, the aforementioned altar's crowning block is the more revealing of the approximate location of the Pythion. Working from the descriptions of Stephanos Koumanoudis, who discovered the altar in 1877, Angelos Matthaiou hypothesized that the altar's fragments were found on Ath. Diakou Street in the area roughly corresponding to numbers 26 to 32, further north than John Travlos' reconstruction (Fig. 4, BM).[57] A recent find, another fragment from the same altar, has nearly confirmed Angelos Matthaiou's reconstruction (Fig. 4, M). I suggest that the original find-spot of the altar may have been located even closer to the rocky hill than previously thought. Following Stephanos Koumanoudis' indications, it must be inferred that the altar was recovered from the courtyard of a poorly built house which, along with others, lay "southwest of the Olympieion."[58] In fact, to the southwest of the temple of Zeus and in the proximity of the area where the last altar fragment was found in 2009, 19th-century photographs show a series of separate houses which seem to match Stephanos Koumanoudis' description more closely than the taller constructions to the south (Fig. 5). They appear as poorly built urban "farmsteads" and are located very close to the rocky

55 This Late Archaic structure, indirectly alluded to by Mitsos as the Pythion, was interpreted by Travlos as the Law Court at the Delphinion; see Mitsos 1947, 262; Travlos 1971, 289, figs 379-80. On the ceramics possibly related to the Pythion, see Amandry 1942, 237-8; Mitsos 1947, 262-4. These fragments were found in pebbly floors dating to the repairs of the building in the 4th or 3rd century BC. One fragment dates to the first half of the 4th century BC and bears the inscription Ἀπ[ό]λλωνο[ς]. The other two fragments date to the middle of the 4th century BC. Both carry the letters ΠΥ on their outer face, which suggests that we may "have the initial letters of the adjective (*Pythio*) of Apollo"; see Mitsos 1947, 262.

56 Travlos 1971, 101, fig. 130.

57 Matthaiou 2011, 265.

58 On this general aspect, see again the contribution of Matthaiou 2011. Koumanoudis 1872, 169: "Παρὰ τὴν δεξιὰν ὄχθην τοῦ Ἰλισσοῦ, πρὸς δυσμὰς τῆς γεφύρας τῆς ἀγούσης πρὸς τὸ νεκροταφεῖον, εἶναι τινὲς οἰκίαι, κτισθεῖσαι οὐ καλῶς πρὸ ὀλίγων ἐτῶν ἐπ' αὐτῆς σχεδὸν τῆς γραμμῆς τοῦ περιβόλου τοῦ ἄστεος". Koumanoudis 1877, 149 "ἔν τινι αὐλῇ οἰκίας ἐπὶ τάδε τοῦ Ἰλισσοῦ καὶ νοτιο δυτικῶς τοῦ Ὀλυμπιείου".

Fig. 5. Detail of the area south of the Olympieion at the time of the discovery of the altar's fragments (1877). The photograph shows the poorly built houses possibly referred to by Koumanoudis 1872, 169 (centre of the photograph). They are located against and on top of the rocky outcrop south of the Olympieion. Looking southeast (American School of Classical Studies at Athens, Archives, Archaeological Photographic Collection).

outcrop south of the Olympieion (in the same general area as the inscribed ceramic fragments). Thus, the best and most prudent solution is to extend the "buffer area" of the altar's find-spot from plot on 3 Iosif ton Rogon Street (where the last fragment was found) to the region of the houses northeast of it. The most likely conclusion is that if the fragmentary altar is seen as the most reliable topographical indicator for the location of the Pythion, there is good reason to believe that the core of the shrine was very close to the rocky outcropping which extends southwest of the Olympieion.

Before proceeding with the reconstruction of the processional path across the city, it is worth considering the following. As already mentioned, the Pythaïs was probably a ritual involving more complex activities than the simple journey to Delphi, one that touched several landmarks within and outside the city and comprised many distinct ritual movements. The Pythion at the Ilissos may also have been involved in other steps of the Pythaïs, rather than merely being used as a departure and arrival point for the pilgrimage. As mentioned before, it is possible that the celebration of the Athenian Pythaïs involved the sending of two simultaneous sacred delegations, to Delphi and to Delos respectively, as this was also the case with the Marathonian Pythaïs.[59] In analogy to the ritual carried out in the Tetrapolis, which involved the Pythion at Oinoe and the Delion at Marathon, the Athenian Pythaïs may also have included a possible Delion in Athens (not identified). In this regard, Angelos Matthaiou suggested

59 The ritual carried out in the Tetrapolis is described by Philochoros (*FGrH* 328 F 75).

Fig. 6. Topographical plan of the ancient road network in southeast Athens (as reconstructed in Ficuciello 2008, pl. I. Map prepared by the author).

that the cult of Apollo Delios in the city may indeed have had a share in the Pythion.[60]

There is more to consider. Laura Ficuciello has hypothesized a relationship between the Pythaïs procession (or a lesser procession as part of the rite) and Prasiai: the traditional departure points for Athenian delegations to Delos – I mentioned this possible connection earlier in this chapter. The Pythaïs or a procession connected with it could have been sent to Delos along one of the roads across the Mesogaia connecting the city to Porto Raphti, in the southern part of which lay the deme of Prasiai (Fig. 1).[61] Therefore, hypothetically, from Prasiai a procession would have made its way back to Athens, as a re-enactment of Apollo's landing and triumphal arrival into the city, before continuing its journey across Attica and central Greece. This procession would have gained access to the city in the sacred Ilissos area, whence, as suggested in this work, the urban Pythaïs departed to seek the Prytanenion. In short, the urban stretch of the procession might be seen as a middle segment of a larger mythical itinerary of the Pythaïs from Delos to Delphi. Even if the sacred topography and the order of the events involved in the celebration can only be reconstructed hypothetically, the Pythion by the Ilissos was certainly the hub of the ritual, at least in its original and early form.

From the Pythion, the procession moved to the Prytaneion; and the discussion above concerning the *pyrphoria* along with the prominence of Hestia within the Pythaïs ritual makes this hypothesis very probable. The identification of the general site of the Prytaneion is a relatively recent achievement. Pausanias, the best source for the contextualization of the Archaic town hall, describes it as being close to the Aglaurion.[62] This latter shrine was identified with certainty in the early 1980s, in the cave on the southeast crag of the Acropolis.[63] In a recently published work, G. Schmalz has re-examined all textual and archaeological evidence for the topographical contextualization of the Prytaneion; he believes it is located under the modern Agia Aikaterini Square, identifying the colonnaded complex underneath the square as the actual Prytaneion.[64] Although this identification has not been definitively proven, it is probable that

60 Matthaiou 2003, 91-2.

61 Ficuciello 2008, 32.

62 Paus. 1.18.2-3.

63 Schmalz 2006, 40, n. 27. The location of the general areas occupied by the Prytaneion and the Archaic Agora has been possible thanks to the identification of the Aglaurion in the 1980s; see Dontas 1983; Schmalz 2006, 40-3. See also Kalligas 1994; Lippolis 1995.

64 Schmalz 2006. The most recently recovered evidence concerning the discussion of the approximate location of the Prytaneion is an inscription (Π 1247 1st Ephoreia of Antiquities inventory number) found at 32 Tripodon Street. This possibly dates to the second quarter of the 5th century BC and concerns regulations for the prytaneis and the Prytaneion.

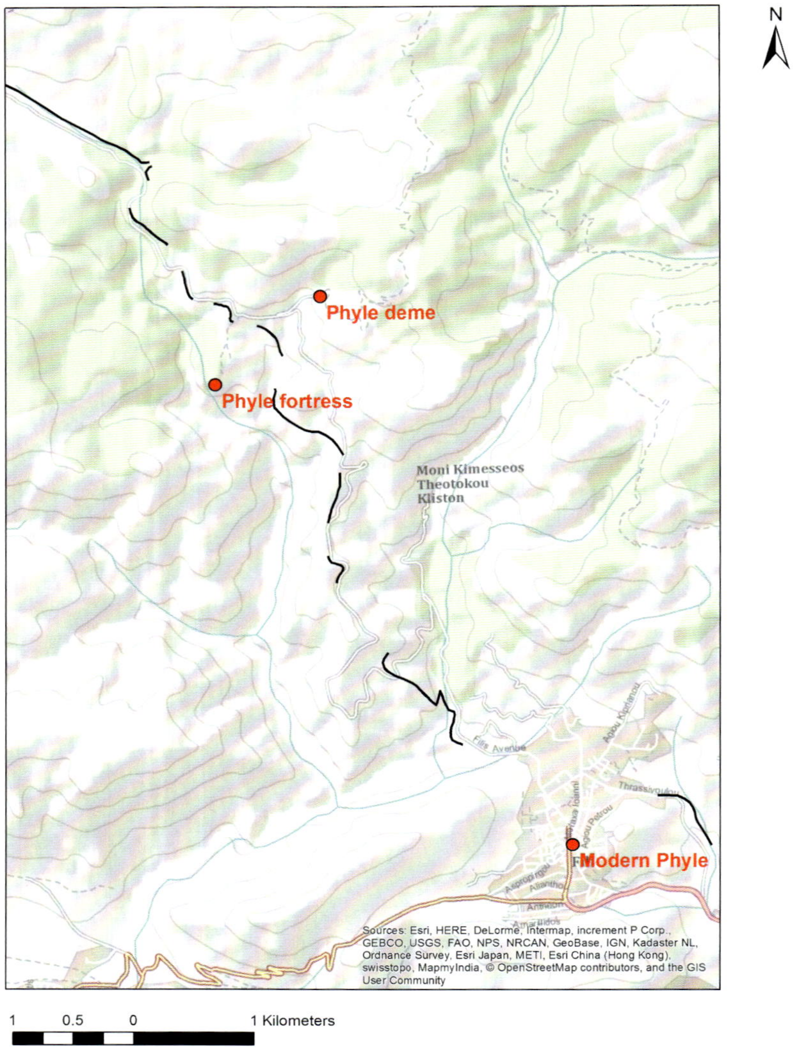

Fig. 7. Path of the ancient Phyle road (indicated by black lines). Reconstruction based on field-collected data (map prepared by the author).

the Prytaneion actually stood in the general area of Lysikrates Square or the immediate surroundings.

From the Pythion area, several roads and road segments may have been connected to the Prytaneion. One stretch of road in particular deserves special attention: this is the thoroughfare that crossed the sacred area southwest of the Olympieion and served John Travlos' city's Gate X on the east section of the Valerian wall (Fig. 6).[65] Given its northwest-southeast orientation, it is plausible that this road headed directly towards the area of the Archaic Agora and the Prytaneion, like other ancient roads which entered the city from the main gates. However, its course can only be reconstructed hypothetically, as part of it was destroyed, probably quite soon after the construction of the Olympieion terrace under Hadrian.[66] The area surrounding the road was occupied

65 Costaki 2006, 587-8. It is possible that the Valerian Gate replaced an earlier predecessor, as indicated by the road itself which must have been connected with a city gate there.

66 Ficuciello 2008, 79. This street may have gone temporarily out of use in the Late Hellenistic period; see Costaki 2006, 587-8.

Fig. 8. Longitudinal wheel ruts carving. The remnants of the carving on the left measure approximately 3.5m in length. The rough road surface is also visible. Photograph taken from north (photographer: author).

without interruption from the Late Helladic through the Byzantine period, and at least from the 6th century BC it developed as one of the focal points of religious life in Athens.[67] This road must have been very important, and early. In fact, the history of the area and the orientation of the road course between major religious buildings, such as the so-called temple of Apollo Delphinios to the south and the Olympieion to the north, suggests that this was a very ancient way which had likely served religious functions since earliest antiquity.[68] As such, this was most probably used as a processional road for many of the deities worshipped there, including Apollo Pythios. Indeed, as already shown, the Pythion was probably closer to this road than previously thought.[69] It is reasonable to believe that this very road (and its extension) may have corresponded to the first urban stretch of the processional road of the Pythaïs.[70]

Two key factors in particular create difficulty in reconstructing the path of the procession across the rest of the city from the location of the Prytaneion: first, the urban course of the processional route was most probably related to the extra-urban route as

67 This area was extensively excavated by Threpsiades and Travlos in the early 1960s; see Threpsiades & Travlos 1963. However, the excavation has not been fully published. On the development of the primitive city in this area, see Thuc. 2.15.4.

68 Costaki 2006, 588 suggests that this might be the ancient road to Sounion.

69 In this regard, it has been proposed by N. Robertson to identify the Pythion in the so-called temple of Apollo Delphinios, which closely borders the street to the south; see Robertson 2005, 52-5.

70 On this hypothesis, see also Ficuciello 2008, 79.

well, and this latter route can only be reconstructed hypothetically; second, it is not certain whether the course of the procession might have changed over time, given the long life of the ritual.

A plausible hypothesis can still be advanced, however. From the general area of the Prytaneion, the Pythaïs probably moved towards the Classical Agora (possibly along the Street of the Tripods, perhaps entering the square in the area of the City Eleusinion, which might have been a station along the procession. In fact, it is in the Classical Agora, more precisely at the northeast corner of the square, that the boundary stone of the sacred road of the Pythaïs was discovered.[71] This boundary stone was not found in its original position, yet it is one of the best topographical indicators for the reconstruction of the path of the route across the city.

The Pythaïdes might have begun to use the area of the future Classical Agora as early as the second half of the 6th century BC, when the ritual was probably introduced to Athens. The area occupied by the Classical Agora gradually developed as a common public space with Peisistratos and the Peisistratids.[72] Among the buildings of the Agora in this early phase, the Altar of the Twelve Gods is of particular relevance in the context of this reconstruction. Dedicated during the archonship of Peisistratos the Younger in 522/521 BC (the same Peisistratos who dedicated the altar in the Pythion), it was used as the point from which all distances to Athens were measured; as such, it became the physical centre of the city, and was certainly an important reference for all outbound travellers.[73] This monument fits well as a landmark in the path of the Pythaïs, since this pilgrimage was, according to mythical tradition, the outbound Athenian journey by definition. The Altar of the Twelve Gods was conveniently located at the convergence of major thoroughfares; indeed, the axes of some of the main roads to the city gates originated near the altar. In this respect, we should observe that the aforementioned road marker for the sacred road of the Pythaïs was found not too far from this altar and, as I will discuss, this boundary stone may have marked the beginning of the sacred road in that area of the Agora.

As with the case of the region southeast of the Acropolis, reconstructing the ritual in this other part of the city is arduous due to the absence of detailed information. Apart from the Classical Agora, the Pythaïs may have also involved the Acropolis (the priestess of Athena features among the participant of the Pythaïs in *IG* II^2, 1136 dating to 106/105 BC). In addition, it has already been observed that the paean by Limenios inscribed in the 2nd century BC seems to point to the Acropolis as a landmark for Apollo's mythical visit to Athens.[74] Indeed, Euripides' *Ion* seems to connect Apollo Pythios, at least at the mythical level, to the aforementioned cave in the north slope of the Acropolis, where the god was officially worshipped as Hypo Makrais (or Hypoakraios).[75] In this respect, this cave may have had a share in the ritual. Moreover, in the Cave of Apollo Hypo Makrais the Pythian god is associated with his function of Patroös as, in that cave, he fathers Ion, an eponymous fatherly figure to all Ionians.[76] The link between Apollo Patroös and Pythios had already been firmly established by the 4th century BC. Therefore, it is probable that even the temple of Apollo Patroös in the west end of the Agora may have been among the places attended during the Pythaïstic celebrations.[77] In short, the complexity

71 Agora 19, H 34.

72 Camp 2005.

73 Thuc. 6.54.6-7. On the altar as a central milestone, see Hdt. 2.7; *IG* II^2, 2640. On the architecture and function of the altar, see Travlos 1971, 458-61; Camp 2010, 89-90.

74 *FdD* III^2, 138.

75 The cult of Apollo Hypo Makrais in the cave is ascertained for the 5th century BC, see Gawlinski 2007.

76 Eur. *Ion* 10, 283, 494, 937, 1400. See Hedrick 1988, 204.

77 On the relationship between Apollo Patroös and Pythios, see Hedrick 1988, 200-3. With regard to other possible Apollonian elements in the Classical Agora,

of the ritual is clear and the reconstruction is open to numerous possible solutions.

While the proposed general direction of the procession from the Pythion at the Ilissos to the area of the Classical Agora, via the Prytaneion, can be considered reasonably probable, proof of the continuation of the procession from the Classical Agora towards one of the city gates is much less clear. Indeed, the course of the procession within the city was certainly related to the direction of its route outside the walls, as the urban and sub-urban Athenian road network was obviously closely connected with the location of the city gates. In short, heading towards one gate rather than another would have most likely determined the route of the pilgrimage outside the city as well.[78]

Extra-Urban Routes

The course of the Athenian Pythaïs across Attica has drawn attention from scholars since the first decades of the 19th century;[79] by the end of that century, scholarship had already indicated three possible itineraries for the extra-urban route of Pythaïs (Fig. 1):

1. A western route across Mount Kithairon via Eleusis.[80]
2. A central route across Mount Parnes via Phyle and Harma.[81]
3. An eastern route by which the path of the Athenian Pythaïs would have merged with that of the Marathonian Tetrapolis' sacred road.[82]

This third possibility has not received much credence in later scholarship, as this northeastern sacred route was probably a feature of the Marathonian Pythaïs, but not of the Athenian. Indeed, Boëthius has convincingly suggested that the Athenian and the Marathonian Pythaïdes were two distinct theoriai that followed different routes before joining the course of the "international" sacred road through Boiotia.[83]

To the three aforementioned routes, we should add a fourth. I will refer to this as the "conciliatory" route, as it combines the western path via the Eleusinian sacred road and the Parnes routes into one, defining a rather indirect itinerary. This route was proposed by scholars such as A.W. Parsons and, more recently, L. Ficuciello. The pilgrimage would have followed the Eleusinian *Hiera Hodos* to the temple of Apollo located in the area of the Daphni monastery. It would then have continued

a hypothetical relationship between the "omphalos"-shaped stones recovered in the Classical Agora and the *gylloi*, the movable stones that marked the route of the processional way between Miletus and Didyma, has recently been proposed by Laura Ficuciello; see Ficuciello 2008, 30-1, nn. 181-2. The temple of Apollo Patroös on the west side of the Classical Agora lies on what is possibly its mid-6th-century BC predecessor.

78 This is evident for the Pythaïs of the 5th century BC, since for this period the enceinte is archaeologically documented. In fact, we do not possess much evidence for the Archaic walls, let alone its possible gates. However, the city gates of the Themistoclean enceinte are in many cases oriented along the axis of the Archaic city road system. Therefore, in the Archaic period the procession must have followed the same general direction as that of the following centuries. On the Archaic Athenian walls, see Theocharaki 2011, 73-6. On the Archaic road system, see Costaki 2006.

79 For a recent, more detailed discussion of the possible extra-urban route of the Pythaïs across Attica, see Fachard & Pirisino 2015, 147-8.

80 The earliest advocate of this route is Müller 1824, 239-40.

81 The route across central Parnes was suggested by Milchhöfer 1873, 56-7; 1895, 14.

82 The possibility that the path of the Athenian Pythaïs could have merged with the Marathonian sacred road was advanced by Curtius 1855, 20-7.

83 The two sacred delegations, and subsequently their routes, merged in the second half of the 2nd century BC. As long as the theoriai were sent separately, they followed different routes; see Boëthius 1918, 38-51. On the "international" sacred way to Delphi, see Hdt. 6.34.2.

past Egaleo, but rather than going up to Eleusis and beyond, it would have turned northeast at Rheitoi or shortly thereafter, making its way into Parnes and Harma across the Thriasian plain.[84] However, my field walks across western Parnes made it clear that this route is not only very taxing physically, but also almost impossible to follow along its shortest path through this region of Parnes. In conclusion, the evidence for the extra-urban route of the Athenian Pythaïs narrows down to two possible routes: either through Eleusis and Kithairon, or by way of Acharnai towards Harma and Phyle.

The sacred road to Eleusis is very well documented in both literary and archaeological records; it is considered by many the definitive *hiera hodos*.[85] For this reason, there is a natural inclination in existing scholarship to consider this route the prime candidate for the Pythaïs. However, no evidence unambiguously associates the Eleusinian *Hiera Hodos* with the Pythaïs. The most discussed element of the route of the Pythaïs along the road to Eleusis is the presence of a temple to Apollo on the road, located at today's monastery of Daphni.[86] Boëthius, as well as others including Parsons, considered this shrine decisive evidence for the course of the Pythaïs.[87] What is particularly relevant about this temple is its foundation myth. According to Pausanias' account, the shrine was built by the descendants of Kephalos, Chalkinos and Daitos, at the request of the god himself as they were travelling back from Delphi to Athens.[88] This has led to the conclusion that the shrine of Apollo lay on the well-trodden route from Athens to Delphi and that this route was also that of the Pythaïs.

The first possible rebuttal of this argument is that the route of the Pythaïs did not necessarily coincide with the regularly used road to Delphi, and furthermore, travellers could follow different routes into Boiotia and back into Attica according to their departure points outside and within Attica. Even considering the route through Kithairon via Eleusis as a possible candidate for the Pythaïs, the foundation myth of the temple of Apollo at Daphni does not constitute conclusive evidence. In addition, apart from the shrine at Daphni, Pausanias devotes little space to Apollo among the heroes and deities mentioned on his way to Eleusis.[89] However, Apollo was certainly venerated near Eleusis as well, as indicated by a 4th-century BC boundary stone of a not-yet-located shrine of the god, even though it specifies no cult epithet. The only references to the god as Pythios in an Eleusinian context are very indirect, and by no means can they be definitively associated with a cult of the Pythian god in the sanctuary.[90] In brief, a cult of Apollo Pythios at

84 Parsons 1943, 237-38; Ficuciello 2008, 28-32.

85 The Eleusinian sacred road was the object of monographic studies as early as the second half of the 19th century, with Lenormant 1864. For recent contributions on the *Hiera Hodos* and the roads through the Thriasian plain into Boiotia, see Drakotou 2009; Papangeli 2009; Steinhauer 2009, 41-4.

86 For a recent discussion of the archaeological evidence for the temple at Daphni, see Despinis 2011; Delinikolas *et al.* 2016. The temple at Daphni might have been dedicated to Apollo Pythios, but there is no absolute certainty in this regard. A marble base from the monastery carries a dedication to Apollo, but the god's epithet is debatable; see SEG XVIII, 90.

87 Boëthius 1918, 50; Parsons 1943, 238.

88 Paus. 1.37.6.

89 Paus. 1.38.1-7. Beyond Reithoi, the only reference to Apollo is a very indirect one. Pausanias mentions a shrine of the hero Zarex, to whom Apollo would have taught music (Paus. 1.38.4). Apart from Demeter and Kore, the main deities of the Eleusinans seem to be Triptolemos, Artemis, and Poseidon, with no mention of Apollo (Paus. 1.38.6). It is, however, well known that Pausanias purposely omits the description of the Eleusinian sanctuary itself (Paus. 1.38.7).

90 A boundary stone (*IG* II^2, 2601) of uncertain provenance, possibly dating to the first half of the 4th century BC, bears witness to the presence of a shrine of Apollo somewhere near Eleusis. However, this boundary presents no cult epithet specification. See Clinton 2005-2008, vol. 1, no. 677, 496; 2008, no. 677, 426. A law concerning the Mysteries, dating to the first half of

Eleusis is plausible, as the sanctuary was also home to other major deities of the Athenian Pantheon, but its presence has not been ascertained by hard evidence.[91]

Parsons brought forward an additional argument for a possible relationship between the Pythaïs and the temple of Apollo at Daphni. He pointed out that of the many votive plaques originally dedicated to Apollo Hypo Makrais (or Hypoakraios), two were recovered at the Dipylon Gate and at the Daphni Monastery respectively.[92] Parsons, who believed that the Pythaïs started from Apollo Hypo Makrais' cave, connected these findings with the route of the Pythaïs. However, these two plaques are relatively late in date, either 1st or 2nd century AD, and the chronology of the entire body of these votives fluctuates between the middle of the 1st century AD to the end of the 3rd century AD. None of these plaques refers to Apollo Pythios; all of them are dedicated to Apollo Hypo Makrais (or Hypoakraios). I suggest that a hypothetical connection between Apollo Hypo Makrais and the shrine at Daphni may well have been established in the context of another celebration or official offering to Apollo, and not necessarily the Pythaïs, since, as is upheld in this chapter, the ritual started from the Pythian shrine by the Ilissos. Furthermore, even if the Cave of Apollo Hypo Makrais had a share in the Pythaïs together with the shrine at Daphni, this still does not indicate the course of the processional route. In fact, a lesser procession conducted in the broader frame of the Pythaïs celebration may well have touched different shrines of Apollo located in different areas of the city and even outside it. In short, neither the location of the shrine of Apollo at Daphni (whether Daphnephoros or Pythios) nor the two fragmentary plaques represents unmistakable evidence for the course of the Pythaïs. Theoretically, if the Pythaïs followed the Eleusian *Hiera Hodos*, it would have obviously headed to the *Hiera Pyle* (Sacred Gate), either along the western stretch of the Panathenaic Way or the urban stretch of the sacred road. The pilgrimage would have left the city from the Sacred Gate and followed the Sacred Way. From Eleusis, the route would have passed into Boiotia through Kithairon at Eleutherai.

The Phyle Route

The direction of the Pythaïs across Athens and Attica should be primarily reconstructed with no other evidence than that concerning the Pythaïs. Indeed, the information available on this specific sacred route to Delphi indicates no other places than Harma and Mount Parnes and does not explicitly include Eleusis.[93]

the 4th century BC (a copy of which was found in the City Eleusinion) refers to an innovation according to Apollo's oracular response, see Clinton 2005-2008, vol. 1, no. 138, l. 10, 124; 2008, no. 138, 119. Apollo Pythios appears at Eleusis in an entry in an Eleusinian sacrificial calendar (*IG* II², 1363) possibly dating to the second half of the 4th century BC, see Dow 1965, 21-30. Clinton 2005-2008, vol. 1, no. 175, l. 9, 182; 2008, no. 175, 170, 172. The calendar mentions offerings to Apollo Pythios on the part of the Eleusinian personnel brought during the celebration of the Pyanopsia festival in Athens. This entry is witness to the Eleusinian representatives going to Athens rather than a Pythian procession going to Eleusis. In this regard, Eleusinian officials took part in the Thargelia at the Pythion in Athens (*LSS* 14.36). In an honorary decree recovered at Eleusis, which dates to the first half of the 1st century BC, a list of priesthoods held by the Kerykes is featured, and among them an official of Apollo Pythios, see Clinton 2005-2008, vol. 1, no. 300, ll. 14-5, 300; 2008, no. 300, 306-7. However, it is possible that this official of Apollo Pythios referred to the cult at Athens, not at Eleusis.

91 On the deities worshipped at Eleusis, see Lippolis 2006, 110-5.

92 These two plaques are *IG* II², 2897, and *IG* II², 2909. All the plaques (*IG* II², 2891-2931) have been collected and studied by Peter E. Nulton; see Nulton 2003.

93 Lambert 2002, fr. 1 A, column 2, 26-7; *POxy.* 2430 (*PMG* 519 fr.35); Rutherford 1990, 169-71; Strabon 9.2.1.

The only real evidence which bears on a discussion of the path of the Pythaïs from the Classical Agora to its extra-urban continuation is the above-mentioned boundary stone of the *Hiera Hodos* of the Pythaïs. This 4th-century BC road marker had been reused as a threshold and was found in 1938 in a Late Roman fill (dating to the 4th-5th century AD) in the northeast area of the Agora. The topographical problem is to understand which road it related to. In the years immediately following its discovery, the boundary stone was first associated to the Panathenaic way.[94] However, in the period between 1969 and 1972, another theory was proposed for the contextualization of the boundary stone, as the ancient road system of the northeast part of the Agora became clearer with the discovery of the East-West street and the North-South street. Stephen Miller, who excavated those streets, writes the following in a topographical note to its excavation report:[95]

> Since the *horos* was found just 30 metres southwest of the intersection of the North-South Street and the East-West Street ... we can better imagine that the Pythaïs came down the Panathenaic Way to the point where the North-South Street branched off. The procession will have proceeded up this street, out the Acharnian Gate of Athens, and northward through the Attic plain to Parnes and the Phyle pass. Our *horos* stone will have stood at some point along this street, most likely at the point where the North-South street branches off the Panathenaic way, or else at the intersection of the former with the East-West street.

This is a likely interpretation, and I would add the following: as discussed earlier in this paper, the term *hiera hodos* is used in antiquity as a toponym proper and distinct to a specific road. Indeed, the inscription on the stone clearly expresses an unequivocal relationship between a distinct sacred road and that very procession: "Marker of the Sacred Road by which the Pythaïs proceeds to Delphi." This should probably discourage any association of this boundary stone to the Panthenaic Way or to the Eleusinian *Hiera Hodos*.

Fig. 9. Narrow, deep wheel rut. Photograph taken from southeast (photographer: author).

The Pythaïs may have actually made its way into Boiotia through Parnes via Harma and Phyle. After leaving the Agora from the northeast corner, it may have headed for the Acharnian Gates, and possibly reached the Phyle road through Acharnai. This was the largest deme in Attica, with a considerable demographic weight in the Athenian state, and strategically located in the heart of the Athenian

94 See Shear 1939, 212; Parsons 1943, 238.

95 Miller 1971, 3.

Fig. 10. Parallel carved wheel ruts, spaced 1.40m from each other. Photograph taken from south (photographer: author).

road network of northern Attica.[96] The deme was certainly a communication hub for the different routes that entered the Athenian *pedion* from the northwest, north, and northeast, and of course *vice versa* it was an important reference for travellers leaving the city towards northern Attica and beyond. The much-used Acharnai road connecting Athens to the deme was under the special protection of Apollo, in his capacity as guardian of the streets and averter of evil. Indeed, an inscription referring to a shrine of Apollo Agyieus Alexikakos was found at the Acharnian Gates; furthermore, the god was worshipped as Agyieus at the deme as well.[97]

The influence of Apollo as protector of roads and travellers probably did not only involve the first segment of the road to the deme, but may have extended along the continuations of this axis that, by means of its extensions, was projected towards long-distance, extra-territorial travels. The particular connection of the Acharnian road with Apollo fits well into the mythical narrative of the Pythaïs. In this regard, it has already been noted that in the Athenian version of Apollo's legendary journey to Delphi, the god appears in the guise of the wandering divinity *par excellence*. Indeed, this Athenian tradition presents Apollo in his function of Agyieus, the road itself having pride of place in the myth. It can therefore be hypothesized that the road to Acharnai may in fact have been used in the sub-urban segment of the pilgrimage. It was at the Acharnian Gates that the usually travelled

96 Thuc. 2.19.2, 2.20-23. See Camp 2001, 274-5.

97 This inscription was found in 1825 at the Acharnian Gates (*IG* II², 4850). On the cult of Apollo Agyieus at Acharnai, see Paus. 1.31.6.

Fig. 11. View of a carved stretch of the ancient Phyle road. Sections of the retaining wall are found throughout its length. Photograph taken from northwest (photographer: author).

road to Boiotia via Parnes began, as shown by maps as early as the 17th century AD; furthermore, the Phyle road was the most direct road into Boiotia.[98] The Turkish public postal service and the courier system (*ulaklik*) had an important horse-changing station (*menzil*) at Phyle.[99] It can be inferred that if the centralized Ottoman Empire preferred the Phyle route for its communication links between Attica and Boiotia, this must have actually meant that the extant (and pre-extant) road assured the most direct connection between the two regions.

Of the possible extra-urban routes of the Pythaïs, the Phyle road has for a long time been probably the least understood and the most underestimated. While the topography and the characteristics of the Eleusinian sacred road and its northward continuations to Kithairon are well known, there has always been great uncertainty concerning the path of

98 See the 17th-century map of Athens drawn by the Capuchin monks as published by G. Guillet (Laborde 1854). Map accessible on the Travelogues website of the Aikaterini Laskaridis Foundation (http://eng.travelogues.gr/item.php?view=32390, last accessed 8 January 2018).

99 Skias 1901, 43; Iotas 2004, 67-8, n. 40. Before the advent of motorized traffic, the speed and means of ancient overland travel did not change for millennia. Therefore, it is reasonable to suggest that the deme of Phyle must also have been an important stop on the Athens-Boiotia road throughout antiquity.

Fig. 12. Polygonal limestone block from a roadside structure flanking the ancient Phyle road. Photograph taken from east (photographer: author).

the ancient Phyle road across Parnes.[100] Therefore, I decided to survey the route traversed by the Phyle road in order to use actual field-collected data and observations to support any discussion surrounding the pilgrimage of the Pythaïs that, however remote to us now, once took place in an actual physical environment – one that cannot be understood unless by first-hand observation.[101] Since recent scholarship has argued that the ancient road may have stopped at the fortress, the main goal of the survey was to verify the true extent of the ancient Phyle road.[102] Other primary aims were to track the course of the road and understand its characteristics, to address questions concerning the suitability of this route to the pilgrimage, and to verify whether the road could have possibly been used by carts.

100 The best description of the Phyle route in previous scholarship (for the segment to the fortress, at least) is that of Wrede 1924. For a recent and detailed analysis of the evidence and contextualization of the route, see Pirisino 2015.

101 Our field surveys were conducted in the western region of Mount Parnes, over the period stretching from September 2013 to December 2014, in order to trace the remains of the ancient routes and road networks that led to Boiotia via Harma and Phyle. The results of these field walks will be described in detail in a further contribution. I would like to express my gratitude to those who volunteered to follow me in my field surveys, especially Miltiades Kylindreas and Artemis Sachtouris, who joined me for almost every mission.

102 Ober 1985, 185.

Our targeted field walks demonstrated that the path of the ancient road can be reconstructed for several kilometres along its most difficult stretch across the mountain (Fig. 7). Wheel ruts (concentrated in a few stretches at the southeastern folds of Parnes), retaining walls, segments of carved road, ancient roadside structures (shrines or funerary monuments), and wells indicate the true course of the road (Figs 8 to 12). This evidence demonstrates that the ancient main Phyle road did not stop at the fortress, as suggested by some scholars, but extended further north to the Skourta plain and Boiotia. In some spots, the ancient Phyle road was carefully laid out and built, and in certain well-preserved segments, it was large enough to accommodate wheeled traffic. Although we cannot be absolutely sure that this road could be used by carts throughout, it may certainly have been used by a large pilgrimage to reach Boiotia. To sum up, the topography of the region certainly indicates that travelling on the Phyle road was not a comfortable journey. However, the scarcity of an obvious monumentalization of this road should not discourage scholarship from considering the Phyle route as a valid alternative to the Eleusis-Kithairon route for the path of the Pythaïs.

While the reconstruction of the general urban course of the Pythaïs suggested in this paper can be considered fairly likely, at least up to the area of the Classical Agora, the continuation of the pilgrimage route across Attica remains difficult to pin down with absolute certainty. It has been shown that a simplistic association between the route of the Pythaïs and the Eleusinian *Hiera Hodos* is inadequate to give an understanding of the relationship between the rite, its ritual space, and its founding myth.[103] In fact, the Pythaïs is best contextualized in a wider scenario that encompasses other areas that probably had a share in the ritual: primarily Parnes. From a multidisciplinary analysis of the data related to the Pythaïs and newly conducted surveys, it can be concluded that a route through western Parnes, via Harma, is a likely candidate for this pilgrimage.

103 As noted, the hypothesis that the Pythaïs followed the *Hiera Hodos* to Eleusis has dominated most scholarship concerned with the pilgrimage since Müller 1824, 239-40.

Abbreviations

Agora = *The Athenian Agora* (Princeton 1953-)

Didyma = McCabe & Plunkett 1985.

FdD = *Fouilles de Delphes*, École Française d'Athènes

FGrH = F. Jacoby, *Fragmente der griechischen Historiker* (Berlin 1923-)

ID = F. Dürrbach *et al.*, *Inscriptions de Délos* (Paris 1926-)

IG = *Inscriptiones Graecae* (1873-)

POxy = *Oxyrhynchus Papyri* (1898-)

PMG = D.L. Page, *Poetae Melici Graeci* (1962)

LSS = F. Sokolowski, *Lois sacrées des cités grecques: Supplément* (1962)

SEG = *Supplementum epigraphicum Graecum* (1923-)

Bibliography

AMANDRY, P. 1942
'Chronique des fouilles et découvertes archéologiques en Grèce en 1940 et 1941. Première partie', *BCH* 64-65, 231-53.

ANDERSON, G. & D. KLUGMANN 2014
'A European Lightning Density Analysis Using 5 Years of ATDnet Data', *Natural Hazards and Earth System Sciences* 14.4, 815-29.

BEKKER-NIELSEN, T. 2009
'Straßen, Heiligtümer und heilige Straßen', *Die Landschaft und die Religion: Stuttgarter Kolloquium zur Historischen Geographie des Altertums 2005* (Geographica Historica 26), Stuttgart, 9-15.

BÉLIS, A. 1992
Les Hymnes à Apollon, vol. 3 of *Corpus des Inscriptions de Delphes*, Paris.

BOËTHIUS, A. 1918
Die Pythaïs. Studien zur Geschichte der Verbindung zwischen Athen und Delphi, Uppsala.

BOUSQUET, J. 1942
'Inscriptions de Delphes', *BCH* 66, 124-36.

CAMP, J.M. 2001
The Archaeology of Athens, New Haven and London.

CAMP, J.M. 2005
'The Origins of the Classical Agora', in *Teseo e Romolo. Le origini di Atene e Roma a confronto. Atti del convegno Internazionale di Studi. Scuola Archeologica Italiana di Atene. Atene, 30 giugno – 1 luglio 2003*, E. Greco (ed.), Athens, 197-209.

CAMP, J.M. 2010
Athenian Agora. Site Guide, Princeton.

CAMP, J.M., M. IERARDI, J. MCINERNEY, K. MORGAN & G. UMHOLTZ 1997
'An Athenian Dedication to Herakles at Panopeus', *Hesperia* 66.2, 261-9.

CHARAMI, C. & V. BARDANI 2011
'New Fragment from the Altar of Apollo Pythios', *Δελτίον της Ελληνικής Επιγραφικής Εταιρείας*, May, www.greekepigraphicsociety.org.gr (accessed 18.11.2017).

CLINTON, K. 2005-2008
Eleusis. The Inscriptions on Stone. Documents of the Sanctuary of the Two Goddesses and Public Documents of the Deme, 2 vols., Athens.

CORCELLA, A. 1993
Erodoto. Le Storie, vol. 4, Milan.

COSTAKI, L. 2006
'The *intra muros* Road System of Ancient Athens', PhD diss., University of Toronto [forthcoming *Hesperia* Suppl.].

CURTIUS, E. 1855
Zur Geschichte des Wegebaus bei den Griechen. Ein Beitrag zur Alterthumswissenschaft, Berlin.

CURTIUS, E. 1877
'Das Pythion in Athen', *Hermes* 12.4, 492-9.

DAUX, G. 1936
Delphes au IIe et au Ier siècle: depuis l'abaissement de l'Étolie jusqu'à la paix romaine 191-31 av. J.-C., Paris.

DAVERIO ROCCHI, G. 2002
'Topografia dello spazio internazionale. La *hierà hodós* da Atene a Delfi', in *Zu Wasser und zu Land – Verkehrswege in der antiken Welt, Stuttgarter Kolloquium zur historischen Geographie des Altertums. Stuttgart 5-9 May 1999* (Geographica Historica 17), E. Olshausen & H. Sonnabend (eds.), Stuttgart, 148-59.

DELINIKOLAS, N., A. MILTIADOU-FEZANS & E. DOUDOUMI 2016
'Συνήθης και ιδιότυπη χρήση Αρχαίων και Ρωμαϊκών σπολίων στο καθολικό της Ι. Μονή Δαφνίου', in *Αρχιτέκτων Τιμητικός τόμος για τον καθηγητή Μανόλη Κορρέ*, K. Zambas, V. Lambrinoudakis, E. Simantoni-Bournia & A. Ohnesorg (eds.), Athens, 175-83.

DESPINIS, G. 2011
'Το ιερό του Απόλλωνα στο Δαφνί', in *Νάματα. Τιμητικός τόμος για τον καθηγητή Δημήτριο Παντερμαλή*, S. Pingiatoglou & Th. Stefanidou-Tiberiou (eds.), Thessaloniki, 21-31.

DONTAS, G.S. 1983
'The True Aglaurion', *Hesperia* 52, 48-63.

DÖRIG, J. 1967
'Lesefrüchte. III. Der Ostgiebel des Apollontempels in Delphi', in *Gestalt und Geschichte: Festschrift Karl Schefold, zu seinem sechzigsten Geburtstag am 26. Jan. 1965*, M. Rohde-Liegle, H.A. Cahn & H.Cr. Ackermann (eds.), Bern, 102-9.

DOW, S. 1965
A Sacred Calendar of Eleusis, Cambridge.

DRAKOTOU, I. 2009
'Ιερά Οδός, ανατολικό τμήμα', in *Αττικής Οδοί. Αρχαίοι Δρόμοι της Αττικής*, M. Korres (ed.), Athens, 112-23.

FACHARD, S. & D. PIRISINO 2015
'Routes out of Attica', in *New Autopsy in Athens: Recent Archaeological Work on Athens and Attica*, M.M. Miles (ed.), Oxford, 139-53.

FARNELL, L.R. 1900
'Questions Concerning Attic Topography and Religion with Reference to Thucydides II.15', *The Classical Review* 14.7, 369-76.

FARNELL, L.R. 1907
The Cults of the Greek States, vol. 4, Oxford.

FICUCIELLO, L. 2008
Le strade di Atene, Athens and Paestum.

FURLEY, W.D. & J.M. BREMER 2001
Greek Hymns: Selected Cult Songs from the Archaic to the Hellenistic Period. Part 1: The Text in Translation (Studien und Texte zu Antike und Christentum 9), Tübingen.

GAWLINSKI, L. 2007
'The Athenian Calendar of Sacrifices: A New Fragment from the Athenian Agora', *Hesperia* 76.1, 37-55.

HEDRICK, C.W. 1988
'The Temple and Cult of Apollo Patroos in Athens', *AJA* 92.2, 185-210.

IOTAS, D.I. 2004
Παλαιά Μοναστήρια της Πάρνηθας, Fyli.

JONES, W.H.S. 1927
The Geography of Strabo, vol. 4, London.

KALLIGAS, P.I. 1994
'Η περιοχή του ιερού και του θεάτρου του Διονύσου στην Αθήνα', in *The Archaeology of Athens and Attica under the democracy. Proceedings of an International Conference celebrating 2500 years since the birth of democracy in Greece, held at the American School of Classical Studies at Athens, December 4-6, 1992*, W.D.E. Coulson, O. Palagia, T.L. Shear Jr., H.A. Shapiro & F.J. Frost (eds.), Oxford, 25-30.

KARILA-COHEN, K. 2007
'La Pythaïde et la socialisation des élites athéniennes aux IIe et Ier siècles avant notre ère', in *Individus, groupes, et politique à Athènes de Solon à Mithridate. Actes du colloque international, Tours 7 et 8 mars 2005*, J.C Coubenhes & S. Milanezi (eds.), Tours, 365-83.

KOUMANOUDIS, S.A. 1872
'Επιγραφαι Αττικής ανέκδοτοι', *Ἀθήναιον* 1, 164-72.

KOUMANOUDIS, S.A. 1877
'Αλλαι Ἐπιγραφαι', *Ἀθήναιον* 6, 149-60.

LABORDE, L. E. 1854
Athènes aux XVe, XVIe et XVIIe siècles, Paris.

LAMBERT, S. 2002
'The Sacrificial Calendar of Athens', *BSA* 97, 353-99.

LENORMANT, F. 1864
Monographie sur la voie sacrée éleusininne, de ses monuments et de ses souvenirs, Paris.

LIPPOLIS, E. 1995
'Tra il Ginnasio di Tolomeo e il Serapeion. La ricostruzione topografica di un quartiere monumentale di Atene', *Ostraka* 4, 43-67.

LIPPOLIS, E. 2006
Mysteria. Archeologia e culto del santuario di Demetra a Eleusi, Milan.

MALKIN, I. 1987
Religion and Colonization in Ancient Greece (Studies in Greek and Roman Religion 3), Leiden.

MATTHAIOU, A.P. 2003
'Ἀπόλλων Δήλιος ἐν Ἀθήναις', in *Lettered Attica. A Day of Attic Epigraphy* (Publications of the Canadian Archaeological Institute at Athens 3), D. Jordan & J. Trail (eds.), Athens, 83-93.

MATTHAIOU, A.P. 2011
'Το Πύθιον παρά τον Ιλισσόν', Επαινος Luigi Beschi, *ΜΟΥΣΕΙΟ ΜΠΕΝΑΚΗ*, Suppl. 7, 259-71.

MCCABE, D.F. & M.A. PLUNKETT 1985
Didyma Inscriptions. Texts and List, Princeton.

MILCHHÖFER, A. 1873
Über den Attischen Apollon, München.

MILCHHÖFER, A. 1895
'Karten von Attika. Heft VII-VIII', in *Karten von Attika. Erläuternder Text*, E. Curtius & J.A. Kaupert (eds.), Berlin, 1-37.

MILLER, S. 1971
'Topographical Notes: Northeast Corner of the Agora', *Athenian Agora Report:1971,* 1-4.

MITSOS, M. 1947
'Inscriptions from Athens', *Hesperia* 16, 262-6.

MOLYNEUX, J.H. 1992
Semonides. A Historical Study, Wauconda.

MÜLLER, K.O. 1824
Die Dorier, Abt. 1, Breslau.

NULTON, P.E. 2003
The Sanctuary of Apollo Hypoakraios and Imperial Athens (Archaeologia Translatantica 21), Providence.

OBER, J. 1985
Fortress Attica. Defence of the Athenian Land Frontier 404-322 B.C., Leiden.

PAPANGELI, K. 2009
'Ιερά Οδός, δυτικό τμήμα', in *Αττικής Οδοί. Αρχαίοι Δρόμοι της Αττικής*, M. Korres (ed.), Athens, 124-37.

PARKE, H.W. 1939
'The Pythais of 355 BC and the Third Sacred War', *JHS* 59.1, 80-3.

PARKER, R. 1996
Athenian Religion. A History. Oxford.

PARSONS, A.W. 1943
'Klepsydra and the Paved Court of the Pythion', *Hesperia* 12.3, 191-276.

PIRISINO, D. 2015
'The Route of the Pythaïs through Athens and Attica', PhD diss., University of Durham.

PODLECKI, A.J. 1989
Eumenides. Aeschylus (reprint, 1992), Warminster.

POLTERA, O. 2008
Simonides lyricus. Testimonia und Fragmente. Einleitung, kritische Ausgabe, Übersetzung und Kommentar (Schweizerische Beiträge zur Altertumswissenschaft 35), Basel.

ROBERTSON, N. 2005
'Athenian Shrines of Aphrodite, and the Early Development of the City', in *Teseo e Romolo. Le origini di Atene e Roma a confronto. Atti del convegno Internazionale di Studi. Scuola Archeologica Italiana di Atene. Atene, 30 giugno – 1 luglio* 2003, E. Greco (ed.), Athens, 43-112.

ROUSSEL, P. 1908
'Les Athéniens mentionnés dans les inscriptions de Délos: Époque de la seconde domination', *BCH* 32, 303-444.

RUTHERFORD, I. 1990
'Paeans by Simonides', *HSCP* 93, 169-209.

RUTHERFORD, I. 2013
State Pilgrims and Sacred Observers in Ancient Greece. A Study of Theōriā *and* Theōroi, Cambridge and New York.

SCHMALZ, G.C.R. 2006
'The Athenian Prytaneion Discovered?', *Hesperia* 75, 33-81.

SHEAR, T.L. 1939
'The Campaign of 1938', *Hesperia* 8.3, 201-46.

SKIAS, N.S. 1901
'Ανασκαφαί παρά την Φυλήν', *Πρακτικά της εν Αθήναις Αρχαιολογικής Εταιρείας*, (1900), 38-50.

STEINHAUER, G. 2009
'Οδικό δίκτυο της Αττικής', in *Αττικής Οδοί. Αρχαίοι Δρόμοι της Αττικής*, M. Korres, (ed.), Athens, 34-73.

THEOCHARAKI, A.M. 2011
'The Ancient Circuit Wall of Athens: Its Changing Course and the Phases of Construction', *Hesperia* 80, 71-156.

THREPSIADES, I. & J. TRAVLOS 1963
'Αρχαιότητες Αθηνών-Αττικης', *ArchDelt* 17B (1961-1962), 9-14.

TÖPFFER, J. 1888
'Die attischen Pythaisten und Deliasten', *Hermes* 33, 321-2.

TRACY, S.V. 1982
I.G.II² 2336. Contributors of First Fruits for the Pythaïs (Beiträge zur klassischen Philologie 139), Meisenheim am Glan.

TRAVLOS, J. 1971
Pictorial Dictionary of Ancient Athens, London.

WEIL, H. 1893
'Inscriptions de Delphes: Nouveaux fragments d'hymnes accompagnés de notes de musique', *BCH* 17, 569-83.

WEIL, H. 1894
'Un nouvel hymne à Apollon', *BCH* 18, 345-62.

WILSON, P. 2007
'Performance in the Pythion: the Athenian Thargelia', in *The Greek Theatre and Festivals,* P. Wilson (ed.), Oxford, 150-82.

WREDE, W. 1924
'Phyle', *Athenische Mitteilungen* 49, 153-224.

Reflections on Pilgrimage at the Acropolis of Brauron during the Late Helladic Period*

Konstantinos Kalogeropoulos

Introduction

The term "pilgrimage" has a very specific meaning in the field of Classical archaeology.[1] In Aegean Bronze Age studies, on the other hand, the term is used frequently and rather loosely – at least in the context of Minoan religion.[2] It describes journeys to various ritually important natural sites, such as ceremonial hills in the proximity of the Minoan palaces and sacred hillsides in remote areas or ceremonial caves.[3] Nevertheless, these pilgrimages constitute an important part of Minoan religious life as practised on Crete since the beginning of the 2nd millennium BC.[4] They involve important social concerns, such as strengthening the solidarity within a given community (indicated by feasting), or male and female initiation. Practical concerns, such as fertility and human healing, are also involved. All these practices are characterized by specific votive offerings.[5]

In the study of mainland Greece, the situation is quite different. The identification of pilgrimage centres has not yet been widely accepted. Even in the few cases where ceremonial centres on hills have been recognized as such, they are at once addressed as or compared with Minoan peak sanctuaries, as in the case of the hill sanctuaries in Kynortion, or the sanctuary of Prophitis Ilias on Mount Arachnaion (Argolid).[6] This emphasis on Minoan religious influence is only partially justified, because it tends to neglect more important issues such as, for example, the reason for the creation and function of ceremonial centres at these particular places.

The site of the acropolis of Brauron in Attica has hitherto been viewed as a Mycenaean habitation site,[7] but in this chapter I will argue that during the Mycenaean period this coastal site was a pilgrimage site and not a settlement. I will also claim that this sacred site is not a Minoan peak sanctuary.

* I would like to express my thanks to Dr Søren Handberg and Dr Wiebke Friese for their invitation to present this paper at the pilgrimage workshop at the Danish Institute in November 2014. This chapter is an expanded version of my presentation and has benefitted from discussions among the participants of the workshop. I am grateful to Dr Vasileios Petrakos, General Secretary of the Archaeological Society at Athens, for allowing me to present material from the Society's excavations at Brauron. My special thanks are due to Dr Vyron Antoniadis, who has critically overseen the various drafts of this paper, and to the anonymous peer reviewer, whose critical reading and helpful comments enabled me to strengthen my argument.

1 Dillon 1997, xii-xviii; Elsner & Rutherford 2005; Rutherford 2013, 12-3.

2 Peatfield 1983, 277; Steel 2013, 23. For the interpretation of Kavos on Keros as a possible EC II pilgrimage site, see Renfrew 2013.

3 Tyree 2001, 41.

4 Watrous 1994, 394.

5 Watrous 1994, 399, 402.

6 Lambrinoudakis 1981, 62 (Kynortion); Psychoyos 2013; Schallin & Tournavitou 2015, 14 (Arachnaion).

7 Wright 2006, 11.

Fig. 1. The crescent-shaped hill of Brauron from the north (adapted from Travlos 1988, fig. 53).

Identifying Pilgrimage Centres

The complexity of the concept of pilgrimage in the ancient world is evident from the number of categories that Jaś Elsner and Ian Rutherford established in the introductory chapter of *Pilgrimage in Graeco-Roman and Early Christian Antiquity: Seeing the Gods*.[8] I use the term "pilgrimage centre" in the sense of Helaine Silverman to describe a sacred place that attracts worshippers from a wide area, a whole region, or even a larger multi-ethnic area.[9]

This chapter aims to apply some now commonly accepted criteria for identifying archaeological sites as pilgrimage centres. The criteria applied here derive mainly from several relevant articles published in 1994 in a special issue of the journal *World Archaeology* entitled *Archaeology of Pilgrimage*. Based on this and on later related published work,[10] the following three criteria are considered relevant to take into account in our attempts to identify possible pilgrimage centres: (1) a site's natural setting, (2) a site's archaeological remains, and (3) a site's spatial patterns and finds in comparison to those found at other contemporary or earlier sacred sites that are believed to have been pilgrimage centres. Each category contains specific questions that can be addressed quantitatively or qualitatively.

(1) Since pilgrims are not (in the majority) residents of the sacred site but must travel to the pilgrimage centre,[11] pilgrimage centres should ideally be geographically isolated from their home community. Pilgrimage centres should be able to attract a fluctuating population of worshippers and host them for a short period. For this reason,

8 Elsner & Rutherford 2005.

9 Silverman 1994, 2; similarly Coleman & Elsner 1994, 74.

10 Adams 2010, 36-55 (components of pilgrimage).

11 Silverman 1994, 2.

the special connection of the proposed pilgrimage centre with one or more specific natural elements should be documented. Sites believed to be situated at the centre of the world (*axis mundi*) also have an impact on the attraction of worshippers.

(2) The archaeological record should demonstrate the existence of religious activity at the site. The aim here is to show how the preserved architecture and finds can be interpreted as objects relating to pilgrimage. This can be confirmed, for example, through the demarcation of sacred space, usually by a low wall that encloses a courtyard area, a temenos. Inside the enclosure should, in theory, be found a focal point of veneration such as an altar, platform, natural cleft, or rock.[12] Other important architectural features, ceramic styles, etc., should be highlighted.

(3) As Helaine Silverman has demonstrated in the case of the interpretation of Cahuachi in southern Peru, the identification of a pilgrimage centre should also rely on a comparison of the site's spatial patterns and material remains to those found at other contemporary or earlier sacred sites that are believed to have been pilgrimage centres.[13] Identified pilgrimage centres should be compared with sacred centres from the same cultural and chronological sphere. The character of the various pilgrimage centres varies significantly from region to region. This is reflected by different social, cultural, economic, and ecological factors.

Brauron
I. The Natural Setting

The coastal acropolis of Brauron is located along the eastern border of Attica, on the eastern edge of the fertile plain of Mesogeia, 10 kilometres northeast of Markopoulo, between Loutsa to the north and Porto Raphti to the south. The 46 metre high limestone hill is roughly crescent-shaped and lies at the estuary of the Erasinos River (Fig. 1).[14] To the north, the coastal plain is separated from the surrounding region by the Agrielista Hill, to the south by the hill of Kommeno Lithari, and to the southeast by the Tsoungari Hill (Fig. 2).[15] Even to the east, the plain of Brauron or Livadi was separated from the sea by a lagoon, a stretch of salt water created by a sandbank. The deep bay of Brauron (Figs. 3 and 4) is a well-protected natural harbour that could accommodate a considerable number of boats and thus fulfilled one of the criteria of a trade junction point.[16] There was plenty of arable land to the west of the site to sustain the local population (Fig. 5). Recent palynological analyses of samples from the coastal plain of Brauron indicate that the cultivation of cereals intensified during the Mycenaean period.[17]

The site has a special connection to water. It is not only connected to the sea and the river Erasinos, but it is also rich in underground streams and springs, such as the famous sacred spring west of the temple of Artemis. In addition, the area in front of the crescent hill was in earlier periods filled by a saltwater lagoon, giving the impression that the crescent hill cradled the water. This lagoon is no longer visible today because it gradually turned into a freshwater marsh (Fig. 2).

Recent analyses of coastal deposits have confirmed that the coastal plain of Brauron had a constant fresh water supply during the entire 3rd and 2nd millennium BC.[18] Consequently, Brauron fulfils all the aforementioned geographical criteria of a sacred landscape and particularly of a pilgrimage

12 Adams 2010, 100.
13 Silverman 1994, 9.

14 Kalogeropoulos 2010, 212.
15 Iakovidis 1969.
16 Fimmen 1921, 7; Kalogeropoulos 2010, 212, n. 2. According to Tartaron 2013, 176, river mouths were generally favored as natural harbours in the Aegean Bronze Age.
17 Triantaphyllou *et al.* 2010, 18.
18 Triantaphyllou *et al.* 2010, 18-20, fig. 6.

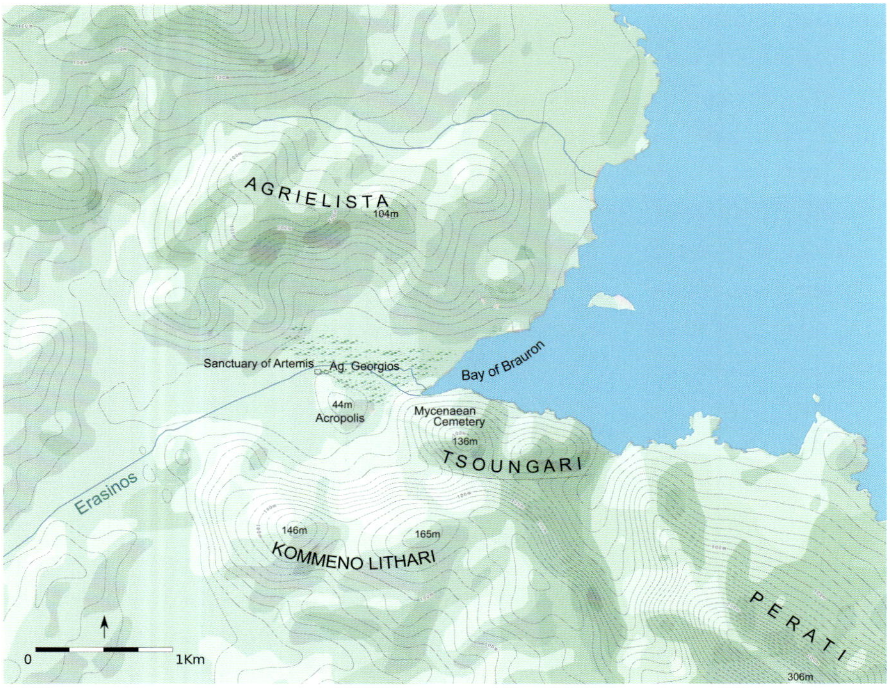

Fig. 2. Brauron's natural setting (map prepared by Vyron Antoniadis. Basemap: Mapbox).

centre. The most important of these features are the following:

a. The liminal character and remoteness of the site (Fig. 2).
b. The presence of a natural port (Fig. 4) and the economically strategic position of the setting.
c. The crescent form of the hill (Fig. 1), which evokes the crescent shape of the waxing or waning moon.
d. The special association of the site with the element water.
e. The status of the site as a "centre of the world". In its connection with heaven (crescent), the sea, and the earth, Brauron constitutes an *axis mundi.*

II. The Acropolis

The first systematic excavations were carried out in 1950, 1955-1956, and 1962 under the auspices of the Archaeological Society at Athens. The excavations, directed by Ioannis Papadimitriou, focused on the top of the hill. Excavations on the acropolis of Brauron were resumed between 1999 and 2001, again under the auspices of the Archaeological Society at Athens and this time under the direction of the late Klairi Efstratiou. Both investigations revealed significant quantities of Bronze Age material, particularly on the highest terrace of the acropolis.[19]

For the sake of convenience, the Bronze Age material is divided into two broad chronological horizons: from EH II to MH II and from MH III/LH I to the end of LH IIIB2/beginning of LH IIIC.

From EH II to MH II

Any attempt to understand the site of Brauron during the period from EH II to MH II requires some evidence (i.e. structures with associated finds or at least some find-spots with a number of contemporary objects related to them). The

19 Kalogeropoulos 2010, 213-4, nn. 4-24 (references); see also Privitera 2013, 147-8.

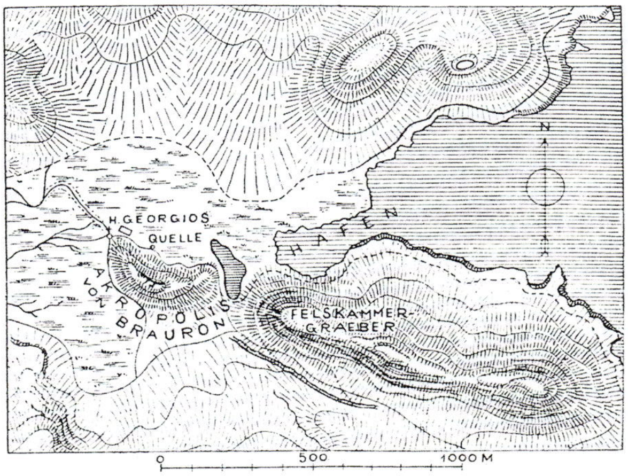

Fig. 3. Plan of the Brauron bay area indicating the acropolis-cemetery relation (adapted from Fimmen 1921, 7, fig. 1).

Fig. 4. The harbour of Brauron from the acropolis (photographer: Kostas Kousouris, February 2006).

excavations revealed no certain evidence of house structures from this period. Furthermore, it remains difficult to prove an association between EH II-MH II artefacts at certain find-spots, since the contextual setting of the finds is often likely to have been affected by post-depositional processes, such as ploughing, or geomorphological factors, such as subsidence and erosion. Proving an association between objects that have been subjected to such processes is problematic since they are not found near their original place of deposition. On the other hand, the absence of data in Brauron cannot be seen as a gap in activity within the site.

Combining published data, the excavation diaries of Ioannis Papadimitriou kept in the Archive of the Archaeological Society at Athens, and the inventory book of the Archaeological Museum in Brauron, we can safely conclude that an Early Cycladic (EC) marble figurine fragment of the Spedos variety was found in the area of the foundations of the Archaeological Museum of Brauron on the eastern slopes of the hill. However, due to the lack of stratigraphy, the figurine cannot be confirmed as being directly linked to any structures. On the contrary, the area that produced the most reliable EH II material in Brauron is the north slope of the acropolis, where datable ceramic finds belong to several phases of EH II. This could have been the figurine's original place of deposition. The type, variety, technique, and material suggest that the figurine of the Spedos variety was brought to Brauron from the Cyclades, probably but not necessarily from Naxos, where the best parallel has been found.[20] The EC figurine fragment was probably in use during the period when the acropolis of Brauron was an important centre of social and perhaps ceremonial interaction, as is suggested by a great number of fine undecorated EH II sauceboats,[21] a shape which according to Martha Wienckie may represent ceremonial vessels.[22]

Besides the EC figurine, the presence of imported EC pottery from the Cyclades is indicative of the fact that during the Keros-Syros phase, if not earlier, the

20 On this figurine, see in detail Kalogeropoulos forthcoming a.

21 Identified by Demetrios Theocharis as the most common fine undecorated pottery shape on the acropolis of Brauron (Theocharis 1950). On the date of these sauceboats in Brauron in early EH II, see Kalogeropoulos forthcoming a.

22 Wienckie 2011.

Fig. 5. View from the acropolis over the plain of Mesogaia (photographer: Kostas Kousouris, February 2006).

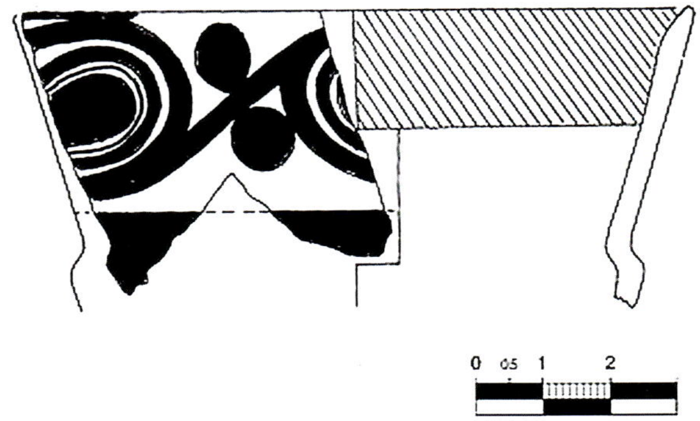

Fig. 6. Brauron, top of the hill, LH I Vapheio cup (adapted from Kalogeropoulos 2010, fig. 4a).

acropolis of Brauron attracted attention from the Cyclades.[23]

Cycladic artefacts were apparently also preferred in Brauron in the early part of the Middle Bronze Age. This is attested by a Cycladic duck vase, a luxury item circulating on the Greek mainland and the Cycladic islands during the first half of the 2nd millennium BC.[24]

From MH III/LH I to the End of LH IIIB2/Beginning of LH IIIC

We possess much more evidence from this period than from the previous period, which comprises:

(a) Structural features (*in situ*), which can assist us in understanding temporal relations within Brauron.

(b) The presence of a great number of pottery assemblages near to these structures.

I will focus on the highest terrace of the acropolis, because it provides the most detailed information about the cultural activity on the acropolis for at least 500 years, from c. 1700-1200 BC.

a) In Situ *Structural Features*

The most important structures, which can be identified beyond doubt in the plan of Ioannis Papadimitriou, are the following:

- The central structure on the plateau of the hill, which Papadimitriou called the "Middle Helladic house" and whose period of use should be dated between MH III or early LH I and LH IIB (fig. 12, no. 1).
- A pit found immediately to the northeast of the MH house, which was filled with cult debris (fine decorated pottery and ritual equipment)
- A post-LH IIB/LH IIIA1 wall on a higher level.

The So-Called Middle Helladic House

The so-called MH house (rather an Early Mycenaean room) measures approximately 2.5 m x 3 m (Fig. 12, no. 1). The presence of at least two floors within this Early Mycenaean structure indicates that it must have had at least two phases: an earlier phase, between the so-called first MH and second MH floor,

23 On these imported pottery fragments, see Kalogeropoulos forthcoming a.

24 Rutter 1985, 17, 31, IV (Incised), G (Miscellaneous), no. 5.

Fig. 7. Brauron, top of the hill, LH I Polychrome Aeginetan Krater (adapted from Kalogeropoulos 2010, fig. 5a).

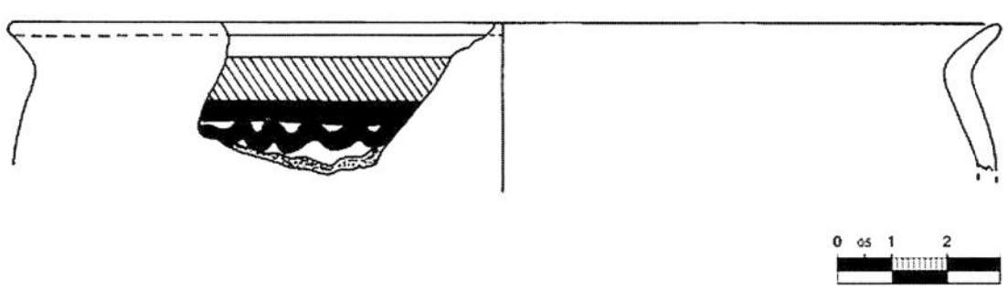

Fig. 8. Brauron, top of the hill, LH I Polychrome Mainland Krater, probably Boeotian (adapted from Kalogeropoulos 2010, fig. 5b).

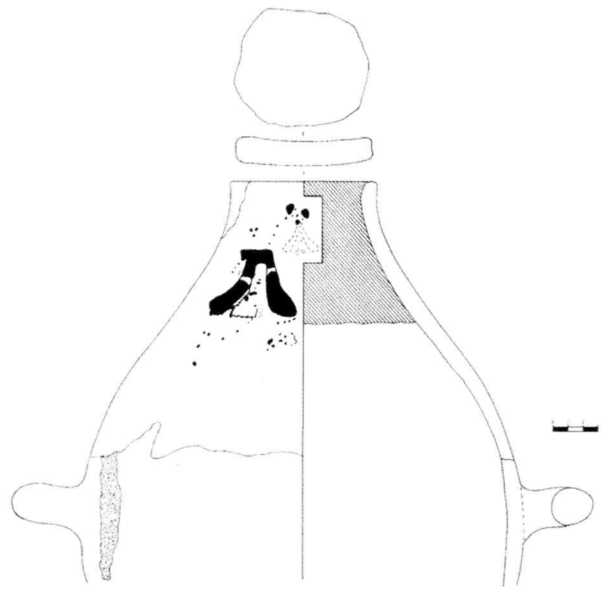

Fig. 9. Brauron, top of the hill, Minoanizing elongated LH I lidded jar with crocus decoration. Possibly from Kea (adapted from Kalogeropoulos 2010, fig. 6d).

which can be dated to an early stage of LH I, and a later phase above the so-called first MH floor, where a circular clay platform was found which can be dated to a late phase of LH I or perhaps also to LH IIA.[25] A fragmentary ring-handled cup, F(urumark) S(hape) 237, which comes from the layer directly above the later floor,[26] gives us a hint about the date of the abandonment of the MH house. It should be placed in the intermediate period between LH IIA and LH IIB. The material from the surface strata of the MH house, on the other hand, was mainly LH IIB/IIIA1.

The pottery groups associated with this structure from both layers are of a similar character and constitute feasting equipment. Many drinking vessels, such as goblets of different types and wares, cups, such as Vapheio cups (Fig. 6), kraters of Aeginetan (Fig. 7) but possibly also Boeotian origin (Fig. 8), and several bowls, indicate an extensive consumption of wine. Fragments of cooking pots on the other side indicate that meals were cooked here. Among the fragments of the lower level, early LH I according to our definition, Ioannis Papadimitriou found the upper part of an elongated, narrow-necked jar with a lid (Fig. 9). This is a Minoan shape unknown on the Greek mainland. The clay of the jar found in Brauron is reddish, relatively fine, and contains a large amount of silver mica, which is typical for the pottery from the Minoanizing island of Kea. Therefore, it probably represents an import from Kea.[27] The presence of a crocus-like floral motif that decorates the area directly below the neck of the jar is the motif *par excellence* of the Great Minoan Goddess. She is best known from the LM IA Saffron Goddess fresco from Xeste 3 at Akrotiri, where the depicted female deity, a "Goddess of vegetation",[28] or

25 Efstratiou 1999, 45, pl. 32α.

26 On this find see Kalogeropoulos forthcoming b.

27 Kalogeropoulos 2010, 217, n. 48.

28 Laffineur 2001, 388.

more specifically a "Potnia of moisture and rain",[29] is shown in an open-air setting,[30] receiving offerings of crocus plants from young girls.[31] Since our vessel from Brauron dates roughly to the same period, when the act of collecting and offering crocus plants was a common ritual connected to female maturation rites in the Minoan and Minoanizing world (LH I / LM IA),[32] it is not unreasonable to suppose that the crocus plant on the Minoanizing container from the MH house was not merely a meaningless decorative feature, but that it may have had a special symbolic meaning with a female connotation.[33]

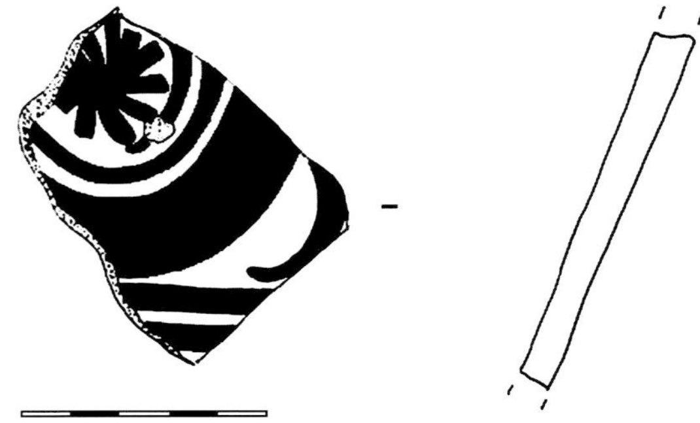

Fig. 10. Brauron, top of the hill, LH IIA palatial jar fragment (drawing: author).

The Pit Found Immediately to the Northeast of the "MH House"

The excavators recognized several pits or holes (so-called alepotrypes). Without soil profiles or a careful examination of all the physical features of the pits, it is impossible to say whether these were storage areas or something else. It is also difficult to work out the relation, if any, between the various pits and the archaeological material found nearby. Only in one case is it clearly stated that the material is associated with one of the pits, but scattered material has also been found. This is the pit found immediately to the northeast of the MH house. Ritual objects have been found here, such as the fragment of a painted plaster offering table (Fig. 11)[34] and a clay miniature composite vessel, called a "kernos" by the excavator,[35] indicating that this installation was pos-

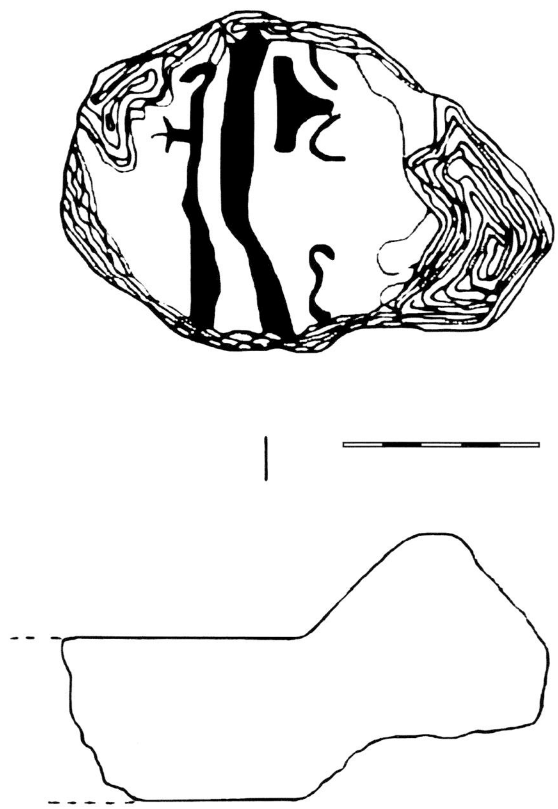

Fig. 11. Brauron, top of the hill, LH II painted offering table fragment (drawing: author).

29 Koehl 2001, 241, n. 52; Vlachopoulos & Zorzos, 2014, 194, pl. LXV-LXVI.

30 Blakolmer 2014, 127.

31 Rehak 2007, 208.

32 Boloti 2009, 46, n. 13-14.

33 Hiller 2001, 296, n. 27.

34 On the type, see Shaw 2006, 763, pl. 4.38.

35 Museum of Brauron, room 1, first display case with prehistoric objects from the acropolis of Brauron, no. 54.

sibly a repository for ritual equipment or for offerings or perhaps a foundation deposit.[36] The kernos constitutes a combination of a cross-shaped base and four miniature cups of the same size, apparently for holding offerings. It is interesting to note that the miniature cups are imitating a cup shape that was dominant in Agia Irini on Kea during the Early Mycenaean period (town VII).[37]

The Post-LH IIB/LH IIIA1 Wall

The third structure from the acropolis that deserves attention in this context is a post-LH IIB/LH IIIA1 wall (Fig. 12, no. 2). It is 168 metres long and 0.85-1.20 metres thick, overlaid the so-called MH house, and surrounded the top of the hill on three sides. This is clearly neither a fortification wall nor a simple retaining wall, but a low boundary wall in the form of a Π, which encloses and delineates a courtyard area of approximately 800 to 1000 square metres. The wall has only one opening in the middle, which may indicate a central entrance at exactly the place where the previously mentioned pit with the earlier ritual equipment was found.

b) Pottery Assemblages Found near the Structures

Within the area of the highest terrace and in close proximity to the structures mentioned above, a great number of pottery assemblages of this period were discovered and kept during the excavations. Although the exact location of each ceramic find is not always provided, comments in the diary by Ioannis Papadimitriou and the level of detail available is sufficient to be able to suggest a likely relationship between them. Detailed analysis of the ceramic finds is not attempted here, but let me comment on some particular aspects of the assemblages.

The assemblages consist predominantly of fine, almost exclusively imported wares. Ceramic material that is undiagnostic or that does not fit well into typological series is, surprisingly, almost nonexistent. However, most sherds may be dated with a reasonable amount of precision, depending on their condition and decoration.

A rigid method such as a statistical analysis cannot be applied here, but comments of a general nature on the assemblages are possible. They show that during the Shaft Grave period Brauron witnessed a sudden and astonishing increase in communication with the outside world. The contacts especially continued with Boeotia and the central Greek mainland, as can be assumed from the presence of great quantities of kraters of high-quality Polychrome Mainland ware (Fig. 8) and with the Cyclades, as can be seen in the case of the Cycladic light-on-dark pottery.[38] However, although there were sporadic connections to Crete as well, the most significant change in the pattern of the imports is the predominance of the Aeginetan gold mica fabrics. The main categories were the Polychrome Aeginetan ware, the Aeginetan Monochrome Matt-Painted ware (among them several rims of Aeginetan pithoi of the barrel-jar type), the Aeginetan cooking pots, and the Aegina Red-Slipped ware.[39] The so-called Acropolis Burnished Pottery, which seems to have been imported from Athens, is another important group of ceramics found on the acropolis of Brauron during this period.[40]

36 I thank Walter Gauß for this suggestion.

37 Cummer & Schofield 1984, pl. 47 (type 5).

38 Efstratiou 1999, pl. 34β.

39 Kalogeropoulos 2010, 215-6.

40 The ware was already recognized by Pantelidou 1975, 170-1 as a special burnished class in the Minyan tradition when publishing the four wells south of the Acropolis, wells 2-5, 115-35, pl. 54-70 and defined in Mountjoy 1995, 25 as a kind of fine Athenian local pottery.

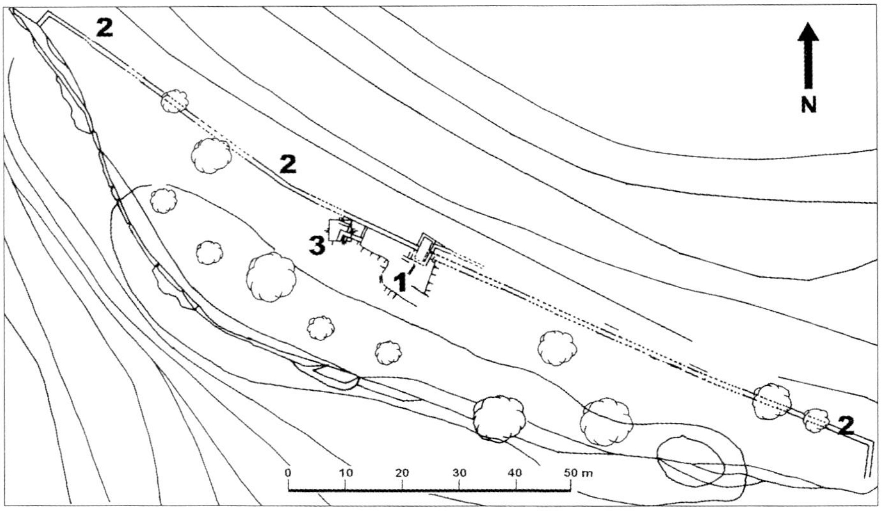

Fig. 12. Brauron, plan of the top of the acropolis. LH IIB/IIIA1 peribolos wall indicated with the number 2 (adapted from Kalogeropoulos 2010, fig. 2).

Among these great quantities of pottery from the area of the highest plateau of the acropolis, clear cases of local pottery were not detected. It seems that an important aspect of the Early Mycenaean pottery found on the acropolis at Brauron is the fact that almost all identifiable wares were imported from elsewhere.

Similar conclusions can be drawn from the data provided by the study of the Mycenean decorated pottery from the acropolis. The LH I Mycenaean decorated pottery on Brauron consists mainly of Vapheio cups (Fig. 6) and semiglobular cups with tangent spiral decoration. Because this ware is poorly represented in the whole of Attica and almost non-existent in LH I contexts of the settlement of Kiapha Thiti, one could assume that the many small fine vases decorated in the LH I manner may also represent imports. The special character of the Mycenaean decorated pottery found on the acropolis is further indicated by the presence of fragments of several LH IIA palatial jars (Fig. 10).[41] These are monumental vases decorated with sophisticated decorative patterns known from tholos and rich chamber tombs, peak sanctuaries of palatial character, and storerooms in palatial buildings but not known from Early Mycenaean domestic contexts like Tsoungiza or Korakou.[42]

The material of the Mycenaean palatial period (LH IIIA2 to LH IIIB2/IIIC Early) of the acropolis of Brauron is not as numerous as the material from the previous period, but the composition of the assemblages remains similar.[43] Feasting equipment (especially deep bowls) continues to dominate. It is also striking that Aeginetan cooking pottery was imported in relatively large quantities, as is evidenced by a great number of tripod jar legs in contrast to the non-Aeginetan cooking pots, which in Brauron are represented only by a few sherds. Ritual activities can be postulated on the basis of the surprising presence of one Phi B type and one Psi figurine found on the acropolis during the excavation of 1956 by Ioannis Papadimitriou. Another special find also points in the direction of ritual activities, namely a LH IIIB deep bowl found by Klairi Efstratiou on the acropolis during the excavations of 2000 which depicts two antithetically arranged deer.[44] The important detail here lies in the decoration of the head of the deer,

41 Kalogeropoulos 1998, 130, no. 7, pl. 28c-d (Kakovatos).

42 Kalogeropoulos 1998, 177, nn. 958-9.

43 On these finds, see Kalogeropoulos forthcoming b.

44 Efstratiou 2000, 40, fig. 2.

which consists of a feather crown, suggesting a rather supernatural setting for the animal.

III. The Cemetery

A group of chamber tombs known as the cemetery of Lapoutsi are approximately contemporary with the Mycenaean cultural activities on the acropolis. They date from LH I and especially from LH IIA (soon after human activity on the acropolis began to increase) until LH IIIC Middle and perhaps LH IIIC Late.[45] These tombs are clustered around the northwest slopes of the hill of Chamolia, overlooked by the acropolis (Fig. 3). The small cemetery, which was recently published by Thanasis Papadopoulos and Litsa Kontorli-Papadopoulou, consists primarily of Mycenaean chamber tombs of modest size. This degree of uniformity can also be seen in the case of the grave goods and the body treatment of the 53 buried individuals.[46] The variations that do exist are consistent with age distinctions (child burials) or with differences based on rather personal factors, such as was the case with the exceptional LH IIIA1 cremation in "Verdelis Tomb A".[47] Egyptian objects, such as a scarab of Ramses II, point to external contact with foreign peoples,[48] but there is no evidence of a skeleton holding, for example, a sceptre or other *insignia dignitatis* usually associated with a king or a leader, at least in Early Mycenaean times. In sum, certain rules according to which social groups could participate in trade or a special body treatment cannot be convincingly postulated. The character of the local society reflected in the cemetery does not seem to suggest differences in status and wealth among its members, unless of course there are other unexplored graves in the area which are much richer. Furthermore, it is noteworthy that two or three generations after the activity on the acropolis ceased, at the end of LH IIIB2/LH IIIC Early (around c. 1200 BC),[49] the cemetery was abandoned.

IV. The Valley of Brauron or Livadi

As already mentioned, there were agricultural activities during the Mycenaean period in the valley (Fig. 5). This has been noted by some scholars,[50] but there is no secure evidence for either an Early or a Late Mycenaean settlement in the vicinity of the acropolis or in the valley. On the other hand, this does not exclude the possibility at least that part of the valley was used to house a large population, especially when one considers the limited excavations conducted in the vicinity of the acropolis. For the time being, the only excavated evidence of a domestic assemblage is a small "house" with a rounded hearth outside the enclosure wall at the eastern foot of the hill in the area of the Museum, which was dated by Papadimitriou to LH IIIB.[51]

V. The Mycenaean Acropolis of Brauron as an Atypical Domestic Site

Summing up, while the limitations of the data are evident, some preliminary developments and trends which emerge from the available archaeological evidence of the site can indeed be traced and described:

- Several Early and Middle Cycladic finds from the acropolis imply that Brauron was already a meeting place between people from Eastern

45 Papadopoulos & Kontorli-Papadopoulou 2014, 162-3.

46 Luxury wares of the type discovered on the acropolis, such as palatial jars, have not been found in the cemetery.

47 Papadopoulos & Kontorli-Papadopoulou 2014, 121-2.

48 Papadopoulos & Kontorli-Papadopoulou 2014, 159-60.

49 Kalogeropoulos forthcoming b.

50 Papadopoulos & Kontorli-Papadopoulou 2014, 1, 161.

51 Orlandos 1962, 35.

Attica and the Cyclades during the 3rd and the first half of the 2nd millennium BC.

- The Mycenaean acropolis of Brauron seems to maintain its special relationship with the Cyclades and especially its strong affinities to the island of Kea. This stands in contrast to the situation observed at the main centres of the northeast Peloponnese, such as Mycenae, where the development of the Early Mycenaean culture appears to have progressed independently of the Cycladic factor, so dominant in the previous periods.[52]
- The frequency of fine drinking wares and, to a lesser degree, cooking pots spanning the period from MH III/LH I to LH IIIB2/LH IIIC Early leads to the conclusion that large quantities of wine were consumed and meals were prepared and eaten on the plateau of the Brauronian acropolis during the entire Mycenaean period. As stated above, several fragments of Aeginetan pithoi were also found inside the enclosure, which suggests storage potential, possibly of grain, within the demarcated space. This, however, does not necessarily imply household-based storage, since agricultural storage is also firmly connected with Minoan and Mycenaean religious sites and ritual spaces.[53] Another explanation could be that these pithoi were used for the storage of water and wine for the people who came to Brauron for a limited period of time. The absence of abundant pottery and the lack of any other evidence of cultural activity on the acropolis after LH IIIB2/LH IIIC Early suggest that all activities ceased there after that period. But the evidence from the Mycenaean cemetery, which was topographically and chronologically related to the acropolis, suggests that after the abandonment of the acropolis around 1200 BC, there were people at Brauron who continued to live and be buried nearby.

52 Dietz 1991, 297-8, 300, 314-5, 325-6.

53 Kyriakidis 2001.

Compared to ordinary Mycenaean domestic contexts, the assemblages on the highest plateau on the acropolis of Brauron are atypical in two respects:

The lack of domestic architecture. Excavation on the highest plateau of the hill within the three-sided (Π-shaped) enclosure, which was apparently built in post-LH IIB/IIIA1 times (Fig. 12, no. 2), did not produce a dense agglutination of Mycenaean habitation remains, as one would expect based on the picture we have from other contemporary walled harbour sites. The early Late Bronze Age settlement of Ayia Irini on Kea, for example, consists of several large building units, surrounded by alleys confined to a fortified area of no more than a hectare.[54] The LH IIIA2 to IIIB Mycenaean harbour settlement of Kalamianos on the Corinthian coast of the Saronic Gulf, where by the end of the 2010 season 50 buildings (four-room buildings and multi-roomed complexes) with 120 rooms and more than 24 further structures had been mapped by the SHARP,[55] demonstrates a similar dense settlement pattern as on Kea.[56] These buildings occupied 3.5 of the total 7.2 hectares of the enclosed space, while the remaining space was left empty.[57] However, on the 800 to 1000 square metres of open space at the plateau of Brauron, no evidence of a large residential domestic occupation was found. The focus of the activities here seems, according to our present state of knowledge, to only concern a single set of superimposed structures in one area at the centre of the plateau. Apart from these features, the excavators found througout the plateau fragments of pithoi (indicating storage) and grinding stones (indicating some kind of food preparation that required millina arain). Of course, this does not exclude the presence of a possible domestic site nearby, as is evidenced by the presence of the My-

54 Cummer & Schofield 1984, V, pl. 5; Mountjoy 1993, 134, fig. 362.

55 Saronic Harbors Archaeological Research Project.

56 Pullen 2015, 378, figs 2.9-12.

57 Pullen 2015, 383, fig. 7.

cenaean cemetery and of the LH IIIB small "house" with the rounded hearth in the area of the museum. However, the latter is downhill from the suggested non-domestic area of the acropolis plateau, so it is doubtful that the domestic assemblage of the "house" would have washed in.

The absence of local wares. In contrast to ordinary settlements a distinctive feature of Brauron during the Mycenaean period is that almost all the ceramic vases found on the plateau of the acropolis, which were not Mycenaean decorated ware, were not produced locally but at other sites, such as Kea, Aegina, Athens, Boeotia, and Crete. This picture is further strengthened by the observation that fine drinking vessels, like those found on the plateau of the Brauronian acropolis such as the Early Mycenaean decorated Vapheio cups (Fig. 6) and goblets as well as decorated kylikes and vases with pictorial decoration of the Mycenaean palatial period, were considered as "luxury objects", which "were probably traded for themselves".[58] This leads to the reasonable hypothesis that the focus of the economy of Brauron both in Early and in Late Mycenaean times was not the local craft production, as was normally the case in habitation sites like Mycenae, Pylos, or Zygouries.[59] Besides the lack of associated domestic architecture and local wares, the presence of some special classes of objects found on the acropolis such as the fragments of the LH IIA palatial jars (Fig. 10) as well as the paucity of artefacts of daily character (e.g. loom weights) further supports the non-domestic character of the plateau.

A series of ritual objects indicates the existence of religious activity at the site during the whole Mycenaean period. Although plaster offering tables are also known from domestic contexts and therefore cannot be considered exclusively as ritual objects,[60] the association in Brauron of the plaster offering table (Fig. 11) with the composite vessel with miniature vessel (kernos), which due to the miniature character of its vases almost certainly constitutes ritual equipment,[61] leads to the conclusion that both objects were used to perform ritual actions. The same holds true for the later Mycenaean figurines, but also for several imported vases with depictions of religious motifs, such as the crocus plant on a LH I closed vase from Kea (Fig. 9) and the antithetic deer with a feather crown on a LH IIIB deep bowl.

Religious activity can be also postulated through the construction of a Π-formed enclosure in LH IIB/IIIA1 (Fig. 12, no. 2). This low, three-sided wall encloses the top of the hill, thereby creating an interior courtyard area, a place suitable for gatherings, accessible through a central entrance and at the same time converting the natural rock into a distinct cultural or sacred space.

The Mycenaean cemetery of Brauron was topographically and chronologically related to the "acropolis" (Fig. 3). The most noteworthy aspect of the tombs at Brauron is the fact that none of them would be considered excessively elaborate or wealthy when compared to each other or to graves from other Mycenaean cemeteries in Attica. Mortuary rituals in Brauron show less evidence of status differentiation (e.g. no tholos tombs, no palatial jars). From the available evidence from the cemetery, it seems that Brauron did not have a large residential population, and therefore did not necessarily have a hierarchy of power or leadership like one that would be expected at a complex habitational site. It may also mean that only a small part of the population had the right to be buried there.[62]

58 Mountjoy 1993, 163.

59 Wright 2015, 216, n. 34.

60 Doumas 2008, 337, n. 20.

61 For the miniature vases as ritual objects during the Mycenaean period, see Kilian 1992, 25; Hägg 1994, 389; Demakopoulou & Valakou 2001, 188.

62 On the subject of access to formal burial in cemeteries, see Morris 1987; Whitley 1991; Cavanagh 1996; Dickinson 2006, 174-8. For a recent case study on the same subject, see Antoniadis 2017, 44-53.

Brauron and Contemporary and Earlier Pilgrimage Centres

The aim of the previous section was to demonstrate that the acropolis of Brauron was not a canonical domestic site. In this section, I will review some sacred centres which are believed to have been pilgrimage sites. If my arguments are compelling and the acropolis of Brauron should be identified as a pilgrimage centre, it would be appropriate to test this hypothesis by comparing Brauron with the following pilgrimage centres from the same and related cultural and chronological spheres.

Kato Syme

The mountainside sanctuary of Kato Syme is one of the few places in the Aegean where the continuity of a cult can be demonstrated from the 2nd millennium to the Archaic period (in later periods known as the cult centre for Hermes and Aphrodite).[63] This sanctuary is considered a destination of large-scale pilgrimage, with pilgrims coming from several regions of Crete. It is located at an elevation of 1130 metres above sea level, looking out over the Libyan Sea, in a natural concavity on the south slope of Mount Dikte. The setting resembles not so much Brauron, but more that of Delphi.[64] According to the excavator, Angeliki Lebessi, the focal point of veneration was a spring with cold water ("krya vrysi").[65] In Neopalatial times, a paved road for accommodating pilgrims was constructed.[66] It led up to an enclosure that contained a large rectangular built structure, a platform, the focal point for the deposition and presentation of offerings as well as a gathering point for feasting.[67] Between the enclosure wall and the interior platform, there were traces of burning and evidence of ritual equipment (stone offering tables, clay tubular stands, thousands of chalices, figurines),[68] as well as ceramic types common both in cultic and in domestic contexts (huge numbers of conical cups, tripod cooking pots, goblets and jugs).[69] The site's open-air ritual activity is associated with a "black stratum", which – due to the absence of an altar and animal bones – was understood by the excavators as evidence for ritual meals rather than for animal sacrifices.[70]

Jouktas

In contrast to the situation at Kato Syme, which does not show signs of palatial activity, the peak sanctuary of Jouktas, which is located about 13 kilometres southwest of the palace of Knossos and which is clearly linked not only to this palace,[71] but also to the palace-style town of Archanes (Fig. 13).[72] The focus of veneration of the shrine – a chasm in the rock – was kept throughout the Protopalatial and the Neopalatial until the Geometric period: a period of at least 12 centuries. As in Syme, the period from MM III to LM I (Marina Zeimbekis' use phase IV) was the most prestigious period of the sanctuary's use. Its structures comprise three terraces (I-III), a stepped altar on terrace I, which stood near the chasm,[73] and a row of rooms on terrace III. As in Kato Syme, the MM III-LM I altar (an early form

63 Lebessi & Muhly 1990, 315; Rehak & Younger 1998, 171.
64 Rehak & Younger 1998, 142.
65 Lebessi 2009.
66 Lebessi & Muhly 1990, fig. 3 (processional road).
67 Lebessi & Muhly 1990, 329 fig. 3 (podium); Davis 2014, 55.
68 Lebessi & Muhly 1990, 324, figs 8 (tubular stands), 10-11 (chalices), 12 (libation table), 14 (bronze adorant); Davis 2014, 57, table 10.
69 Lebessi & Muhly 1990, 324; Davis 2014, 57, table 10.
70 Lebessi & Muhly 1990, 326.
71 Karetsou 1981, 137; Peatfield 1994, 22.
72 Lebessi & Muhly 1990, 334; Sakellarakis 2013, 122.
73 Karetsou 1981, fig. 7, no. 2 (altar), fig. 6, 7, no. 3 (chasm).

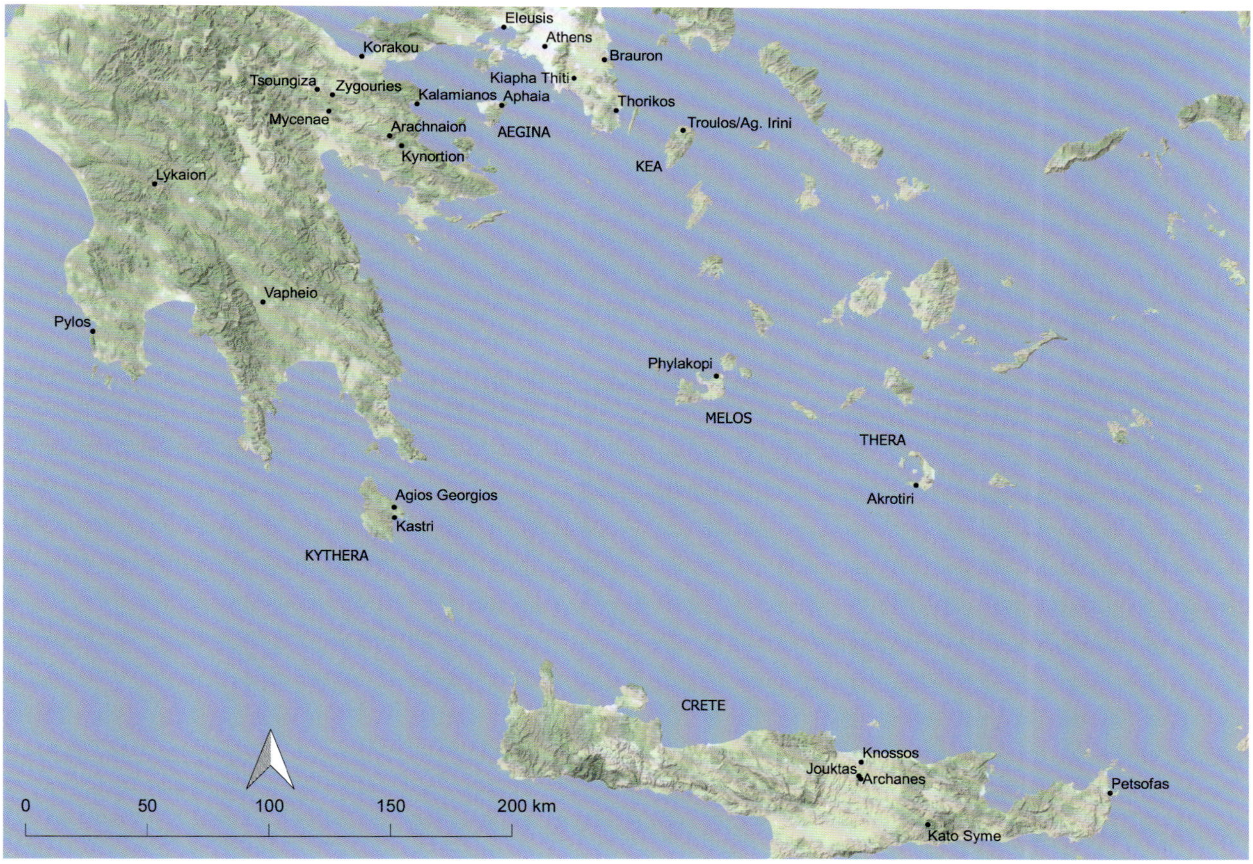

Fig. 13. Location of LBA sites mentioned in text (map prepared by Vyron Antoniadis. Basemap: Mapbox).

of which was already erected there during MM IB to MM II)[74] and a bench running along the outer wall of the row of rooms on terrace III were used for the deposition of objects. Apart from that, the site's open-air ritual is associated with an ash layer, which has been connected with activities related to the use of fire, and many votives,[75] such as stone tables of offerings.[76] The most substantial, nearly undisturbed, evidence of MM III-LM I open-air activity is related to the use of terrace Ill, where there is a great concentration of votives, including bovine figurines and figures;[77] a dominant representational element of the cult at Jouktas throughout its life. To the south of the altar, a pit was found measuring 0.40 x 0.85 m, containing a hoard of Bronze Age double axes and a kernos within a protopalatial ash layer.[78] The excavators interpreted this pit, located not far from the southern retaining wall of terrace I, as a possible foundation deposit of the period from MM III to LM I (?).[79] Here we may see a similarity with the pit with the kernos and the offering table in Brauron. Another conspicuous feature of Jouktas, which also applies to Brauron, is the presence of palace-style closed vessels (jars?).[80]

74 Zeimbekis 1998, 34-5 (Phase II).
75 Zeimbekis 1998, 46-7.
76 Zeimbekis 1998, 37.
77 Zeimbekis 1998, 44 (Context 1).
78 Karetsou 1981, 145-6, figs 11, 13-4.
79 Zeimbekis 1998, 264.
80 Karetsou 1978, 255, pl. 168γ (LM IB marine style pottery); 168δ (LM II palace-style closed vessels).

Agios Georgios

The peak sanctuary of Agios Georgios *sto vouno* ("on the mountain") is located on the summit of a mountain at the southeast side of the island of Kythera 355 metres above sea level.[81] It overlooks the Minoanizing settlement at Kastri, which lies 3 kilometres south of it (Fig. 13).[82] The latter is a site that has been plausibly characterized as a Minoan colony already in existence since EM II.[83] No architectural remains survive,[84] but the archaeological finds, which, although they represent both the Old and especially the New Palace Period,[85] show predominance in the period from MM III to LM I/IB. They have great similarities to those of Brauron. The artefacts from this site, published by the excavator, Jannis Sakellarakis and his collaborators,[86] include traces of painted plaster offering tables,[87] rhyta,[88] a very interesting local form of palatial or palace style jars,[89] kernoi,[90] cups,[91] and bowls.[92] The crocus plant, which seems to have a special connection to Brauron, dominates the decoration of the pottery recovered from excavations at Agios Georgios (16 cases),[93] suggesting a further parallel. A difference between this site and the hill of Brauron is the abundance of bronze figurines (84 pieces during the 300-year lifespan of the sanctuary),[94] which represent mostly male (74) but also a few female (10) dedicants of the Minoan type,[95] and for models of body parts, which are symbols of healing.[96] As Sakellarakis pointed out,[97] the finds have many similarities to Jouktas and Petsophas, but in contrast to the situation in the Minoan peak sanctuaries, the 84 human bronze figurines from Agios Georgios (many of them representing members of the elite)[98] by far outnumber those in clay (21).[99] The animal clay representations, on the other hand, mostly consist of clay bovine figurines.[100] Fine ware pottery of high quality, such as the palatial jars and a lot of bronze figurines, but also isolated prestigious finds such as an inscribed ladle,[101] and an unusual bronze scorpion,[102] underline the palatial character of the sanctuary,[103] which is somehow connected with the concept of the Minoan colonization of Kythera.[104] As Sakellarakis points out, the ritual participants (pilgrims) were members of the elite.[105] Besides votive offerings, at least one fireplace and numerous fragments of cooking pots indicate that ritual meals were cooked here.[106]

Troullos

The hilltop sanctuary of Troullos on northwest Kea is associated with the Cycladic town of Agia Irini (it lies only c. 500 metres northwest of it) and similarly emphasizes the integration of Minoan religious practices on the site. The summit of the Troullos Hill is 65 metres above sea level and provides an excellent

81 Sakellarakis 2011, 13.
82 Sakellarakis 2011, 16.
83 Sakellarakis 1996, 83.
84 Sakellarakis 2013, 12.
85 Sakellarakis 2013, 130.
86 Sakellarakis 2011; 2012 and 2013; Sapouna-Sakellaraki 2012; Banou 2012; Tournavitou 2014.
87 Banou 2012, 323-327, nos Π172 – Π178, pl. 13, figs 78-80.
88 Tournavitou 2014, nos K 803-K 871, figs 69-76.
89 Tournavitou 2014, nos K 548-K 562, figs 43-45.
90 Sakellarakis 2013, 66.
91 Tournavitou 2014, nos K 150-K 257, figs 10-15
92 Tournavitou 2014, nos K 258-K 351, figs 16-20.
93 Sakellarakis 2013, 31, n. 158.
94 Sapouna-Sakellaraki 2012, 7.
95 Sapouna-Sakellaraki 2012.
96 Sakellarakis 1996, 85, pl. 13d.
97 Sakellarakis 1996, 84-8.
98 Sakellarakis 2013, 119, fig. 46.
99 Sakellarakis 2013, 71.
100 Sakellarakis 2013, 73.
101 Sakellarakis 2013, fig. 22.
102 Sakellarakis 2012; Banou & Davis 2015.
103 Sapouna-Sakellaraki 2012, 5.
104 Steel 2013, 26.
105 Sakellarakis 2013, 122.
106 Sakellarakis 2013, 69, 96, n. 587.

view not only of the town of Agia Irini, but also of the Greek mainland. In 1966, John Caskey excavated a rectangular enclosure of 11.5 m x 15 m at the top of the hill, paved with large slabs of local limestone and coarse plaster flooring.[107] There was an entrance in the middle of the east side and another one at the southwest corner. The interior was occupied by a "drum-shaped structure" (5 metres in diameter and 0.80 metres high), possibly an altar. Another round structure (6 metres in diameter) lies outside the enclosure.

Troullos does not meet all the criteria set by Alan Peatfield and others to be characterized as a "Minoan peak sanctuary"[108] and the site also lacks the abundance of anthropomorphic and zoomorphic figurines so typical of Minoan peak sanctuaries. But this is partly due to the nature of the archaeological discovery, as the recovery of a human bronze figurine from this site suggests.[109] Nevertheless, several objects of ritual character also known from Jouktas or Agios Georgios such as libation tables and a ladle were found here.[110] Furthermore, 149 plain conical cups of types known from the Minoanized town VII of Agia Irini (LM IB/LH IIA)[111] suggest that some kind of communal ritual drinking took place there during the Early Mycenaean period. This could be related to Agia Irini and its urban temple, which was located just inside the main gate of the town.

It is possible therefore that the rituals performed in Troullos were somehow connected with the famous freestanding LM IB/LH IIA clay female statues of Minoan character. They possibly both "represent the adoption of Cretan ideology on Keos".[112] These statues range in size from 70 cm to 120 cm and their estimated number lies between 32 and 55. Their main characteristics are that they wear the Minoan elite dress, their breasts are uncovered, they wear a heavy torque around their necks, and their hair is arranged in long single locks flowing down the back.[113] Ancient repairs, such as replastering of the worn surface, indicate that they were in use over a long period of time and that they were moved in some way.[114] Since they were brought out of the temple, it is possible that they were meant to be seen by the Keian community. These female statues have been interpreted – I think plausibly so – by Miriam Caskey as initiates or dancers ensuring the epiphany of the deity.[115]

Aphaia

The open-air hilltop sanctuary of Aphaia is located on the northeast corner of the island of Aegina (Fig. 13) some 160 metres above sea level. The site fulfils all the aforementioned formal geographical criteria for a pilgrimage centre: It is located in a remote place, on top of a rocky outcrop, in the middle of a pine forest, there is no settlement in the vicinity, the steep northern slope of the sanctuary leads to a fertile plain (Mesagros), to the south lies a harbour (Agia Marina), and it is located in a visible point for sailors coming from Crete.[116] Korinna Pilafidis-Williams' publication of the Late Bronze Age material discovered by Adolf Furtwängler in 1901-1902

107 Caskey 1971, 392-5.

108 Peatfield 2009, 253; compare also Sakellarakis 2013, 156, n. 112.

109 Sakellarakis 2013, 156, fig. 62.

110 Caskey 1971, 394, fig. 14, pl. 84; a-b (ladle); c-d (libation tables).

111 Caskey 1971, 394.

112 Davis 1984, 165. Even though a direct connection between the Troullos ritual practices and the ones in Agia Irini cannot be established, it is interesting to note that both date to the same period (LM IB/LH IIA), both have a communal character, and both have connections with Crete.

113 Gorogianni 2011, 640.

114 Steel 2013, 28.

115 Caskey 1981, 133; 1986, 41-2.

116 Pilafidis-Williams 1998, 1, 149.

and Dieter Ohly from 1966 to 1978 has shown that the Mycenaean period is represented in a total of eleven find-spots located within the east terrace of the "late Archaic" temple.[117]

The most important of these find contexts is the LH IIIA2-LH IIIB deposit 76/2, which lies in crevices in the rock south of the ramp of the Aphaia temple.[118] It was the only sealed deposit among the 11 find contexts of the East Terrace and consisted of solely Mycenaean material. Numerically predominant were open shapes, especially kylikes (21 pieces, 14 decorated, 7 unpainted) and Mycenaean figurines (50 pieces). The most common were of the Phi and Psi type, but there was also an extremely rare Kourotrophos fragment, a special female figurine, part of a triple group, which adds a distinctive element to the deposit. Those triple groups consist of two joined Phis (generally considered as representing divine nurses)[119] and of a divine child seated on their shoulders,[120] resembling the famous ivory group that share a shawl found 1939 by Alan Wace in the palace – area of Mycenae.[121] Special vases such as composite vessels and hedgehog-shaped rhyta were possibly connected with agricultural fertility,[122] and a large number of Kourotrophoi with hopes of a successful childbirth.[123] Pilgrims would have prayed "for a good crop and the well being of their children".[124]

Some pieces from the sanctuary may have been very old when finally discarded in the crevices. Chief among them are a MM IIIA rhyton fragment[125] and two Minoan-style seals,[126] which, according to Pilafidis-Williams, could be understood as evidence for "Cretans, who had made the journey from their island, landed in Ag. Marina and started worshipping one of their own goddesses".[127] No secure cult buildings or evidence for a Mycenaean enclosure have been identified, but according to Pilafidis-Williams, the focus of pilgrimage was a specific feature of the natural landscape (perhaps the wooded nature and the clearing in the middle) at which apparitions might have been seen.[128]

Kynortion

The Early Mycenaean elite ideology is certainly reflected in the Minoanizing finds of the LH I-LH II open-air mountainside sanctuary of Maleatas on Mount Kynortion in the Argolid. Here, the excavations of Ioannis Papadimitriou and Vassileios Lambrinoudakis brought to light a terrace supporting a Late Helladic altar that lies directly underneath the Archaic altar.[129] This Early Mycenaean altar, which opens up to a paved courtyard to the west,[130] was apparently designed to hold a crowd of people, probably coming from Mycenae itself or from other sites in the Argolid. It contained ashes, burned animal bones, feasting equipment (especially Vapheio cups),[131] and many prestige items, among them gold rings and bronze weapons in particular.[132] These prestige items are clearly associated with the rich material from Grave Circle A in Mycenae and, as has been noted, there is a special warrior ideology behind this connection.[133] The preference for weapons at the mountainside sanctuary of Kynortion constitutes a major difference from the situation at Aphaia, but also from that at Brauron, indicating that religious

117 Pilafidis-Williams 1998, 3, fig. 2.
118 Pilafidis-Williams 1998, fig. 2, no. 11.
119 Korres 1968.
120 Pilafidis-Williams 1998, 35, no. 176, pl. 2, 43; 164.
121 Pilafidis-Williams 1998, 32, n. 94.
122 Pilafidis-Williams 1998, 108, nos. 793-4, 110, 138.
123 Pilafidis-Williams 1998, 135-44.
124 Pilafidis-Williams 1998, 152.
125 Pilafidis-Williams 1998, 83, no. 553, pl. 6, 62.
126 Pilafidis-Williams 1998, 117.
127 Pilafidis-Williams 1998, 146.
128 Pilafidis-Williams 1998, 149.
129 Lambrinoudakis 1981, 59.
130 Lambrinoudakis 1981, 62.
131 Lambrinoudakis 1981, fig. 6.
132 Lambrinoudakis 1981, 62, n. 14, fig. 13.
133 Pilafidis-Williams 1998, 140; Whittaker 2014, 192.

pilgrimage in the Early Mycenaean period was a rather complex social phenomenon with many, partly contradictory, aspects. At the Maleatas site, great quantities of Mycenaean figurines, in addition to the presence of figures, wheel-made bovids, and precious objects, demonstrate continuous cult activity from the Early Mycenaean into the Late Mycenaean period.[134]

Lykaion

Recent excavations (2004-2010) on the highest peak of Lykaion in Arcadia, near the ancient boundaries between Arcadia, Messenia, and Elis,[135] have significantly added to our knowledge of the concept of pilgrimage in the Peloponnese during the Late Helladic period. At this summit, where most of the Peloponnese is visible, a previously unknown Mycenaean peak sanctuary has been discovered. The sacred place, which seems to have served pilgrims from several Peloponnesian sites, was set on the southern peak of the mountain, in an area of c. 700 square meters. It was covered by a large ash layer containing "pulverized bone from burned animal sacrifice" ("altar").[136] Furthermore, it includes a large number of fragments of drinking vessels (kylikes, goblets, cups, stemmed bowls) dating from LH IIB through to LH IIIC, suggesting that ritual feasting took place there.[137] Since 2007, the excavators, David G. Romano and Mary E. Voyatzis, have uncovered several groups of small votive offerings from the altar. Characteristic of the finds is a group of bull terracotta figurine fragments dating from LH IIIA2 to LH IIIB.[138] The importance of the bull symbolism in this context is underlined by an exceptional find, a LM II rock-crystal lentoid seal-stone depicting an impressive bull,[139] which was probably imported from Crete. The seal-stone had been found buried in a hole and was understood by the excavators as one of the earliest offerings marking the beginning of the ritual activity in the sanctuary.[140] The structural remains that could be traced consisted of stones which were placed on bedrock at the highest point of the sacred area (trench Z).[141] According to the excavators, they may have served as a platform for depositing offerings, such as a LH IIIB bull figurine,[142] which was found nearby.

Prophitis Ilias on Mount Arachnaion

This is the final site of our Late Bronze Age pilgrimage sanctuaries group. Recent excavations (2009-2010) on its summit yielded evidence for a ritual use of its highest peak during the Mycenaean palatial (LH IIIA2 to IIIB) and postpalatial (LH IIIC) period.[143] The bedrock, especially in its eastern part, was flat and suitable for gatherings. It was found covered with remains of bonfires (hearths)[144] mixed with potsherds (jars, tripod cooking pots, kylikes, trefoil-mouthed jugs, feeding bottles, shallow cups, tripod alabastra, squat stirrup-jars, and miniature vessels),[145] anthropomorphic figurines (Phi and Psi types), but also zoomorphic figurines, Mainland Popular Group seals, and stone conuli.[146] By drawing attention to its remote appearance and its prominent position (1199 metres), at a visible point for those coming from both the Argolic and the Saronic Gulfs,[147] the excavators concluded that the sacred place functioned "as

134 Whittaker 2014, 192.
135 Romano & Voyatzis 2014.
136 Romano & Voyatzis 2014, 579, n. 33.
137 Romano & Voyatzis 2014, 628; Salavoura 2015, 307.
138 Romano & Voyatzis 2014, nos 100-2.
139 Romano & Voyatzis 2014, 104.
140 Romano & Voyatzis 2014, 616.
141 Romano & Voyatzis 2014, fig. 9.
142 Romano & Voyatzis 2014, no. 100.
143 Psychoyos & Karatzikos 2015, 268.
144 Psychoyos & Karatzikos 2015, fig. 4.
145 Psychoyos & Karatzikos 2015, 267, fig. 11.
146 Psychoyos & Karatzikos 2015, 267, fig. 12.
147 Psychoyos & Karatzikos 2015, 261; 2016, 313, n. 15.

an ideal focal point for periodic pilgrimages and communal feasts for people from further away".[148] More specifically, since the summit was topographically suitable for conducting ceremonies of territorial unifications, the rituals performed on this sacred place were understood by the excavators as being possibly devoted to ceremonies of palatial character like those known from Mycenaean palatial iconographic and epigraphic sources as being held in mountainous destinations, e.g. for the celebration of the initiation of the wanax.[149]

I have presented an overview of eight pilgrimage sites from three related cultural spheres in order to test our initial hypothesis. Similarities to earlier and contemporary pilgrimage sites from Crete (Kato Syme, Jouktas), contemporary pilgrimage sites from the Minoanized "mainland islands" (Kea, Kythera, Aegina), and pilgrimage sites from the Greek Mainland (Kynortion, Lykaion, Arachnaion) indicate that the so-called acropolis of Brauron served as a pilgrimage site during the Mycenaean period.

With respect to the examined material, we can discern four basic similarities:

1. The Pattern of the Material Remains

The pattern of material remains at several Minoan or Minoanizing pilgrimage sites corresponds not exactly but quite closely to the situation found at Brauron. The presence of palatial-style jars in Brauron (Fig. 10) is, for example, comparable to the situation at Agios Georgios, but also to Jouktas. The Vapheio cups (Fig. 6) and the bowls correspond to those found on Kynortion, in Troullos, or in Agios Georgios, while offering tables (Fig. 11) and composite vessels (kernoi) are two of the most typical ritual paraphernalia found at the pilgrimage sites of Kato Syme, Jouktas, Aphaia, and Agios Georgios on Kythera.

2. The Spatial Concept (the Combination of Natural Setting and Human-Constructed Entities)

The reviewed pilgrimage sanctuaries of the 2nd millennium BC fall roughly into two groups, partially representing two different types of pilgrimage sites. The first group seems to have been chosen for its height. Jouktas on Crete, Agios Georgios on Kythera, Kynortion and Arachnaion in the Argolid, and Lykaion in Arcadia belong to this category. They have the following profile: They were constructed on a high or very high place, usually but not always (e.g. Kynortion) at the highest peak of the chosen mountain. The main emphasis of this group was clearly on creating a fireplace or several bonfires on these summits. One of the most prominent aspects here is the use of bovine figurines, and in general the bull symbolism. The important criterion for the second group was not the height, but rather a specific physical feature of the given site, usually surrounded and highlighted by an artificial or physical enclosure. Kato Syme on Crete (spring surrounded by an enclosure), Aphaia on Aegina (rocky opening surrounded by a forest), and Troullos on Kea (enigmatic drum-shaped structure defined by an enclosure as sacred) belong to this group.[150]

The comparison of Brauron's spatial patterns to those found at the above-reviewed pilgrimage centres on Crete and at Minoanizing sites shows that Brauron's features correlate especially with those of the pilgrimage sanctuaries of the second group. The

148 Psychoyos & Karatzikos 2016, 314, n. 21.

149 Psychoyos & Karatzikos 2015, 270-1.

150 Although we should always be cautious in making interpretations using sources from much later times, it is worth pointing out that in "historic" times, later sources connected the pilgrimage centres of the first group with Zeus (Jouktas, Lykaion), Zeus together with Hera (Arachnaion), and Apollo (Kynortion), and those of the second group with Aphaia (Aegina) and with Aphrodite together with Hermes (Kato Syme).

most important feature among these is Brauron's central enclosure. Chief among the sites which share this feature with Brauron is Kato Syme, which was the pilgrimage centre *par excellence* on Crete during the whole of the 2nd millennium and the first half of the 1st millennium BC on Crete. Troullos on Kea is also important because it lies in the neighbourhood of Brauron (Fig. 13).

3. The Absence of Representations which Can be associated with the venerated Deity on These Sites

The study of the pilgrimages sites of the 2nd millennium from Crete, the Minoanized islands, and Mainland Greece does not reveal to which deity the sacred spaces were dedicated. There are no cult statues in the examined pilgrimage sanctuaries and, consequently, there are no temples as a shelter for these divine images. The same stands for Brauron.

4. The Elite Character of the Votives and/or Objects

Similarities between specific categories of objects which can be characterized as prestigious or related to the Early or Late Mycenaean elite ideology, such as palatial or palace-style jars in Jouktas, Agios Georgios, and Brauron, gold rings in Kynortion, the image of the divine child in Aphaia, or the abundance of bronze figurines and the presence of unusual objects such as the bronze scorpion in Agios Georgios indicate that these pilgrimage sites (at least the non-Cretan ones), which in their majority were founded or flourished in the Shaft Grave period (MH III to LH I or MM III to LM IA) had a special relationship to members of the elite. This observation is particularly important since it suggests that in the Shaft Grave period (or in Early Mycenaean times at the latest), the elite of the (Minoanized) mainland Greece developed a system of pilgrimages to various sacred sites. Thus, a new religious concept seems to have emerged. The socio-political implications of this for Brauron and Attica will be discussed in the following section.

Implications

The acceptance of Brauron as a pilgrimage centre already during the beginning of the Late Helladic period raises two questions: What kind of ritual activities occurred on the plateau of the acropolis and who were the gods for whom these rituals were performed? Who were the pilgrims or ritual participants in Brauron and where did they come from?

At the current stage of research, we cannot provide definite answers to these questions. However, some general remarks can be made. Regarding the first issue, there is no direct evidence for a specific religious activity addressed to a specific god or goddess, which is a prerequisite for any ceremonial site. But contemporary iconographic evidence can help here. Depictions on rings indicate that in the earlier Late Bronze Age hills and mountains were favourite sites for the epiphanies of gods. This was not only the case in Crete, as we can see on a well-known ring impression from Knossos,[151] perhaps depicting the peak sanctuary of Jouktas, but also on the Greek mainland, as can be seen on a golden ring from Ano Englianos, Pylos.[152] These epiphanies of the deities were attracted either by "tree shaking", as can be seen on the famous gold ring from Vapheio,[153] or by "ritual dances" performed by female participants, as on the gold ring from Isopata,[154] where four women are performing a dance between blossoming lilies. In the air above them appears a differently

151 Gill *et al.* 2002, 397, no. 256 (= CMS II.8 256); Sakellarakis 2013, 36, n. 187 (references), fig. 19.

152 Sakellariou 1964, 329, no. 292 (= CMS I 292); Vassilicou 2000, 41, fig. 26; Sakellarakis 2013, 37, n. 191 (references), fig. 20.

153 Sakellariou 1964, 253, no. 219 (= CMS I 219).

154 Platon & Pini 1984, 61-2, no. 51 (CMS II.3 51); Vassilicou 2000, 53, fig. 35.

dressed smaller figure, which could be understood as the visionary epiphany of the goddess.[155] This iconographic evidence supports the hypothesis that during the Late Helladic period the focal point on the plateau of the acropolis in Brauron could have been a tree, a dancing space, or both.

Regarding the provenance of the pilgrims, as I have indicated, the presence of palatial jars as offerings on the plateau indicates that the actors who celebrated communal rituals at Brauron at least during the LH IIA period, i.e. the 15th century BC, were members of an Early Mycenaean elite.[156] The connection with rituals performed by a palatial elite also explains why the abandonment of the acropolis at Brauron chronologically coincides with the collapse of the Mycenaean palatial system (LH IIIB2/LH IIIC Early).

Since palatial jars, characteristic grave offerings among elite members in the Early Mycenaean communities including those of Attica,[157] have not been found in the contemporary graves in Brauron, we could argue that these "aristocrats" did not reside in Brauron. Their origin (home community) should be sought in regions beyond Brauron. Where could these elite members have come from? Several hypotheses can be formulated here. The following two or three possibilities are, in my opinion, currently the most plausible ones: from the palatial site of Agia Irini/Troullos on Kea (approaching Brauron by sea); from a palatial site in Attica (approaching Brauron overland); or from both sites.

Especially important is the connection of Brauron to Agia Irini on Kea. Agia Irini, a significant palatial site during the Early Mycenaean period, surely had an impact in the Early Mycenaean world of Brauron, as indicated by possible ceramic imports already during the Shaft Grave and Early Mycenaean periods.[158] Given the proximity of this west Cycladic town to Brauron, Agia Irini is a reasonable possibility for a home community of ritual participants in Brauron even if one does not go so far as to accept Anne-Monika Dürk's and Anne P. Chapin's suggestion that the impressive homogeneous group of the Minoan elite style LM IB/LH IIA clay dancing girls from Kea should be understood as a form of Bronze Age *arktoi*, the famous young girls who in Classical times would perform sacred dances in honour of Artemis (in a period of ritual "wildness" before puberty) in Brauron.[159]

The second possibility (from a palatial site in Attica approaching Brauron overland) presupposes a certain understanding of the archaeological and historical context of the Shaft Grave and Early Mycenaean periods in Attica within which the possible pilgrimage centre in Brauron was in use. This will be briefly discussed in the last section.

Political and Social Centrality in Attica during the Shaft Grave and Early Mycenaean Periods

Evidence for political and social centrality in Attica is not confined to LH IIIB2 Athens, the period of the construction of the Cyclopean wall at the Acropolis of Athens, a fortification which, according to Spyros Iakovidis, should rather be understood as a symbol of status established under royal rule in order to control trade and production.[160] During the Shaft Grave period, several sites in Attica, Brauron included, suddenly became important. Some of them, such as Kiapha Thiti, were fortified.[161] Furthermore, there is evidence for unusually richly equipped tombs for a

155 Morris & Peatfield 2004, 42; Ruppenstein 2011, 260-2, figs 1-3.
156 Kalogeropoulos 1998, 174-9; 2011, 207.
157 Kalogeropoulos 1998, 150-3.
158 Davis 1977; Kalogeropoulos 2010, 217.
159 Dürk 1996, 20; Chapin 2000, 19-20.
160 Iakovidis 1999, 202-3; 2006, 190-6 (argues for the existence of a palace on the acropolis).
161 Maran 1994, 68; Lauter 1996, Beilage 18.

minority, as is attested in a distinguished warrior grave in Eleusis (Grave E.III.6) with a high concentration of boar's tusks.[162] The same occurs in Thorikos (tholos V),[163] which contained Minoan stone vases, along with the intensification of metallurgical production at the latter site (evidence for silver mining).[164] These finds suggest a submerging ideology of power in Attica during that period. However, the lack of conformity in the funerary architecture as well as in settlement geography indicates that these sites were probably not organized under one ruler. It seems that an increasingly competitive political landscape of elites established their own sites. It appears that during this period, Attica broke up into several independent political units.

In contrast to the previous period, the 15th century BC (LH IIA to B), a period of great importance for Brauron, was clearly a time of major change in Attica, and for Athens in particular, both on the Acropolis and around it. High-quality LH IIA ceramics from the area of the later Agora and high-status items, such as the LH IIA palatial jars from the still unfortified Acropolis,[165] as well as the production of high-quality local ceramic wares, the so-called "Acropolis Burnished Pottery", which were exported to several other Attic sites such as Kiapha Thiti,[166] Eleusis,[167] and Thorikos[168] as well as Agia Irini on Kea and Korakou in Korinthia,[169] indicate a general increase in Athenian activity from the early 15th century BC onwards. This view is strengthened by Athenian LH IIA pottery exported to Phylakopi on Melos.[170] The existence of a social group in Athens who was occupied with large-scale pottery production required surplus production by the whole society in order to support these craftsmen.

A smaller cemetery to the west of the Athenian Acropolis in the area of the later Kerameikos and large amounts of LH IIB-IIIA1 material from wells and deposits in the area of the later Olympieion to the southeast determine the approximate limits of the central settlement of Athens during the Early Mycenaean period.[171] Within this extensive area, two important cemeteries (the North Cemetery in the area of the later Athenian Agora[172] and the South Cemetery at Koukaki)[173] and also numerous excavated deposits, mainly wells rich in pottery and artefacts, have been found.[174] They indicate that the whole area was in domestic use between LH IIB and LH IIIA1.

As is seen in tomb I, one of the largest and wealthiest tombs in the North Cemetery, images of power emerge which use animals as an allegory for the forces of life. It has a rectangular chamber with a rock-cut bench along each side of the walls. The famous large ivory pyxis was found standing on the east bench together with some vases. It depicts the classical image of power: the strong predator (two winged griffins) attacking the weak (deer and fawns).[175]

The density of settlements at the west coast of Attica during LH IIB/IIIA1 (even if evidence derives mainly from funerary contexts) lasting until LH IIIC Early, (i.e. more than 250 years)[176] indicates a certain degree of sociopolitical stability, which

162 Cosmopoulos 2014b, vol.1, 185; Papadimitriou 2001, 90.
163 Papadimitriou 2001, 91-3.
164 Servais & Servais Soyez 1984, 61-6.
165 Rutter 1975 (Agora); Mountjoy 1995, 16, n. 36, fig. 6, bottom left; Kalogeropoulos 1998, 150-1 (Acropolis).
166 Maran 1992, 136-9.
167 Cosmopoulos 2014b, vol.1, 375; 2014c, 178, fig. 2.
168 Mountjoy 1995, 25, n. 69.
169 Mountjoy 1995, 25, n. 68 (Agia Irini); 26, n. 71 (Korakou).
170 Mountjoy & Pointing 2000, 173.
171 Pantelidou 1975, fig. 16 (T18-T22), figs 15-6 (Θ9-Θ10, Φ4-Φ6); Benvenuti 2014, 206.
172 Privitera 2013, 84-92 (references).
173 Privitera 2013, 79-83 (references).
174 Pantelidou 1975 (passim); Mountjoy 1981 (south slope).
175 Langenbucher 2006, 88-9, fig. 91.
176 Privitera 2013, 109-18 (references).

implies some form of government. The question of whether these sites were simply farmsteads or part of a larger planned settlement can only be determined if we knew the function of each site. Considering the homogeneity of the material culture, however, something like a central planning seems more likely. Athens, with its monumental architecture, would be the most appropriate candidate for such a process.

The situation in contemporary Eleusis also leads us in the direction of a palace-centred society in Attica during the Early Mycenaean period. Of great importance during this period is the so-called "Megaron B", situated on the east side of the acropolis hill. The sanctity of this central building during this phase has been rejected by Pascal Darcque and Gerhard Hiesel,[177] mainly because of the absence of a real peribolos and Mycenaean figurines. However, new research conducted by Michael Cosmopoulos has shown that "Megaron B" was a long room with an exedra/altar at one end and that it was indeed – as in Brauron – surrounded by a peribolos from LH IIB to IIIA1.[178] He has therefore plausibly re-interpreted the construction as a building of religious function.[179] There is also evidence of an elaborate wall painting connected with Megaron B. It shows a large eye of a female figure in fresco technique.[180] This evidence of a wall painting is certainly a feature of architectural elaboration that, in combination with the ceremonial architecture (peribolos, exedra), can be understood as structures of a complex society.[181]

To sum up: The archaeological evidence from Athens and Attica points strongly to a development towards centrality in the Early Mycenaean period. A formal setting (e.g. a monumental building) for the residence and display of the leader is to be expected.[182]

Conclusion

The aim of the present chapter was to investigate the function of the so-called acropolis of Brauron based on the available evidence. Even though there are details awaiting further development, the evidence suggests that it became a pilgrimage site possibly as early as LH I. It was not only the natural setting, nor the objects found on the acropolis in themselves, nor the spatial concept alone that lead to this conclusion, but rather the combination of all these parameters in the specific archaeological and historical context.

Since the pilgrimage pattern on highland destinations was in use earlier on Minoan Crete than in the Greek mainland, it is reasonable to suggest that the general idea was borrowed from Crete, or more probably indirectly from the neighbouring Minoanized island of Kea. However, we should be careful not to interpret this Early Mycenaean development on the acropolis of Brauron as a transformation of the hill to a Minoan "peak sanctuary". The elite status of – at least some – of the individuals who participated in the ritual acts performed on the hill (mainly ritual meals), who according to our analysis were not resident in Brauron but rather came from other areas, seems to have played an important role in this development. It has been argued that such a development is related to state formation processes in Early Mycenaean Attica.

177 Darcque 1981; Hiesel 1990, 45-6.

178 Cosmopoulos 2003, 8-11, 18; 2014a, 416-8; 2014b, vol. 1, 175-8.

179 Cosmopoulos 2003, 16-8; 2014a, 417.

180 Cosmopoulos 2014a, 404, fig. 6, left; 2014b, vol. 1, 92, fig. 90.

181 Dabney & Wright 1990, 47.

182 In the case of Athens, this monumental building could have been erected on the Acropolis. In this respect, it is interesting to note that Mountjoy 1995, 24 has already suggested the presence of a "LH IIIA1 proto-palace" on the Acropolis (similarly Benvenuti 2014, 198).

Bibliography

ADAMS, K.L. 2010
'Textual and Archaeological Evidence for Pilgrimage in the Central Hill Country of the Southern Levant during the Late Bronze Age – Iron I Transition Period, ca. 1300-1000 BCE', PhD diss., University of Arizona. Available online: http://arizona.openrepository.com/arizona/handle/10150/194308 (accessed: 07.03.2015).

ANTONIADIS, V. 2017
Knossos and the Near East. A Contextual Approach to Imports and Imitations in Early Iron Age Tombs, Oxford.

BANOU E. 2012
'Μικροαντικείμενα μινωικών χρόνων από πηλό, λίθο και πολύτιμες ύλες', in *Κύθηρα. Το μινωικό ιερό κορυφής στον Άγιο Γεώργιο στο Βουνό 2. Τα ευρήματα*, J. Sakellarakis (ed.), Athens, 249-507.

BANOU, E. & B. DAVIS 2015
'The *Symbolism of the Scorpion* in Minoan Religion. A Cosmological Approach on the Basis of Votive Offerings from the Peak Sanctuary at Ayios Yeoryios Sto Vouno, Kythera', in *Metaphysis. Ritual, Myth and Symbolism in the Aegean Bronze Age. Proceedings of the 15th International Aegean Conference, Vienna, Institute for Oriental and European Archaeology, Aegean and Anatolia Department, Austrian Academy of Sciences and Institute of Classical Archaeology, University of Vienna, 22-25 April 2014* (Aegaeum 39), E. Alram-Stern, F. Blakolmer, S. Deger-Jalkotzy, R. Laffineur & J. Weilhartner (eds.), Leuven, 123-8.

BENVENUTI, A. 2014
'Πριν από Αίδ' εισ' Αθήναι Θησέως η πριν πόλις', *ArchEph*, 197-234.

BLAKOLMER, F. 2014
'Meaningful Landscapes: Minoan "Landscape Rooms" and Peak Sanctuaries', in *Physis. L'environnement naturel et la relation homme-milieu dans le monde égéen protohistorique, Actes de la 14e Rencontre égéenne internationale, Paris, Institut National d'Histoire de l'Art (INHA), 11-14 décembre 2012* (Aegaeum 37), G. Touchais, R. Laffineur & F. Rougemont (eds.), Leuven and Liège, 121-8.

BOLOTI, T. 2009
'Τελετουργική προσφορά υφασμάτων και ενδυμάτων στον αιγαιακό χώρο της ύστερης Χαλκοκρατίας', Αράχνη 3, 44-71.

CASKEY, J. 1971
'Investigations in Keos: Part I: Excavations and Explorations, 1966-1970', *Hesperia* 40, 359-96.

CASKEY, M.E. 1981
'Ayia Irini, Kea: The Terracotta Statues and the Cult in the Temple', in *Sanctuaries and Cults in the Aegean Bronze Age. Proceedings of the First International Symposium at the Swedish Institute in Athens, 12-13 May, 1980*, R. Hägg & N. Marinatos (eds.), Stockholm, 127-36.

CASKEY, M.E. 1986
The Temple at Ayia Irini Part I: The Statues, vol. 2 of *Keos*, Princeton.

CAVANAGH, W.G. 1996
'The Burial Customs', in vol. 2 of *Knossos North Cemetery. Early Greek Tombs* (BSA Suppl. 28), J.N. Coldstream & H.W. Catling (eds.), London, 651-75.

CHAPIN, A.P. 2000
'Maidenhood and Marriage. The Reproductive Lives of the Girls and Woman from Xeste 3, Thera', *Aegean Archaeology* 4, 7-25.

COLEMAN, S. & J. ELSNER 1994
'The Pilgrim's Progress: Art, Architecture and Ritual Movement at Sinai', *World Archaeology* 26.1, 73-89.

COSMOPOULOS, M.B. 2003
'Mycenaean Religion at Eleusis. The Architecture and Stratigraphy of Megaron B', in *Greek Mysteries. The Archaeology and Ritual of Ancient Greek Secret Cults*, M.B. Cosmopoulos (ed.), London, 1-24.

COSMOPOULOS, M.B. 2014A
'Cult, Continuity, and Social Memory: Mycenaean Eleusis and the Transition to the Early Iron Age', *AJA* 118, 401-27.

COSMOPOULOS, M.B. 2014B
The Sanctuary of Demeter at Eleusis. The Bronze Age, 2 vols., Athens.

COSMOPOULOS, M.B. 2014C
'Ιστορία δύο πόλεων. Η Ελευσίνα και η Αθήνα στην Εποχή του Χαλκού', *Ο Μέντωρ* 109, 173-86.

CUMMER, W.W. & E. SCHOFIELD 1984
Ayia Irini. House A, vol. 3 of *Keos*, Mainz am Rhein.

DABNEY, M.K. & J.C. WRIGHT 1990
'Mortuary Customs, Palatial Society and State Formation in the Aegean Area. A Comparative Study', in *Celebrations of Death and Divinity in the Bronze Age Argolid, R. Hägg & G.C. Nordquist (eds.), Stockholm,* 45-53.

DARCQUE, P. 1981
'Les vestiges *Mycénien découverts sous le Télestérion d'Éleusis*', *BCH* 105, 593-605.

DAVIS, B. 2014
Minoan Stone Vessels with Linear A Inscriptions (Aegaeum 36), Leuven.

DAVIS, J.L. 1977
'Brauron and Keos in the Shaft Grave Period', *AAA* 10, 270-2.

DAVIS, J.L. 1984
'Cultural Innovation and the Minoan Thalassocracy at Ayia Irini, Keos', in *The Minoan Thalassocracy. Myth and Reality. Proceedings of the Third International Symposium at the Swedish Institute at Athens, 31 May – 5 June, 1982*, R. Hägg & N. Marinatos (eds.), Stockholm, 159-66.

DEMAKOPOULOU, K. & N. DIVARI-VALAKOU 2001
'Evidence for Cult Practice at Midea. Figures, Figurines and Ritual Objects', in *Potnia. Deities and Religion in the Aegean Bronze Age. Proceedings of the 8th International Aegean Conference. Göteborg, Göteborg University, 12-15 April 2000* (Aegaeum 22), R. Laffineur & R. Hägg (eds.), Liège, 181-91.

DICKINSON, O.T.P.K. 2006
The Aegean from Bronze Age to Iron Age: Continuity and Change between the Twelfth and Eighth Centuries B.C., London.

DIETZ, S. 1991
The Argolid at the Transition to the Mycenaean Age. Studies in the Chronology and Cultural Development in the Shaft Grave Period, Copenhagen.

DILLON, M. 1997
Pilgrims and Pilgrimage in Ancient Greece, London and New York.

DOUMAS, C. 2008
'Η θρησκεία στο Ακρωτήρι', in *Ακρωτήρι Θήρας. Τριάντα χρόνια έρευνας 1967-1997. Επιστημονική συνάντηση 19-20 Δεκεμβρίου 1997*, C. Doumas (ed.), Athens, 333-62.

DÜRK, A.-M. 1996
'Bronzezeitliche Arktoi? Zum Verständnis der Tonfiguren von Ayia Irini', *Thetis* 3, 1996, 13-20.

EFSTRATIOU, K. 1999
'Ανασκαφή Βραυρώνος', *Prakt*, 43-6.

EFSTRATIOU, K. 2000
'Ανασκαφή Βραυρώνος', *Prakt*, 37-40.

ELSNER, J. & I. RUTHERFORD 2005
'Introduction', in *Pilgrimage in Graeco-Roman and Early Christian Antiquity. Seeing the Gods*, J. Elsner & I. Rutherford (eds.), Oxford, 1-40.

FIMMEN, D. 1921
Die kretisch-mykenische Kultur, Leipzig & Berlin.

GILL, M.A.V., W. MÜLLER & I. PINI 2002
Die Siegelabdrücke von Knossos, unter Einbeziehung von Funden aus anderen Museen, vol. 8 of *Corpus der Minoischen und Mykenischen Siegel. Iraklion Archäologisches Museum, Band II*, Mainz am Rhein.

GOROGIANNI, E. 2011
'Goddess, Lost Ancestors, and Dolls. A Cultural Biography of the Ayia Irini Terracotta Statues', *Hesperia* 80, 635-55.

HÄGG, R. 1994
'State and Religion in Mycenaean Greece', in vol. 2 of *Politeia. Society and State in the Aegean Bronze Age. Proceedings of the 5th International Aegean Conference, University of Heidelberg, 10-13 April 1994* (Aegaeum 12), R. Laffineur & W.-D. Niemeier (eds.), Liège and Austin, 387-91.

HIESEL, G. 1990
Späthelladische Hausarchitektur. Studien zur Architekturgeschichte des griechischen Festlandes in der späten Bronzezeit, Mainz am Rhein.

HILLER, S. 2001
'Potnia/Potnios Aigon. On the Religious Aspects of Goats in the Aegean Late Bronze Age', in *Potnia. Deities and Religion in the Aegean Bronze Age. Proceedings of the 8th International Aegean Conference. Göteborg, Göteborg University, 1-15 April 2000* (Aegeaum 37), R. Laffineur & R. Hägg (eds.), Liège, 293-304.

IAKOVIDIS, S.E. 1969
Περατή. Το νεκροταφείον Α. Οι τάφοι και τα ευρήματα, Athens.

IAKOVIDIS, S. 1999
'Late Helladic Fortifications', in vol. 1 of *Polemos. Le contexte guerrier en Égée à l'Âge du Bronze. Actes de la 7e Recontre égéenne internationale Université de Liège. 14-17 avril 1998* (Aegaeum 19), R. Laffineur (ed.), Liège and Austin, 199-204.

IAKOVIDIS, S.E. 2006
The Mycenaean Acropolis of Athens, Athens.

KALOGEROPOULOS, K. 1998
Die frühmykenischen Grabfunde von Analipsis. Mit einem Beitrag zu den palatialen Amphoren des griechischen Festlandes, Athens.

KALOGEROPOULOS, K. 2010
'Middle Helladic Human Activity in Eastern Attica: The Case of Brauron', in *Mesohelladika. La Grèce continentale au Bronze Moyen. Actes du colloque international organise par l'École française d'Athènes, en collaboration avec l'American School of Classical Studies at Athens et le Netherlands Institute in Athens, Athènes, 8-12 mars 2006*, A. Philippa-Touchais, G. Touchais, S. Voutsaki & J. Wright (eds.), Athens, 211-21.

KALOGEROPOULOS, K. 2011
'The Social and Religious Significance of the Palatial Jars as Grave Offerings', in *Honouring the Dead in the Peloponnese, Proceedings of the Conference Held at Sparta 23-25 April 2009*, H. Cavanagh, W. Cavanagh & J. Roy (eds.), Nottingham, 207-36.

KALOGEROPOULOS, K. FORTHCOMING A
'Fragment of an Early Cycladic Folded-Arm Figurine from the Acropolis of Brauron', in *Early Cycladic Sculpture in Context. Athens, 27-29 May 2015*, M. Marthari, C. Renfrew & M. Boyd (eds.), Athens.

KALOGEROPOULOS, K. FORTHCOMING B
'The Acropolis of Brauron during the 2nd Millennium BC: An Overview', Arch Eph 2009.

KARETSOU, A. 1978
'Το ιερό κορυφής Γιούχτα', *Prakt*, 232-58.

KARETSOU, A. 1981
'The Peak Sanctuary of Mt. Juktas', in *Sanctuaries and Cults in the Aegean Bronze Age. Proceedings of the First International Symposium at the Swedish Institute in Athens, 12-13 May, 1980*, R. Hägg & N. Marinatos (eds.), Stockholm, 137-53.

KILIAN, K. 1992
'Mykenische Heiligtümer der Peloponess', in *Kotinos. Festschrift für Erika Simon,* H. Froning, T. Hölscher & H. Mielsch (eds.), Mainz am Rhein, 10-25.

KOEHL, R. 2001
'The "Sacred Marriage" in Minoan Religion and Ritual', in *Potnia. Deities and Religion in the Aegean Bronze Age. Proceedings of the 8th International Aegean Conference. Göteborg, Göteborg University, 12-15 April 2000* (Aegaeum 22), R. Laffineur & R. Hägg (eds.), Liège, 237-43.

KORRES, G. S. 1968
'Διπλαί θεότητες εν Κρήτη και μυκηναϊκή Ελλάδι (διπλαί ή τριπλαί θεότητες εν τη υπηρεσία του θείου βρέφους)', in vol. 2 of *Πεπραγμένα του Β' Διεθνούς Κρητολογικού Συνεδρίου, Χανιά, 1966*, N.M. Panagiotakis (ed.), Athens, 107-19.

KYRIAKIDIS, E. 2001
'The Economics of Potnia. Storage in "Temples" of Prehistoric Greece', in *Potnia. Deities and Religion in the Aegean Bronze Age. Proceedings of the 8th International Aegean Conference. Göteborg, Göteborg University, 12-15 April 2000* (Aegaeum 22), R. Laffineur & R. Hägg (eds.), Liège, 123-30.

LAFFINEUR, R. 2001
'Seeing is Believing. Reflections on Divine Imagery in the Aegean Bronze Age', in *Potnia. Deities and Religion in the Aegean Bronze Age. Proceedings of the 8th International Aegean Conference. Göteborg, Göteborg University, 12-15 April 2000* (Aegaeum 22), R. Laffineur & R. Hägg (eds.), Liège, 387-92.

LAMBRINOUDAKIS, V. 1981
'Remains of the Mycenaean Period in the Sanctuary of Apollon Maleatas', in *Sanctuaries and Cults in the Aegean Bronze Age. Proceedings of the First International Symposium at the Swedish Institute in Athens, 12-13 May, 1980*, R. Hägg & N. Marinatos (eds.), Stockholm, 259-65.

LANGENBUCHER, J. 2006
'The Mycenaean Era in the Athenian Agora', in *The Art of Antiquity. Piet de Jong and the Athenian Agora*, J.K. Papadopoulos (ed.), Athens, 75-92.

LAUTER, H. 1996
Kiapha Thiti. Ergebnisse der Ausgrabungen III (Die bronzezeitliche Architektur), Marburg/Lahn.

LEBESSI, A. 2009
'Σύμη Βιάννου', http://www.archetai.gr/site/content.php?artid=373 (accessed 14.03.2015).

LEBESSI, A. & P. MUHLY 1990
'Aspects of Minoan Cult. Sacred Enclosures. The Evidence from the Sanctuary (Crete)', *AA*, 315-36.

MARAN, J. 1992
Kiapha Thiti. Ergebnisse der Ausgrabungen II2 (2. Jt. v. Chr.: Keramik und Kleinfunde), Marburg/Lahn.

MARAN, J. 1994
'Structural Changes in the Pattern of Settlement during the Shaft Grave Period on the Greek Mainland', in vol. 2 of *Politeia. Society and State in the Aegean Bronze Age. Proceedings of the 5th International Aegean Conference, University of Heidelberg, 10-13 April 1994* (Aegaeum 22), R. Laffineur & W.-D. Niemeier (eds.), Liège and Austin, 67-72.

MORRIS, I. 1987
Burial and Ancient Society: The Rise of the City-State, Cambridge.

MORRIS, C. & A. PEATFIELD 2004
'Experiencing Ritual: Shamanic Elements in Minoan Religion', in *Celebrations: Sanctuaries and the Vestiges of Cult Activity. Selected Papers and Discussions from the Tenth Anniversary Symposion of the Norwegian Institute at Athens, 12-16 May 1999*, M. Wedde (ed.), Bergen, 35-59.

MOUNTJOY, P.A. 1981
Early Mycenaean Wells from the South Slope of the Acropolis at Athens, Ghent.

MOUNTJOY, P.A. 1993
Mycenaean Pottery. An Introduction, Oxford.

MOUNTJOY, P.A. 1995
Mycenaean Athens, Jonsered.

MOUNTJOY, P.A. & M.J. POINTING 2000
'The Minoan Thalassocracy Reconsidered. Provenance Studies of LH IIA/LMIB Pottery from Phylakopi, Ayia Irini and Athens', *BSA* 95, 141-84.

ORLANDOS, A. 1962
'Βραυρών', *Ergon* 1962, 25-39.

PANTELIDOU, M. 1975
'Αι προϊστορικαί Αθήναι', PhD diss., University of Athens.

PAPADIMITRIOU, N. 2001
Built Chamber Tombs of Middle and Late Bronze Age Date in Mainland Greece and the Islands, Oxford.

PAPADOPOULOS, T. & L. KONTORLI-PAPADOPOULOU 2014
Vravron: The Mycenaean Cemetery, Uppsala.

PEATFIELD, A. 1983
'The Topography of Minoan Peak Sanctuaries', *BSA* 78, 273-80.

PEATFIELD, A. 1994
'After the 'Big Bang' – What? Or Minoan Symbols and Shrines beyond Palatial Collapse', in *Placing the Gods. Sanctuaries and Sacred Space in Ancient Greece*, S.E. Alcock & R. Osborne (eds.), Oxford, 19-36.

PEATFIELD, A. 2009
'The Topography of Minoan Peak Sanctuaries Revisited', in *Essays on Ritual and Cult in Crete in Honor of Geraldine C. Gesell, Hesperia Supplement* 42, 251-9.

PILAFIDIS-WILLIAMS, C. 1998
The Sanctuary of Aphaea on Aegina in the Bronze Age, Munich.

PLATON, N. & I. PINI 1984
Die Siegel der Neupalastzeit, vol. 3 of *Corpus der Minoischen und Mykenischen Siegel. Iraklion Archäologisches Museum. Band II*, Berlin.

PRIVITERA, S. 2013
Principi, Pelasgi e pescatori. L' Attica nella Tarda Età del Bronzo, Athens and Paestum.

PSYCHOYOS, O. 2013
'A Mycenaean Sanctuary on Proph. Ilias at Mt. Arachnaion in the Argolid', paper read at the Mycenaean Seminar of the University of Athens on Thursday, 24.01.2013. Available online: http://www.aegeussociety.org/images/uploads/lectures/2013/psychoyou-myc-sem-athens.pdf (accessed 02.03.2015).

PSYCHOYOS, O. & Y. KARATZIKOS 2015
'Mycenaean Cult on Mount Arachnaion in the Argolid', in *Mycenaeans up to Date. The Archaeology of the Northeastern Peloponnese – Current Concepts and New Directions*, A.-L. Schallin & I. Tournavitou (eds.), Stockholm, 261-76.

PSYCHOYOS, O. & Y. KARATZIKOS 2016
'The Mycenaean Sanctuary at Prophitis Ilias on Mount Arachnaio within the Religious Context of the 2nd Millennium B.C.', in *Metaphysis. Ritual, Myth and Symbolism in the Aegean Bronze Age. Proceedings of the 15th International Aegean Conference, Vienna, Institute for Oriental and European Archaeology, Aegean and Anatolia Department, Austrian Academy of Sciences and Institute of Classical Archaeology, University of Vienna, 22-25 April 2014* (Aegaeum 39), E. Alram-Stern, F. Blakolmer, S. Deger-Jalkotzy, R. Laffineur & J. Weilhartner (eds.), Leuven, 311-9.

PULLEN, D.J. 2015
'How to Build a Mycenaean Town. The Architecture of Kalamianos', in *Mycenaeans up to Date. The Archaeology of the Northeastern Peloponnese – Current Concepts and New Directions,* A.-L. Schallin & I. Tournavitou (eds.), Stockholm, 377-90.

REHAK, P. 2007
'Girls as Acolytes in Aegean Ritual and Cult', in *Constructions of Childhood in Ancient Greece and Italy*, A. Cohen & J.B. Rutter, Princeton, 205-25.

REHAK, P. & J.G. YOUNGER 1998
'Review of Aegean Prehistory VII: Neopalatial, Final Palatial, and Postpalatial Crete', *AJA* 102.1, 91-173.

RENFREW, C. 2013
'The Sanctuary at Keros: Questions of Materiality and Monumentality', *Journal of the British Academy* 1, 187-212.

ROMANO, D.G. & M.E. VOYATZIS 2014
'Mt. Lykaion Excavation and Survey Project, Part 1: The Upper Sanctuary', *Hesperia* 83, 569-652.

RUPPENSTEIN, F. 2011
'Zu Bedeutung und Funktion der mykenischen und minoischen Terrakottafiguren mit erhobenen Armen', in *Österreichische Forschungen zur Ägäischen Bronzezeit 2009, Akten der Tagung am Fachbereich der Paris Lodron-Universität Salzburgvom 6. bis 7. März 2009*, F. Blakolmer, C. Reinholdt, J. Weilhartner & G. Nightingale (eds.), Vienna, 253-70.

RUTHERFORD, I. 2013
State Pilgrims and Sacred Observers in Ancient Greece: A Study of Theoria and Theoroi, Cambridge.

RUTTER, J.B. 1975
'Evidence for a Mycenaean Tomb of the Late Helladic IIA Period in the Athenian Agora', *Hesperia* 44, 375-8.

RUTTER, J.B. 1985
'An Exercise in Form vs. Function: The Significance of the Duck Vase', *TUAS* 10, 16-41.

SAKELLARAKIS, J. 1996
'Minoan Religious Influence in the Aegean. The Case of Kythera', *BSA* 91, 81-99.

SAKELLARAKIS, J. 2011
Κύθηρα. Το μινωικό ιερό κορυφής στον Άγιο Γεώργιο στο Βουνό 1. Τα προανασκαφικά και η ανασκαφή, Athens.

SAKELLARAKIS, J. 2012
'Μινωικά χάλκινα μικροαντικείμενα', in *Κύθηρα. Το μινωικό ιερό κορυφής στον Άγιο Γεώργιο στο Βουνό 2. Τα ευρήματα*, J. Sakellarakis (ed.), Athens, 218-29.

SAKELLARAKIS, J. 2013
Κύθηρα. Ο Άγιος Γεώργιος στο Βουνό. Μινωική λατρεία και νεώτεροι χρόνοι, Athens.

SAKELLARIOU, A. 1964
Die minoischen und mykenischen Siegel des Nationalmuseums in Athen, vol. 1 of *Corpus der Minoischen und Mykenischen Siegel*, Berlin.

SALAVOURA, E. 2015
Μυκηναϊκή Αρκαδία. Αρχαιολογική και τοπογραφική θεώρηση, Athens.

SAPOUNA-SAKELLARAKI, E. 2012
'Χάλκινα ειδώλια', in *Κύθηρα. Το μινωικό ιερό κορυφής στον Άγιο Γεώργιο στο Βουνό 2. Τα ευρήματα*, J. Sakellarakis (ed.), Athens, 1-212.

SCHALLIN, A.-L. & I. TOURNAVITOU 2015
'Introduction', in *Mycenaeans up to Date. The Archaeology of the Northeastern Peloponnese – Current Concepts and New Directions*, A.-L. Schallin & I. Tournavitou (eds.), Stockholm, 9-18.

SERVAIS, J. & B. SERVAIS SOYEZ 1984
'La tholos 'oblongue' (tombe IV) et le tumulus (tombe V) sur le Vélatouri', in *Thorikos VIII, 1972/1976. Rapport Préliminaire sur la 9e, 10e, 11e et 12e Campagnes de Fouilles*, Ghent, 15-71.

SHAW, M. 2006
'Plaster Offering Tables', in *The Monumental Minoan Buildings*, vol. 5 of *Kommos*, J. W. Shaw & M. C. Shaw (eds.), Princeton, 751-70.

SILVERMAN, H. 1994
'The Archaeological Identification of an Ancient Peruvian Pilgrimage Center', *World Archaeology* 26.1, 1-18.

STEEL, L. 2013
Materiality and Consumption in the Bronze Age Mediterranean, New York and London.

TARTARON, T.F. 2013
Maritime Networks in the Mycenaean World, Cambridge and New York.

THEOCHARIS, D.R. 1950
'Εκ της προϊστορικής Βραυρώνος', *Prakt*, 188-93.

TOURNAVITOU, I. 2014
'Κεραμεική της εποχής του Χαλκού', in *Κύθηρα. Το μινωικό ιερό κορυφής στον Άγιο Γεώργιο στο Βουνό 4*, J. Sakellarakis (ed.), Athens, 1-664.

TRAVLOS, J. 1988
Bildlexikon zur Topographie des antiken Attika, Tübingen.

TRIANTAPHYLLOU, M.V., K. KOULI, T. TSOUROU, O. KOUKOUSIOURA, K. PAVLOPOULOS & M.D. DERMITZAKIS 2010
'Paleoenvironmental Changes since 3000 BC in the Coastal Marsh of Vravron (Attica, SE Greece)', *Quaternary International* 216, 14-22.

TYREE, E.L. 2001
'Diachronic Changes in Minoan Cave Cult', in *Potnia. Deities and Religion in the Aegean Bronze Age. Proceedings of the 8th International Aegean Conference. Göteborg, Göteborg University, 12-15 April 2000* (Aegaeum 22), R. Laffineur & R. Hägg (eds.), Liège, 39-50.

VASSILICOU, D. 2000
Mycenaean Signet Rings of Precious Metals with Cult Scenes, Athens.

VLACHOPOULOS, A. & ZORZOS, L. 2014
'Physis and Techne on Thera: Reconstructing Bronze Age Environment and Land-Use Based on New Evidence from Phytoliths and the Akrotiri Wall-Paintings', in *Physis. L'environnement naturel et la relation homme-milieu dans le monde égéen protohistorique, Actes de la 14e Rencontre égéenne internationale, Paris, Institut National d'Histoire de l'Art (INHA), 11-14 décembre 2012* (Aegaeum 37), G. Touchais, R. Laffineur & F. Rougemont (eds.), Leuven and Liège, 183-97.

WATROUS, L.V. 1994
'Some Observations on Minoan Peak Sanctuaries', in vol. 2 of *Politeia. Society and State in the Aegean Bronze Age. Proceedings of the 5th International Aegean Conference, University of Heidelberg, 10-13 April 1994* (Aegaeum 12), R. Laffineur & W.-D. Niemeier (eds.), Liège and Austin, 393-403.

WIENCKIE, M.H. 2011
'Ceremonial Lerna', in *Our Cups Are Full: Pottery and Society in the Aegean Bronze Age. Papers Presented to Jeremy B. Rutter on the Occasion of his 65th Birthday*, W. Gauss, M. Lindblom, R.A.K. Smith & J.C. Wright (eds.), Oxford, 345-54.

WHITLEY, J. 1991
Style and Society in Dark Age Greece: The Changing Face of a Preliterate Society 1100-700 BC, Cambridge.

WHITTAKER, H. 2014
Religion and Society in Middle Bronze Age Greece, Cambridge.

WRIGHT, J.C. 2006
'The Formation of the Mycenaean Palace', in *Ancient Greece. From the Mycenaean Palaces to the Age of Homer*, S. Deger-Jalkotzy & I.S. Lemos (eds.), Edinburgh, 7-52.

WRIGHT, J.C. 2015
'The Nature of Mycenaean Occupation of the Watersheds That Comprise the Longopotamos, Nemea and Asopos Valleys', in *Mycenaeans up to Date. The Archaeology of the Northeastern Peloponnese – Current Concepts and New Directions*, A.-L. Schallin & I. Tournavitou (eds.), Stockholm, 211-9.

ZEIMBEKIS, M. 1998
'The Typology, Forms and Functions of Animal Figures from Minoan Peak Sanctuaries with Special Reference to Juktas and Kophinas, PhD diss., University of Bristol. Available online: https://research-information.bristol.ac.uk/files/34492850/DX214653_1.pdf (accessed 21.12.2017).

EPILOGUE

Ritual in Its Space

Fritz Graf

Background

The study of Greek religion is in quest for new paradigms. The paradigm shift of the 1960s, connected with the work of Jean-Pierre Vernant and Walter Burkert seems to have run its course, and new approaches are being tried out. Whereas in the earlier shift archaeology and material culture did not play a major role – symptomatically, Vernant's Centre Louis Gernet was rather slow to admit at least icononography to its interests – among the new paradigms, material culture in all its forms plays an important role; this goes together with the rise of an interest in materiality in ancient archaeology in general that reacts to the dominance of sociological ways of reading archaeological data that has dominated the field in the past decades.

The range of the approaches to Greek religion is large. I start with the paradigm that has provoked most resistance among scholars of the ancient world. Mainly thanks to the work of Pascal Boyer, over the last few decades a cognitive approach to the study of religion has became attractive to many historians of religion, including to a few historians of the ancient world. Here, its impact became most visible in the collective volume *Theorizing Religions Past. Archaeology, History, and Cognition,* published in 2004 by Harvey Whitehouse and Luther H. Martin and, more recently, in Jennifer Larson's monograph on Greek religion (2016); but overall, the impact has remained small. Memory is almost as cerebral as cognition, but less provocative. It has been a long-standing topic in social anthropology after the ground-breaking work of Maurice Halbwachs, *Les cadres sociaux de la mémoire* (1925), made accessible to the Anglo-Saxon world especially by Paul Connerton's short *How Societies Remember* (1989); more recently, the issues have been rethought in a magisterial way by the philosopher Paul Ricoeur in his *La mémoire, l'histoire, l'oubli* (2000; English 2004). The application of memory in the study of the ancient world was pioneered by the Egyptologist Jan Assmann: both the longevity and the modern reception of Egyptian culture and religion was favorable to such an approach, and Assmann did pioneer work on the modern reception of Egypt.[1] Its application to ancient archaeology is less obvious: here, it was *Le sombre abîme du temps: mémoire et archéologie* by the French prehistorian Laurent Olivier (2008) that theorized its conditions and possibilities.

Then there is space. Its contemporary theory goes back to Henri Lefèbvre's seminal *La production de l'espace* (1974, English 1991); for the ancient world, it was pioneered in a much less theorized way in the collective volume on *Placing the Gods. Sanctuaries and Sacred Space in Ancient Greece*, edited by Susan Alcock and Robin Osborne (1994).[2] The recent collective volume *Cityscapes*

1 Assmann, J. 1992; for a wider overview see Assmann, A. 1999.

2 Somewhat an outlier is the interesting collection of papers from the ninth Stuttgart colloquium on historical geography, Olshausen and Sauer 2009.

and Monuments of Western Asia Minor. Memories and Identities, edited by Eva Mortensen and Birte Poulsen (2017), efficiently combines memory with space and adds identity, a somewhat overused topic after Edward Said's reclaiming of cultural and political identity against colonialist appropriation made it into a politically hot topic; Martina Seifert's short introductory essay to the volume sketches the complex methodological background. The other very recent collective volume, Troels Myrup Kristensen and Wiebke Friese's *Excavating Pilgrimage: Archaeological Approaches to Sacred Travel and Movement in the Ancient World* (also from 2017), combines space with long-established ritual studies, and adds the perspective of movement and mobility. The emphasis on pilgrimage in the title follows the application of what originally was a concept of Christian liturgy to the ancient world which goes back to Matthew Dillon's *Pilgrims and Pilgrimage in Ancient Greece* (1997) and to the collection of essays edited by Jaś Elsner and Ian Rutherford, *Pilgrimage in Graeco-Roman and early Christian antiquity: Seeing the Gods* (2005). But it is not their term: a generation ago, Victor and Edith Turner's rather controversial study on *communitas* in Christian pilgrimage, *Image and Pilgrimage in Christian Culture. Anthropological Perspectives* (1978), had the effect of making the term 'pilgrimage' appear as a justifiable term of religious anthropology, with the result that recently Ian Rutherford could distinguish between scholars of antiquity who used pilgrimage "in a more general sense, such as we find in anthropological literature," and those who insisted (like myself) on a "narrower, more specific sense known from Christianity".[3]

Space is almost inseparable from matter; and the seriousness of matter, not surprisingly, has also returned to archaeology. After decades of following models developed by social studies, ancient archaeology has taken up the focus on materiality that goes together with the more wide-spread material turn in cultural studies; Bjørnar Olsen, *In Defense of Things: Archaeology and the Ontology of Objects* (2010) is a recent and influential theoretical presentation. Another collective volume, again a hybrid, shows its impact on ancient studies: Jennifer Knust's and Claudia Moser's *Ritual Matters: Material Remains and Ancient Religion* (2017) applies the new materiality to ritual studies, the mainstay of research on ancient religions during the last century. John Scheid's memorable title of his book on Roman sacrifice, *Quand faire, c'est croire* (2005), is the most fitting epigraph to ancient ritual studies, not only for the Roman world. Scheid's title also makes abundantly clear that the generation of researchers to which he belongs did not think about ritual in terms of materiality but in mental and conceptual terms, as had done already Vernant, Burkert and Dumézil.

The present collection

The present collection may appear to be a companion volume to the 2017 volume *Excavating Pilgrimage* edited by Kristensen and Friese. But unlike that volume with its narrow thematic but wide geographical focus, the present collection widens its thematic and methodological approach but focuses its geography mostly on Athens, with some glances at other parts of the Greek world. In his introduction, Troels Myrup Kristensen opens up also the range of methodologies by presenting what he sees as the leading theoretical approach in mobility studies by the urban architect Ole B. Jensen in his *Staging Mobilities* (2013); this paradigm, developed for modernity, proves useful and attractive for the ancient world as well. But the present collection does not focus on mobility alone, not even in a much wider sense than the narrow pilgrimage: it adds an interest in processions (that

3 Rutherford 2013, 14. A splendid example for communitas in a Christian procession is Leonardo Sciacia's description of a Sicilian visit to Lourdes, Sciascia 1990, 66-67.

are less problematical than pilgrimage but also need more theoretical thinking) and what it calls rather loosely 'religious travel'. Furthermore, it adds the analysis of cultic space as an assemblage of shrines in a coherent spatial arrangement that can be explored through walking. Uniquely in the Greek world, the unusually dense data of Athens allows us to analyze two such spaces; in both cases, this space is organized along a walking path on which a visitor could move from shrine to shrine. In what follows, I will regroup the eleven case studies under these three headings of procession, religious travel and space.

1. *Processions*

One of the most fundamental expressions of mobility in religion is the procession. In the ancient Mediterranean Bronze Age already, processions are well attested for Egypt and ancient Mesopotamia.[4] They become especially well-documented in the visual culture of the Greek cities of the Imperial Age; but the Greek term πομπή became technical well before the common culture under the emperors, as its early Roman adoption as *pompa* shows.[5] Processions still remain under-researched for the ancient world: they always have invited more the antiquarian writing of inventories and typologies than theoretical analysis, from Nilsson's 1911 attempt at classification to the rich inventory with which *ThesCRA* opened its first volume in 2004.[6]

The present collection with its several case studies attempts a much richer theoretical look on the phenomenon. For Athens, it is the Panathenaic procession (Erin Warford, and for an important detail on space Kristensen's introduction) and the procession of the initiates to Eleusis (Kevin Clinton and Soi Agelidis); in an appendix, Clinton adds the procession of the mysteries of Andania, a ritual act codified rather late in a famous inscription that recently has received two book-length treatments.[7] Ariadne Konstantinou looks at the Dionysiac *oreibasia* in Athens that is less easily classified, but also rather neglected in recent scholarship.

Warford and Agelidis share an interest in the personal experience of participants and onlookers, although the perspectives of the two authors vary. In the wake of a recent interest in emotions, Warford concentrates her approach on the sensory perceptions surrounding the procession, a topic that is here addressed for the first time ever and that certainly deserves this interest. Although no ancient text talks about what the participants (or for that matter the onlookers) of the Panathenaic procession felt, a few texts on other processions show an openness for personal experience. For the procession to Eleusis, the figure of Iakchos epitomizes the personal experience of the participants that verges towards the ecstatic. This made Athenians read Iakchos as a divinity expressing the enthusiastic and ecstatic state of mind and saw him as a form of Bakchos as early as Sophocles' *Antigone*.[8] In the *Frogs*, Aristophanes has his Dionysos and especially the slave Xanthias react to the sensory stimuli of the Eleusinian procession as performed by the initiates in the underworld that provoke both culinary and erotic desire. Later, novelists such as Xenophon in his *Ephesiaka* or Heliodorus in the *Aithiopika* are very open to the visual and erotic stimuli of the processions they describe and use them as starting point for the ἐρωτικὰ παθήματα of their heroes; to a certain extent, the description of the Great Procession of the Alexandrian Dionysia under Ptolemy Philopator already builds upon these sensual stimuli, albeit for

4 Assmann, J. 1991; Pongratz-Leisten 1994; for the architectural framework see already Andrae 1941.

5 Attested as early as Plautus, *Cistellaria* 90 (Dionysia) and, in a legal context, *CIL* I^2.593.65 (*in pompam ludeis circensibus agei*; lex Iulia municipalis, a. 45 BCE).

6 Nilsson 1916 = 1951; *ThesCRA* 1, 1-58.

7 Gawlinski 2011; Deshours 2006; on the date of the text see the convincing re-dating by Pirenne-Delforge 2010.

8 Graf 1974, 40-58; but see Clinton 1992, 64-78.

the on-lookers only as a way of enhancing royal greatness.[9] The visuality of these processions is underlined and heightened by the objects carried past the on-lookers, from the Dionysiac phallos to the divine images that provoked the anger of Christian fathers; when Vibius Salutaris in 104 CE constructed his Ephesian procession with its impressive, if not almost oppressive splendor of the many gold and silver images that his law carefully lists, he was fully aware of this visual effect.[10] Warford emphasizes the importance of these objects in Athenian processions; in the wake of Victor Turner, she calls them symbols, analyzes a selection of them in their cultural contexts and thinks that they are to imprint themselves unto the individual and collective memories of a city. The Salutaris procession can serve as a powerful confirmation of this view, with its many references to the mythical and historical past and present of Ephesos that construct a visual map of the city's history and organization that is directed at citizens and foreigners alike, with a special emphasis, it seems, on the young; the imprinting is taken care of by the many repetitions of the procession in the course of the Ephesian year.[11]

Agelidis on the other hand works out individual agency in the preparation and performance of the procession to Eleusis, about which we do not know much, but again less than we could know. Both our sources and our research have always been much more interested in institutions and structures than in individual agency; it is only the hierophant about whose actions we have some details of knowledge, from the scant fragments of the liturgy, the few images and the rare grave epigrams for a hierophant. It is only in very exceptional cases that we hear the voice of an *initiandus* on details of emotional impact, such as in the fear of Aristophanes' Strepsiades (provided the *Clouds* mirror Eleusinian ritual), in Plato's remark in the friendship resulting from mystery initiation, or in some remarks of Plutarch.[12] Sometimes iconography also allows a glance on individual experience, as with the Niinnion pinax that depicts the arrival in Eleusis, or the images of the Urna Lovatelli and related images that show to the stages of an initiation and oscillate between representation and symbolism.[13] Given that participation was the consequence of an individual decision and that at least some individuals remain audible and visible, I share Agelidis' surprise about the scant research.

Iconography is also one of the sources of information for Ariadne Konstantinou in her paper on the *oreibasia* as reflected in Athenian images. Of course, one could as endlessly as uselessly debate whether *oreibasia* qualifies as a procession or a ritual gathering in the *eschatiē*: it is both, and to a certain extent, then, the definition is a matter of perspective. A famous Hellenistic epigram from Miletus introduces the city priestess of Dionysos at the head of her menads on their way to the mountains, in a way not radically different from Iakchos and the Eleusinian priests who lead the Mystery procession from Athens to their mystical experience in Eleusis, and if, as I agree with Agelidis, the way to Eleusis is a πομπή and not a pilgrimage, the *oreibasia* is the same – in both cases the group of initiates leads and accompanies (πέμπει) each other and the sacred objects (the symbols, in Warford's terminology) to the place where they experience the encounter with the divine. A sacred law from Hellenistic Physkeis in Lokroi expresses this with the term "to go together to the mountain" (εἰς ὄρος ...

9 See Callixenus of Rhodes, in Athen. 197C-203B, with Hazzard 2000, 59-80.

10 *Inschriften von Ephesos* 27.

11 Painstakingly analyzed by Rogers 1991, with too much emphasis on the Roman side; for a recent analysis see Graf 2015, 41-51.

12 Plato, *Epistula* 7, 333e; Plutarch, *De progrediendo* 10, 81 DE and frg. 178 Sandbach.

13 Niinnion Pinax: *ThesCRA* 1.13 no. 78 = *LIMC* 4 Demeter 392; Urna Lovatelli and related images: *ThesCRA* 2. 96 nos. 34-40.

συνελθὼν) as a compulsory ritual for each member of the thiasos. The strenuous experience of the walk up to the mountain must explain the reluctance of some members to participate in what would in the end, one hopes, become an experience of bliss, and that mirrors the reluctance of wealthy Athenians to walk to Eleusis instead of being driven which lead the authorities in 422/421 BCE to built a very narrow bridge over the Rheitoi "so that vehicles cannot pass but one has to walk to the rites".[14] But Konstantinou's main interest is not with the "walk to the mountain" (the literal meaning of ὀρει-βασία), but with the space of arrival, the space of the Dionysiac ecstasy in the liminal ritual space of the mountain; this shifts the perspective from the processional aspect to the ritual experience outside the boundaries of civilisation. For her analysis of this space, she follows the mildly structuralist understanding of the mountains that after others Richard Buxton had laid out, but she unfolds its impact on experience and emotions, for which the first song of Euripides' *bakchai* remains the most impressive text.[15]

2. Sacred Travel and the Problem of Pilgrimage

In past research, the opposition between procession and pilgrimage had been widely debated, especially by those scholars who hesitated to use the term 'pilgrimage' for Greek religion; already Nilsson's 1911 article tried to differentiate between processions, pilgrimages and *theoriai*, "festival embassies", and in recent years the debate has become more intensive. It was important for the 2017 collection on *Excavating Pilgrimage*, and it is in the background to this volume where it surfaces more visibly in the contributions of Agelidis, Handberg, and especially in the introduction to Maria Pretzler's essay on Pausanias; here the author addresses Jaś Elsner's influential characterization of Pausanias' *Perihegesis* as a pilgrimage. Elsner consciously (and, I suspect, somewhat provocatively) built on the Christian associations of the term; to do so, he took up the lead of Victor and Edith Turner who remained focussed on Christian pilgrimage but through their theoretization opened it up as a technical term for the history of religions and cultural studies.[16] Elsner thought the writers of the Second Sophistic idealized the Greek past with clear religious undertones; Pausanias, of course, was such a member of this movement, and his travels, again in Elsner's reading, could be compared with a Christian pilgrim's travels in quest of the experience of the holy. There are problems with this, as Pretzler after earlier critical analyses is pointing out; although I agree with her, I am also aware that the resistance to the use of pilgrimage among scholars of the ancient world might not just stem from an aim for precise lexicography but also have something to do with the secular bias Classics had after the late 19th century. However that may be, two objections seem relevant. On the one hand, the Second Sophistic was not a religious but a cultural and educational movement. The idealization of the Greek past was far from being confined to the second century CE, as Tim Whitmarsh has pointed out, but a key feature of the reception of earlier Greek culture in late antiquity; Eunapios, to whom we owe the term sophists for the members of this movement, is only one later exponent of this late antique and Byzantine reception of classical Greek culture.[17] More importantly, in Pausanias' *Perihegesis* there are few traces of a religious feeling about Greece and its classical antiquities. His is not a religion of classical education in an otherwise secular writer – a stance thinkable only after the Romantic Age. Rather, he

14 Physkeis: *IG* IX,1² 3:670; Eleusis: *IG* I³ 79 (hίνα μὲ hάμαχσαι διελαύνονται ἀλλὰ τοῖς ἰõσιν ἐĩ βαδίζεν ἐπὶ τὰ hιερά).

15 Buxton 1992 and Buxton 1994, 81-96.

16 See the introduction to Elsner & Rutherford 2005.

17 Whitmarsh 2013; for Byzantium Kaldellis 2007.

shares the religious attitudes and scruples of his contemporaries, somewhere between the dedication of Aristides and the irreverence of Lucian. At best, then, the term pilgrimage is a metaphor, a rhetorical device and not a description valid for the history of religion. In this light, I fear that the term creates more confusion than clarity.

Handberg makes a good case for the observation that none of the more specific modern or ancient terms – procession (πομπή/pompa), sacred embassy (θεωρία), pilgrimage – covers all Greek ritual movements, and the less so the further one moves back from later antiquity; this is borne out, among other things, by the complex typology of "pilgrimage" that Elsner and Rutherford offered in 2005.[18] Handberg advocates "sacred travel" as a neutral term that covers what he describes in his essay as the result of an archaeological reconstruction of Geometric finds in two mountain shrines, deliberate private visits by elite members in shrines outside one's own community. This should not be confounded with *theoria* which always denotes a visit by city officials that is sanctioned and often initiated by the community that sends the *theoroi* – "state pilgrims" in Rutherford's terminology whose problems and limits he was the first to point out.[19] "Pilgrimage" on the other hand returns loud and clear in Kalogeropoulos' contribution. He reconstructs the very same phenomenon of religious visits in a shrine outside one's community in even earlier times, in Late Helladic Brauron; this makes for a wide and loose application of the term. In both papers it is the analysis of archaeological objects – to be precise, of objects that are foreign in the local find material – that leads to a specific assumption of religious movement connected with the import of objects: these were brought along by foreign visitors. The discrepancy between the two papers demonstrates that a chief virtue of volumes like this one is to help understanding the limits of terminology simply by embedding the debated terms in very specific contexts; it is then up to the reader's discretion whether they prefers the narrow approach of Handberg or the wide by Kalogeropoulos. What is important, though, is that both approaches come with their price-tags attached: the wide approach obscures specific differences by inserting the phenomenon in a very wide frame of interdisciplinary reference that imposes a certain reading on the data precluding other readings, whereas the narrow approach honors the local and historical specificities of the data that, however, remain comparable only in a narrow frame-work, excluding any wider comparability; to work against this problem, Handberg introduced the extremely wide term "religious travel". In the end, this come down to the opposition between two different styles of historiography, universalist and historicist.

In both these early cases, the archaeological remains as such only show a mixture of local and foreign, non-local objects. The analysis makes sense of this mixture of objects by extrapolating to the agency and presence of foreigners at a sacred place and their participation in the rituals celebrated by the locals in this place. The assumption that the foreigners came as guests in order to celebrate with the locals is easy, but not the only one: alternative scenarios are possible, such as the cult of foreigners without locals (absent relevant inscriptions, we do not know whether this was prohibited in these shrines), or the chance arrival of the foreigners at the time of the sacrifice, the way Telemachos and "Mentor" arrive in Pylos at the time of a sacrifice to Poseidon. Telemachos, however, did not leave Ithacan drinking vessels behind. At any rate, in neither case do we have information about the space these foreigners travelled, whether they visited other places as well, or whether tradition compelled them to follow a specific route.

This is markedly different in later processions, such as the ones from Athens to Eleusis or from

18 Elsner & Rutherford 2005, 9-30.

19 Rutherford 2013, 12-14.

Miletus to Didyma. Here, texts describe the complex ritual that is much more than a movement from A to B; for Miletus, it is Molpoi inscription (mid-fifth-century), for Eleusis, the famous description given by Pausanias.[20] In both cases, the movement from the city to the outlying shrine was several times interrupted by rituals performed at specific sacred spots that evoked and thus kept alive or even created a memory of the past of the cult, as Pausanias explains for Eleusis – yet another good instance for the connection of processions (or, more generally, space) with memory. In both cases, we learn that the route was not just traditional: it was "staged" from above through permanent constructions ("procession roads" that in the case of Didyma show the influence of Egyptian models) that were initiated by the political community and for which wealthy benefactor could spend money and earn respect and fame of the community; and as a permanent construction, its boundaries were marked by boundary markers or statuary, and being in the service of the gods, it was called "sacred street", ἱερὰ ὁδός or, in Roman Anatolia, ἱερὰ πλατεῖα.[21] The Eleusinian bridge was even used as a stage to impose correct ritual behavior on the participants.

Much of this also applies to the Pythaïs discussed in Daniele Pirisino's contribution; unlike the two preceding cases, however, here we lack a literary or epigraphical master text and have to rely on the tricky business of reconstruction. Like the procession to Eleusis or to Didyma, the Pythaïs is not just a case of sacred travel from place A to place B. Its performance includes many rituals on the way and connects the performers with a number of sacred places that again construct a memory of Apollo's history in Athens or, if the Athenian part continues the first part from Delos, in the Greek world. If the compelling combination of a Delian with a Pythian part is correct, we end up with a ritual that effectively corrects the earlier memory as expressed in the Homeric Hymn to Apollo; it might not be a coincidence that this foundational text is recorded on Delos at about the time when the Pisistratids changed the route. But the most intriguing feature of the Pythaïs is its structural complexity that move it well beyond either πομπή or θεωρία. The performers not only "conveyed a sacrifice" to Delphi (πέμπουσι τὴν θυσίαν in Strabo's words that leave it open whether he meant the Athenian tripod or a herd of sheep or cattle; Jason of Pherai had proven that the latter was well doable[22]), they also brought back another tripod and the sacred fire from Apollo's altar (φέρουσι πῦρ). This double movement fits neither the template of *theoria* nor pilgrimage, and that of procession only loosely and if one compares its structure with the Ephesian procession of Vibius Salutaris that moved from the temple of Artemis Ephesus to the theatre as the place of public assembly and, after the assembly, back to the temple, albeit on a different route. Examples like these (rare in the epigraphical and literary record) show that my own paradigm of centrifugality and centripetality was too simplistic.[23]

3. Cultic Space

The term ἱερὰ ὁδός and its later synonym, ἱερὰ πλατεῖα, show that often enough processions and comparable ritual movement created a permanent space for moving towards the communication with the divine, provided these rites were cyclical or otherwise recurrent. As Pirisino underlines, the existence of boundary markers for procession ways proves the permanence of such a stage for

20 Herda 2006; Pausanias 1.37.

21 In Roman Perge, *IK* Perge 322, a photo *ZPE* 199 (2016) 81 no. 5. There is also a ἱερωτάτη πλατίᾳ in Apameia in Phrygia, presumably an association for the emperor cult organized by the inhabitants of the street where this temple was (with, presumably, processions as well), *MAMA* vi 66 n. 176.

22 Xenophon, *Hellenica* 6.4.29.

23 Nilsson 1916 = 1951.

rituals, as does, I would add, the existence of Imperial Age associations that permanently united the neighbors along the ἱερὰ πλατεῖα in Perge and Phrygian Apameia.[24] Such paths or streets are not only attested on the territory of Athens by a beautiful fourth-century border marker for the Pythaïs, but also in a few other places:[25] two rock inscriptions on Naxos marked the path up to the mountain precinct of Zeus Melosios, used, according to the attractive hypothesis of Maria Barbara Savo, for a procession in a weather ritual.[26] When the movement ritually connected several city shrines, as in the Pythaïs or in the procession to Eleusis that already inside the city walls connects the Eleusinion above the agora with the Iakcheion near the Sacred Gate, this constellation recalls zones the of a surprising density of shrines such as the one along the *peripatos* described by Wiebke Friese or along the Ilissos that Maria Salta analyzed. These shrines were interconnected by a built footpath such as the *peripatos* round the Acropolis or the path on which Socrates and Phaedrus strolled along the Ilissos, albeit with the vital difference that these paths were, for all we know, simple utilitarian walking paths and had no ritual function.[27]

This density of shrines in a single area of the city is in need of an explanation, especially since the fourth-century boundary inscription of the *peripatos* staged its existence not very differently from any *hiera hodos,* procession street. Friese implies an answer by her careful recording of the very specific development of each shrine: the shrines have no functional connection in Athenian religion, and each had its own independent archaeological and cultic life, with the possible exception of the Asklepieion and the source of the Nymphs nearby, which is grounded in the need Asklepios' cult had of a permanent water source. This is satisfactory on a pragmatic level: the *peripatos* shrines were not founded as a system but put together piecemeal over several centuries. Still, the question arises why a given sanctuary had to be placed at a given spot: there are other permanent water sources in Athens beyond the one with which in the late fifth century the city Asklepieion was connected. Scholars such as myself who wanted to insert the pragmatic description into a wider context, without focusing on the problem of content, tried a structural description and called these sanctuaries "liminal", in the wake of Arnold van Gennep as read by Victor Turner. Such a structural description, it seemed, would not distort the archaeological reality. But this might be a mirage: the label "liminal" suggests that one should also include in the group of shrines the Eleusinion halfway up to the acropolis on the *hiera hodos* but outside the *peripatos* that branches off the sacred road further uphill, that is again in a liminal position. Its role as a local Thesmophorion, as suggested by Kevin Clinton, would go well together with such a reading: the Eleusinion shares its position with most shrines of Demeter that are located on a hill side, as observed long ago by Yves Béquignon, and the shrine of Demeter in Priene is almost a picture book illustration of this fact.[28] But doing so is harmless only if the *peripatos* really is a utilitarian foot path without ritual functions.

The same problem is posed by the cults along the Ilissos and their equivalent cults on the Southwest slope of the acropolis that Maria Salta describes with again a great wealth of archaeological detail. In her analysis, she chooses a different approach from Friese's that resolutely focuses on shared content,

24 Apameia *MAMA* vi 66 n. 176; Perge *IK Perge* 322 and *ZPE* 199 (2016) 81 no. 5. – On the meaning of πλατεῖα as "neighborhood association" see Pont (2013).

25 See the overview in Bekker-Nielsen (2009).

26 *IG* XII:5, 48 and *SEG* 54. 792, both 4th cent. BCE; see Savo 2004a and 2004b; I owe the references to Oliver Pilz.

27 *IG* II² 2639, mentioned by Friese; as a minimum, such an inscription demonstrated the pride of the people responsible for its construction and maintenance.

28 Béquignon 1958.

in her case expressed by the term "chthonic" and translated in her programmatic title as "under the care of the daemons": with this, the author means cults that mainly have a relationship to the world of the dead. This difference between Friese's and Salta's approach opens up an important problem of methodology: do we, as Friese the pragmatic historian does, propose a very careful description without attempting to seek a unified explanation, or do we think that the shared topography points to a shared function? As historians, we are under some pressure to read meaning into the data, and so Salta's attempt at a unified explanation is intriguing, even if I am somewhat hesitant to use the term "chthonic" that as a technical term is not older than Carl Otfried Müller?[29] To phrase it differently: in a purely structuralist view of things, the cults that Salta discusses all share the fact that they are outside city (*asty*), and her connecting them with some cults on the acropolis slope suggests that this might be true also for the cults discussed by Friese. Is this correct, and if so can the common structure also be filled with a common meaning?

It might be too much to expect an answer in the framework of this book. The question is much larger: it concerns the connection between cult topography and function of a cult. The question has never been addressed with a general theory. For some temples outside the city, François de Polignac attempted an answer based on the model of the Heraion of Argos;[30] other scholars followed, but it never triggered a larger historical or theoretical approach,[31] and there is not even a scholarly consensus whether the ancient description of a divinity as πρὸ πόλεως talks about the topography of the shrine, the function as protecting the city, or both.

Summary

Thus, the workshop and the present volume that represents its result do not just demonstrate the vitality and feasibility of some of the new approaches to Greek religion and the importance of archaeological data. The papers together point at problems of terminology that await further elucidation, and be it only the insight that some terms are not indigenous and need careful explanation by each user (pilgrimage, chthonic). And, at least as important for future scholarship, they point to areas that ask for more work and promise new insights for more research, be it the relationship between topography and religious meaning, the role of individual emotions and agency in processions, or a general history and theory of processions in ancient and other religions.

Abbreviations

ThesCRA = *Thesaurus cultus et rituum antiquorum (2004-2005).*

IG = *Inscriptiones Graecae (1873-).*

Inschriften von Ephesos = *Die Inschriften von Ephesos. (Inschriften griechischer Stadte aus Kleinasien).*

IK Perge = *Die Inschriften von Perge. (Inschriften griechischer Städte aus Kleinasien).*

LIMC = *Lexicon Iconographicum Mythologiae Classicae (1981-2009).*

MAMA = *Monumenta Asiae Minoris Antiqua (1928-1953).*

29 Schlesier 1994.

30 de Polignac, 1984.

31 But see Scheid & de Polignac 2010 and the articles that follow.

Bibliography

ANDRAE, W. 1941
Alte Feststrassen im Nahen Osten, Leipzig.

ASSMANN, J. 1991
'Das ägyptische Prozessionsfest,' in *Das Fest und das Heilige. Religiöse Kontrapunkte zur Alltagswelt*, J. Assman and T. Sundermeier (eds.), Gütersloh, 95-112.

ASSMANN, J. 1992
Das kulturelle Gedächtnis. Schrift, Erinnerung und politische Identität in frühen Hochkulturen, Munich.

ASSMANN, A. 1999
Erinnerungsräume. Formen und Wandlungen des kulturellen Gedächtnisses, Munich.

BEKKER-NIELSEN, T. 2009
'Strassen, Heiligümer und heilige Strassen', in Olshausen and Sauer 2009, 9-15.

BÉQUIGNON, Y. 1958
'Déméter, déesse acropolitaine,' *Revue Archéologique* 2, 149-177.

BUXTON, R. 1992
'Imaginary Greek Mountains,' *Journal of Hellenic Studies* 112, 1-15.

BUXTON, R. 1994
Imaginary Greece, Cambridge.

CLINTON, K. 1992
Myth and Cult. The Iconography of the Eleusinian Mysteries, Stockholm.

DE POLIGNAC, F. 1984
La naissance de la cité grecque. Culte, éspace et société, VIIIe-VIIe Siècles Av. J.-C., Paris.

DESHOURS, N. 2006
Les mystères d'Andania. Étude d'épigraphie et d'histoire religieuse, Pessac.

ELSNER, J. & I. RUTHERFORD (EDS.) 2005
Pilgrimage in Graeco-Roman and Early Christian Antiquity. Seeing the Gods, Oxford.

GAWLINSNKI, L. 2011
The Sacred Law of Andania. A New Text with Commentary, Berlin.

GRAF, F. 1974
Eleusis und die orphische Dichtung Athens in vorhellenistischer Zeit, Berlin.

GRAF, F. 2015
Roman Festivals in the Greek East, Cambridge.

HAZARD, R.A. 2000
Imagination of a Monarchy: Studies in Ptolemaic Propaganda, Toronto.

HERDA, A. 2006
Der Apollon-Delphinios-Kult in Milet und die Neujahrsprozession nach Didyma. Ein neuer Kommentar der sog. Molpoi-Satzung, Mainz.

KALDELLIS, A. 2007
Hellenism in Byzantium. The Transformation of Greek Identity and the Reception of the Classical Tradition, Cambridge.

LARSON, J. 2016
Understanding Green Religion, London.

LEFÈBRE, H. 1974
La production de l'espace, Paris.

NILSSON. M.P. 1916/1951
'Die Prozessionstypen im griechischen Kult. Mit einem Anhang über die dionysischen Prozessionen in

Athen,' *Archäologisches Jahrbuch* 31, 309-339, again in *Opuscula Selecta* 1, Lund 1951, 166-214.

OLSHAUSEN, E. AND V. SAUER (EDS.) 2009
Die Landschaft und die Religion (Stuttgarter Kolloquium zur Historischen Geographie des Altertums 9, 2005 = Geographica Historica 26), Stuttgart.

PIRENNE-DELFORGE, V. 2010
'Mnasistratos, the 'Hierophant' in Andania (*IG* 5.1.1390 and *Syll.*[3] 735),' in *Myths, Martyrs, and Modernity. Studies in the History of Religions in Honor of Jan N. Bremmer*, J. Dijkstra, J. Kroesen and Y. Juiper (eds.), Leiden, 219-235.

PONGRATZ-LEISTEN, B. 1994
Ina Sulmi Īrub. Die kulttopographische und ideologische Programmatik der akitu-Prozession in Babylonien und Assyrien im 1. Jahrtausend v. Chr., Mainz.

PONT, A.-V. 2013
'Les groupes de voisinage dans les villes de l'Asie Mineure Occidentale à l'époque impériale," in *Groupes et associations dans les cités grecques, III*[e] *siècle av. J.-C. – II*[e] *siècle apr. J.-C.*, P. Fröhlich and P. Harmon (eds.), Geneva, 129-156.

ROGERS, G.M. 1991
The Sacred Identity of Ephesos. Foundation Myths of a Roman City, London.

RUTHERFORD, I. 2013
State Pilgrims and Sacred Observers in Ancient Greece. A Study of Theōriā and Theōroi, Cambridge.

SAVO, M.B. 2004A
Culti, Sacerdozi e Feste delle Cicladi dall'Età Arcaica all'Età Romana, Rome.

SAVO, M.B. 2004B
'Lo Zeus con μηλωτης: una nuova iscrizione dal monte Zas di Nasso,' *Ricerche di antichità e tradizione classica* 3, 149-171.

SCHEID, J. & F. DE POLIGNAC 2010
'Qu'est-ce qu'un 'paysage religieux'? Représentations cultuelles de l'espace dans les sociétés anciennes. Avant-Propos,' *Revue de l'histoire des religions* 4, 427-434.

SCHLESIER, R. 1994
'Olympische Religion und chthonische Religion,' in *The Notion of 'Religion' in Comparative Research. Selected Proceedings of the XVI IAHR Congress*, U. Bianchi (ed.), Rome, 301-310.

SCIASCIA, L. 1990
Candido Ovvero Un Sogno Fatto in Sicilia, Milan.

WHITMARSH, T. 2013
Beyond the Second Sophistic: Adventures in Greek Postclassicism, Berkeley.

List of Contributors

SOI AGELIDIS
Ruhr-University Bochum
Institute of Archaeological Studies
Am Bergbaumuseum 31
D-44791 Bochum
Germany
Soi.Agelidis@ruhr-uni-bochum.de

KEVIN CLINTON
Cornell University
Department of Classics
Goldwin Smith Hall
Ithaca, NY 14853
USA
kmc1@cornell.edu

WIEBKE FRIESE
Hamburg
Germany
wiebke.friese@me.com

FRITZ GRAF
Ohio State University
Department of Classics
414 University Hall
230 N. Oval Mall
Columbus, OH 43210
USA
graf.65@osu.edu

SØREN HANDBERG
University of Oslo
Department of Archaeology, Conservation and History
Blindernveien 11
N-0371 Oslo
Norway
soren.handberg@iakh.uio.no

KONSTANTINOS KALOGEROPOULOS
Academy of Athens
Research Center for Antiquity
Anagnostopoulou 14
GR-10673 Athens
Greece
kkaloger@academyofathens.gr

ARIADNE KONSTANTINOU
Bar-Ilan University
Department of Classical Studies
Ramat Gan 5290002
Israel
ariadne_kon@yahoo.com

TROELS MYRUP KRISTENSEN
Aarhus University
Department of History and Classical Studies
Jens Chr. Skous Vej 5
DK-8000 Aarhus C
Denmark
tmk@cas.au.dk